LATIN AMERICAN ENVIRONMENTAL POLICY IN INTERNATIONAL PERSPECTIVE

—————— ▪ ——————

Latin America in Global Perspective

The fundamental purpose of this multivolume series is to broaden conceptual perspectives for the study of Latin America. This effort responds to a perception of need. Latin America cannot be understood in isolation from other parts of the world. This has always been so; it is especially true in the contemporary era.

Accordingly, the goal of this series is to demonstrate the desirability and the feasibility of analyzing Latin America in comparative perspective, in conjunction with other regions, and in global perspective, in the context of worldwide processes. A subsidiary purpose is to establish a bridge between Latin American "area studies" and mainstream social science disciplines, to the mutual benefit of both. Ultimately, the intent is to explore and emphasize intellectual challenges posed by dynamic changes within Latin America and in its relation to the international arena.

The present volume examines the competing forces acting on Latin American governments as they grapple with challenges posed by environmental neglect, and by way of comparison it offers case studies from Southern Africa, Russia, and Indonesia. The series thus far includes:

Latin America in Comparative Perspective: New Approaches to Methods and Analysis, edited by Peter H. Smith;

EnGENDERing Wealth and Well-Being, edited by Rae Lesser Blumberg, Cathy A. Rakowski, Irene Tinker, and Michael Monteón;

Cooperation or Rivalry?: Regional Integration in the Americas and the Pacific Rim, edited by Shoji Nishijima and Peter H. Smith;

Institutional Design in New Democracies: Eastern Europe and Latin America, edited by Arend Lijphart and Carlos H. Waisman; and

Civil Military Relations: Democracy and Regional Security in Latin America, Southern Asia, and Central Europe, to be edited by David Mares.

This series results from a multiyear research program organized by the Center for Iberian and Latin American Studies (CILAS) at the University of California, San Diego. Principal funding has come from the Andrew W. Mellon Foundation.

LATIN AMERICAN ENVIRONMENTAL POLICY IN INTERNATIONAL PERSPECTIVE

———— ■ ————

edited by

Gordon J. MacDonald, Daniel L. Nielson, and Marc A. Stern

WestviewPress

A Division of HarperCollins*Publishers*

Latin America in Global Perspective

Copyright © 1997 by Westview Press, A Division of HarperCollins Publishers, Inc.

Published in 1997 in the United States of America by Westview Press, 5500 Central Avenue, Boulder Colorado 80301-2877, and in the United Kingdom by Westview Press, 12 Hid's Copse Road, Cumnor Hill, Oxford OX2 9JJ

A CIP catalog record for this book is available from the Library of Congress.
ISBN 0-8133-2423-8
ISBN 0-8133-2424-6 (pb)

The paper used in the publication meets the requirements of the American National Standard for Per-manence of Paper for Printed Library Materials Z39.48-1984.

10   9   8   7   6   5   4   3   2   1

Contents

Tables and Figures

Acknowledgments

We thank the set of interdisciplinary scholars who came together to share generously their insights and data on environmental policy and policy making in Latin America and throughout the globe. The suggestions and hypotheses generated by this diverse group have greatly enriched the contributions to this volume.

We thank Peter H. Smith, the director of Latin American Studies at the University of California, San Diego, who has served as editor of this series. His encouragement and direction on this project have been vital to its realization.

We thank Margaret MacDonald, whose editing on nearly every page of this volume has proved invaluable. We owe deep gratitude to Patricia Rosas, editor at the Center for Iberian and Latin American Studies, who likewise edited the manuscript thoroughly and guided us through the preparation process.

We thank the Andrew W. Mellon Foundation and the Institute on Global Conflict and Cooperation of the University of California for their financial support of this project.

Finally, we owe thanks to our editor at Westview Press, Barbara Ellington, whose support and guidance made the idea for this volume a reality.

Gordon J. MacDonald
Daniel L. Nielson
Marc A. Stern

Acronyms

ACDESS	African Centre for Development and Strategic Studies (Nigeria)
AMDAL	environmental impact assessment process (Indonesia)
ANC	African National Congress
ASEAN	Association of Southeast Asian Nations
BAPEDAL	Environmental Impact Management Agency (Indonesia)
CAP	Compañía de Aceros del Pacífico (Chile)
CARE	CARE International
CARICOM	Caribbean Community and Common Market
CFC	chlorofluorocarbon
CI	Conservation International
CILAS	Center for Iberian and Latin American Studies
CIPMA	Centro de Investigación y Planificación del Medio Ambiente (Chile)
CITES	Convention on International Trade in Endangered Species of Fauna and Flora of 1973
CODEFF	Comité Pro-Defensa de Fauna y la Flora (Chile)
CODELCO	Corporación Nacional del Cobre (Chile)
COHDEFOR	Corporación de Forestería de Honduras
CONADE	National Ecology Commission (Chile)
CONAF	Corporación Nacional Forestal (Chile)
CONAFOR	National Forestry Commission (Chile)
CONAIE	Confederation of Ecuadorian Indigenous Groups
CONAMA	Federal Council for Environmental Quality (Brazil)
CONAMA	National Commission on the Environment (Costa Rica)
CORMA	Corporación de la Madera (Chile)
CSD	Commission on Sustainable Development (Venezuela)
DL	Decree Law
DML	Dana Mitra Lingkungan (Indonesia)
EAP	environmental action plans
ECLAC	Economic Commission for Latin America and the Caribbean
EBRD	European Bank for Reconstruction and Development
EDF	Environmental Defense Fund
EIA	environmental impact assessment

ENGO	environmental nongovernmental organization
EMINWA	Environmentally Sound Management of Inland Waters
EPA	Environmental Protection Agency
FDN	Frente Democrático Nacional (Mexico)
FECOM	Federación Costarricense para la Conservación del Medio Ambiente (Costa Rica)
FN	Fundación Natura (Ecuador)
FSU	former Soviet Union
G-77	Group of 77 (Lesser Developed Nations)
GATT	General Agreement on Tariffs and Trade
GDP	Gross Domestic Product
GEF	Global Environmental Facility
GEM	Group for Environmental Monitoring
GNP	gross national product
GNU	Government of National Unity
GP	Green Party (Brazil)
GOI	Government of Indonesia
GSO	grassroots service organization
HDI	United Nations Human Development Index
HRW/A	Human Rights Watch/Asia
IBAMA	Institute for the Environment and Natural Resources (Brazil)
IBASE	Institute of Social and Economic Analysis (Brazil)
IDA	International Development Association
IDB	Inter-American Development Bank
IMF	International Monetary Fund
INBIO	National Institute for Biodiversity (Costa Rica)
INFOR	Silviculture Research Agency (Chile)
IRDC	International Research and Development Council
ISAR	Institute for Soviet-American Relations
ISI	import substitution industrialization
IUCN	International Union for the Conservation of Nature
LNGO	Latin American nongovernmental organization
MAG	Ministry of Agriculture (Chile)
MDB	multinational development bank
MERCOSUR	Southern Cone Common Market
MFN	most favored nation
MinKhimMash	Chemical and Petroleum Machine Building Ministry (Russia)
MinVod	Ministry of Water Amelioration (Russia)
Minpriroda	Ministry of Environmental Protection and Natural Resources (Russia)
MIRINEM	Ministerio de Recursos Naturales, Engergía y Minas (Costa Rica)
MO	membership organizations
NAFTA	North American Free Trade Agreement

NC	Nature Conservancy
NEPA	National Environmental Protection Act (Brazil)
NGO	nongovernmental organization
NIS	newly independent states (former Soviet Union)
NNGO	Northern nongovernmental organization
NPB	National Parks Board (South Africa)
NUM	National Union of Mineworkers (South Africa)
NWF	National Wildlife Federation
OAS	Organization of American States
ORNL	Oak Ridge National Laboratory (United States)
OTS	Organization for Tropical Studies (Costa Rica)
PDC	Christian Democratic Party (Chile)
PDVSA	Petróleos de Venezuela, S.A.
PEM	Partido Ecologista Mexicana (Mexico)
PEMEX	Petróleos Mexicanos (Mexico)
PHPA	Directorate General of Forest Protection and Nature Conservation (Indonesia)
PPD	Democratic Party (Partido por la Democracia, Chile)
PRI	Partido Revolucionario Institucional (Institutional Revolutionary Party, Mexico)
PSDB	Party of Brazilian Social Democracy
PT	Workers' Party (Brazil)
PUR	Partido de la Unidad Republicana (Ecuador)
RBM	Richards Bay Minerals (South Africa)
RDP	Reconstruction and Development Program (South Africa)
SADC	Southern African Development Community
SADCC	Southern African Development Coordination Conference
SAICEM	Southern African International Conference on Environmental Management
SARDC	Southern African Research and Documentation Centre
SEDESOL	Secretariat of Social Development (Mexico)
SEDUE	Secretaría de Desarrollo Urbano y Ecología (Mexico)
SEGPRES	General Secretariat of the Presidency (Chile)
SEMA	Special Secretariat of the Environment (Brazil)
SFF	Society for Industrial Development (Chile)
SIA	Social Impact Assessment
SINAC	National System of Conservation Areas (Brazil)
SNAPSE	Sistema Nacional de Areas Silvestres Protegidas (National Wilderness Protection System, Chile)
SOFOFA	Manufacturing Development Association (Chile)
SUDAM	Superintendency for the Development of the Amazon (Brazil)
TETS	thermoelectric power plant north of Moscow
TFAP	Tropical Forest Action Plan

UGAM	Union of Environmentalist Groups
UNCED	United Nations Conference on Environment and Development
UNDP	United Nations Development Programme
UNEP	United Nations Environment Programme
USAID	U.S. Agency for International Development
USSR	Union of Soviet Socialists Republics
WALHI	Indonesian Environmental Forum
WWFN	World Wide Fund for Nature
WWF	World Wildlife Fund
Zacplan	Zambezi River Action Plan
Zesco	Zambia Electricity Supply Corporation
Zesa	Zimbabwe Electricty Supply Authority

CHAPTER ONE

— ■ —

Environmental Politics and Policy in Latin America

Gordon J. MacDonald and Marc A. Stern

Across Latin America, environmental policy has progressed in recent years from symbolism toward substance. Recognizing that environmental concerns are no longer a luxury only affluent nations can afford, leaders across the hemisphere have begun to realize that the long term costs of ignoring environmental protection are steep. Although the pace of reform varies from country to country, virtually every nation in Latin America is making progress toward addressing both the enormous environmental deficits created by past development and the need for some controls on present and future growth.

What explains this startling shift in policy priorities? A set of interrelated changes in both international and domestic politics may be responsible for this regionwide trend toward environmental policy reform. First, the international development community—composed of multilateral development banks, national development institutions, and United Nations-based development agencies—has undertaken a substantial effort to integrate environmental concerns into traditional models of economic development. This trend has converged with the remarkable economic reforms that have opened domestic economies to international market forces as never before. In both development and trade-related affairs, environmental concerns have emerged as a central issue on the North/South agenda.

Economic liberalization has coincided with political reform in most countries within Latin America, permitting environmental nongovernmental organizations (ENGOs) to proliferate. Their effectiveness has been bolstered by two developments. First, the mounting environmental costs of industrialization and population growth have mobilized communities throughout the hemisphere and have elevated the political costs to politicians of ignoring the demands of these

1

ENGOs. Second, international ENGOs have launched serious programs to share financial, technical, and organizational resources with local groups in the region.

Finally, it merits notice that the nations of Latin America have played an important role in forging formal international agreements on the global environment, such as the Montreal Protocol, the Convention on Biodiversity, and the Climate Change Convention. Latin American leadership was notable as well at the United Nations Conference on Environment and Development (UNCED) in Rio de Janeiro in 1992. Subsequently, Mexico and Brazil have made important contributions to the work of the Commission on Sustainable Development—the UN body charged with promoting compliance with the declarations completed at the Rio meeting and coordinating the activities of the international development community in environmental matters. The negotiation of these and other international environmental agreements can help spur policy reforms within individual countries in related areas such as treatment of industrial waste, energy efficiency, forestry, and natural resource conservation, while simultaneously educating national bureaucracies and politicians about the long-term economic and political costs of poor environmental management. For all of these activities, government agencies must come together to hammer out a national position, an activity with significant educational value.

Contributors to this volume address the competing forces now acting on Latin American governments as they attempt to grapple with the dual challenges posed by past environmental neglect and future growth. Unlike most discussions of this topic, this volume includes works by specialists on environmental policy in other regions of the world in an effort to gain a comparative perspective on Latin America's progress to date. In the first two sections of the book, chapters address the domestic and the international factors that shape the course of environmental policy in Latin America. A third section then offers three comparative case studies—on Southern Africa, Russia, and Indonesia—that demonstrate the common challenges facing developing nations worldwide.

If our optimism about the future of environmental protection in Latin America is tempered by these international-level concerns, however, the domestic obstacles to sound environmental policy making are even more troubling. As William Ascher documents in his chapter, political tampering with the management of the region's natural resources continues to undermine efforts to rationalize resource policy. Furthermore, the democratic opening underway in the hemisphere is less than robust in many places. Stephen P. Mumme and Edward Korzetz point out that legal and administrative remedies for environmental complaints are weak, and public participation in the policy-making process in general is still inadequate in many nations. Eduardo Silva's chapter demonstrates the considerable political influence that prodevelopment interest groups exercise over resource policy in Chile. Political and economic difficulties can also undermine the progress already accomplished in the region. As Eduardo Viola explains, the political and economic turmoil that Brazil experienced following the Rio de Janeiro

"Earth Summit" of 1992 eroded the ability of both the government and ENGOs to advance Brazil's environmental agenda. Recent events in Mexico underscore this point. Economic resources for environmental protection in Mexico are threatened by the economic crisis that engulfed the Zedillo government in 1994 and 1995. Should Mexico's financial troubles undermine other economies in Latin America, funding for environmental activities throughout the region is likely to suffer.

Three of the contributions to this volume examine the aggregate influence of international factors on the pace and scope of environmental reform in Latin America. The findings are mixed. Heraldo Muñoz investigates the relationship among free trade, economic integration, and environmental protection, and he argues that, even where reform is reactive instead of anticipatory or strategic, there exists a clear positive relationship between open trade and policy reform. Analyzing the role of the multilateral development banks in the region, Daniel L. Nielson and Marc A. Stern argue that although environmental lending has ballooned in recent years, most of the funding targets urban pollution problems at the expense of natural resource conservation projects. This focus on urban health issues may be due in part to a recognition that increased mortality and days of work lost due to contaminated air and water slow economic development. Finally, Blanca Torres examines the linkages between ENGOs in developed and developing nations and finds that friction over competing priorities can threaten the benefits offered by cooperation.

The comparative essays offer context for the Latin American experience by highlighting the challenges posed by institutional weakness, political and economic turmoil, nonparticipatory decision making, and rapid development on effective policies to protect the environment in other regions of the globe. As Larry Swatuk explains, changing political contexts have created increased pressures on water resource problems through cooperative policy mechanisms in Zimbabwe and South Africa. As new social movements and environmental groups press their agendas, they often confront hostility from entrenched interests. Given the changing local and global economic and political contexts, however, such movements in Southern Africa are meeting with marginally more success than in the past. Barbara Jancar-Webster's chapter on Russia's policy response to the daunting environmental legacy of the Soviet Union underscores the linkages among environmental protection, economic growth, and political stability. Carl Petrich and Shelby Smith-Sanclare highlight the political motives that underlie the severe deforestation problem that plagues Indonesia. In each of these cases, parallels to Latin America's environmental challenges are apparent as policymakers exploit natural resource endowments to satisfy short-term political pressures, largely ignoring the negative externalities generated by their activities.

In this chapter, we briefly examine both the opportunities and the difficulties that shape environmental politics and policy in Latin America. As this review indicates, the dynamism of the first half of the 1990s offers reason for cautious optimism about the future of environmental protection in the region, tempered by a recognition of the real political and economic problems that this region faces in the coming decades.

THE INTERNATIONAL DEVELOPMENT COMMUNITY

The changing consensus within the international development community solidified following the 1987 publication of *Our Common Future*. In the late 1980s, many in the development and environmental communities embraced the influential concept of sustainable development. This is a convenient phrase meaning different things to different people. Its virtue is that it allows people to think of compromises, "of ways to temper the impact of growth without sacrificing it entirely."[1]

In many developing nations, the first United Nations Conference on the Human Environment, held in Stockholm in 1972, cultivated the idea that the environment was an issue that would not go away. In the years following Stockholm, country after country developed an institutional base, often in the form of an environmental ministry, to deal with pollution and natural resource issues. The international development assistance programs were slow to incorporate environmental considerations, focusing attention on issues such as structural adjustment during the 1970s and early 1980s. The common assumption during this period was that economic growth would be the panacea for environmental quality. Economic affluence would lead to attention and action on the environment.

The concept of sustainable development emphasizes the content of growth—the composition of inputs, including environmental resources, and outputs, including waste products—and argues that pure economic growth is not the main issue. The economic and environmental institutions within a country in part determine this content. These institutions must be designed to provide the right incentives to protect the resilience of natural ecosystems. Such measures will not only promote greater efficiency in the allocation of environmental resources at all income levels, but also will ensure a sustainable scale of economic activity within the ecological system.

International development assistance programs are beginning to incorporate the concepts of sustainable development. Latin American countries caught up in trade liberalization and democratization have been slow to move forward in structuring the appropriate institutions. Exceptions do exist, such as Bolivia's recent establishment of a Ministry of Sustainable Development. Other countries, such as Chile and Colombia, have established environmental ministries with broad powers. In Argentina and Brazil, the state has delegated major responsibility for the environment to the provinces and states.

International efforts to promote sound environmental policy in the developing world helped educate bureaucrats and politicians in these countries in new ways for assessing the costs and benefits of their development policies. As the leaders of these countries became familiar with the range of environmental problems that affected their citizens, they began to formulate their own environmental agendas. Input from these leaders on issues such as deforestation, ozone, and climate change has transformed the politics of international cooperation in these areas. Whereas industrialized nations were likely to focus primarily on the role of the developing world in contributing to global environmental problems, the G–77 (a group of developing nations founded in 1967) believed that the industrialized North was largely responsible for creating the very same global crises that the G–77 countries were being asked to help solve.

As a consequence of this shift in priorities in the international community, financial and technical assistance is now available for a wide array of projects aimed at transforming development strategies hitherto largely devoid of environmental content. These projects include building institutions, establishing technical and legal standards, improving enforcement capacity, undertaking research on environmental problems, and subsidizing solutions to specific environmental crises. As Nielson and Stern document in chapter 7, the multilateral development banks have provided ever-increasing support for critical infrastructure projects such as water supply and sewerage, air-quality improvements, and solid-waste disposal. With these funds, many projects that otherwise would not have been undertaken have achieved notable results. In many cases, local technocrats and engineers are gaining important experience in valuing and protecting fragile natural resources. In addition to the capacity-building efforts undertaken in recent years, the financial support has had an impact on resource management and development policies that have been part of the political landscape in the developing world for decades. However, despite significant changes in multilateral development institutions' goals and organizational structures, Nielson and Stern note that macroeconomic needs are often emphasized in multilateral development projects at the expense of sustainability goals. Swatuk corroborates this argument with evidence from Southern Africa, noting that in the Zambezi basin in particular, multiple multilateral initiatives have overemphasized the macro benefits of electrical generation capacity at the expense of local social and environmental needs.

ECONOMIC INTEGRATION

By the end of the 1980s, nearly every government in Latin America had committed itself to market-based development strategies. Underwritten by monetary and fiscal discipline, tax reforms, and large-scale privatization of state-owned industries, these reforms have produced an unprecedented convergence of economic policy in the hemisphere. As a result and due to increased levels of international trade, the economies of the region are integrating ever more tightly. The U.S. government, a strong supporter of these reform efforts, has responded with a new emphasis on trade relations as the central plank of its Latin American diplomacy.[2]

In place of direct aid, the United States has shifted its diplomatic energies toward trade liberalization as a means of furthering its interests in the region. As trade policy takes a central role, nontrade issues—such as environment, labor, human rights, and democracy—have been linked to trade in an effort to maintain some leverage over them. The trade/environment linkage is, to date, perhaps the most noteworthy. Simultaneously, policy experts working on trade issues view weak or poorly enforced domestic regulations in such areas as environment, labor, health, and safety as indirect subsidies to industry. As a result, these experts have taken an unprecedented interest in the environmental policies of developing nations now pursuing liberal trading relations with the North.

The linking of environmental demands to the negotiation of the North American Free Trade Agreement (NAFTA) represented the triumph of these views. It transformed the politics of environment not only in Mexico but also in other Latin American nations contemplating joining the agreement: Progress toward the creation and strengthening of environmental ministries throughout the region has accelerated in anticipation of future integration with the North American economies. In this context, the analysis offered by Muñoz may provide a useful template for further studies of the motives behind environmental reform in the hemisphere.

Economic liberalization has also unleashed powerful capital flows into the region that are helping to finance economic growth and development. As a result, it has become increasingly clear that companies throughout Latin America will play a major role in determining environmental quality. In the United States and Europe, the 1980s saw a greater confluence of ideas between moderate environmentalists and well-run companies. This has been fostered by a wide appreciation of the "sustainable development" approach to economic growth. When environmentalism reached a peak in 1972, some environmentalists argued fiercely that economic growth was incompatible with wise environmental policies. Hostility to growth from radical "greens," however, essentially sent environmentalism up a blind alley. When faced with the stark choice between environmental concerns and economic growth, most people chose growth. Moving beyond such simplistic interpretations of the environment/development dynamic allows for public sympathies toward "green" objectives to be harnessed in the service of successful and cooperative policy innovation.

However, some people hope that economic growth can be made environmentally benign. Unfortunately, it never truly can be. Most economic activities use energy and raw materials, which in turn create waste that the planet must absorb. "Green growth" is thus a chimera, but "greener growth" is possible. Many industries in the developed world have learned the lesson that reduced consumption of raw materials and energy in response to changes in production processes can increase profitability. Further, industries—driven by bottom-line considerations, concerns about liabilities, and pressures from the insurance industry—are reducing the release of waste products.

Many multinational corporations have, in large part, adopted better environmental practices and are participating in the transfer of appropriate technologies to Latin American countries. In contrast, medium-sized and small firms throughout the region continue to rely on inefficient processes, and to date, most governments have not created the incentives for these smaller companies to use raw materials and energy more frugally. Recent evidence from Mexico, however, suggests that competitive pressures may play an important part in motivating smaller firms to find low-cost methods to increase efficiency, reduce waste, and pollute less.[3] Furthermore, as export markets demand better environmental performance from exporters, important sectors of industry that cater to these markets (as well as their subcontractors) will be compelled to modernize their production processes and improve their environmental-management practices. It should be noted, however, that export markets can also strengthen resource-exploiting industries whose interests typically run counter to sound resource management polices. As Silva documents in his essay on Chilean forestry policy, the forestry industry worked to undermine efforts to introduce greater conservation measures into Chile's forest management law.

RISING COSTS OF
ENVIRONMENTAL NEGLECT

Urbanization, population growth, poor resource management, and rapid industrialization have contributed to widespread discontent about deteriorating environmental conditions in the region. Latin American governments have begun to recognize the very large cost to their economic development resulting from pollution, particularly in urban areas. Numerous studies in the developed world have demonstrated the social costs of air and water pollution.

Most of the costs, though not all, are associated with health and well-being. Dirty water leads to loss of labor productivity as debilitating intestinal infections lower worker efficiency. In a similar way, respiratory problems resulting from air pollution lower efficiency and keep workers away from the job. Pollution also raises the cost of government-provided health care.

The total drag on the economy from the direct social cost of pollution depends on a variety of factors, including nutritional levels and the percentage of the population who smoke. We do not know of any economic evaluation of social costs of pollution for Latin American countries. In other regions, existing estimates indicate that the social cost of pollution can be a significant percentage of Gross Domestic Product (GDP).[4] For example, the estimated social cost of air pollution alone for Eastern Europe in the late 1980s averaged about 10 percent of GDP.[5]

In the "mega-cities" of Latin America, vehicular pollution has been the main source of air pollution. Combined with other urban pollutants such as toxic waste and chemical residues, these hazards impose especially heavy costs on children and the elderly. Political mobilization in response to the deterioration of the urban environment has been especially marked in such major Latin American cities as Mexico City, Rio de Janeiro, São Paulo, and Santiago de Chile.

DEMOCRATIZATION AND
ENGO PRESSURES

Political liberalization has created space for ENGOs to organize and lobby where previously such activity had been discouraged or repressed. As Mumme and Korzetz document in chapter 3, environmental movements in Latin America have benefited significantly from institutional and legal reforms instituted under newly democratic regimes. These reforms have permitted more extensive political activity such as organizing and lobbying, and they also have generally been accompanied by a more liberal interpretation of media freedom. Less fearful of official sanction, newspaper and television editors have been able to publish investigative reporting on environmental problems that in many cases were not previously disclosed. In 1992, for example, the Brazilian media responded to the United Nations "Earth Summit" in Rio de Janeiro by saturating the airwaves with environmental reporting and documentaries. This sort of media attention, in conjunction with extensive efforts by ENGOs in the region, has contributed to a radical transformation of public attitudes toward the natural environment.

Democratization alone, however, does not guarantee that environmental concerns will gain support in the government. Scarce fiscal resources ensure fierce competition for government funds. The outcome of these battles can easily undermine effective resource management or pollution-control policies. As Ascher argues in this book, natural resources controlled by democratic governments can become convenient sources of patronage for political clients. Forests in Indonesia have suffered a similar fate under an authoritarian regime, according to Petrich and Smith-Sanclare.

Even if resource management is not threatened by corruption or inefficiency, democratically determined policies can still favor commercial exploitation rather than conservation. Reforms that permit ENGOs to thrive also support the growth of industry and sectoral lobbying groups. If their interests conflict with those of the ENGO community, democratic institutions ensure little more than an orderly resolution of the debate through a recognized process of consultation and decision making. As Silva illustrates in his chapter, revisions to forestry policies established under the Pinochet government were substantially blocked in recent years by a well-organized lobbying effort by the forest-products industry.

Nevertheless, the net effect of democratization is likely to be positive. Authoritarian regimes are generally supported by narrow coalitions of interest groups that promote policies with concentrated benefits for themselves at the expense of the diffuse interests of the general public. Democratically elected regimes, although still capable of promoting policies that benefit narrow segments of the electorate, must build broader coalitions to govern without resort to repressive tactics. Meanwhile, greater freedom of the press and expanding educational activities by ENGOs are likely to result in a gradual shift in public attitudes toward conservation and environmental protection. Moreover, greater openness in political discourse often provides forums for environmental and social action that previously did not exist. Swatuk makes such a case about the effects of political liberalization in Southern Africa. In both Zimbabwe and South Africa, democratization has resulted in a greater likelihood of international and local ENGOs having a voice in communities and therefore affecting public policy.

INTERNATIONALIZATION OF REGIONAL ENVIRONMENTAL ISSUES

Finally, several environmental issues of particular relevance to Latin America have become the focus of international attention in recent years. Since the early 1980s, tropical deforestation has occupied a place near the top of the agenda for ENGOs in developed nations. Forest destruction in the Amazon was a key catalyst to this movement. In conjunction with losses in Asia and Africa, deforestation in Latin America generated extensive concern in the international development community that such unsustainable land use patterns would contribute significantly to global problems such as climate change and loss of biodiversity. Deforestation contributes to carbon dioxide buildup in the atmosphere while simultaneously destroying potential "sinks" for CO_2.

Tropical deforestation also threatens a rich habitat that supports a vast array of biological diversity. Estimates suggest that extinction rates in the tropical forests of Latin America may range from 10 to 50 percent in the near term.[6] Because the loss of biodiversity represents a global concern, the Global Environmental Facility (GEF) (a multilateral fund jointly administered by the World Bank, the United Nations Environment Programme, and the United Nations Development Programme) has dedicated a significant portion of its funds to grants to assist developing nations protect critical habitats and endangered species. Latin American countries received numerous such grants during the GEF's pilot phase.

A broader fear exists that the rapid industrialization of the developing world may substantially compound today's global environmental problems in the space of a few decades. International efforts are already focusing on the use of "green" technology and environmentally sensitive management practices to help the South avoid the North's costly path of dirty development. Development banks have been particularly helpful in supporting integrated national environmental plans in many countries.

LATIN AMERICA IN COMPARATIVE PERSPECTIVE

The comparative cases in this volume highlight a set of common challenges present in Latin America and elsewhere. Political transitions, for example, complicate policy making by undermining old administrative structures and uprooting established political coalitions. Although these developments can serve to catalyze new departures in policy making that favor the environment (as in Chile), they can also signal the breakdown of existing regulatory structures, however flawed they may be (as in Russia). Experiences in Russia and Indonesia also highlight the importance of autonomous resource management institutions to the attainment of sound resource-use patterns.

Economic transformations can also be a mixed blessing. It is now widely accepted that protected and state-owned industries are generally far more polluting and wasteful than those facing real competition in the market. And though integration into the world economy can promote efficiency gains and modernization, integration can also increase the burden on natural resources. Export opportunities may spur the unsustainable exploitation of forests and fisheries. In addition, unregulated growth can produce scale effects that show up in reduced air and water quality. Recognizing that economic growth is the top policy priority for developing countries on every continent, international, regional, and national efforts must press forward with solutions that integrate environment and development. Proposals that favor one side of this equation over the other are not likely to prove sustainable in the long term, either politically or environmentally.

Reflecting on the future of environmental policy in the region, it is encouraging to find increased attention to and funding for conservation, cleanup, and prevention—topics that were highlighted at the Summit of the Americas held in Miami in December 1994. If this volume offers any single lesson, however, it is that the politics of environmental policy making remain contentious, both in Latin America and elsewhere. Even though technical and financial barriers to sustainable development remain, achieving a political commitment to overcoming them is frequently a more fundamental problem. Where political institutions rely on competing interest groups to define and promote policy alternatives, ENGOs are generally confronted by well-organized and well-funded opposition from industry. Even where international partners assist local ENGOs with technical and organizational matters, institutional and cultural factors can prove decisive for their efforts to overcome the daunting collective action problems they face.

In other cases documented in this volume, political institutions do not adhere to this genteel model of politics. Privileged individuals or groups exercise disproportionate influence over government policies, frequently securing preferential access to natural resources owned by the state. In other cases, political leaders manipulate natural resource policies to produce patronage for selected members of their political coalition, thereby undermining sound resource management. Resource policy can also fall victim to power struggles within the government.

Finally, where the state's capacity to administer policy is severely undermined due to financial or political crisis, the environment is clearly at risk. Natural resources are plundered; pollution costs are largely externalized. Under such circumstances, even well-crafted policies are ineffectual, as economic incentives operate unencumbered by regulatory efforts intended to reflect the larger costs to society of individual actions.

If political interests shape policy choices, then the growing involvement of the international community in environmental issues in Latin America and elsewhere may play a critical role in reinforcing and assisting those domestic forces pressing for environmental reform. Financial and technical assistance not only helps solve problems but also bolsters likeminded groups in civil society and within the state. International conferences provide opportunities to introduce new scientific findings, new technologies, and new ideas to national leaders and their advisers. They also inspire increased media coverage of the environmental costs of development, thereby increasing public awareness and education about these issues. In sum, the linkages between domestic and international developments are mutually reinforcing.

With this perspective in mind, we conclude with a cautious optimism that the progress made so far toward sustainable development in Latin America offers a promising start toward a more sustainable future. Snapshots of environmental policy and practice from the region indicate that a great deal of work remains. Considered against the history of development in the region, we believe the trend is strongly positive. In Latin America, as elsewhere, we are witnessing what appears to be a fundamental transition among both governing elites and the general public in their beliefs about the appropriate costs of development. The challenge of the next decade will be to consolidate these beliefs politically and to transform them into concrete policy decisions that actually guide economic activity. Our hope is that this book contributes in some small way to this endeavor.

NOTES

1. World Commission on Environment and Development, *Our Common Future* (New York: Oxford University Press, 1987).

2. Alexander F. Watson, "U.S. Environmental Policy in Latin America and the Caribbean" (paper presented at conference on "The Policies of Latin American Policy in International Perspective," University of California, San Diego, La Jolla, CA, January 20-23, 1994).

3. C. Foster Knight, Richard P. Wells, and Lawrence Pratt, "After the Crisis," *The Environmental Forum* 12, no. 3 (May-June 1995): 22–27.

4. Gordon MacDonald, "Economic Cost of Pollution in Eastern and Central Europe" (unpublished paper, 1995).

5. Ibid.

6. Latin American and Caribbean Commission on Development and Environment, *Our Own Agenda* (Washington, DC: Inter-American Development Bank, 1992), p. 39.

PART ONE

Domestic Politics And Policy

CHAPTER TWO

———————— ■ ————————

The Politics of Rent Distribution and Latin American Natural Resource Policy

William Ascher

In many Latin American countries, state management and government regulation of natural resources have led to overly rapid exploitation, inefficiency in development and extraction, conversion to inferior resource bases, inequitable distribution of benefits, and gratuitous environmental damage. Development and exploitation of renewable natural resources have rarely been sustainable, and the exploitation of nonrenewable resources has failed to obtain the greatest benefits for existing and future populations from these finite endowments. This chapter explores a subset of these problems: the wasteful, overly rapid, and excessive natural resource exploitation in Latin America, involving renewable resources such as forests, nonrenewable resources such as oil and hard minerals, and quasi-renewable natural resources such as water and land, which can suffer declines in quality, productivity, and access.

The simplest potential explanation for this mismanagement—technical ineptitude in understanding and managing natural resources—is not compelling. Economics and natural science are sufficiently developed to make it rather obvious that many resource exploitation approaches are unwise from a societal perspective. There is also growing recognition that ineffective state control, rather than truly communal ownership, results in an "open access" situation that induces unsustainable exploitation. At the root of incompetent, deleterious state control is often an identifiable policy that accounts for the weakness. For example, in Costa Rica ineffectual policing of forests can be attributed to the Dirección General Forestal's minimal budget for gasoline and other operational (as opposed to personnel) expenditures, which has largely kept forest guards out of the jungle. The

15

argument that the state's reach exceeds its grasp has merit, but it raises the question of why governments offer up for exploitation state-controlled resources without extracting "natural resource rent."

This natural resource rent is the potential surplus intrinsic in a natural resource. John Hartwick and Nancy Olewiler define natural resource rent in the following way: "Rent is a surplus—the difference between the price of a good produced using a natural resource and the . . . costs of turning that natural resource into the good. The . . . costs include the value of the labor, capital, materials, and energy inputs used to convert the natural resource into a product. What remains after these factor inputs are netted out is the value of the natural resource itself— the land, or . . . minerals, fish, forests and environmental resources such as air and water."[1]

Robert Repetto defines the rent in trees (called "stumpage value") as "an economic rent, a value attributable not to any cost of production, but to the strength of market demand and favorable natural resource endowments and location. . . . Rent, by definition, is a value in excess of the total costs of bringing trees to market as logs or wood products, including the cost of attracting the necessary investment."[2]

As the initial value of the resource, the natural resource rent might be expected to be the target of often desperate efforts by governments to capture as many financial resources as possible. Another explanation for poor natural resource policies might therefore be that governments try to capture the resource rent even at the expense of maximizing benefits over time. Maximizing *present* extraction may be irresistible, since the losers are often those with the least political power to resist such policies or to impose costs on the government: typically small groups of people in remote locations and future generations. In an alarming number of cases however, the state neither maximizes its gains from natural resource extraction nor safeguards resources for the future.

To understand why this occurs, this chapter explores yet another distributional-politics explanation that is both compelling and troubling. It is compelling because it seems to account for both overexploitation of natural resources *and* inefficient resource development across a broad range of world regions and types of resources. It accounts for the paradox of resource-exploiting institutions that, despite the benefit of lucrative resources, are both heavily indebted and undercapitalized. For a resource-exploiting institution, adequate capitalization is necessary to exploit the resource at the optimal rate and to secure equipment and technology to operate efficiently. Undercapitalization is a problem if, for example, expectations of future price declines call for heavy current production; undercapitalization can thus prevent the enterprise from following the optimal time path for extraction. Overcapitalization is often a problem for the economy as a whole, since unnecessary investment in the resource sector denies capital to other sectors and to the enterprise per se if overcapitalization leads to overspending and overproduction.

The theory also accounts for the bewildering complexity of state institutions entrusted with natural resource exploitation, a factor that contributes strongly to the lack of transparency and accountability in resource management and in converting the resource endowment into worthwhile investment. It is troubling because it raises the possibility that suboptimal resource development and exploitation may be socially optimal under given institutional constraints, where the conventional means of governmental allocation of economic benefits would be normatively inferior.

THE THEORY

The most compelling explanation for problematic natural resource policies and state management is that high-level government and state officials engage in the deliberate violation of John Stuart Mill's principle of separation of production and distribution. Mill argued for treating the maximization of production and the pursuit of just distribution as separable tasks. In this view, production is to be conducted wholeheartedly for maximum efficiency. Just distribution is to be pursued through government spending that provides benefits to the needy and the worthy, financed by revenues from differential tax rates. Production need not be concerned with inequity because inequities arising from production (for example, a worker receiving wages that are too high or too low from a distributive-justice perspective) can be addressed in the subsequent phase of reallocation through fiscal policy (taxation and spending). This presumes that government spending will not introduce inefficiencies in production and that taxes can be implemented that do not lead to production-reducing reactions.[3]

Apart from the feasibility of separating production from distribution, the rationale behind the notion is anchored in the need to maintain the single-minded goal of efficiency. Production activities structured to reward particular individuals or groups cannot be expected to maximize economic returns. For example, paying Bolivian tin miners more than the market-clearing wage raises unit costs, thereby prematurely reaching the "choke point" at which further extraction is no longer financially viable. Conversely, delaying the closing of a depleted mine to keep miners employed requires excessive extraction and the loss of revenues.

Prescriptive natural resource theory implicitly accepts the Millian view. Optimizing refers to maximizing the overall returns of resource development and extraction, taking into account time preferences and discounting in short, optimal, efficient production in Mill's terms.[4] For privately or communally held natural resources, the government ought to regulate for maximum societal efficiency, including the imposition of Pigovian taxes (that is, taxes levied against actions that produce societal costs otherwise not borne by the actor) to force private exploiters to internalize negative externalities. There is no need either to tax some natural resource development or extraction activities more than others or to tax them more or less than nonresource exploitation activities, because the government can tax incomes or consumption "later" and thus avoid driving natural resource exploiters away from the most productive prospects.

For state-controlled natural resources, accomplishing efficiency and distributive justice together is even more straightforward. The state can develop and extract its own resources or sell the rights to private (or communal) actors, thus receiving revenues amounting at least to the intrinsic starting value (natural resource rent) of the resource endowment. Those revenues can then be allocated to obtain distributive justice. In simple terms, the Millian approach secures the greatest monetary value from the resource, and then *channels proceeds through the government's conventional allocative mechanism.*

There is an important conjunction of two objectives: When the government collects the full natural resource rent, it adds to its revenues, and resource exploiters can respond to price signals, enabling them to exploit the resource efficiently. If the government allows rents to be distributed *in the course of* exploiting the natural resource, however, the full rent will not be captured by the state. It is thus likely that the resource-exploitation activities chosen to serve distributive goals (for example, higher wages for mine workers, greater incomes and infrastructure for the population in particular sites, and artificially low consumer prices) will not coincide with productivity-maximizing and, therefore, state-revenue-maximizing activities. Subsidies above those that provide just enough incentive to achieve positive externalities lead to price distortions and fiscal drains. For exploitation of privately owned resources regulated by the state, government actions (aside from those averting negative externalities) favoring certain sectors will distort relative prices and reduce net economic activity. For example, export bans on round logs are designed to favor a domestic wood products industry by lowering log prices on the domestic market.

Channeling rents from public lands through the central fiscal apparatus fulfills the following objectives:

1. increasing the state's capacity to extract fiscal resources;
2. allowing central governmental officials (who, at least in democratic systems, have greater accountability by virtue of their need to stand for election) to determine the distribution of benefits provided by public resources; and
3. increasing the transparency of public resource allocation, insofar as the central budgetary process typically requires broad dissemination of detailed budget information.

From these considerations, it may seem that the Millian approach would be attractive to governments for a host of reasons, including the fundamental political objective of keeping the resource flow within the central government. Despite this I argue that government officials and agencies are strongly motivated to circumvent the fiscal apparatus even at the cost of inefficient resource exploitation. Under certain circumstances various governmental actors—often including some involved in the central budgetary process—have institutional incentives to violate

Millian principles. The pursuit of other objectives may lead to a failure to maximize resource exploitation and central government revenues.

REASONS FOR VIOLATING
THE MILLIAN PRINCIPLE

If we begin by identifying the three fundamental motives that drive government officials to abuse natural resources, we can understand why some of the strategies they adopt lead to resource policy failures. The following motives sometimes lead to such abuses:

1. *Political power.* The motive to increase the power of the actor, agency, the government in general, or particular partisan political organizations leads to concern over

    1.1. the *net external political support* for government officials coming from outside of government (but note that power has other bases beyond political support, such as control over information, monopoly over expertise, or control over coercion).

    1.2. *bureaucratic political power*, encompassing the capacity of an agency both to prevail in policy conflicts with other agencies and to control key resources.

2. *Economic self-aggrandizement.* Economic rewards for the government officials and close associates are sometimes sought as ends in themselves.

3. *Programmatic objectives.* Government officials have programmatic objectives beyond simply enjoying the rewards of government office, most prominently

    3.1. to distribute (or redistribute) income and wealth, and

    3.2. to pursue particular development strategies.

Objectives may be considered as programmatic when the outcomes are sought for their own sake, rather than simply for political or economic advantage for the government officials.

These motives are obviously related, yet they are analytically quite distinct. There are times when an actor's political power enhances his or her capability to pursue programmatic objectives, and the achievement of programmatic goals can strengthen the standing of particular government officials and agencies. Yet, there are other times when the pursuit of programmatic objectives runs the risk of reducing political support. Similarly, political power can expand the opportunities for economic venality by officials and their associates. Economic power is often a base for political power, yet political standing sometimes requires forgoing economic opportunities, and vice versa. By separating these motives, rather than reducing them to a single motive, we avoid the pitfall of characterizing government officials too narrowly as simply power hungry, avaricious, or naively idealistic.

These motives, particularly the motives of power and the pursuit of programmatic objectives, do not necessarily result in resource policy failures. One could imagine officials gaining greater political support and power from the economic growth that results from efficient resource management. One could also imagine programmatic objectives that are consistent with good resource management, such as seeking benefits for regions where natural resources can be exploited efficiently or launching sensible resource-based industries. Yet the focus of this chapter is on the instances in which the pursuit of these goals leads to poor resource policies.

Three strategies for pursuing these motives can be identified as follows:

1. *Granting economic benefits via the natural resource exploitation process.* Insofar as economic benefits elicit political support from their recipients, officials who can make the beneficiaries aware of the benefits can often count on enhancing their political power. The ability to grant economic benefits gives government officials the economic power to aid potential supporters or undermine opponents and to enhance the bureaucratic standing of government agencies. One crucial form of exchange is the opportunity for private actors to avail themselves of special privileges (so-called rent-seeking opportunities)[5] provided through government policies that restrict competition by other actors, thus enabling the beneficiaries to enjoy higher and often more secure rates of return than the competitive market would provide. For example, logging concessions are in essence exclusive licenses: If the government does not charge for the full value stumpage value, then the concessionaire enjoys the opportunity to capture greater returns than if the forest concession were auctioned off to the highest bidder. Providing these "rents" can often induce their recipients to reciprocate to the responsible government officials, whether through bribes, political support, or the willingness to undertake other actions at the direction of those officials. The economic surpluses involved in resource exploitation can also provide capital for income redistribution and the financing of development initiatives as well as financial rewards for the officials themselves. The problem posed for the productivity of natural resource exploitation, as mentioned in the previous section, is that there is no reason why directing resource exploitation to serve these purposes would coincide with the best resource practices.

2. *Gaining or maintaining discretion over the allocation of economic surpluses.* The government official bent on using the surpluses for the purposes outlined above needs to control them. Yet wresting control over allocation often requires, or results in, misuse of natural resources. For example, a government agency or state enterprise may develop a particular resource because it could have control over the allocation of the benefits. A surplus may be buried in an inefficient resource investment in order to keep it from being captured by other officials.

3. *Evading accountability for actions that might increase political opposition or provoke the withdrawal of political support if these actions are attributed to governmental actors.* The capacity to evade accountability can protect against the erosion of political support when publicized governmental actions would antagonize various actors or when officials would be discredited because of their venality and offers of rent-seeking opportunities. Reduced accountability can also make the pur-

suit of programmatic objectives more politically viable insofar as lower account-ability allows government officials to pursue objectives that otherwise would be too risky politically. However, the evasion of accountability often entails suppress-ing information that resource exploiters need in order to choose the most appro-priate resources to exploit and to establish optimal rates of resource development and extraction. Evasion of accountability also often involves adding complexity to the structure of resource-exploiting institutions, leading to both greater waste and greater difficulty in determining optimal strategies. Lack of accountability in itself allows the agents of the resource owner to indulge their own interests at the expense of those of the owner. In particular, state enterprises in natural resource exploitation are prone to gross inefficiency when their personnel find that they cannot be held accountable for inappropriate practices.

Orientations of Actors in the Conventional Central Budget Process

The "conventional fiscal authorities" include all officials involved in obtaining and spending funds of the central treasury. Some of these actors, such as the tax ad-ministration, are involved only in taxation, including establishing the target mag-nitudes of revenues, setting the levels and kinds of revenue sources (such as taxes and royalties), establishing the rules for administering revenue collection, and im-plementing tax policy. Other officials spend the revenue by setting allocations via ministerial and agency budgets. Many of the most important fiscal authorities are involved in both activities in order to deal with the problems of balancing rev-enues and expenditures. Thus the office of the chief executive, the finance (or eco-nomics) ministry, the executive branch planning agency, the legislature, and the legislative branch budgeting agency all have some degree of influence on both revenue targets and spending limits.

For some actors, financial resources are at their disposal only once the re-sources are in the central treasury. To the degree that discretion over fiscal re-sources and the balance between revenues and expenditures are major objectives, these actors have strong institutional motives to be Millians. The finance ministry and executive planning agency in particular are typically concerned with main-taining macroeconomic balance by ensuring that the maximum funds reach the treasury. Indeed, these actors may be so eager to increase treasury revenues that they are willing to go beyond the Millian position by imposing royalties on re-source extraction that exceed the value of the publicly owned natural resource rent and by denying subsidies that are warranted by the positive externalities they would generate. The spending ministries that depend predominantly on the bud-get also favor high levels of treasury revenues.

Legislators and the chief executive face greater complexities in deciding on how far to follow Millian principles. Legislators who play a major role in central bud-get decision making gain politically when recipients of government spending credit them with having provided the benefits. Government spending may directly subsidize inputs for natural resource development, for example, through inexpensive fertilizer from state companies or cheap government credit. Tax credits and exemptions for natural resource development activities, however, are benefits that reduce overall tax revenues. Legislators may also encounter political pressures to reduce overall spending and maximize tax revenues; others are fiscally conservative for ideological reasons or to manifest opposition to the executive's fiscal expansiveness. In short, specific political and ideological configurations determine the extent to which the Millian approach is favored.

The executive dominates both the allocation of the central treasury and the spending and investment decisions made by natural resource exploiters. Preference, therefore, may depend on which mode of allocating resources is more firmly under the president's control and provides the greatest political credit. Often the presidency has greater control over nonministerial spending, such as that for decentralized state agencies and public enterprises. Moreover, when the president wants to evade accountability for politically embarrassing investments or consumption decisions, the complexity of resource exploitation allocations will be more attractive.

Orientations of Actors in the Natural Resource Sector

The natural resource sector spans government agencies, state enterprises, and private actors involved in the development, extraction, and regulation of natural resources. Government agencies sometimes develop or extract natural resources directly. They also oversee and regulate resource development and extraction, from the smallest operating units to the highest levels of the ministries of mining, petroleum, forestry, and so forth. In regard to conservation, government agencies involved in both resource exploitation and regulation exhibit ambivalence.

Private resource exploiters want to maintain maximum control over resources for which they have property or user rights, including freedom from government regulation that would restrict profit-making opportunities. They also want to capture as much of the natural resource rent from publicly owned resources as they can. Although they may favor conservation, this occurs mostly when exploiters are confident it will benefit them in the future. Hence, their confidence in long-term access to natural resources is crucial.

Whether public or private, natural resource exploiters favor keeping rents within the sector and maximizing central treasury funds earmarked for resource development. By assuring that resources stay in the sector, government agencies controlling natural resources can expand their budgets and win the support of private exploiters. Even those government agencies mandated to regulate natural resource exploitation form political alliances with state enterprises and large-scale private firms, which can generate large surpluses without requiring the agencies to agonize over surplus-limiting issues such as conservation or catering to low-income, marginal resource exploiters.

In summary, finance ministries and executive planning agencies place high priority on macroeconomic balance and increasing institutional discretion over financial surpluses; sectoral spending ministries place high priority on the availability of ample funds in the central treasury. Therefore, these institutions favor bringing the maximum amount of surplus derived from natural resources into the central treasury. Presidents and legislators place high priority on maintaining discretion over, and maximizing political credit from, the allocations of both resource-derived surpluses and budgetary funds. Based on the calculus of both intragovernmental and electoral politics, they may favor either bringing surpluses into the central treasury or circumventing the treasury. However, they may prefer to withhold treasury funds from resource development in order to allocate them elsewhere, or they may favor spending those funds on development activities, although it is not justified by the logic of positive externalities. Government agencies in the natural resource sector and their allies among private resource extractors favor increased resources coming into and being retained by the sector. These actors attempt to place the maximum volume of treasury funds into resource development.

Mechanisms for Violation of Millian Principles

Three mechanisms make possible the violation of Millian principles. First, the government may undercharge the resource exploiter by setting formal royalty rates below the value of the resource rent (stumpage value, value of oil or mineral in the ground, and so forth). This allows the exploiters to capture a very large surplus. In the extreme, undercharging takes the form of granting user or property rights to nongovernmental actors for resources previously under governmental control (for example, land grants to colonists, ceding forest rights on state-owned land, and awarding mineral claims on state land). Undercharging also occurs when government agencies fail to devote sufficient resources to monitoring and enforcing royalty collection, despite the existence of a full-rent-capture policy. In addition, governments can obscure whether royalties are being paid (for example, by allowing exploiters to claim community service as a payment).

Yet another form of undercharging appears in the failure to collect Pigovian taxes. Since the value of the resource is both its market value and the value of the environmental services it provides, reduction or elimination of the resource would entail a loss, for which the state on behalf of the people should be compensated.

A crucial step in undercharging occurs when the officials direct or coordinate the allocation of the captured surplus by the recipient. Often the state undertakes actions that mask its failure to collect appropriate revenues, including suppression of information or utilization of complex financial and ownership arrangements.

Second, Millian principles are violated when circumstances may require the exploiter to deviate from optimal-return practices in order to provide a transfer to a particular group. It might do so by requiring excessive employment or wage rates above the market-clearing wage; setting low output prices to benefit the purchasers and downstream consumers; banning exports of raw resources to provide a cheaper supply for domestic processors; directing the resource exploiters to perform social and developmental functions (for example, providing educational facilities for local communities); and choosing an exploitation site in order to provide higher incomes to its residents, even if the area is not optimal for resource exploitation. These mechanisms deny income to the resource exploiter and revenues to the fiscal authorities, who suffer as the tax base erodes under suboptimal policies.

Third, Millian principles are violated by subsidizing the development, expansion, or restoration of natural resources (for example, reforestation programs) beyond the amount justified to pursue the positive externalities of resource enhancement. This is equivalent to rent seeking that wastes fiscal resources.

Those who defend a reliance on conventional fiscal processes to control public resource rents do not sit still in the face of these efforts. Inasmuch as they anticipate efforts to circumvent their control, the fiscal authorities will try to strengthen their hold over the resource rent by (1) developing mechanisms (such as higher royalties, taxes, dividends from state enterprises, mandatory loans) in order to extract surplus from the exploiters; (2) controlling financial resources available to the resource-exploiting or resource-regulating institutions; (3) increasing the monitoring of resource exploiters or resource regulators; (4) requiring approval over operational decisions by the resource exploiters or resource regulators; (5) forcing replacement of officials perceived as circumventing the fiscal authorities; and (6) restructuring the government to strengthen control over resource rents.

These measures are very difficult to calibrate. Therefore, when the fiscal authorities "win," the resource institutions face the risks of excessive financial extraction (for example, royalties in excess of the rent of the resources extracted), inadequate budgets for resource development, cumbersome bureaucratic controls, inefficient and inexpert micromanagement, excessive job insecurity, and institutional instability. The first two lead to suboptimal resource exploitation.

Finally, in reaction to these problems resource exploiters often undertake another round of protective maneuvers that exacerbate inefficiency in resource exploitation. Resource managers in the state sector often "hide" surpluses by investing them, without regard to the quality of the investment. By diversifying, they risk exceeding the boundaries of their technical and managerial competence, even when they succeed in escaping the areas in which fiscal authorities have restricted the exploiter's autonomy or in which those authorities can most easily extract the surplus. They build overspending into their structures and operations. They conspire with other bureaucratic warriors to get the fiscal authorities dismissed or weakened. As for the private resource exploiters, they quickly learn to withhold information from heavy-handed fiscal authorities. When faced with the prospect of losing rent-seeking opportunities, private resource exploiters rush to extract as much as possible as fast as possible before privileges may be withdrawn.

Pitfalls of the Millian Approach

The Millian approach presumes that distributive justice can be achieved through the conventional fiscal mechanism. When this is not true, inefficiency in resource exploitation that leads to greater distributive justice cannot be considered gratuitous. Efficient resource exploitation may be a casualty of distributional struggles, but that does not necessarily mean that exploitation efficiency should override other societal values. In other words, should we consider a moderate loss of efficiency tolerable if it allocates some of the resource surplus directly to poor mine workers or loggers who would not receive their "fair" share of government benefits from fiscal authorities bent on directing conventional government spending to their wealthy friends? Should the marginal Bolivian mine be kept open in light of the fact that laid-off mine workers may receive very few of the benefits generated by a sounder mining policy? However, resource developers and exploiters are themselves not always worthy of greater benefits (organized oil and mining workers, in particular, are generally at the top of the "labor elite"). Consequently, it is not easy to determine the distributive superiority of steering natural resource rents away from the conventional spending authorities. It requires contextually sensitive analysis of a case-by-case nature.

What about fiscal authorities bent on indulging resource developers with subsidies that lead to detrimental natural resource conversions? It is possible that the cycling of natural resource rents into the fiscal apparatus and then into unwise resource-development subsidies would be detrimental to resource endowments. In the case of Mexico, for example, oil wealth captured by the conventional apparatus has been channeled into counterproductive irrigation and forest clearing for low-yield pasture.

EMPIRICAL SUPPORT FOR THE THEORY

How can we determine whether these dynamics are truly important in accounting for the natural resource policy failures so prevalent in Latin America? Several broad-based tests are conceivable to demostrate that

- governments with relatively less internal division and bureaucratic rivalry are less prone to diversion of the state's natural resource rent through resource exploitation;
- governments in countries with general consensus on development strategies are less prone to diversion of the state's natural resource rent through resource exploitation;

- governments offering low rents (such as Chile, where promoting rent seeking exposes the government to political or legal sanctions) rely less on natural resource exploitation to provide special privileges to favored groups;
- the chief executive's support for fiscal authorities over resource exploiters shifts according to the executive's satisfaction with the fiscal allocations;
- efforts at rent capture will increase when the resource exploiters' investments no longer fit the priorities of the government officials;
- competing explanations may be dismissed, including those that claim that, (a) officials simply try to maximize rent capture; (b) officials simply try to maximize rent-seeking opportunities; (c) officials blunder into resource-policy failures; and
- there is consistency of explanation with the interpretations provided by key individuals (elicited through interviews).

These broad tests face subtle difficulties. For example, while it would seem appropriate to hypothesize that a strong chief executive could dispense with the suboptimal strategy of diverting the state's natural resource rent or otherwise maximizing long-term returns from natural resource exploitation, in fact the basis of the chief executive's strength may be in maintaining a rent-seeking arrangement and benefiting certain groups to a greater degree than would be politically possible with transparent budget allocations. Indeed, all of these multicountry tests are fraught with the risks of measurement error. A more "micro," thick-description approach based on case histories is sounder. This is in keeping with an epistemology that is content to identify patterns that ought to be examined for their explanatory relevance in specific cases, rather than asserting and testing general laws. Space does not permit truly thick description, but I offer brief and stylized cases for consideration.

Corporación Nacional del Cobre (CODELCO)

Can a resource-exploiting agency, even under formal jurisdiction of fiscal authorities, evade the efforts of these authorities to capture the resource rent? In the mid–1980s, the Chilean Finance Ministry informed the Corporación Nacional del Cobre (CODELCO), the world's largest copper company, that its investment budget would be cut from roughly US$400 million to below US$300 million, so that Chile could meet its macroeconomic targets of reduced spending. As a parastatal completely owned by the Chilean government, CODELCO was legally obligated to accept the investment budget authorized by the Finance Ministry, as well as to submit its investment projects for review by several other governmental agencies, such as the Ministry of Mines, the Chilean Copper Commission, and the Office of Planning. Since CODELCO is obliged to surrender its entire surplus each year, both true profit as well as resource rent, it has no autonomously controlled investment fund.

However, CODELCO was in the midst of a crucial expansion of the Chuquicamata facility, the world's largest open-pit copper mine. Because the ore grades at a particular deposit generally decline over time (inasmuch as miners try to identify and extract the highest-grade ores first), Chuquicamata's expansion was essential to keep CODELCO's production costs down. The expansion was considered sound and important by all of the technical and economic analyses conducted within and outside of CODELCO. The long-term expansion plan was approved by the government in 1981, and the Finance Ministry approved the five-year investment program (1984 to 1988) which called for annual investments of nearly US$400 million. However, in 1985, in the context of a commitment to the International Monetary Fund to curtail overall investment, the Finance Ministry imposed an annual investment ceiling of US$300 million for 1985 and 1986. With the apparent backing of the Ministry of Mines, CODELCO proceeded to spend US$369 million in 1985 and US$378 million in 1986.[6] After the investment expenditures of 1986 became known, CODELCO was compelled to reduce 1987 investments very sharply, to less than US$300 million, and the CODELCO senior management team was dismissed. The cutback had very serious consequences for the Chuquicamata expansion, including delays of up to a year and a half in getting components on line and a lack of coherence of the subsequent investment program.

The CODELCO case demonstrates the fiscal authorities' motivation to surpass Millian limits of extracting natural-resource-sector surplus; the budget approved by the Finance Ministry would have captured the resource rent and the capitalization needed for reasonable resource development. Finance Ministry officials surely knew of the severity of the problems that the budget cutbacks would cause. Their actions reflected not only the centrality of the macroeconomic stabilization objective but also the long-standing struggle over the allocation of the resource rent. This struggle dated to the Allende period (1970–1973) when CODELCO reported that high wages had left no profit and hence no resource rent for the government. Even today, CODELCO truck drivers and guards are paid roughly double the wages of their counterparts in Chile's private copper mines. The Finance Ministry's concern that CODELCO had been absorbing the natural resource wealth of the country at objectionable levels therefore had some basis. The institutional interests of the corporation clearly prevailed over the agenda of the Finance Ministry. Ultimately, the formal authority and/or intragovernmental political influence of the Finance Ministry outranked CODELCO, and the critics of CODELCO exacted a high price for the corporation's attempt at autonomy.

The most prevalent interpretation of the dismissal of the senior management team in 1987 is that the Finance Ministry was punishing the senior management in order to ensure greater compliance in the future. This is borne out by the fact that the government then installed a management team with little experience in copper and soon replaced that team with another of similarly limited experience. Although it is impossible to definitively pin down the government's rationale for bringing in these inexperienced teams, this pattern of replacing management is consistent with a tactic of reducing autonomy by selecting agents who lack both the capability to manipulate the system to increase their autonomy and prior loyalties to the corporation. The performance of both teams was judged unsatisfactory when CODELCO fell seriously behind in meeting its sales commitments. In January 1989, the government finally appointed a highly experienced team.

The budget episode also demonstrates that the formal control by fiscal authorities, in this case the Finance Ministry, does not definitively translate into de facto control. The top CODELCO management presumably had enough influence with the president to defy the Finance Ministry for two years. It also resorted to creative labeling and accounting in developing the Las Pampas copper deposit, near Chuquicamata. By relabeling the deposit "Chuquicamata Norte," and charging its development to Chuquicamata's operating costs, CODELCO circumvented both restrictions against exploiting deposits outside its mandated area and Finance Ministry restrictions on its capital budget. Thus, CODELCO has exemplified the motivation and the capacity of a resource-sector actor to evade control by fiscal authorities despite the formal jurisdiction of these authorities.

Another, more enduring aspect of the relationship between the government and CODELCO reveals the willingness of the president and the Chilean Congress to circumvent their own conventional budgetary process. Since the late 1960s, a law has earmarked 10 percent of copper revenues to go directly to the armed forces, rather than allowing the military budget to be fully allocated in the conventional fiscal process. The law was enacted before the Chilean military played its pivotal role in the 1970s. Therefore, rather than representing the mere power of the armed forces, the law reflected the political convenience for the president, Congress, and the armed forces to have an automatic appropriation rather than having to annually debate and justify the full military budget. Once the law became a fixture of Chilean political economy, executives and legislators were no longer held accountable for this component of military spending.

Petróleos Mexicanos (PEMEX)

The government strategy of capturing the resource extractor's surplus—even to the point of undercapitalization—is not unique to CODELCO. Also in response to the resource extractor's past retention of the resource rent, the Mexican Finance Ministry has driven Mexico's state petroleum monopoly, Petróleos Mexicanos (PEMEX), into both serious indebtedness and chronic undercapitalization. PEMEX was unable to expand production when petroleum prices were high, costing Mexico hundreds of millions of dollars.

Beginning with the oil boom of 1974, PEMEX expanded rapidly. It also spent lavishly, both directly and through complicated transfers to the Petroleum Workers Union. PEMEX chief executives and Mexican presidents reportedly collaborated continuously on allocating the vast oil earnings to meet political needs. PEMEX's chief executive, Jorge Díaz Serrano, was extraordinarily prominent and was considered a leading candidate for the presidential nomination of Mexico's dominant Partido Revolucionario Institucional (PRI) party. Díaz Serrano made numerous public statements extolling the vastness of Mexican oil reserves at the same time that President José López Portillo was cautioning the public about the need to preserve the national patrimony. Yet these two men reportedly collaborated intimately in deciding how to allocate oil wealth to address political needs. PEMEX accounting was extremely opaque. Some of the eventual fallout included Díaz Serrano's imprisonment and the disgrace of López Portillo. One estimate, published in the respected journal *Proceso*, estimated the discrepancy within PEMEX's own accounting of oil sales as being equivalent to US$3.56 billion for 1980 alone![7]

In 1978, a new tax regime imposed by the Finance Ministry resulted in transfers often above PEMEX's net revenues. Oscar Guzmán wrote:

> The federal government's policy was to appropriate most of PEMEX's international earnings and redistribute them according to the priorities established in government programs; thus, the oil industry's remaining profit, which was to be used for investment, was severely reduced. In 1982 the government again increased its tax on the sale of refined products to 27 percent; for petrochemicals it was set at 15 percent and exported crude at 58 percent plus 3 percent *ad valorem*. Consequently, the federal tax PEMEX had to pay in 1982 amounted to 91 percent of its before-tax profits, that is, around US$11.724 billion, which was 5.4 times more than it had paid in 1979 in constant 1977 currency.[8]

As PEMEX borrowed internationally (apparently with a credit ceiling separate from that of the Mexican government, even though PEMEX debt is theoretically sovereign debt), the taxes still drew resources out of the company, resulting in the paradoxical situation of a heavily indebted, undercapitalized company in a lucrative industry.

The PEMEX case also reflects high-level struggles over bureaucratic-political power. Before Díaz Serrano's fall, he and President López Portillo presided over much of the pivotal resource allocation in Mexico, to a degree bypassing both the Finance Ministry and the spending ministries. The early reputation of PEMEX as "a state within the state" reflected both the lack of transparency of PEMEX finances, used frequently by Mexican presidents to avoid accountability for spending in politically key areas, and PEMEX's power vis-à-vis fiscal authorities. The eventual confiscation of PEMEX surplus and investment capital is marked by an excessiveness that reflects the outcome of a winner-take-all bureaucratic-political conflict, in which the fiscal authorities resorted to extreme rent confiscation in order to ensure that the resource extractor and its allies could not hide the surplus in various operations and new investments, as had occurred in the CODELCO case.

Petróleos de Venezuela, S.A.

The Venezuelan oil company, Petróleos de Venezuela, S.A. (PDVSA), is yet another resource-extracting parastatal that illustrates the "second-round" maneuvers, taken by management at the expense of efficiency, to evade efforts by the fiscal authorities to drain away surplus. Again, the scenario develops when the treasury attempts to capture the resource rent. PDVSA's investment fund held surplus because the preexisting formula of profit retention did not foresee the windfall oil revenues of 1979–1981. However, in the case of Venezuela, much of the resource rent eluded the fiscal authorities. PDVSA avoided the capture of its surplus to the point of undercapitalization, but the resulting investment pattern was, according to the judgment of outside observers, highly problematic.

PDVSA developed out of privatized international companies and the original state corporation in 1976. The competition among the three PDVSA operating companies, the preexisting professional culture, and PDVSA's right to retain its profits reinforced its culture of efficiency. While the majority of oil revenues went directly to the government through royalties and taxes (amounting to around 80 percent of "profits"), the initial arrangement between PDVSA and the Venezuelan government provided the company an unusually high level of autonomy, including retention of its after-tax profits in its own investment account. Beginning with its original capital outlay, the fund approached US$8 billion by 1981 in the wake of the second oil price shock.

PDVSA's considerable financial (and operating) autonomy then eroded in less than a decade, beginning with the 1979 amendment to the nationalization law that required the Ministry of Hydrocarbons and Mines to approve all PDVSA budgets and reduced the terms of PDVSA directors from four years to two.[9] Government officials charged PDVSA with mismanagement of funds as a prelude to a September 1982 decree that assigned the Central Bank control over all state enterprises' foreign exchange earnings. PDVSA was assigned control over a US$300 million revolving fund to meet its international obligations in other currencies, and the rest of the US$8 billion account was converted into public bonds. In December 1982, the government asked PDVSA to provide US$1.8 billion to bail out the bankrupt Workers' Bank. When the board refused, the government called a special shareholders' meeting and ordered the board to acquire US$1.8 billion in public debt bonds. In the same month, the Central Bank ratified the use of up to another US$1.8 billion for the acquisition of more debt bonds to underwrite government budget deficits. As a result, PDVSA was forced to freeze its heavy-crude project in the Orinoco. By April 1986, 85 percent of PDVSA's investment fund had been channeled into long-term government bonds. Doubt abounds concerning the government's ability or willingness to redeem these bonds, as opposed to simply rolling them over, because of the very high level of indebtedness of the Venezuelan government and its reluctance to relinquish the surplus it captured from PDVSA.[10]

PDVSA's reaction, naturally enough, has been to distrust its investment fund as a secure haven for its surplus. Shortly after the raids by the government, PDVSA spent the bulk of its reserves on questionable investments in refineries and gas stations. The purchase of outmoded refining facilities in Louisiana was particularly criticized, but to the degree that these facilities had value, purchasing them allowed PDVSA to retain some control over its surplus.

Corporación de Forestería de Honduras (COHDEFOR)

While the preceding cases all depict the intragovernmental struggles over the natural resource rent, in forestry cases the conflict is extended to private actors, both commercial loggers and traditional, low-income forest users. The struggle in Honduras began in 1974 when the government formed the state forestry company, Corporación de Forestería de Honduras (COHDEFOR). That same year the state took formal control over all trees in the country.

Despite its status as a Honduran government forestry agency and a state enterprise, COHDEFOR's budget is drawn primarily from its own revenues from operations and leasing. COHDEFOR's sustainable-yield philosophy in its management of its commercial pine forests arose because it earns its own budget from those harvests. COHDEFOR's capacity to retain its profits gives it an incentive to be cost conscious, and this has led to harsh restrictions for keeping local people—the traditional, low-income forest exploiters—from extracting resources, even when they have customary rights to do so. The long-term perspective of its personnel, based largely on expectations that they will remain in the agency, also contributes to resisting the temptation to overharvest. Yet the government's denial of user rights to local people contributes to hostility not only toward the government but also toward the forest: There is widespread removal of fuelwood; squatting by farmers on forest land claimed by the government; and illegal burning of forests to plant crops and to extend pastures.[11] The conflict over the right to the resource rent, expressed in the simple terms of ownership over the trees, has triggered wasteful exploitation and inappropriate conversion of this resource by local people where COHDEFOR policing is weak. Given the remoteness of many forest sites, even an intimidating agency such as COHDEFOR cannot enforce its restrictions in much of the Honduran forest lands.

The situation in the Honduran broadleaf forests, rich in game and other forms of biological diversity, is worse. They have been disappearing rapidly, in part because COHDEFOR has little commercial interest in them and has devoted even fewer resources to their conservation.[12] COHDEFOR also squandered large forest revenues through its abortive wood products subsidiary, Corfino, and other ventures in "downstream" processing. This is another example of government earmarking of surplus for particular beneficiaries—in this case the owners and workers of the wood products industry—instead of allowing the central planning and budgeting process to develop a sectoral strategy. From the mid-1970s through the mid-1980s, the Honduran presidency and the relevant sectoral ministries pushed the expansion of wood products despite the deteriorating prospects for private sawmills. Corfino, located in the pine forest reserve of Olancho, was heavily in debt and essentially bankrupt by the mid-1980s. COHDEFOR inherited Corfino's debts and those of other wood products ventures, demostrating the failure of questionable investments that would have been extremely difficult to justify in any analysis undertaken by the conventional fiscal authorities.[13]

Forestry in the Brazilian Amazon

The effort by the Honduran government to capture the forest resource rent is curiously inverted in the case of the Brazilian Amazon. Investigators estimate that, as of the mid-1980s, the value of industrial round logs was US$1.7 trillion.[14] Yet, with the establishment of the Superintendency for the Development of the Amazon (SUDAM) in the mid-1960s, the Brazilian government opened the region to accelerating deforestation and unsound land conversion, receiving very little return from marketing, as opposed to burning, the trees. Cattle ranching and smallholder agriculture are the major sources of deforestation. Little effort has been devoted to either timber extraction or conservation, despite formal requirements to keep the land forested.[15] Private concerns have been responsible for exploitation, which predominantly involved wholesale clearing more than deliberate logging of commercial timber.

In a solid analysis of the Brazilian Amazon's economic potential, John Browder points out that "the industrial wood sector plays a small but growing role in the Brazilian economy. . . . In the Amazon . . . [f]our of the region's six states and federal territories depend on wood products for more than 25 percent of their industrial output. . . . In Rondonia and Roraima, wood products account for more than 60 percent of industrial output."[16]

However, industrial output in the Amazon is quite small compared to crop and livestock production. Thus, Browder concludes that "Notwithstanding this tremendous industrial growth potential . . . Brazil's stewardship of its tropical forest patrimony has allowed, in fact promoted, its destruction."[17]

Why have the Amazonian forests been treated as if they are of so little value? Subsidized credit and tax benefits made the resource development of the Amazon—ostensibly intended to turn "low-value" forest into agricultural land and pasture—into a prime rent-seeking opportunity of the 1980s, at least until the policy reforms of the Collor administration. Resource management thus proceeded as if the private resource rent of a typical piece of Amazonian land was minimal; its value is not so much in the trees nor in the soils, which are generally poor for agriculture and even for livestock, as in the opportunities to receive government largesse.

Of course, there has been some recognition of the long-term economic and environmental importance of the Amazon and occasional policy responses. The greatest societal value of the Amazon forest lies in gradual extraction of valuable hardwoods (facilitated by government policies to encourage the marketing of more than the handful of species currently utilized in significant volumes) and in the environmental and habitat services provided by the intact forest.[18] Once the Southeast Asian forests are depleted, the Amazon, thus far less exploited because of the lower density of commercial species, will become far more attractive for commercial logging. In the 1960s, a reforestation plan allowed forestry companies to retain up to half of their income tax obligations for the purpose of replanting.

Official sources claimed that 1.8 billion trees were replanted on 820,000 hectares between 1970 and 1975, but serious doubts have been raised as to whether either viable plantations were established or natural forest restoration was actually accomplished.[19] The clear policy failures in resource development arose because the Brazilian reforestation plan was vulnerable to privately profitable strategies by forestry companies designed to do the minimum required to qualify for the tax credits.

The potential rent of the Brazilian Amazonian forests has been reduced by several factors. First, the long-standing prohibition on the export of round logs constricts the effective export market.[20] It forces loggers either to sell more cheaply to the more limited domestic processing industry, thereby reducing the rents that the loggers can capture, or to become vertically integrated. Vertical integration, in requiring domestic loggers to establish sawmills and other facilities, is often a suboptimal economic venture. Browder points out that Brazil has nearly a third of the world's hardwoods but accounts for only a tenth of hardwood exports.[21] The round-log export ban only denied income to the timber harvesters in favor of the processors and also reduced the total rent by subjecting the timber to inefficient processing. The government's preference for channeling the rents to the processing industry is also reflected in the tax holidays provided for these industries, a practice still in effect in Brazil even though it has been eliminated in many other countries where these subsidies have been recognized as shortsighted.[22] The Brazilian government launched a downstream forest-products strategy similar to that of Corfino in Honduras without allowing the central budgetary process to determine whether this strategy would yield sufficiently high rates of return. In the Brazilian case, however, the government has relied on the private sector rather than on the state itself to undertake the strategy. Part of the rationale was that powerful private interests, particularly from São Paulo, were attractive allies in offering rent-seeking opportunities.

Thus, most importantly, the low private economic value of Amazonian land (aside from its public goods value) reflected the fact that it was merely a prop for the real rent-seeking game: using landholding to qualify for fiscal rents—subsidized government credit, tax credits, free or cheap inputs, and so forth. Tax credits were equivalent to up to 75 percent of the investment costs in Amazonian projects, such as cattle ranches.[23] Land giveaways in the Brazilian Amazon thus have been more a pretext for rent-seeking extraction than efficient conversion to sustainable agriculture. Despite the formality of obtaining private land titles, the Amazon became an open-access resource, with the predictable waste in its exploitation. In this case, the natural resource endowment (that is, the trees, the biodiversity, and the ecosystem as a whole) essentially got in the way of the most convenient form of rent seeking. The convenience came from the remoteness of the Amazon and the consequent lack of transparency of what was going on, and it could be rationalized in terms of politically potent rhetoric of national security and bold development.

Forestry in Costa Rica

Three aspects of forestry policy bring into question Costa Rica's vaunted reputation for natural resource conservation: subsidies for cattle ranching (now eliminated), low stumpage prices on state lands, and poorly designed subsidies for reforestation. Like Brazil but unlike Honduras, funds have been transferred primarily from the central treasury to ostensible resource developers. The rent-seeking component of all three policies has led to disappointing development and alarming depletion of sustainable resource-extraction opportunities.

The cattle ranching subsidies in Costa Rica are a well-known story. There are strong indications that the promotion of cattle ranching was a rent-creation device. In the 1970s, credit for ranching, coming predominantly from the nationalized banking sector, surpassed credit for agriculture; by 1982, ranching accounted for 23 percent of *all* state credit.[24] Little was applied to serious ranching efforts, as indicated by many loan defaults, which signals that the credit might have been used for consumption rather than investment in livestock. By the end of 1985, over 70 percent of the delinquent farm loans were from livestock operations, and delinquency rates for large livestock producers were 63.1 percent (compared to 28.3 percent for small-scale ones).[25]

In the face of these delinquencies, the Costa Rican government proposed a debt rescheduling program as part of the 1987 Ley Fodea, an agricultural promotion law initially aimed at small and medium-sized producers. In the course of the congressional deliberations, large-scale ranchers lobbied for its passage and in the end became the beneficiaries, receiving nearly half of the rescheduling credits provided by the Banco Nacional.[26] Fortunately, the renewal of the legislation (Ley Fodea II) did not pass, partly because the World Bank objected that it would have violated the terms of Costa Rica's structural adjustment loan.[27]

The stumpage prices charged loggers who operate in public reserves are remarkably low, amounting to 3 percent of the value of logs delivered to the mill.[28] The minimal field presence of the government forestry agency, the Dirección General Forestal, does little to prevent illegal logging; checkpoint inspection of logging trucks has stopped only a small fraction of the illegal timber. The comprehensive Abt Associates survey of Costa Rican resource policies notes: "Checkpoints have been unsuccessful for many. . . reasons, including bribery of officials. High officials have announced their intended actions in advance, ostensibly for political purposes. On one occasion, a leading newspaper carried an article that mentioned dates, times, and the area of the highway where checkpoints would be set up to deter transport of logs after dark."[29]

Thus, weak enforcement reduces the government's rent capture even further and provides a straightforward opportunity for both rent seeking and rent dissipation in the form of bribes.

Rent-seeking opportunities were also extended into reforestation. Costa Rica's tree-planting incentive system that operated during the 1980s was based on highly faulty economic analysis. The policy was ostensibly designed to restore forest cover and to encourage plantations to meet domestic timber demands. In exchange for planting specified species, planters would receive a tax-credit certificate, tradeable on the Costa Rican stock exchange, that pays off at given percentages over five years.

Regulations identified which tree species would qualify (for example, fast-growing species, especially exotics such as gmelina and eucalyptus) but did not specify geographical areas in which each species could or could not be planted to qualify for the fiscal benefit. Consequently, some planters planted only the least expensive species in areas where soil or climate conditions were inappropriate for their long-term survival; then they neglected to care for the maturing trees. Companies with little or no experience in forestry took advantage of the incentives. In some cases, natural forests were cleared to make way for plantations. Because societal costs of natural forest and biodiversity destruction have not been offset by good yields, this policy of permitting forest removal is widely regarded as the most serious failure of the reforestation incentives.[30]

The Costa Rican reforestation subsidies have also amounted to fiscal transfers without valid justification from a societal perspective. Although expansion into the Amazon propelled by rent-seeking opportunities was explained in terms of national security and development, reforestation rent seeking in Costa Rica has been excused with the even more hypocritical rhetoric of conservation.

The case of Costa Rica demonstrates the pervasiveness of rent-seeking opportunities in the natural resource sector, even in a country as self-conscious about conservation issues as Costa Rica. It also illustrates how the weak bureaucratic standing of the agency mandated to enforce forest conservation can lead to the siphoning off of publicly owned rents into private hands.

MORE BASIC EXPLANATIONS AND POSSIBLE DIRECTIONS OF REFORM

What do these cases tell us? First, they show the pervasiveness of the strategy of using resource exploitation to provide economic transfers and the seriousness of the suboptimal exploitation that ensues. In Brazil and Costa Rica, the efforts to make logging, land grants, and reforestation into vehicles for benefiting favored groups resulted in gross misuse of land and forest, and they even "reversed the flow" so that fiscal rents channeled into the forest sector resulted in both economic waste and the destruction of natural forest. The Mexican state oil company, PEMEX, has a long history of poor exploration and investment patterns driven by efforts to channel benefits to oil workers, residents of particular regions of that country, and various groups close to Mexican presidents and the PRI. Chile's CODELCO diverted a huge portion of the country's copper earnings to the copper workers in the early 1970s, and this problem still exists, though at a much reduced level.

Second, the cases demonstrate the importance of the second strategy of capturing discretion over the surplus and the costs officials are willing to impose on resource exploitation to gain that control. In Chile, overzealous efforts to control CODELCO so that full rent extraction can occur has sometimes resulted in lethargic and inept management. The confiscation of true profit in order to capture all rent has made CODELCO relatively disinterested in cost containment, including the limitation of copper workers' wages, which constitute an important retention of rent that would otherwise go to the central treasury. In Venezuela, the government's effort to capture the rent accruing in the PDVSA investment fund provoked oil company authorities to circumvent this by making poor investments in downstream petroleum processing and marketing and hence to suffer the destruction of resource rents. Honduras's COHDEFOR similarly squandered forest wealth in its downstream processing ventures, but in this case under the pressure of the top government leadership. In Mexico, the fiscal authorities have been so eager to capture PEMEX's oil rents that the company has become severely undercapitalized, and there is little incentive for profit-maximizing cost consciousness.

The cases show a wide variety of motivations that are served by capturing control over the disposition of the resource rent. Each of the three categories of motives for circumventing the conventional fiscal allocation mechanism opens up a distinct, if somewhat overlapping, set of predisposing factors and possible strategies of reform.

The creation of rent-seeking opportunities directed to building political coalitions is complicated in that it pertains to the fundamental political-economic formula of many countries. Latin American countries many be particularly prone to rent-seeking-based political-economic formulas.[31] Nevertheless, the degree to which a particular regime needs to rely on creating rent-seeking opportunities to maintain its political support can vary widely over time, depending on its political security and the acceptability of mixing political and economic exchanges according to the country's political culture. The viability of creating rent-seeking opportunities as a political strategy can be reduced, for example by increasing the transparency of rent-creating maneuvers. Finally, a very important consequence of the liberalization movement of the 1980s is the reduction in the political acceptability of the vehicles of fiscal rent seeking, including cheap credit, tax exemptions, protectionism, and domestic monopolies. These developments have increased both the awareness of the economic costs of rent seeking and the political costs to governments that persist in creating rent-seeking opportunities.

The consequences of intragovernmental power struggles may also be amenable to reform. The specific conditions that trigger interagency rivalries include party or factional divisions within the governing coalition, ideological divisions, conflicting institutional missions, large discrepancies in the economic and deference rewards accruing to "winning" and "losing" government units, divisive governance strategies of chief executives, executive-legislative schisms, and legacies from previous conflicts. Fortunately, it is possible to reform governmental structures to reduce at least some of these conditions. This is particularly true with respect to conflicting missions, the stakes of winning or losing, and the degree to which divisions within the governing coalition are allowed to sour relations among bureaucratic units. The chief executive often has considerable discretion in choosing between unifying or divisive styles, including:

1. *Economic Self-Aggrandizement.* When the exchange relationship that underlies the creation of rent-seeking opportunities is motivated by the venality of public officials high and low, a reformist can try to either reduce the priority of the motivation or increase corrupt officials' costs of manipulating the resource rents back to their own pockets. For example, it is commonplace to point out that reasonable official compensation of lower-level bureaucrats can go a long way in reducing petty rent seeking of the sort that permits illegal logging. It is equally true that increasing the transparency of all transactions involving natural resource exploitation will increase the political and legal risks of relying on resource exploitation for personal economic gain on the part of public officials. As rent-seeking opportunities become scarcer or more risky politically, the benefits of corruption decrease. There is a virtuous circle in the fact that reducing the scope of rent transfers through resource exploitation increases transparency, and transparency reduces the net rewards of using resource exploitation for venal ends.

2. *Programmatic Objectives.* The clear precondition for programmatic objectives to be a cause of the struggle over allocating the resource-rent surplus is significant disagreement over distributional outcomes and economic strategies. Obviously, consensus within a government on economic objectives and strategies would make circumventing the fiscal apparatus irrelevant in terms of pursuing these objectives and strategies.

We can also ask why there is an absence of consensus, political or developmental, within the governing coalition. At the level of the polity, a basic lack of agreement about the nation's economic model may permeate single party or even coalition governments. A coalition government would more likely be prone to disagreement on distributive and economic strategy, and officials would not be averse to undermining other units to win in this struggle.

The professionalization of either the fiscal authorities or the resource management authorities can be another important factor. First, the professionalization of *part* of the state may create different epistemic communities, thereby increasing the gulf in the perception of what constitutes appropriate economic strategies. Second, professionalization may increase the commitment as to the "right" strategies, so that actors are willing to tolerate the risks of trench warfare within the government. The CODELCO officials in the mid-1980s clearly cared enough about the importance of a successful Chuquicamata expansion to risk their jobs by defying the Finance Ministry.

3. *Political Power.* Several conditions predispose officials to manipulate natural resources in order to increase their political power. In terms of the broad political factors that make government officials more or less desperate to sacrifice natural

resource efficiency in order to gain support, such as the closeness of political competition or the degree of polarization among political opponents, there is little that can be changed through institutional reform short of revamping the entire political system. However, reliance on the creation of rent-seeking modalities of politically motivated exchange can be addressed.

The third strategy of evading accountability undoubtedly arises where rent seeking is very prevalent, but it also arises where political support for the regime rides predominantly on perceptions of the distribution of material rewards. Top-level government officials try to reduce their accountability for distributional decisions when they believe that benefiting one group, whether for reasons of political calculus or distributional justice, would risk losing crucial support (or at least acquiescence) from others. Clearly, we would expect politically secure leaders to be less willing to sacrifice resource exploitation efficiency in order to benefit particular groups surreptitiously.

Even where leaders are motivated to obscure their distributional decisions, efforts to increase transparency by government officials or nongovernment actors can block this strategy. The myriad institutions overseeing CODELCO have reduced the likelihood that either the Chilean government or CODELCO officials could keep distributional maneuvers from the public eye. Increased press coverage of Brazilian and Costa Rican forestry issues made certain that past subsidy programs of both governments were more of a political embarrassment than a political benefit.

We may conclude that the bases for the distributional struggles resulting in suboptimal natural resource exploitation can be diagnosed—on a case-by-case basis—and often can be addressed by reforms in structure, policies, and governance strategies.

NOTES

1. John Hartwick and Nancy Olewiler, *The Economics of Natural Resource Use* (New York: Harper and Row, 1986), p. 23.

2. Robert Repetto, "Overview," in Robert Repetto and Malcolm Gillis, eds., *Public Policies and the Misuse of Forest Resources* (Cambridge: Cambridge University Press, 1988), p. 18.

3. John Stuart Mill, *Principles of Political Economy, With Some of Their Applications to Social Philosophy* (London: Longmans, Green and Co., 1909), esp. chapter 2.

4. See Harold Hotelling, "The Economics of Exhaustible Resources," *Journal of Political Economy* 39 (1931): 137–175, for the classic paradigm.

5. Conceptually, the provision of rent-seeking opportunities can be distinguished from general income distribution by the fact that rent seeking typically entails such reciprocity. See Robert Tollison, "Rent Seeking: A Survey," *Kyklos* 35 (1982): 576–602, for a review of rent-seeking theory.

6. World Bank, *Chile Mining Sector Memorandum* (Report No. 7509-CH, Washington, DC, June 15, 1989), p. 24.

7. Juan Mora, *Esto nos dió López Portillo* (Mexico City: Editores Anaya, 1982), p. 43.

8. Oscar Guzmán, "PEMEX's Finances," in Miguel Wionczek, Oscar Guzmán, and Roberto Gutiérrez, eds., *Energy Policy in Mexico* (Boulder: Westview Press, 1988), p. 395.

9. Edwin Lieuwen, "The Politics of Energy in Venezuela," in John Wirth, ed., *Latin American Oil Companies and the Politics of Energy* (Lincoln: University of Nebraska Press, 1985), p. 220.

10. Gustavo Coronel, *The Nationalization of the Venezuelan Oil Industry* (Lexington, MA: Lexington Books, 1983), pp. 221–232; and Laura Randall, *The Political Economy of Venezuelan Oil* (New York: Praeger, 1987), pp. 47–48.

11. Jeffrey Jones, "Socio-Cultural Constraints in Working with Small Farmers in Forestry: Case of Land Tenure in Honduras," in Louise Fortmann and John W. Bruce, eds., *Whose Trees? Proprietary Dimensions of Forestry* (Boulder: Westview Press, 1988), pp. 157–158.

12. Abt Associates, "Honduras Natural Resource Policy Inventory," Vol. II (Bethesda, MD, May 1990).

13. Marie Lynn Miranda, Olga Marta Corrales, Michael Regan, and William Ascher, "Forestry Institutions," in Narendra Sharma, ed., *Managing the World's Forests* (Dubuque, IA: Kendall-Hunt Publishing Company, 1992).

14. John Browder, "Public Policy and Deforestation in the Brazilian Amazon," in Repetto and Gillis, eds., *Public Policies and the Misuse of Forest Resources*, p. 247.

15. William Ascher and Robert Healy, *Natural Resource Policymaking in Developing Countries* (Durham, NC: Duke University Press, 1990), pp. 82–89.

16. Browder, "Public Policy and Deforestation in the Brazilian Amazon," pp. 248–249.

17. Ibid., pp. 250–251.

18. Ibid., pp. 249–250.

19. Malcolm Gillis, "Forest Concession Management and Revenue Policies," in Narendra Sharma, ed., *Managing the World's Forests*, p. 166.

20. Marianne Schmink, "Big Business in the Amazon," in Julie Sloan Denslow and Christine Paduch, eds., *People of the Tropical Rain Forest* (Berkeley: University of California Press, 1988).

21. Browder, "Public Policy and Deforestation in Brazil," p. 248.

22. Gillis, "Forest Concession Management and Revenue Policies," p. 166.

23. Browder, "Public Policy and Deforestion in the Brazilian Amazon," p. 257.

24. Ernst Lutz and Herman Daly, "Incentives, Regulations, and Sustainable Land Use in Costa Rica," World Bank Policy, Planning and Research Staff, Environmental Department, *Environment Working Paper*, no. 34 (Washington, DC, July 1990), p. 16.

25. Ibid., pp. 16–17.

26. Victor Baltodano, Roberto Chávez, Francisco Sequeira, and Laureano Montero, *FODEA* (Heredia, Costa Rica: Universidad Nacional, 1988), pp. 46–48.

27. Lutz and Daly, "Incentives, Regulation, and Sustainable Land Use in Costa Rica," p. 17.

28. Abt Associates, "Costa Rica Natural Resource Policy Inventory," p. 69.

29. Ibid., p. 68.

30. L. González, E. Alpizar, and R. Muñoz, *Problemática del sector forestal* (San José: Centro Científico Tropical, 1987).

31. Gary Wynia, "Opening Late Industrialized Economies: Lessons from Argentina and Australia," *Policy Sciences* 23, no. 3 (1990): 185–204.

CHAPTER THREE

———— ■ ————

Democratization, Politics, and Environmental Reform in Latin America

Stephen P. Mumme and Edward Korzetz

The upsurge in civic participation in Latin America in the 1980s is now commonly associated with the restoration of democratic, electorally driven political regimes.[1] Environmentalism is generally identified as one of the most prominent new social movements benefiting from the recent liberalization of the Latin American regimes. To date, however, the linkage between the liberalization of Latin American politics and the emergence of organized environmental concern has received scant attention in regional discussions of political change.

This chapter offers a preliminary exploration of the relationship between political liberalization and the new environmental mobilization found in the hemisphere. Our goal is to identify linkages between political liberalization and the new potential for inserting environmental concerns into the policy processes of Latin American governments. Our analysis is limited, since we cannot draw on a systematic review of the emergence and development of environmentalism as a political force in the region. Instead, we draw selectively from three cases—Brazil, Mexico, and Ecuador, with occasional references to other countries—to support our observations. Insofar as our purpose is to examine the political dimensions of environmental politics in Latin America, we do not address important economic and fiscal aspects of environmental policy reform. We do assume that the resumption of economic growth is a critical variable influencing the capacity of Latin American governments to successfully undertake environmental policy initiatives.

With these qualifications in mind, we aim to identify some of the basic opportunities political liberalization has afforded environmental organizations and to illustrate various constraints that persist due to the limited nature of political liberalization in the region. Our review suggests that liberalization is positively associated with changes at the formal, political, policy, and societal levels that are conducive both to the mobilization of environmental concern and to government action in support of environmental protection and natural resource conservation. However, Latin America's emerging environmentalism confronts formidable obstacles as it presses to place environmental concerns on national policy agendas and campaigns for effective implementation of government commitments. Such constraints fall into two broad categories: those that are manifestly political in nature and those embedded in Latin America's legal and administrative systems. The structural nature of these problems suggests to us that the prospects for environmental policy reform in Latin America are currently limited, and they are heavily contingent both on the region's economic resurgence and on environmentalists' ability to locate environmental solutions in sustainable development strategies that speak to the basic needs of groups and communities within the region.

DEMOCRATIZATION AND ENVIRONMENTAL CONCERN IN LATIN AMERICA

Environmental activism as a form of associative civic expression bloomed late in Latin America, emerging in the 1980s in the wake of both rising international concern with environmental conditions and relaxed restrictions on political mobilization following the eclipse of military regimes and a shift away from more rigid forms of bureaucratic-authoritarianism in the region. The usual benchmark for establishing the emergence of environmental concern is the 1972 United Nations Conference on the Human Environment held in Stockholm, in which a number of Latin American governments participated.[2] After the Stockholm meeting, Latin American regimes hastened to invest some form of environmental agency with at least nominal responsibility for administering laws that, broadly speaking, might affect the environment. Often this meant a simple consolidation of legislation related to sanitation and health or the creation of an additional administrative body to supervise the development of such laws in their environmental aspects. By design, a good deal was neglected. The region's heavy economic dependence on extractive activities encouraged the avoidance of natural resource conservation policies aimed at arresting destructive forms of economic development.[3] Domestic awareness and popular mobilization around environmental concerns remained uniformly low throughout the region in the 1970s. Government officials, professional associations, and a handful of elite environmental nongovernmental organizations (ENGOs) with strong linkages to influential groups in the industrialized countries dominated what discussion did take place.

By the late 1980s, however, environmental activism exerted a significant role in health and conservation policy in the more advanced Latin American countries. Virtually all Latin American countries had designated environmental agencies.[4] At least a half-dozen countries had elevated environmental policy to cabinet rank, and even more had a ministry of natural resources,(see Table 3.1). A few "green" parties had even made their appearance on the electoral stage.[5] Although electoral mobilization on ecological and environmental lines remained marginal in the more liberal and economically advanced nations of the hemisphere where green

TABLE 3.1   Cabinet-level Environmental Agencies in Latin America, 1984–1995

Country	Agency
Argentina	none
Belize	Environment, 1991–1995
Bolivia	Sustainable Development, 1994–1995
Brazil	Environment, 1990–1995
Chile	Natural Resources, 1990–1995
Colombia	Environment, 1995
Costa Rica	Natural Resources, 1990
	Natural Resources, Energy, & Mines, 1991–1994
Dominican Republic	none
Ecuador	Natural Resources & Energy, 1984–1990
Guatemala	none
Guyana	none
Haiti	Agriculture, Natural Resources, & Rural Development, 1984–1995
Honduras	Natural Resources, 1984–1995
Mexico	Urban Development & Ecology, 1984–1992
	Environment, Natural Resources, & Fisheries, 1995
Nicaragua	Environment, Natural Resources, 1995[a]
Panama	none
Paraguay	none
Peru	none
Suriname	Natural Resources & Energy, 1984–1995
Uruguay	Housing & Environment, 1990–1995
Venezuela	Environment & Natural Resources, 1984–1995

Table lists only cabinet-level ministries with the terms "environment," "ecology," and "natural resources" in the title for the period 1984–1995. Single-purpose agencies devoted to health, agriculture, forests, mines, or water resources are not listed. We began searching in 1984, and this should not be construed as the year of origin for listed ministries.
[a]Position remained unfilled in January 1995. See *Keesing's Record of World Events*, Reference Supplement 41, 1995.

SOURCES: Arthur S. Banks, ed., *Political Handbook of the World*, Vols. 1984–1995 (Binghamton, NY: CSA Publications); *Environment Watch Latin America* 4 (1994), 5 (1995); *Facts on File* 54 (1994) and 55 (1995).

parties emerged, their appearance signaled the growing political salience of environmental concern.

The emergence of popularly based groups and parties advocating environmental causes in the 1980s is at least loosely correlated with political liberalization, although it may also be tracked to the gradual dispersion of public awareness through the media, the legitimation of environmental protection at the national level by the new post-Stockholm environmental laws and institutions, and the unflagging efforts of international environmental organizations—the International Union for the Conservation of Nature (IUCN), the Conservation Foundation, and the World Wildlife Fund (WWF), among others—to stimulate environmental concern in the region. Unlike environmental organizations in Eastern Europe in the late 1980s, those in Latin America, with the possible exception of Brazil, were not influential in spearheading the movement for political liberalization, though they unquestionably benefited from political transformation.

The transition from military or political authoritarianism in the region was advantageous for civic associations mobilizing around environmental and ecological themes. In those nations experiencing repressive political controls, liberalization meant not only a restoration of electoral contestation and civilian government but also frequently the relaxation of restrictions on the press, reassertion of legislative powers, restoration of freedom of assembly, new opportunities for lobbying and pressuring public officials, and greater sensitivity of public officials to political constituencies and clienteles. In limited authoritarian regimes, such as Mexico, where liberalization ushered in opportunities for greater political contestation, there emerged a broad range of political parties and, partly in consequence, state sponsorship of environmental concern as a means of enhancing regime legitimacy in the face of growing public awareness of environmental problems.

Brazil

The previously listed conditions were structurally advantageous for the emergence of ENGOs. In Brazil, an incipient environmental movement emerged in the early 1970s in response to the modest liberalization by the military government of Ernesto Geisel and the creation in 1974 of the Special Secretariat of the Environment (SEMA). The gradual process of liberalization was accompanied by formation of a number of ENGOs between 1974 and 1981, including several national-level associations.[6] This "environmentalist," or "apolitical," phase saw the development of social networks, new publications, and protests directed at extant or potential sources of environmental degradation.[7]

Following restoration of competitive elections in the early 1980s, a new, more political environmentalism emerged. Environmental organizations inserted themselves in the politics of several Brazilian states, sponsoring candidates supportive of environmental interests and organizing candidate debates on environmental questions. Electoral contestation saw the proliferation of NGOs, both grassroots service organizations (GSOs) and membership organizations (MOs), which provided additional impetus for the development of ENGOs.[8] A survey by Goldstein found nearly 900 ENGOs in Brazil by the late 1980s.[9] Although small in number and lacking the resources of large ENGOs in the industrialized countries,[10] these new organizations were able to exert modest influence at various levels of government.

Environmentalists also mobilized to influence the Constituent Congress, convened in 1987 to draft a new constitution for Brazil. In response, the Brazilian Congress convoked public assemblies to debate environmental questions in preparation for the Constituent Congress. By means of these forums and further parliamentary lobbying, environmentalists were successful in inserting an ecology chapter into the new constitution, which was promulgated in 1989.[11] Moreover, debate within the environmental community resulted in the creation of a green party in 1988.

Mexico

In Mexico, and particularly in Mexico City, electoral liberalization initiated in 1977 coincided with rising public concern over deteriorating environmental conditions. The administration of Miguel de la Madrid, which assumed office in 1982, saw the environment as a new social issue with which the government should be positively identified. It actively placed the resources of the government behind group mobilization in the environmental arena. The government campaign boosted the visibility and popularity of environmental concern nationwide and gave a considerable impetus to the recruitment efforts of Mexican environmental groups as well as to their mobilization of public opinion. Several national-level umbrella associations of environmental groups emerged between 1982 and 1984, such as the Pacto de Ecologistas and the Mexican Ecology Movement, along with numerous local groups. By the end of the 1980s, more than one hundred groups had organized.[12] Not coincidentally, media coverage of environmental issues increased. The social mobilization campaign was accompanied by the creation of a cabinet-level environmental agency, the Secretaría de Desarrollo Urbano y Ecología (SEDUE), and the revision in 1983 of the nation's decade-old comprehensive environmental law. During the de la Madrid *sexenio*, environmental organizations drew attention to the government's policy failings in the environmental area, contributing to the rapid turnover of government ministers at SEDUE and the development of a new national ecology law in 1988.

By the 1988 general election, most political parties had formally incorporated an environmental component in their campaign platforms. Mexico's first green party, created in 1987, joined with other minor parties to support the coalition-party candidate Cuauhtémoc Cárdenas, who ran on the Frente Democrático Nacional (FDN) ticket in 1988. Subsequently, the green party reconstituted itself as the Partido Ecologista Mexicana (PEM) to contest local and congressional seats in the 1991 general elections. The increasing salience of environmental issues in Mexican national politics contributed to the government's policy activism on this issue during the administration of Carlos Salinas de Gortari (1988–1994).[13]

Ecuador

In Ecuador, the first modern environmental legislation was enacted in 1976 under the auspices of the military regime in power from 1972 to 1979. Constitutional revision in 1979 accompanying the transition to civilian government further guaranteed "the right to an environment free of contamination."[14] The transition also provided new opportunities for civic association and participation in national politics. An array of new social forces joined together to challenge the old politics of corruption and *personalismo*, fueling the campaign of Jaime Roldos, victor in the 1979 presidential election. Roldos appealed to numerous social groups, particularly peasant and working-class interests neglected during the military interregnum. He also mobilized younger voters, the *voto nuevo*, who placed on the political agenda a number of nontraditional demands, including environment and health issues.[15]

Ecuador's first national ENGO, Fundación Natura (FN), was created in this liberalized context in part as a vehicle for channeling international developments to deserving projects, bypassing the discredited state sector. During the first four years of its existence, grants from the U.S. Agency for International Development (USAID) accounted for 85 percent of FN's funds.[16] Its strong connection with the official policy sector, private industry, and mainstream development projects provoked criticism from various environmental activists and eventually led to the formation of independent and critical splinter groups. The widely publicized despoliation of Ecuadorian forests by the petroleum industry and indigenous opposition to oil exploration in officially designated protected areas provoked considerable criticism of government extractive policies, and it helped catalyze the formation of additional environmental and ecological associations, many of them linked to indigenous associations.[17] By 1992, Carrie Meyer was able to identify at least twenty-four different ENGOs operating in Ecuador.[18]

Just as the processes of liberalization and democratization in Latin America provided a favorable environment for the mobilization of environmental interests, they also stimulated new external linkages supporting the development of environmental groups. As the case of Ecuador indicates, liberalization encouraged foreign governments and NGOs to explore the possibility of working through domestic ENGOs in Latin America to achieve certain policy objectives. By the mid–1970s, major ENGOs based in the industrialized world were likewise expanding their programs in the hemisphere and seeking out indigenous ENGOs as partners. Although the opportunity to fashion ties with Latin American

ENGOs varied from country to country and issue to issue, liberalization certainly facilitated their development.[19]

In sum, liberalization and democratization create a host of new opportunities for environmental mobilization and policy development in the region by altering the formal, political, policy, and societal conditions for the insertion of environmental values into the agendas of Latin American governments. These opportunities exist at several levels. At the *formal* level, political liberalization means the generation of constitutional and statutory changes including the restoration of democratic and representative political institutions, the adoption or modification of rules regulating environment conditions and natural resources, and the establishment of government agencies charged with their administration, all of which contribute to legitimating and strengthening national regimes for environmental protection and conservation. At the *political* level, political liberalization stimulates group formation by suspending or relaxing repressive restrictions on civilian political organization and activism; stimulating state sponsorship of NGOs and ENGOs through direct sponsorship or subsidies for their activities; reintroducing vigorous electoral contestation and debate of a wide range of social issues that were placed on the back burner during the authoritarian interregnum, which, in turn, enhances the opportunity for insertion of environmental agendas in party platforms; and the emergence of independent partisan activity—green parties—in the region. At the *policy* level, political liberalization promotes the development of a wide range of government initiatives related to environmental protection, conservation of natural resources, and public education on environmental issues; enhanced attention to the need for greater public participation in the process of policy formation (if only formal in nature); and greater sensitivity of elected and appointed officials to environmental concerns. At the *societal* level, it is reflected in greater public awareness of environmental problems and their relationship to other social concerns; increased media attention to these issues; and a liberalized environment for the development of transnational linkages between domestic ENGOs and foreign governments and NGOs interested in environmental agendas.

Of course, political liberalization as such was only a necessary condition, not a sufficient condition, for the rapid emergence of environmental groups in the Americas in the 1980s. To paraphrase Eduardo Viola's observations in the case of Brazil, a short list of factors influencing the emergence of environmentalism would, in addition to democratization, include (1) the development of the world environmental movement in the context of global socioenvironmental degradation; (2) the degree to which particular countries are intermeshed in the international economy; (3) the specific character of socio-environmental degradation in any country; (4) the policies of the authoritarian regime before liberalization; and (5) the ideological environment affecting organized discussion and debate of environmental values and policies in any country.[20]

Even so, democratization has provided the institutional and political platform for a broad opening to the emergence of environmental politics in Latin America.[21] Political liberalization is nonetheless fraught with challenges for environmental associations, whether they are constituted as interest groups or parties. Not only do they face conventional organizational and agenda-building problems found in the democratic-industrialized countries, but also they confront a range of problems associated with incipient political liberalization and the constraints of economic development.

THE POLITICAL CHALLENGE
OF LIBERALIZATION

Liberalization's challenges to the political influence of environmental interests in Latin America are mainly traceable to the varied forms liberalization has taken in the region. Political liberalization, of course, is a process, not a static state.[22] Although generally expressed in amplified possibilities for electoral contestation, the process and the policy opportunities it presents to environmental organizations vary from nation to nation. The partial and incomplete nature of liberalization, coupled with the constraints of economic development, present environmental groups and parties with an array of practical impediments to their political and policy influence. These impediments complicate the organizational, institutional, and ideological obstacles that environmental interest groups and parties might normally face in political mobilization and agenda building in the industrialized, well-institutionalized democracies of Asia, Europe, and North America.

Problems of a political or legal-administrative nature are discernible and are directly affected by the character of liberalization in the region. On the political side, the persistence of formal restrictions on political activity in some states, co-optation of environmental interests by the state, mobilization of anti-environmental interests, and policy biases arising from the practices of pre-liberal regimes compose a short list of factors that can limit the policy influence of environmentalists. On the legal-administrative side, statutory formalism, the domination of state bureaucracy by administrative holdovers from pre-liberal regimes, and the lack of legal remedies for environmental problems present substantial handicaps for environmental activists and reformers. This list is certainly not exhaustive, but it should suffice to illustrate the range of challenges confronting Latin American environmentalists under newly liberalized political regimes.

Political Constraints

Nowhere are the political constraints of democratization more dramatic than in the persistence of various formal limitations on political expression and mobilization. Although we have no evidence that such constraints are specifically targeted at environmental organizations, these devices handicap efforts by environmental groups to mobilize support and place their concerns on the public agenda.

Such formal limitations may range from electoral laws to press censorship. Electoral rules and regulations are, of course, basic to democratic government and encompass diverse practices, including the mechanics of electoral representation, the establishment of performance thresholds for the electoral participation of parties, and standards for voter eligibility.[23] Proportional representation systems, the prevalent mode in Latin America for constituting representative assemblies,[24] should favor the development of green parties, whereas single-member-district systems should restrict their emergence. In either system, however, performance thresholds for the legal registry of parties and thresholds for obtaining seats in representative assemblies may bias against minor parties, hindering the emergence of green or ecologically oriented parties. Voter eligibility laws that discriminate on the basis of literacy, property, ethnicity, and other factors may also limit the potential for partisan environmental activity.

Mexico is perhaps the best example of the persistence of formal restrictions on electoral contestation. The series of liberalizing reforms that have been affecting political participation and electoral contestation since 1977 has its limits. A 1996 reform initiative by the Zedillo administration promises significant improvements, to include insuring the independence of the Federal Electoral Tribunal, imposing strict campaign financing limits, opening the electoral process to independent observers, and other changes. Mexico's electoral process is thus likely to become more competitive in the near future. Mexico continues to impose substantial restrictions on electoral contestation by favoring the governing party in national and state electoral commissions, by placing restrictions on independent poll monitoring, and through other devices.[25] Yet another example of restrictive electoral codes is seen in Guatemala, where a distributional principle in the electoral law provides that only national-level parties—those that meet minimal membership thresholds in all the provinces—may nominate candidates for the national ballot, effectively discriminating against its large indigenous groups, which remain concentrated in only one or a few provinces.[26]

Although Latin American thresholds for the electoral registry of parties are not highly restrictive by international standards, green parties in the region have had difficulty with them. Mexico's PEM, for instance, is one of several parties that lost its electoral registry following congressional elections in 1991 because it gained less than 1.5 percent of the vote.[27] The party was reinstated on a conditional basis for the August 1994 presidential election, but despite receiving .09 percent of the vote—nearly 500,000 votes nationwide—its legal registry is again imperiled.[28] Brazil's fledgling Green Party similarly lost its registration in 1990 for failing to meet minimal national membership thresholds for electoral eligibility.[29] Chile's Green Party, on the other hand, won 5.5 percent of the vote in the 1994 general election, qualifying for seats in the national Chamber of Deputies.[30] The success of the Chilean Green Party suggests registry thresholds are not insurmountable barriers, provided green parties mount well-crafted campaigns capitalizing on urban frustration with fouled environments.

With respect to voter eligibility, Ecuador continued to use a literacy test until 1979 to exclude indigenous electoral participation. Since 1979, indigenous populations have participated, although informal mechanisms of ostracism frequently persist. It is instructive that Ecuador's indigenous peoples have found it far more effective to articulate their environmental interests through the national Confederación de Indígenas de Ecuador (Confederation of Ecuadorian Indigenous Groups [CONAIE]) than through electorally based representation.[31]

Press censorship is also a type of formal restriction used against environmental mobilization, although abandonment of formal censorship has been one of the strongest indicators of political liberalization in Latin America. Although press censorship has abated, it nevertheless persists in a variety of forms, ranging from press dependence on government subsidies for financial survival to government restrictions on the use of electronic media. Of our three cases, Mexico is perhaps the best example of persistent "soft" limits on the press. The silent threat inherent in direct state-subsidized advertising in the print media is instrumental in determining coverage of various controversial issues, and it is widely seen as a means of manipulating public information on important policy issues. In Brazil and Ecuador, the restoration of civilian government has been accompanied by a vigorous revival of the independent press system.[32]

A more serious problem for environmental organizations under liberalization is co-optation by government and state authorities. Co-optation, according to Philip Selznick, may be defined as "the process of absorbing new elements into the leadership or policy-determining structure of an organization as a means of averting threats to its stability or existence."[33] As Scott Mainwaring observes in the case of Brazil, co-optation is a double-edged sword.[34] As governments have liberalized, they have extended new opportunities to become involved in the political process. Environmental groups, like others, confront the dilemma of gauging the extent to which the opportunity to participate in government forums, project assessment and implementation, agencies, and even parliaments may compromise their goals, organizational integrity, and public legitimacy. Moreover, in liberalizing regimes the dilemma of co-optation is exaggerated precisely because the question of regime legitimacy is placed in such high relief. The need to conserve group legitimacy may thus prove more compelling than the need to compromise and modify demands while cooperating with other organizations in order to attain certain policy objectives. The dominance of the state in policy development under pre-liberal regimes and the persistence of executive domination afterward puts a premium on legitimate and independent representation, which groups ignore at their peril. Environmental organizations, as nontraditional actors in policy making, may be particularly susceptible to overtures of inclusion in government-dominated policy forums.

The range of co-optation extends from simple participation in discussions of environmental problems within government-mediated forums to providing advice in quasi-formal and formal consultative bodies, to direct participation in government itself. As a rule, the perceived risks of compromise rise along this spectrum. Latin American environmental organizations appear to be quite aware of this problem, though the dilemmas and pressures cannot and should not be trivialized. In Mexico, for example, many environmental activists were dismayed when several group leaders opted to join the new administration of Carlos Salinas de Gortari in 1989. Many prominent leaders professed to have been actively recruited, but they drew the line at joining the government directly.[35] Mexican state sponsorship of environmental groups and functions, however, has kept co-optation high on the list of concerns for environmental groups, and it remains a significant source of cleavage among them.

On the other hand, some ENGOs deliberately amend their goals to take advantage of co-optative opportunities. In Ecuador, what is arguably the most influential ENGO, the FN, has consciously pursued what might be viewed as a co-optative alliance with the state, eschewing policy independence in exchange for influence in natural-resource policy.[36] The attractiveness of corporatist models of representation was seen in environmental reforms by the Patricio Aylwin government in Chile that reversed two decades of political exclusion of environmental organizations from government policy making. The new Comisión Nacional del Medio Ambiente, an interministerial coordinating body for environmental policy, is advised by an eight-member consultative council that includes two ENGO representatives and two representatives apiece from business, labor, and academia.[37]

Electoral contestation also presents a range of challenges for environmental organizations. Although most political parties have begun to incorporate environmental concerns in party platforms, this is not uniformly the case throughout the region. Certain conservative and pro-development parties continue actively to oppose environmental agendas; more frequently, political parties have relegated their green commitments to a low priority as they seek to shape national policy agendas. To a degree, this is due to different ideological perspectives on the implementation of environmental priorities: Conservative parties are more apt to favor the adoption of market and developmentalist approaches to environmental protection whereas liberal and socialist parties lean toward more active forms of state intervention to attain their goals. In Ecuador, for example, recent administrations, while formally espousing environmental values, have regularly disregarded those concerns when environmental preservation conflicted with economic development—petroleum exploration in the Oriente is a case in point. Ecuador's conservative Partido de la Unidad Republicano (PUR) is at present revamping the hydrocarbon law to allow for easier exploitation of national resources.[38] Ecuador's indigenous groups have also expressed environmental concerns with respect to PUR's liberalization of the 1963 agrarian reform code. In mid–1994, the CONAIE undertook nationwide protests over a new agrarian reform law that would have relaxed restrictions on private investment and development of lands claimed by indigenous groups.[39]

Similar dynamics are found in Mexico, Brazil, and Peru. Mexico's governing Partido Revolucionario Institucional, under the liberalizing administration of Carlos Salinas, enacted between 1990 and 1992 a set of far-reaching market-oriented reforms of Mexico's agrarian, water, forestry, and fishery laws.[40] In Brazil, important military leaders with strong connections to the right-wing parties continue to express reservations concerning the environmental conservation in Amazonia.[41] Indeed, the enduring institutional power of the Brazilian military accounts in good measure for the military's domination of environmental policy implementation in that region.[42] In Peru, President Alberto Fujimori's party, Cambio 90 (Change 90), spearheaded constitutional reforms approved in 1993 that provide for the conferral of "real rights" (virtual property rights) with state natural resources concessions, effectively immunizing such concessions against state conservation and environmental regulations.[43]

The persistence of developmentalist norms and policies among liberalizing Latin American regimes can be partly attributed to entrenched resistance of dominant political parties to environmental values. Virtually all the newly liberalized countries are strongly committed to market-oriented, export-centered, developmentalist models even as they have incorporated a degree of environmental concern in national policy instruments. Environmental orthodoxy in the international development community, which sees development as a complement to environmental improvement,[44] provides ample opportunity for parties of various ideological persuasions to embrace the ideal of sustainable development. This occurs despite profound differences over concrete policy objectives and implementation. In the absence of strong green parties with focused environmental agendas, Latin American environmental reformists are thus confronted with the need to collaborate with established parties whose dominant programs may well compromise their values and reputations.

Legal-Administrative Limits

Formalism—the enactment of legislation for strictly symbolic purposes or, often, the failure to implement legislation adopted in good faith—continues to be a prevalent feature of Latin American environmental law. Its rationale is well understood in the literature of comparative public administration and need not be elaborated here.[45] It bears mentioning, however, that formalism presents both opportunities and constraints for environmental activists. On the positive side, the adoption of formal environmental rules—Ecuador's constitutional prescription is a case in point—provides useful symbolism and legitimation for environmental interests. Formal prescription may also provide legislative instruments that are necessary, but not sufficient, for more effective implementation and thus assist activist organizations to focus government attention on pressing environmental problems.

Nevertheless, legislative formalism is also a hindrance to environmental activists and organizations. As a form of symbolic action, it creates the appearance of responsiveness, enabling government officials to deflect pressure from reformists. Whether the legislation is general or specific, formalism endows government with the opportunity to construe its actions with considerable independence from public opinion. It limits citizen initiative aimed at enforcing environmental norms by placing implementation discretion in the hands of government officials. Such conditions tend to undermine public confidence in government performance. Beyond that, as one observer notes, legal decrees establishing protected areas, conservation zones, parks, and other nontraditional uses of natural resources, in the absence of enforcement, may actually aggravate extant conditions by creating a de facto commons to be exploited with impunity by interested parties.[46]

Yet another impediment of a legal-administrative nature—an enduring problem that liberalizing reforms have only begun to correct—is the continued inadequacy of most Latin American legal systems to enforce environmental law. The problem goes beyond the need to perfect criteria for evaluation and enforcement in the field of environmental law—the "technical norms and standards" issue, currently a major weakness of Latin American environmental law. Shaped in the tradition of civil law administrative justice rather than common law, Latin American systems do not as yet grant standing to environmental groups as such, thereby limiting ENGOs' ability to bring actions against the state or private individuals and groups. Although Brazil "opened the door to citizen suits by environmental groups" in 1985,[47] this restriction remains in Mexico, Ecuador, and various other Latin American countries. Roger W. Findley's analysis of Brazilian law also notes that "burden-of-proof" requirements, particularly in cases of multiple-source pollution, created nearly insurmountable obstacles for plaintiffs.[48] Some systems also permit defendants to postpone government action nearly indefinitely through liberal extension of injunctive relief against government regulation—the *amparo* device in Mexico is a case in point.[49]

The informal aspects of pursuing judicial remedies come into play here. Few Latin American environmental groups have the resources to pursue legal sanctions energetically. In some countries, the strong tradition of executive domination of the courts is also a deterrent to civil action. Coupled with the formal barriers outlined above, it is far more expedient to pursue political rather than legal remedies. The perverse irony is that weak legal systems often stand environmental legislation on its head. In Mexico, in fact, it is still easier and a good deal more common for industries to use the national environmental laws to defend themselves against enforcement than the contrary. In Guatemala, plaintiffs desiring to pursue legal action against industrial polluters must first obtain a judgment from the National Environmental Commission, a weak agency that lacks the resources to conduct investigations, creating a catch-22 for environmentalists. Activists have thus opted for using direct political pressure rather than the legal process to spur government action.[50]

Finally, the administrative legacy inherited by liberalizing governments may be viewed as a serious impediment to policy influence by environmentalists. The problems are numerous and cannot be laid exclusively at the feet of repressive military regimes since, as in the case of the legal systems, they have left an enduring legacy of administrative development in the region. Moreover, a number of these problems are common in the most advanced regulatory systems. Even so, the problems confronting environmentalists in Latin America are more pronounced due to the region's historical legacy of bureaucratism and underdevelopment and were certainly not corrected during the repressive military regimes. A short and by no means exhaustive list of administrative obstacles confronting environmental reformers would include (1) regulatory fragmentation; (2) the subsumption of environmental administration within preexisting, more powerful, administrative institutions; and (3) limited avenues for citizen participation in the regulatory process and limited citizen access to official information related to environmental problems. We deliberately do not mention policy design problems since, strictly speaking, these are not structural in nature.

The problem of bureaucratic fragmentation is common throughout the region and, in certain cases, has been demonstrably aggravated by environmental reforms that aimed at consolidating and coordinating environmental policies. The standard objection that the connotative range of what might be subsumed under the term "environment" extends to virtually all government agencies does not alter the fundamental problem: What has been redefined and restructured as "environmental" legislation in fact predated the modern era of environmental reformism—health and sanitation legislation is a case in point—and remains embedded in the jurisdiction of multiple agencies. Such agencies compete for turf and resources with national environmental agencies,[51] which tend to be given lower priority and funds in relation to established sectoral players. Although modern environmental legislation in countries such as Mexico and Brazil has sought to consolidate administrative functions to some degree, much remains beyond the province of the officially designated environmental agency. In Mexico, after the adoption of the 1988 environmental law, nearly a half-dozen major ministries continued to have responsibilities for environmental standard setting, including the ministries of social development—which had ostensible oversight jurisdiction—agriculture and water resources, federal district government, patrimony and industry, and others.[52] Even more, of course, are engaged in the process of implementing environmental regulations. Decentralization of environmental policy and administration to the Mexican states—another recent initiative arising in lieu of providing those states with either adequate resources or clarification of the lines of administrative accountability—has compounded the problem.

In Brazil, the environmental chapter of the 1988 constitution grants concurrent regulatory powers to states and municipalities, stipulating that the most stringent norms should apply.[53] The greater administrative capacity of Brazilian state and local governments suggests that decentralized administration in Brazil may prove more effective than centralized administration.[54] However, current regulatory discrepancies are so great among the Brazilian states that a national environmental protection code applicable to the states was under preparation for presentation to the Brazilian Congress in 1995.[55] Chile's newly devised approach to environmental administration explicitly eschews a centralized model in favor of a decentralized interministerial coordinating commission, effectively accepting bureaucratic fragmentation as the norm instead of attempting to impose centralized administration.[56]

A common predicament in Latin America is the relatively low priority accorded environmental administration and its consequent subsumption within more powerful, established government ministries. Environmental priorities will always compete with other established values on government policy agendas, and attaining cabinet autonomy is no guarantee of their success. But, embedding those functions in the jurisdiction of more established and higher priority missions of existing agencies amplifies the bureaucratic impediments to policy development and implementation. Only three countries (Belize, Brazil, and Colombia) by 1995 had a cabinet-rank ministry exclusively dedicated to the environment. All others either endow their ministries with partial jurisdictions of an environmental nature (for example, natural resources) or attach environmental functions to other, nonrelated ministries (Table 3.1). Under these circumstances, environmental priorities tend to be overridden by competing values.

Yet another impediment is found in limitations on citizen participation and access to information in Latin American systems. Although most Latin American environmental legislation acknowledges and makes some provision for citizen input into policy development, numerous barriers to citizen participation remain. As seen previously, much official participation prescribed in current environmental law is corporatist in nature, stipulating citizen advisory boards or providing for some form of group participation in policy development, yet leaving the determination of specific participants and advisory bodies to the discretion of government officials. This "privileging" of groups is a source of concern and potential cleavage among environmental organizations. The problem may be aggravated by multilateral organizations and foreign foundations as they develop linkages with—and often create—ENGOs in the host country. Particular groups may be better able to press their policy views onto government agendas; in turn, such advantages may nurture "green triangles" between multilaterals, domestic ENGOs, and host government bureaucracies that dominate a policy area to the exclusion of other interested groups.

Finally, there is as yet little tradition of generalized public access to official information, and liberalizing regimes tend to sustain a bias toward privileged access to information. True, a considerable amount of information is generated by Latin American governments, so much that one analyst argues that the availability of information is generally not the critical problem in planning resource conservation in Latin America.[57] Although this may be the case in selected policy areas of various countries, citizens groups confront serious problems accessing information on environmental conditions. As an example, no Latin American government currently has a counterpart to the U. S. Freedom of Information Act. Various governments provide certain types of information, but such information is typically warehoused in a few locations and not widely disseminated.[58] Most of the "state-of-the-environment reports," for example, are not easily accessed by private citizens or groups. Much information on social dimensions of environmental conditions is potentially controversial and therefore protected by government officials.

In sum, the legal-administrative structures of liberalizing governments in the Americas present activists and environmental groups with a formidable array of impediments to advancing environmental values on national policy agendas. As a consequence, Latin American environmental groups continue to labor under austere conditions and must resort to a mix of creative strategies for mobilizing support and generating government attention to critical policy priorities.

CONCLUSION

Environmental mobilization and the political prospects of organized environmental interests have certainly benefited from the climate of political liberalization in the hemisphere. The rapid growth in the number and variety of groups, the appearance of ecology parties, the growth of public environmental concern, and the placement of environmental concerns on national policy agendas all point to more than a coincidental relationship between political liberalization and environmental mobilization.

The political and policy prospects for Latin American environmental groups and parties remain clouded, however. Although this review is certainly not comprehensive, our look at several specific cases suggests that problems will continue to limit the opportunities for effective policy reform that follow from political liberalization. Latin American environmental groups and parties are handicapped by the persistence of formal limitations on interest groups and electoral mobilization in politics. To the extent that they are able to place their concerns on national policy agendas, they are susceptible to co-optation and delegitimation by government and administrative interests. Moreover, the growing influence of environmental organizations has provoked strong opposition to their agendas. Different constructions of sustainable development and differences regarding alternative modes of implementation provide ample opportunities for defenders of prevailing development practices to deflect environmentalists' influence. Extant policy biases held over from authoritarian and pre-authoritarian regimes continue to shape national policy agendas, providing plenty of ammunition to those interests opposing environmental reforms.

At the legal-administrative level, policy implementation continues to suffer from statutory formalism and the low priority typically attached to environmental enforcement. The positive values attached to the adoption of new statutes and regulations may be offset by the erosion of public confidence in the real commitment of governments to invest resources in environmental enforcement, remediation, and conservation. At worst, formalism is an invitation to further environmental abuse. Weak legal systems and the expense of pursuing legal remedies further diminish the impact of the new wave of environmental legislation in the Americas. Finally, the functioning of the relatively young environmental policy domains suffers from entrenched and fragmented national bureaucracies and limited avenues for citizen participation in policy design and implementation.

Such problems are structural and are not likely to change in the near future. Realistically, the prospects for increased environmental enforcement depend heavily on the resumption of economic growth in the hemisphere. Some degree of improvement can be expected to follow from evolving patterns of economic integration and the multilateral structures for environmental accountability that are increasingly associated with these trends. In the end, however, the deepening of environmental policy reform rests heavily on the ability of environmental organizations to broaden public support for environmental improvement, amplifying awareness of the linkage between material quality of life and environmental improvement. Of particular importance is the role of environmental organizations in identifying strategies of local and community development that improve or maintain income and employment as well as environmental quality. Much also depends on their capacity to develop organizationally, building broader links to middle- and working-class organizations and developing their capacity to make such use of existing sources of leverage on national politics as their respective national systems may afford. Thus, as democratization yields new opportunities to civil society to mobilize on behalf of the environment, the strengthening and deepening of current policy reforms require a great deal more of Latin American environmental organizations than they are currently capable of. Whether they are up to the challenge remains to be seen.

NOTES

1. See Oxford Analytica, *Latin America in Perspective* (Boston: Houghton-Mifflin, Inc., 1991), pp. 60–61; and Thomas Skidmore and Peter Smith, *Modern Latin America*, 3d ed. (Oxford: Oxford University Press, 1992), pp. 81–100.

2. See Economic Commission for Latin America and the Caribbean (ECLAC), *Sustainable Development: Changing Production Patterns, Social Equity, and the Environment* (Santiago, Chile: ECLAC, 1991).

3. See, for example, David Goodman and Michael Redclift, *Environment and Development in Latin America* (Manchester: Manchester University Press, 1991) and Michael Redclift, *Development and the Environmental Crisis* (New York: Methuen and Co., 1984).

4. Alicia Barcena Ibarra, "Reflections on the Incorporation of an Environmental Dimension into the Institutional Framework and Operations of the Public Sector in Latin America and the Caribbean" (unpublished paper) cited in Kirk P. Rodgers, "Strengthening Government Capacity for Environmental Management in Latin America," in Denizhan Erocal, ed., *Environmental Management in Developing Countries* (Paris: Organisation for Economic Co-operation and Development, 1991), pp. 323–340.

5. See, for example, country chapters in Arthur S. Banks, ed., *Political Handbook of the World 1993* (Binghamton, NY: CSA Publications, 1994).

6. Eduardo J. Viola, "The Ecologist Movement in Brazil, 1974–1986," *Journal of Regional and Urban Research* 12 (1988): 211–228.

7. Ibid.

8. John W. Garrison, "UNCED and the Greening of Brazilian NGOs," *Grassroots Development* 17 (1993): 2–11.

9. See reference to K. Goldstein, "Searching for Green Through Smog and Squalor: Defense of the Environment in Brazil" (Ph.D. diss., Princeton University) in Enrique Leff, "Environmentalism: Fusing Red and Green," *NACLA Report on the Americas* 25 (May 1992): 35–37.

10. Ronald A. Foresta, *Amazon Conservation in the Age of Development* (Gainesville, FL: University of Florida Press, 1991), p. 157.

11. See Julie Fisher, *The Road from Rio: Sustainable Development and the Nongovernmental Movement in the Third World* (Westport: Praeger Publishers, 1993), p. 16; Roger W. Findley, "Pollution Control in Brazil," *Ecology Law Quarterly* 15 (1988): 1–68; and Roberto P. Guimaraes, *The Ecopolitics of Development in the Third World: Politics and Environment in Brazil* (Boulder: Lynne Rienner Press, 1991), pp. 200–201.

12. E. Kurzinger Wienmman et al., *Política ambiental en México* (Mexico City: Friedrich Ebert Stiftung Instituto Alemán de Desarrollo, 1991); and Leff, "Environmentalism: Fusing Red and Green," pp. 35–37.

13. Stephen P. Mumme, "Clearing the Air: Environmental Reform in Mexico," *Environment* 33, no. 10 (December, 1991): 6–30.

14. Judith Kimmerling, "Disregarding Environmental Law: Petroleum Development in Protected Natural Areas and Indigenous Homelands in the Ecuadorian Amazon," *Hastings International and Comparative Law Review* 14 (1991): 849–903.

15. David Cubitt and David Corkill, *Ecuador: Fragile Democracy* (London: Latin American Bureau, 1988).

16. Carrie A. Meyer, "Environmental NGOs in Ecuador: An Economic Analysis of Institutional Change," *Journal of Developing Areas* 23 (1993): 191–210.

17. Douglas Foster, "Debt for Nature: Dirty Deals?" *Mother Jones* (July-August 1990).

18. Meyer, "Environmental NGOs in Ecuador," p. 200.

19. World Resources Institute, *World Resources 1990–1991* (New York: Oxford University Press, 1990), p. 46.

20. See Viola, "The Ecologist Movement in Brazil," 225–226. For an analysis of the impact of liberalization on Brazil's environmental policy, see Camilla Bustani, "The Forest for the Trees: Explaining Change in Brazilian Environmental Policy" (paper prepared for the XVIII International Congress of the Latin American Studies Association, Atlanta, Georgia, March 10–12, 1994).

21. Charles A. Reilly, "The Road from Rio: NGO Policy Makers and the Social Ecology of Development," *Grassroots Development* 17 (1993): 25–35.

22. Terry Lynn Karl, "Dilemmas of Democratization in Latin America," *Comparative Politics* 23 (October 1990): 1–21.

23. For an enumeration of types of electoral rules that may determine the nature of party competition in modern democracies, see Bernard Grofman and Arend Lijphart, "Introduction," in Grofman and Lijphart, eds., *Electoral Laws and Their Political Consequences* (New York: Agathon Press, 1986), pp. 1–18, esp. pp. 1–3.

24. Ronald H. McDonald and J. Mark Ruhl, *Party Politics and Elections in Latin America* (Boulder: Westview Press, 1989), p. 12.

25. Robert Pastor, "Electoral Reform in Mexico," *The Carter Center of Emory University Occasional Paper Series* 4, no. 1 (1993), pp. 32–35.

26. Stephen P. Mumme, "Clearing the Air: Environmental Reform in Mexico," *Environment* 33, no. 10 (December 1991):7–28.

27. Aurelio Ramos M., "La ley es clara, el PEM tiene derecho a subsidio: González T.," *Excélsior*, September 8, 1994, p. A4. See also "Mexico: Elections," *Facts on File* 54 (August 1994): 40–136.

28. Banks, *Political Handbook of the World 1993*, p. 104.

29. Organization of American States (OAS), *Annual Report of the Inter-American Commission on Human Rights, 1993* (Washington, DC: General Secretariat, OAS, 1994), p. 407.

30. *Facts on File* 53 (December 1993), p. 958

31. "Indians Hail U.S. Court Ruling," *Latin American Weekly Report*, April 28, 1994, p. 173.

32. Council on Hemispheric Affairs (COHA), *A Survey of Press Freedom in Latin America, 1984–1985* (Washington, DC: COHA, 1985).

33. Philip Selznick, *TVA and the Grassroots* (New York: Harper and Row, 1966), esp. p. 259.

34. Scott Mainwaring, "Grassroots Popular Movements and the Struggle for Democracy in Latin America: Nova Iguaçu," in Alfred Stepan, ed., *Democratizing Brazil* (Oxford: Oxford University Press, 1989), see esp. pp. 188–189.

35. See Jolle Demmers and Barbara Hogenboom, "Popular Organization and Party Dominance: The Political Role of NGOs in Mexico" (master's thesis, University of Amsterdam, Faculty of Political and Sociocultural Sciences, 1992); Stephen P. Mumme, C. Richard Bath, and Valerie J. Assetto, "Political Development and Environmental Policy in Mexico," *Latin American Research Review* 23 (1988): 7–34.

36. Meyer, "Environmental NGOs in Ecuador."

37. World Resources Institute, *World Resources 1994–95* (New York: Oxford University Press, 1994), p. 246.

38. "Amazon Indians Take on Big Firms," *Latin American Weekly Report*, November 18, 1993, p. 539.

39. "Más violencia en Ecuador; otro indígena muerto," *La Jornada*, June 21, 1994, p. 45.

40. "Se promulga la Ley Agraria y la Ley Orgánica de los Tribunales Agrarios," *Comercio Exterior* 42 (March 1992): 230; "Nueva Ley de Pesca," *Comercio Exterior* 42 (July 1992): 230; "Ley General de Equilibrio Ecológico y la Protección al Ambiente," *Diario Oficial* (Mexico, DF: Secretaría de Desarrollo Urbano y Ecología, March, 1988); E. Miguel Székely, M. Angélica Sánchez P., and Francisco Abardia M., "The Free Trade Agreement and Constitutional Agrarian Reform: Possible Implications for Forest Exploitation" (paper presented at the XVII International Congress of the Latin American Studies Association, Los Angeles, September 24–27, 1992).

41. "Trying To Defuse the Amazonia Scare," *Latin American Weekly Report*, March 5, 1992, p. 11. For additional background, see Marianne Schmink and Charles H. Wood, *Con-*

tested *Frontiers in Amazonia* (New York: Columbia University Press, 1992), esp. pp. 352–353.

42. Georgia O. Carvalho, "The Evolution of Amazonia Policy in Brazil: An Environmental Perspective, 1979–1993" (paper presented at the annual meeting of the Western Social Science Association, Albuquerque, New Mexico, April 21–23, 1994), pp. 30–31.

43. "Peru Wins New Constitution But Environmental Policy Impact Remains Unclear," *Environment Watch Latin America* (November 1993): 12–13.

44. World Bank, *World Development Report: Development and the Environment* (New York: Oxford University Press), pp. 2–3.

45. Fred Riggs, *Administration in Developing Countries* (Boston: Houghton-Mifflin, 1964).

46. Rodgers, "Strengthening Government Capacity for Environmental Management in Latin America," in Erocal, ed., *Environmental Management in Developing Countries*, pp. 328–329.

47. Findley, "Pollution Control in Brazil," p. 65.

48. Ibid.

49. H.F. Fix Zamudia, "Brief Introduction to the Mexican Writ of Amparo," *California Western International Law Journal* 9 (Spring 1979): 306–348; and Lucio A. Cabrera, "Administrative and Judicial Protection of the Environment in Mexico: Problems Reinforcing the Law," in Garth M. Hansen, ed., *Proceedings of the Rocky Mountain Council on Latin American Studies*, 34th Annual Meeting (Las Cruces, NM: New Mexico State University, 1986), pp. 113–120.

50. "Guatemalan Cities Charge Environment Officials with Negligence," *Environment Watch Latin America* 4, no. 7 (July 1994): 15.

51. William Ascher and Robert Healy, *Natural Resources Policy Making in Developing Countries* (Durham, NC: Duke University Press, 1990), esp. p. 180.

52. "Ley General de Equilibrio Ecológico y la Protección al Ambiente," *Diario Oficial*; and Elsa Laurelli, Pedro Pirez, and Eric Castenares, "Incorporación de la dimensión ambiental en una administración sectoral," in Enrique Leff, ed., *Medio ambiente y desarrollo en Mexico* 2 (Mexico, DF: Grupo Editorial Miguel Angel Porrúa, 1990), pp. 736–737.

53. N. Patrick Peritore, "Brazilian Environmental Thought: A Q-Method Study of Policy Making Elites" (paper presented at the conference on Third World Studies, Omaha, Nebraska, March 1994), p. 10. See also Michele Zebich-Knos, "In Search of a Balanced Environmental Agenda: Politics, Policy and Development in Latin America" (paper presented at the annual meeting of the American Political Science Association, New York, September 1–4, 1994), pp. 18–19.

54. Reilly, "The Road from Rio," p. 30; and "CETESB Returns Hazardous Waste Shipment to UK Following Greenpeace Tip," *Environment Watch Latin America* 4, no. 1 (January 1994): 3.

55. "São Paulo Prepares National Environmental Protection Code," *Environment Watch Latin America* 4, no. 10 (October 1994): 6–7.

56. World Resources Institute, *World Resources 1994–1995* (New York: Oxford University Press, 1994), pp.245–246.

57. Rodgers, "Strengthening Government Capacity for Environmental Management in Latin America," p. 329.

58. For a guide to published government environmental reports, see World Resources Institute, *Directory of Country Environmental Studies* (Washington, DC: Center for International Development and Environment, World Resources Institute, 1990).

CHAPTER FOUR

— ■ —

Conservation, Sustainable Development, and the Politics of Native Forest Policy in Chile

Eduardo Silva*

Most of the burgeoning literature about conservation and sustainable development of native forests in developing countries concentrates on diagnosing the forces behind deforestation in order to advance a set of policy prescriptions to halt the destruction. It has offered solutions as varied as market-friendly economic restructuring, grassroots development, family planning, and the elimination of state subsidies to the problems of economic development, poverty, overpopulation, and perverse government incentives.[1] Few analysts, however, have addressed the factors that induce governments to adopt those policy recommendations—or to adopt one set over another—other than to invoke the need for political will.

In order to uncover some of the underpinnings of political will, this chapter examines when and how ideas, state institutions, social groups, and international factors influenced two outcomes in redemocratized Chile: the government's basic orientation with respect to the conservation and sustainable development of native forests, and the degree of conflict over proposed policies. In this chapter, I argue that the ideas of cohesive policy-making teams and their institutional

*Research for this chapter was made possible by funding from the North-South Center of the University of Miami, the University of Missouri-St. Louis, and the Center for International Studies of UM-St. Louis. I wish to thank Charles Reilly, Andrew Hurrell, William Ascher, and the editors of this volume for their commentary at various points in the genesis and execution of this project. Special thanks to Patricio Rodrigo and Carlos Cuevas. Without them field research would have been immeasurably more difficult. I alone, of course, am responsible for the remaining errors.

sources of power may give initial direction to policy. But politicization occurs if their idea of sustainable development challenges the dominant market-friendly definition, especially in the presence of strong private interests in the forestry sector. Thus, socioeconomic forces strongly condition, or limit, the extent to which government actors can turn their ideas into policy.

The native forest policy debate in Chile is a good case for exploring these relationships. First, it offers an opportunity to examine environmental politics in the context of redemocratization. The military government concentrated on free-market economic reforms and paid scant attention to environmental concerns. As a result, the democratically elected administration of Patricio Aylwin addressed pent-up environmental demands, and native forest policy was among the first initiatives to emerge. Second, the policy outcomes themselves reflected a poor fit with the principles espoused by either government officials charged with developing the policies or societal forces. Third, the issue was highly politicized, and it offers a window on the negotiation of forest policy in other countries with powerful timber industries.

In order to flesh out these arguments, I begin with an exposition of the general interpretive framework and define the central axis of conflict over native forest policy in developing nations: the market-friendly versus the progressive, alternative approaches to sustainable development. The next sections summarize forest policy in Chile and show how the debate over recent policy proposals conforms to the contours of the disagreement between the market-friendly versus alternative approaches. The rest of the chapter analyzes the impact of social forces on the native forest legislation during the formulation stage of the policy process from 1990 to 1994. A concluding section examines the implications of the Chilean case for native forest policy in other Latin American nations.

EXPLAINING THE POLITICS OF CONSERVATION AND SUSTAINABLE DEVELOPMENT

With respect to the interpretive framework, this chapter examines when and how four different factors influenced policy outcomes in the Chilean native forest debate: ideas, institutions, social groups, and external conditions. This methodology builds on recent work about political and economic change that has called attention to the relative futility of seeking to determine which one of these factors has more overall explanatory power.[2] In order to achieve this objective, the chapter explores the utility of synthesizing an emerging literature that has tackled the question of the determinants of environmental politics from two different theoretical approaches.

Following state-centric approaches, Peter Haas focused on the role of ideas and the institutional capacity of the state in order to explain environmental policy outcomes.[3] He argued that networks of experts in government agencies who are bound together by shared values, knowledge, and policy recommendations—

epistemic communities—shape the state's response to environmental problems. According to this model, differences in the cohesiveness and extensiveness of policy depend on the relative autonomy from social forces of the institution charged with developing the policy.

Haas made a significant contribution to the debate, but this approach suffers on at least two accounts. First, it shares the weaknesses of statist approaches in general. It only looks at the relationship of specific interest groups to the state and ignores the effect of broader social coalitions that may support or oppose proposed policy. Second, the epistemic community approach has not taken into account the politicization of environmental issues. There is no one technocratic solution to a problem, which leaves the door open for alliance building between conflicting groups, including social groups and external actors. Moreover, these groups and actors may seek allies within state institutions that do not support the objectives of the ministry in charge of forest policy.

A second explanatory approach focuses on the role that social groups and international factors play in forcing recalcitrant governments to adopt policies that promote the conservation and sustainable development of native forests. These studies mostly focused on the struggle to establish extractive reserves in Brazil.[4] The main problem with this approach is that the state itself remains a black box. Because they concentrated on the sources of resistance to destructive policies and the imposition upon the state of more benevolent policy, these studies say little, if anything, about the role of state actors in devising environmentally conscious native forest policy.

Given the limitations of these approaches when taken individually, this chapter explores two hypotheses about when and how ideas, state institutions, social groups, and international factors influence native forest policy in Chile and its high degree of politicization. One hypothesis is that other things being equal, policy tends to reflect the preferences of the epistemic community that controls the government agencies responsible for designing it. This requires a cohesive technical team and firm backing by the ministry in which it is housed. A second hypothesis addresses the reasons for the relative lack of fit between an epistemic community's policy preference and actual outcomes. It contends that politicization occurs when the incumbent epistemic community has views that differ from the dominant market-friendly approach to the forest issue. But the point only holds when coupled with the presence of well-developed private interests in the forest sector that draw their power from the economic importance of that sector for the national economy. These conditions affect both the interest and the power that competing groups may have in forest policy. A strong, privately held forest industry may deflect the ideas proposed by the incumbent epistemic community by forming alliances with competing epistemic communities (that hold different views on how to deal with environmental issues) in other ministries and with broader political and social forces.

International variables, however, will not be explicitly examined because, unlike the cases of Costa Rica and Brazil, these variables did not directly influence the Chilean debate over native forest policy. Nevertheless, external factors undeniably played background and conditioning roles. In Chile, for example, negotiatiors found foreign trade issues linked to action on environmental concerns. Chile also wanted to put a good face on its participation at the 1992 Earth Summit. These pressures created a perception that the Chilean government was obligated to make advances in environmental policy. Moreover, contending groups in Chile used many of the central concepts adopted from debates in developed nations.

Competing Conceptualizations of Sustainable Development

Given the general interpretive framework, what are the axes of conflict over native forest policy in developing countries? The chapter argues that differences in two major competing views of sustainable development—a market-friendly versus a progressive, alternative approach—lie at the core of dissension in environmental politics. Before characterizing these two approaches, however, it is useful to distinguish the concept of sustainable development from those of preservation and conservation. Both sides of the sustainable development debate use those terms, but to different ends. "Preservation" refers to initiatives that prohibit economic exploitation of natural resources present in an ecosystem. It is the strictest form of protection. Conservation, by contrast, does not rule out the economic use of an ecosystem. Rather, it seeks to rationalize use in order to ensure the availability of resources in the future. Despite these differences, both concepts have a common denominator. The focus is on the resource itself and on whether it should be used. Scant attention is paid to the social consequences of those choices: who gains or loses from them. Moreover, in some circles, the concept of conservation fails to take into account some of the ecological effects of use, such as impacts on biodiversity and the integrity of the forest.

Sustainable development, by contrast, is a concept that attempts to link both ecological and social dimensions to the idea of conservation. It was forged in the 1980s in an effort to bridge a widening gap between the preservationist position and the need for further economic development. The well-documented effects of poverty on environmental degradation gave birth to the concept of sustainable development that was popularized by the Brundtland Commission in its report, *Our Common Future*.[5] That report stressed the need for a style of economic development capable of meeting the basic needs of a developing country's population while maintaining its stock of natural resources so as not to rob future generations of their use.[6] For policy and programmatic purposes, development economists have broken the concept of sustainable development down into three interrelated components: fostering a healthy, growing economy (which may necessitate structural adjustment); maintaining a commitment to social equity (or meeting basic needs); and providing protection of the environment.[7]

This general definition raises two difficulties. First, the terms are too general. As a result, careful attention must be paid to their specific content because it heavily colors policy prescriptions. Second, fulfilling all three conditions, no matter how

they are defined, is problematic due to inherent distributional—and therefore political—tensions among them. Given these considerations, environmental policies, programs, and projects—including those related to the forest—have tended
to cluster around two distinct conceptualizations of the relationship between economic growth, equity, and environment.

The dominant view within the policy establishment, shared by governments
and multilateral institutions, reduces equity and environmental considerations to
market-friendly economic growth.[8] To achieve rapid growth, developing countries must build market economies, integrate them into world markets, and pay
careful attention to private property rights. From this perspective the environmental consequences of economic development are considered to be unfortunate
side effects that must be ameliorated. Consequently, the solution is limited to the
addition of technologies capable of mitigating the environmental impact of industrial processes, rather than finding substitutes for them or alternative methods
of production.[9] Social equity concerns and their link to the environment receive
even less direct attention. At its core, this perspective argues that aggregate economic growth brought about by structural reforms will improve national income
(and therefore housing, education, and wealth), and that rising income levels will
allow people to become concerned about environmental degradation.

These views inspire a number of policy prescriptions for the use of natural renewable resources. Multilateral lending institutions now require the addition of
"environmental" safeguards to large-scale development projects in forestry that
are undertaken with the goal of providing employment and repaying onerous international loans.[10] Many studies have advocated the promotion of private property rights over communal ownership, elimination of government subsidies that
make deforestation profitable, reduction of the role of the state in order to minimize the impact of bureaucratic incompetence, and the strengthening of institutional "capacities" in sharply reduced spheres of state action.[11]

An alternative approach to sustainable development takes each of the terms—
economic growth, social equity, and environment—into account in its own right
and then seeks to find reinforcing linkages among the three. Most of the studies in
this vein begin by explicitly, or at least implicitly, questioning the orthodox view
of economic development. They argue that even with technological fixes and a
more realistic economic accounting of environmental losses,[12] rapid economic
growth on the periphery (and in the center) ultimately will be self-defeating in
terms of environmental and human sustainability. As a result, a number of more
ecologically centered values infuse this alternative approach to development. Its
proponents conclude that efforts should involve decentralization, multiple use of
the forest, exploitation of alternative products and production methods, support
for smaller-scale over large-scale enterprise, and serious participation in project
and policy design and implementation by means of grassroots development.[13]

Equally important, this alternative approach to sustainable development builds
on the assumption that *livelihoods* are at the root of environmental problems in

developing nations—especially for the impoverished rural areas.[14] Thus, the struggle over the environment is inextricably linked to the larger issue of social, economic, and cultural self-determination, which requires offering vulnerable populations alternatives to exclusive reliance on the market. This is particularly true for people who are not yet fully integrated into market economies or who are at the lower end of the socioeconomic scale. In the forest, these include dispossessed or displaced small-scale subsistence farmers and Indian and settler communities, as well as families and individuals that derive their living from multiple extractive activities.

From this perspective, environmental concerns, social equity, and economic development for the rural poor are given equal weight conceptually—not reduced to one or another term—and then they are linked. This more holistic approach requires explicit consideration of the ecological impact of the way human activities cut across economic activities and across social, economic, and political boundaries.[15] This has led to an emphasis on grassroots development, technologies that mimic natural processes, and projects that promote local self-reliance and control over a resource in order to achieve a more equitable distribution of wealth.

As will be seen, these two distinct conceptual views of sustainable development stand at the center of the native forest policy debate in Chile. They define proponents of market-friendly developmentalist solutions versus alternative arrangements. Epistemic communities within the government articulate these points of view, as do societal actors (both economic interest groups and the leaders of social movements). Moreover, each side uses the concepts of preservation and conservation in its discourse to legitimize its environmental credentials. In short, all are "green," but there are clearly different shades with significant political consequences.

FOREST POLICY UNDER MILITARY RULE
AND DEMOCRACY

Before turning to a discussion of present-day forest policy in Chile, we must consider how past policy and the historical development of the forest sector have affected policy responses in the Aylwin administration. In general, current efforts to preserve and develop native forests in a sustainable manner have their origin in the consequences of past policies, which left the forest sector divided into two subsectors. One was a well-developed, economically highly concentrated, domestically owned timber industry, which was based on plantations growing exotics, mainly radiata pine and some eucalyptus. The second subsector, native forests, had little industrial economic value and was under increasing pressure resulting from such things as substitution by timber-industry plantations, clear-cutting for wood chips for export, and change of land use for agriculture. In this context, environmentalists in the Aylwin administration turned their attention to strengthening the native forest subsector.[16] This section reviews these developments, which are the backdrop to the politics of native forest policy during the Aylwin administration.

The Legacy of Military Rule and Pressures on the Forest

Chile has long been known for its mineral resources, principally nitrate and copper. But Chile also has a wealth of renewable natural resources, such as fish and forests, which governments began to exploit in the 1960s. One analyst estimated that native forests covered about half of Chile during early colonial times. Since then, Chile has lost about 50 percent of its forest cover, mainly due to the expansion of agriculture, dairy farming, and ranching in south-central, southern, and the extreme south of Chile. The consequences have been soil erosion, silted streams, dried river beds, extensive coastal dunes, and sand banks at the mouths of rivers. The character of the landscape, of course, was irreversibly changed as well.[17] In the 1960s, the administration of Eduardo Frei began reforestation of deforested areas, especially in regions with land officially classified as appropriate for forests, began to be reforested. The government designed an industrial policy to stimulate forest production with plantations of exotic commercial species, principally radiata pine and some eucalyptus.

That policy gathered momentum during the military government with the 1974 introduction of Decree Law (DL) 701, which the forest industry had helped to formulate. DL 701 subsidized 75 percent (up to 90 percent in some years) of the costs of reforestation for commercial plantations. With this sizable direct subsidy, the total areas forested with exotics shot up from about 200,000 hectares in 1974 to approximately 1.3 million in 1988. Reversing past law, another decree in 1975 authorized the export of wood products regardless of value added; this made possible the export boom in timber and chips.[18]

DL 701, a reaction to the socialist government of Salvador Allende that the military had overthrown, was intended to promote private-sector ownership of this economic resource; it succeeded admirably. Most plantations are in private hands, concentrated in a few large Chilean companies—sometimes in association with foreign firms—that are part of Chile's most powerful conglomerates.[19] Indeed, the economic power of this sector should not be underestimated. Exports of raw logs, wood chips, sawn wood, and cellulose have become leading foreign exchange earners for Chile, amounting to almost US$900 million in 1990.[20]

The expansion of the plantation-based, export-oriented forest industry has put serious pressure on native forests in certain regions in Chile. Initially, forest companies established their plantations in the coal-mining zone of Concepción and then expanded to eroded and sand-covered lands in Regions VII and VIII (The Republic of Chile is divided into thirteen regions.) Eventually, the plantations began to compete with native forests in these regions after the denuded areas near existing forest operations were replanted. After the forest was cut, exotics were planted or the land was given over to agriculture or ranching. Chile's powerful timber companies have now expanded their operations to Regions IX, X, and XII.

The data on the extent of the deforestation of native forest for plantations are not robust. However, one study estimates that approximately 200,000 hectares of native forest had been cleared by 1987. The process accelerated after 1988 due to exploding demand for short-fiber wood chips. Currently, the annual rate of deforestation resulting from substitution for exotics is some 10,000 hectares, about the same as the loss from forest fires and extraction of wood fuel by smallholders and peasants.[21]

In short, by the 1990s companies tied to the international pulp and paper industry were clear-cutting large tracts of native forest to use the short-fiber wood for export and to replace the forests with plantations of faster growing exotic species. Additionally, the widespread practice of "high-grading," (that is, "mining" rather than planned "harvesting") of native forest timber for which there is commercial demand has inflicted extensive damage.[22] Overgrazing has also denuded some areas, as forests are either burned to clear land for cattle and sheep or the animals themselves consume caducifoliate species, damaging their reproductive and developmental cycles and stunting trees.[23]

Reversing the Tide: Policies and Programs
of the Aylwin Administration

The Chilean state has a relatively long history of involvement in the preservation and conservation of its forests. Beginning in the nineteenth century, the government implemented legislation to preserve and conserve this resource. Preservation efforts center on the National Wilderness Protection System (Sistema Nacional de Areas Silvestres Protegidas [SNAPSE]). The SNAPSE encompasses a system of national parks, reserves, and monuments. It covers a total of 13,834,489 hectares, but only about 1.5 million hectares contain native forests.[24] Since the SNAPSE was devised long before the concept of biodiversity was developed and popularized, many unique Chilean forest ecosystems are not covered under this system.

Conservation is basically covered in two pieces of legislation: the forestry law of 1931 and DL 701 of 1974 (as amended in 1979). The 1931 law regulated use and established a few reserves.[25] At present, the provisions of DL 701 are the most relevant for the forestry sector. In addition to stimulating plantations of nonnative species, it sets the criteria that define land use (which lands are suitable for forestry and not for other uses) and regulates the economic use of both plantations and native forests.[26] The focus is strictly economic. Ecological concerns— biodiversity and ecosystem integrity—are not explicitly considered; the social consequences of economic use are also not considered. In practice, however, virtually no one made use of the incentives of DL 701 for the management of native forests. This was largely because forestry is a capital-intensive industry, and DL

701 only reimbursed firms a year after the initial outlay. This meant that large-scale producers found plantations that grow exotics to be much more profitable. Exotics, utilized by the pulp and paper industries and for the production of planks and logs, had ready markets abroad. Smallholders who may have wished to manage their native forests simply could not afford to do so.

In March 1990, the first democratic administration in seventeen years took office. The government of Patricio Aylwin was based in a coalition representing a spectrum of ideological views from center and center-left political parties that was called the Concertación de Partidos por la Democracia, or Concertación for short. Despite its diversity of representation, it was largely dominated by the Christian Democratic Party (PDC). Because the environmental movement had formed part of the opposition to the dictatorship, environmental issues had a place in the Concertación's program, and forest management was one of the first areas addressed. The Aylwin administration took two tacks. First, it initiated new legislation, the Ley de Bosques Nativos. Second, the agency charged with overseeing forests and the national parks system—the Corporación Nacional Forestal (CONAF), under the direction of the Ministry of Agriculture (MAG)—began a set of modest programs to benefit smallholders and peasants in forest areas. Of these two efforts, the Bosques Nativos bill is potentially more significant than the set of small, underfunded programs. Because this legislative initiative was the main focus of the Aylwin administration's effort, this chapter concentrates more attention on it than on the smaller programs.

The bill applied a rigorous economic focus to the preservation and conservation of native forests. Given the success of DL 701 in stimulating plantations to cultivate exotics, the new legislation also offered a 75 percent subsidy for reforesting and managing native forests, and it regulated harvesting of native species. The idea behind the subsidy is to give property owners an economic incentive to improve and manage native forests rather than to cut them down for short-term economic gain. Over time, it is hoped, the internal and international markets for native wood products will develop as well. The law itself refers only to the economic use of timber. Its treatment of the replacement of native forest by plantations cultivating exotics, however, reveals a strong interest in preservation. The bill prohibits replacement of forests on slopes of more than 30 degrees and of those that have a high management potential, are unique habitats for species of flora and fauna, and protect watersheds. The bill also regulates the amount of degraded forest that may be substituted, as well as extraction methods and rates for each species.[27]

As a complement to this major legislative effort, MAG and CONAF also undertook small pilot projects that are more explicitly geared to addressing the equity question in the forestry sector.[28] One of these programs, the peasant reforestation aid program, has two subprograms. One is a credit and technical aid program enabling smallholders (with up to five hectares) to receive subsidies granted by DL

701 in a timely manner. The program is managed by CONAF and financed by the Instituto de Desarrollo Agropecuario of the Ministry of Agriculture, but in order to run the program efficiently, these agencies have encouraged peasant organizing. The second reforestation subprogram addresses the domestic subsistence needs of peasants—fuel, posts, and building materials—and offers aid for the forestation of areas of up to one hectare. This program is administered by CONAF and financed by a special agency created by the new government to administer social programs. The funds come mainly from a tax on corporate profits. Another pilot program explicitly targets peasants with land containing native forests. Through appropriate technology transfers, the program helps peasants learn how to live off the forest without destroying it. DL 701 expired in 1994. Preliminary ideas for its revision center on eliminating subsidies for large-scale corporations and focusing benefits on smallholders.[29]

THE POLITICS OF NATIVE FOREST POLICY IN REDEMOCRATIZED CHILE

What are the politics that influenced forest policy initiatives and outcomes in newly redemocratized Chile? Supporters of the alternative view of sustainable development clearly controlled key government institutions charged with developing the native forest legislative bill. These individuals, sharing both a set of notions of cause and effect concerning deforestation and common policy prescriptions, formed a cohesive epistemic community. Yet, the bill fell far short of what one would expect, given the common perceptions shared by these policymakers. Why did it not more fully reflect their point of view? The evidence suggests that the presence of powerful market forces in Chile, and a strong forest industry sector in particular, exerted direct and indirect pressure that forced the alternative epistemic community to compromise. Moreover, the policy debates clearly showed that the alternative and market-friendly views of sustainable development divided both societal and state actors. This meant that societal interests formed complicated alliances with like-minded rival epistemic communities in the government that cut across political party lines. These coalitions both limited and helped the alternative epistemic community.

Two Views of Sustainable Development in Chile and Agenda Setting During the Transition to Democracy

If two competing groups—the alternative approach and the market-friendly view—exist in Chile, why does the former dominate the forestry sector in redemocratized Chile? One part of the answer lies in the development of the environmental movement in Chile. The other has to do with the relationship between the supporters of the alternative position and the political opposition during the transition to democracy from authoritarian rule (that is, in the agenda-setting stage of the policy process).

The alternative view of sustainable development in Chile began as early as the 1960s and 1970s. A group working with Francisco de Castri in the University of Chile linked ecology to social and economic problems.[30] The debate was picked up by forestry schools at the University of Chile and the Universidad Austral de Chile. Harald Schmidt and Claudio Donoso and their students clearly linked ecological concerns and the sustainable economic use of native forests with an appreciation for social equity in rural areas.[31] As members of the political opposition, many found work in academic think tanks and ENGOs critical of the dictatorship, such as the Grupo de Investigaciones Agrarias and the Comité Pro-Defensa de Fauna y la Flora (CODEFF). In short, supporters of the alternative conception of sustainable development were well defined in Chile and had long advocated policy in accord with those views. They formed the backbone of the alternative environmental social movement. Many were also members of the Christian Democratic and center-left political parties, such as the Partido por la Democracia (PPD) and the Partido Humanista Verde.

The alternative group's involvement in policy debates began in the middle of the 1980s during the military dictatorship. Concerned over the impact of DL 701 on economic concentration and the replacement of native forests, they developed a native forestry bill for CONAF, which accepted the idea. Although the bill never made it to the legislative commissions of the junta, one of the principal ideas of the current bill—subsidies for the management of native forests—was first developed there.[32] The very narrow economic focus of the effort was largely due to the fact that the forestry ecologists were trying to convince an agency stacked with pro-military government administrators to do something for native forests. Moreover, because the bill was modeled after existing practice, the framers hoped that it would not suffer outright rejection. Other values had to be suppressed for the time being.

In 1988, the Concertación defeated General Augusto Pinochet's bid for eight more years of rule and began to prepare its platform for general elections in December 1989. During that process, supporters of sustainable development set the basic agenda for native forest policy because they dominated the native forestry subcommission of the Concertación's environmental commission.[33] They believed policy should help conserve and improve forests, protect them from replacement with exotics, give incentives to create industrial demand for native species (to reduce pressure for replacement), and improve the living conditions of peasants and smallholders in forested regions. Their writings recognized the need to promote the multiple use of the forest and grassroots development efforts for communities in the forest sector. They expressed concern over the biodiversity of flora and fauna and the integrity of old-growth and secondary forests.[34]

By contrast, supporters of the market-friendly approach to sustainable development were not active in setting the initial policy agenda because they were not well represented in the forest policy subcommission. Market-friendly advocates placed little importance on environmental issues and assumed they would influence policy at a later point. The advocates were located mainly in the private sector, primarily through the Empresarios por un Desarrollo Sostenible and the Corporación de la Madera (CORMA). The former was a working group of the Chilean industrial sector's peak association, the Society for Industrial Development (SFF). CORMA was the powerful association of the forest industry proper, which was affiliated with the SFF. Other adherents of this view included a few think tanks, the most important of which was the Centro de Investigación y Planificación del Medio Ambiente. The presence of this think tank in the market-friendly camp is evidence that the environmental movement itself was split between the two concepts of sustainable development. Moreover, some socialists who gave preference to rapid industrialization over ecology, and who affirmed that environmental problems could be solved by adding technology to existing industrial processes, also supported the market-friendly developmentalist view.[35]

With respect to the forestry sector, the proponents of the market-friendly developmental approach to sustainable development preferred policies that establish clear distinctions between private and public property. To this end, they believed that state regulation and conservation efforts should confine themselves to public lands. Since most forests suitable for exploitation are in private hands, these efforts were limited to some degree to forested areas unsuitable for productive use (i.e., commercial exploitation). However, the proponents believed that the state should not regulate exploitation of the five to seven million hectares of private lands appropriate for forestry activities. Moreover, they felt that the state should pay the owners of such forests for the opportunity costs of restrictions on their economic use.[36]

Policy Formulation: The Alternative Epistemic Community and the Indirect Effect of Socioeconomic Forces

Supporters of the alternative view of sustainable development not only dominated the agenda-setting stage of the policy-making process but also formed a significant epistemic community in government agencies charged with formulating native forest policy. This meant that from the state-centric perspective, and before politicization set in, native forest policy should have reflected more fully the alternative position. The relative lack of fit between the alternative epistemic community's point of view and policy as implemented arose due to the indirect influence of market-friendly socioeconomic groups. As time passed, these groups came to apply more direct pressure.

CONAF was the principal locus of the alternative community. Members of the community headed key departments within CONAF, although they did not initially control the directorship. They owed their positions to the fact that they were militants who had worked on this issue and belonged to political parties that were part of the Aylwin administration's governing coalition. CONAF, ordinarily not a powerful department, is under the wing of the Ministry of Agriculture, whose minister, Juan Agustín Figueroa, supported—and thus immeasurably strengthened—the position of the alternative epistemic community's central policy recommendations. From the beginning, Minister Figueroa took a consistent stance against replacement of native forests with plantations.[37]

Soon after the Aylwin inauguration, MAG and CONAF set about designing, without interference from other groups or government institutions, a native forest bill to submit to Congress.[38] The alternative community revived the idea of subsidies that would create economic incentives for the sustainable-use management of native forests. Their proposal would have facilitated the qualification of smallholders and peasants for the subsidies by making them available on demand. In clear opposition to the powerful forestry industry, the alternative epistemic community was adamantly against the replacement of native forest by plantations cultivating exotics.

These key elements of the bill incorporated only a limited range of the central tenets of the alternative epistemic community's view of sustainable development. On the positive side, the proposals emphasized preservation and conservation by linking the fate of the forest to its economic use. They also sought to preserve large tracts to promote biodiversity.

This approach, however, clouded a number of points—clearly articulated in their writings during the military government—which would have strengthened the holistic vision of the alternative sustainable development approach. Most significantly, the alternative epistemic community took a narrow economic approach to the problem. It was narrow in the sense that the subsidies provided only a general incentive to conserve native forests, based primarily on the establishment of an industry and a market for native forest wood products. Ironically, the alternative community's central idea was just as market oriented as that of the forest industry. The difference lay only in the species of trees that the incentives targeted.

The issue of social equity was also less distinct than it might have been. Incentives for the economic use of native woods were never linked explicitly to the livelihood of peasants and smallholders. Instead, the issue was addressed in an oblique manner that assumed economic incentives would help smallholders, who controlled much of the remaining native forest but were not linked directly to large forestry enterprises.[39] The alternative community stopped short of proposing that smallholders needed help with marketing, the establishment of cooperative ventures, and the fostering of autonomous grassroots development—all ideas which it had proposed in the past.

Finally, a number of concepts that the alternative epistemic community had espoused—which gave it its holistic cast—were entirely lacking in the proposals. With the focus exclusively on the economic use of timber, it failed to address potential multiple uses of the forest (including aesthetic value). In addition to the lack of attention to grassroots development, the guiding principles overlooked the importance of local ecological factors affecting exploitation methods and biodiversity. Although biodiversity concerns and measures to strengthen CONAF's oversight and programmatic capacities were absent from the bill, they were incorporated into CONAF's small projects and thus certainly were recognized as a priority by the alternative epistemic community.

Given that this community began its legislative task in a strong position (it had a cohesive policy-making team in CONAF and the firm backing of the MAG, a major state actor), what lay behind the conceptual ambivalence of those who previously had articulated the alternative view so clearly? The answer is that the indirect pressure exerted by market-friendly socioeconomic forces on the alternative epistemic community forced it to make strategic choices.

Market-friendly groups of Chilean socioeconomic elites had gained strength during the authoritarian period, when they enjoyed a solid structural advantage as the country was emerging from the economic crisis of 1982–1984. In response to that crisis, they had formed a cohesive economic policy coalition which successfully negotiated a modified version of the neoliberal economic model imposed on the authoritarian regime by orthodox monetarists—the so-called Chicago boys. Policy was generally responsive to the capitalist group that was largely responsible for the sustained high growth in the newly created free-market economy emerging during that time.[40]

From this position of strength, business and landowning elites expressed concern over the post-transition fate of the market economy. To ease their fears and to gain their support for democracy, the Concertación had promised to retain the free-market economic policies of the authoritarian period, including a commitment to high economic growth rates, fiscal restraint, and a limited role for government in the economy. In addition to this political agreement, market-friendly socioeconomic forces also enjoyed important institutional protections. The electoral rules of the authoritarian constitution of 1980 virtually guaranteed the dominance of right-wing political forces in the Senate, which had an absolute veto power over all legislation.[41]

Nevertheless, as the political opposition to a harsh dictatorship, the Concertación also promised to address social equity issues, an area sorely neglected by the previous military government. The slogan "economic growth with equity" captured the dual nature of the Concertación's commitment to the hard task of forging national reconciliation after so many years of embittered antagonisms: the obligation to retain what were perceived to be the positive legacy of the dictatorship (a steadily growing economy) coupled with the need to redress the dictatorship's shortcomings in the social arena.

But the Concertación's commitment to economic orthodoxy and the accompanying liberal, minimalist, night-watchman state had significant negative consequences for the new administration's ability to deliver on its promises of social equity (including resolving growing income inequality, improving government services in health and education, and reviewing labor laws). The military government had stripped public administration resources to the bone, and the Aylwin administration was committed to the same principles of fiscal austerity that the military government had labored so hard to set. As a result, the new government was more successful at maintaining economic growth than in redressing equity questions. The administration lacked the disposition to expand the provision of social services into universal programs. Instead, it channeled funds from a new 15 percent corporate tax on profits to the programs that were designed under the military government. These perpetuated a dualist welfare model, whereby the middle sectors received health and other services from private businesses while the government provided welfare support only to the poorest segments of society.[42]

These circumstances strongly conditioned the strategic choices on native forest policy available to the otherwise institutionally well-positioned alternative epistemic community. The legislative initiative's narrow economic focus and lack of more explicit commitment to social equity for peasants and smallholders arose largely as a result of these circumstances. The alternative community realized that the policy-making process made it impossible for CONAF and MAG to push through legislation that asked for funding to implement a wide range of programs, such as multiple use of the forest, cooperative ventures, the purchase of forests for purposes of preservation, changes in labor laws, and so forth. Given these limitations, the alternative epistemic community decided that the only way to save native forests was to create an industry for its timber. This step might effectively counteract the powerful plantation-based private interests. If native forests managed in a sustainable manner could contribute to both the nation's GDP and balance of trade, then that might reverse the lack of interest in conservation.[43] By the same token, this context explains why the social questions were relegated to pilot programs designed by CONAF. As programs, rather than laws, CONAF had far greater discretionary authority over them. The programs, in turn, were necessarily small due to fiscal constraints and staffing restrictions, a result of the Concertación's commitment to a liberal state model.[44]

Despite the strong position of the alternative epistemic community, it found itself constrained at the outset by the structural position of Chile's private sector. Business derived its power from a number of sources. One was its privileged position in a thoroughly market-based socioeconomic system: Its investment was crucial to continued rapid economic growth. Second, private interests also had decisive allies in the Senate, a gatekeeping institution. Third, the Concertación had explicitly agreed to conserve the market policies that had formed the basis of rapid economic growth in Chile while reinforcing the structural power of capitalists. In this context, so unfavorable to challenges to economic orthodoxy, the real significance of a solid institutional position and a cohesive policy-making team for the alternative epistemic community was that it was able partially to imbue policy proposals with its ideas despite these systemic constraints.

Direct Social Pressure and Politicization: The Forest Industry and the Market-Friendly Developmental Epistemic Community

The alternative epistemic community soon found itself in a more direct struggle with the market-friendly groups. Events demonstrated that in the presence of powerful private-sector actors, alternative epistemic communities can expect resistance to their proposals. This resistance was a major source of politicization in Chile and confirms that environmental issues are more than purely technical matters. The ensuing conflict revealed that the Aylwin administration itself was riven by the two rival epistemic communities. The conflict was heightened as complex alliance patterns emerged between these competing epistemic communities and like-minded social forces. The combination of strong industry groups, rival epistemic communities, and alliance building among state and societal actors made the struggle particularly sharp, and it revealed that tensions between the competing conceptions of sustainable development cut across party lines.

Although forest industry interests and the representatives of the market-friendly epistemic community were not initially involved in the design of native forest policy, they formed an alliance of like-minded state and societal interests and quickly raised a challenge to the alternative community. By the end of 1990, the battle lines were drawn over the question of property rights, including the freedom to clear-cut privately owned native forests for short-term economic gain or for longer-term planting with exotics.

The diversification of the Compañía de Aceros del Pacífico (CAP), a large Chilean conglomerate, into the lucrative short-fiber wood chip export industry galvanized the native forest issue. CAP's directors negotiated a joint venture with a Japanese consortium, Terranova, that owned substantial native forest in Region X. In order to obtain a permit to clear-cut the lands, Terranova circumvented CONAF by approaching the Ministry of Economy, which granted its approval of the project. The Ministry of Economy was far more interested in meeting economic growth targets than in ecological concerns.[45]

Supporters of this project rationalized the operation with market-friendly sustainable development arguments. Both the Ministry of Economy and the industrialists argued that there was nothing improper about clear-cutting native forests because they had no other economic value. Moreover, they argued, the environmental function of the trees would still be met by the plantations that would replace the native forests. These views clearly distinguish this position from that held by the alternative approach to sustainable development. The latter values ecosystems and their preservation for more than just their contributions to global environmental conditions (for example, the role of trees as natural "scrubbers" and preventers of soil erosion). The market approach clearly contradicted the alternative approach to sustainable development, which values these ecosystems for their intrinsic worth as contributors to biodiversity and to quality of life (in the sense that the community enjoys enhanced environmental quality and the fruits of economic activity, which traditionally were siphoned off by large corporations).

If private timber interests had found an ally in the representatives of the market-friendly developmentalist epistemic community in the Ministry of Economy—notably Carlos Ominami, the minister himself—the societal interests that supported the alternative view did not remain quiet. They quickly mounted a highly visible media campaign to denounce the timber interests' attempted end run around CONAF. This was led by CODEFF, the best known of the alternative ENGOs, and it was also supported by preservationist ENGOs.[46] In a very real sense, these groups became the societal allies of the beleaguered alternative epistemic community in CONAF and MAG. Together these like-minded social and state interests formed a countervailing alliance.

The presidency, true to its consensual policy-making style, formed an interministerial commission to set guidelines in this issue area pending the promulgation of the native forest law. The commission included the ministers of agriculture, economy, and finance, as well as the General Secretariat of the Presidency (SEGPRES) and the Ministry of National Property (Bienes Nacionales).[47] SEGPRES is a powerful agency, the strategic and tactical planning nerve center of the presidency. Bienes Nacionales is a relatively minor ministry not unlike the Department of the Interior in the United States. The positions they took revealed the existence of broader, competing epistemic communities in the government and laid bare their institutional power bases. The most intractable antagonists were the Ministry of Agriculture, which sided with the alternative approach, and the Ministry of Economy, on the market-friendly developmentalist side. The latter's approach was largely created by its commitment to the government's economic growth targets. Generally less adamant, yet still clearly identifiable, were the positions of the Christian Democratic-led Ministry of Finance and of SEGPRES, which supported the market-friendly view, and the Ministry of National Property (headed by the Partido Socialista and PPD), which argued for the alternative approach.[48]

The divisions clearly ran deep and cut across party lines within center-left political parties, with socialist groups being the most pro-growth on the left (they headed the Ministry of Economy). Had it not been for the cohesiveness and steadfastness of the alternative epistemic community, in alliance with the Ministry of Agriculture, the combined influence of the Ministries of Economy and Finance and of SEGPRES would probably have defeated its proposals. In any case, the interministerial commission failed to arrive at a consensus. However, the highly public and acrimonious debate exposed the degree of polarization over the native forest issue.

The Search for Consensus: The National Forestry Commission

The public conflict over the Terranova case involved both government agencies and societal forces, and it revealed the alliances among them. The necessity of forming the interministerial commission was a testament to the power of market-friendly social forces—the forest industry. Their strength, the public conflict, and the impasse in the interministerial commission also meant that the Ministry of Agriculture and CONAF could no longer formulate the general native forestry bill alone. To stay within the bounds of the Aylwin administration's commitment to a consensual policy-making style, the formulation stage of the policy-making process would now have to include the relevant government, societal, and academic forces. To this end, in the first quarter of 1992, MAG formed an advisory group called the National Forestry Commission (CONAFOR), and within it a native forest subcommission. MAG and CONAF were supposed to use the subcommission's recommendations as a foundation for the native forest legislation.

Like the interministerial commission before it, CONAFOR again revealed that rival conceptualizations of sustainable development demarcated the polarization in the native forest policy debate. These conceptualizations ran deep in government and society alike, and CONAFOR's structure lent itself to complex alliance patterns between state and societal actors. Government actors in CONAFOR and the native forest subcommission included CONAF and the Instituto Nacional Forestal (INFOR, the agency in charge of silvicultural investigation), as well as the Ministries of Finance and Economy. As it turned out, none of these supported the alternative view because CONAF's Christian Democratic director, under great pressure and in accord with his party's wishes, sided with the developmentalist epistemic community. By the same token, the societal forces represented in CONAFOR were also mostly market friendly. These included CORMA (the industry peak association) and the Centro de Investigación y Planificación del Medio Ambiente (CIPMA). Both of these were well financed and had very capable technical teams. The academic community was more divided. CODEFF, which took the alternative view, had been invited but declined because it felt that it would legitimize a foregone conclusion: The commission would probably support the market-friendly developmentalist view.[49] The forestry workers' union— the Confederación de Trabajadores Forestales—also participated. However, the alternative epistemic community considered it to be an unrepresentative organization. Its leaders were mainly intent on securing personal advantages.[50] As CODEFF feared, the subcommission's "consensus document" reflected the preferences of the market-friendly developmentalist epistemic community. At its core, the document advocated the creation of three categories of forests: preservation, protection, and production. The first two categories covered an area of some 22 million hectares combined, and the third one covered about 7 million.[51] Forests to be designated as preservation areas were not to be touched and were to be included in the SNAPSE. Protected forests could not be exploited either because they were near watersheds, contained species legally prohibited from cutting, or were on slopes of over 80 degrees. Most importantly, the document argued that productive forests should be divided into restricted- and unrestricted-use categories. Restricted-use forests were those in areas with slopes of over 45 degrees or that contained protected species. These could be exploited by selective logging rather than clear-cutting. In unrestricted-use productive forests, the document argued that owners should be allowed to use the forest in any way they wished, which usually coincided with the short-term economic gain. In practice, this gave owners the right to replace natural forests with plantations. The consensus document also contained provisions for subsidizing native forest management.[52]

The main areas of restricted use clearly fall in remote areas of Magallanes and Aysén (Regions XI and XII). The unrestricted-use areas are close to the existing operations of the forest companies or in the more infrastructurally well-developed Regions VII, VIII, IX, and X. (Region X has far more forestlands than the other three.)

The Alternative Epistemic Community Strikes Back

Subsequent events clearly confirm the importance for policy outcomes of a cohesive team of experts and strong state institutional sources of power. The subcommission's recommendations had reflected an uncompromising posture on the part of the forest industry and their government allies with respect to the key issue of replacement by exotics. By classifying forests according to areas of preservation, protection, and production, the document advocated virtually unrestricted use of the "productive" areas. This condemned forests in accessible areas to extinction. The subcommission, however, was only an advisory board, and the minister of agriculture, a key member of the alternative epistemic community, rejected that position. He then strengthened the alternative epistemic community by replacing the director of CONAF with a more flexible person, one who was not completely in favor of the market-friendly developmentalist position.[53] Nevertheless, market-friendly societal actors—industry groups and their allies in the environmental movement—were still a force to be reckoned with. The general context of the policy-making process still favored them. This meant that the market-friendly developmentalist desire for substitution would also have to be addressed by the policymakers who favor the alternative approach, although from a weaker position as far as industry interests were concerned.

President Aylwin ordered supporters of the timber interest in the state bureaucracy (primarily in the Ministry of Economy) to end their rigid resistance and to compromise with the alternative epistemic community groups in CONAF and the Ministry of Agriculture. The alternative epistemic community's position was further strengthened by the fact that President Aylwin himself had some sympathy for the minister of agriculture's position.[54] In a sense, then, the president of the republic himself became a "soft" supporter of the alternative epistemic community.

The choice for the directorship of CONAF reflected the presidential disposition. The Christian Democrats under Patricio Aylwin dominated the administration. Accordingly, the new director still had to be of that party but more flexible than the outgoing director, more open to the position of the Ministry of Agriculture without completely ignoring the market-friendly developmentalist view. Juan Moya, who had been a member of the original native forest subcommission in the Concertación presidential campaign, met the criteria.

In early 1992, the native forestry subcommission met behind closed doors to work out a compromise between the alternative and market-friendly developmentalist positions. Neither CORMA and the NGOs nor academics participated in these meetings. Nevertheless, these social forces still played a role in the outcome, albeit a more indirect one. They relied on the alliances they had already established with the rival epistemic communities. Thus, CONAF, National Property, and the Ministry of Agriculture defended the position of the alternative environmental movement. The Ministries of Finance and of Energy, SEGPRES, and others bodies supported the position of CORMA.[55]

The reformulated bill retained the idea of subsidies as an incentive for native forest management. It discarded the notion of three types of land classification, which was the basis for the idea that productive lands should not be subject to restrictions. Instead, it addressed preservationist concerns by stating that forests in the SNAPSE, in state reserves, and near watersheds could not be exploited. Most telling, however, were the across-the-board restrictions on clear-cutting, the basis for replacement. Clear-cutting was prohibited on slopes of over 30 degrees (as opposed to 45 degrees in the consensus document). In addition to this measure, CONAF introduced the category of "manageable native forest", meaning native forests suitable for harvesting or selective cutting. These often coincided with areas in which the private sector had wanted unrestricted rights. Moreover, in order to preserve biodiversity, forests that were habitat to endangered fauna or flora could not be replaced unless they had substantially degraded and would be very hard to regenerate. Moreover, only 25 percent to 50 percent of a landowner's forest could be replaced, depending on conditions.[56]

President Aylwin approved the bill and formally sent it to Congress—the House of Deputies—in April 1992. As of August 1993, it had emerged from the lower chamber with few significant modifications.[57] Key to this partial victory was that the bill gained some support from the Ministry of Finance, where the bill was sent for a fiscal feasibility study in the middle of 1993. Otherwise, lobbying by SEGPRES and Energy, which supported the market-friendly developmentalist epistemic community, might have killed the bill. At first, the Ministry of Finance study opposed both the subsidy and the restrictions on replacement. But after long conferences with CONAF officials, the study team realized that the economic rationality by which it had made its calculations did not apply to peasants and smallholders. CONAF and the Ministry of Finance reached a compromise. Rather than blanket subsidies, there would be eligibility rules. But the strictness of those rules would vary according to objective socioeconomic and regional geographic considerations. CONAF would also be empowered to aid smallholders in generating the necessary requirements.[58]

From the House of Deputies, the bill was scheduled to go to the Senate. Its supporters expected to meet stiff opposition there by right-wing political forces that dominate that branch of the legislature. And they did.

As a result, in 1996, during the second government of the Concertación under President Eduardo Frei, the bill was still pending in the Chilean Senate. If a native forest bill emerges from that august body, Chile will have to wait even longer, if ever, before this or other legislation offers incentives for native forest management. For, in an attempt to satisfy Senate objections, the Frei administration altered the content of the bill sufficiently to warrant a reconciliation bill between the House of Deputies and the Senate. The gulf that separates the two is great and may never be bridged.

Although the Congress has not yet passed a native forestry law, the examination of the policy-making stages over which MAG and CONAF had the most direct influence and control—the period before the bill went to the Congress—confirmed two expectations. First, that ideas and state institutions in the form of cohesive epistemic communities clearly influenced policy content. They framed the bill in terms of the alternative approach to sustainable development. Second, the outcome also depended on the direct and indirect action of social forces. They limited the extent to which the alternative epistemic community could imbue the bill with its view of sustainable development. In so doing, market-oriented social groups forced the alternative epistemic community to relegate such ideas to small projects where they could not have larger implications for the forest industry.

CONCLUSION: COMPARATIVE IMPLICATIONS

This chapter argued that the central axis of conflict in environmental politics is rooted in two rival conceptualizations of sustainable development: a dominant, market-friendly one and a progressive, alternative approach. Furthermore, neither the state- nor the society-centric explanations alone are sufficient to explain environmental policy outcomes in Chile and, by extension, in other cases like it. It showed that a cohesive team of experts in key government agencies that share notions of cause and effect and policy proposals—epistemic communities—do orient policy initiatives. It would probably be strange if they did not. However, disgruntled societal forces—to the extent they exist—may seek alliances with competing epistemic communities in other state institutions and force compromises. In today's climate of economic orthodoxy, this will be particularly true when the epistemic community in charge of designing policy has views that differ from the dominant market-oriented approach.

What are the implications of the Chilean case for native forest policy in the rest of Latin America? At the most general level, international factors should strengthen market-friendly approaches to native forest policy. The United States and the World Bank are the most significant external actors, and they advocate these approaches through "green conditionality" in trade and aid. As will be seen below, however, the available evidence suggests that their impact varies from country to country. This means that the effect of domestic politics must also be taken into account in every case, although its weight may be stronger in some instances than in others.

A brief examination of Chile in comparison to Venezuela, Mexico, and Costa Rica illustrates these points—an exercise that is by necessity only suggestive of a possible hypothesis and that awaits further study for more conclusive evidence. In all of these cases, with the exception of Venezuela, national forestry policy leans more to the market-friendly approach than to the alternative one. Moreover, in Chile and Costa Rica, the epistemic community in charge of the forest agencies tended to favor the alternative view of sustainable development. But in both instances, albeit for different reasons, they were overwhelmed by their adversaries. The concluding paragraphs suggest how the analytical framework introduced at the beginning of this chapter might help to tease out some of the reasons for these outcomes.

Why was Venezuela an exception to the general trend toward market-friendly native forest policy? To begin with, in both Chile and Venezuela domestic factors weighed more than international ones, which were more of a background variable rather than a direct influence. Without negating the importance of other factors, a comparison of Chile and Venezuela suggests that the structure of the economy, and by extension the relative economic power of private interests, made a crucial difference. As we saw in the Chilean case, the timber industry was key to economic development, and the business sector was well organized and placed to form alliances with state actors against the alternative epistemic community. The situation is quite different in Venezuela. It is an oil economy, a country that was rich enough not to depend heavily on foreign aid or diversified trade, and timber is not a nationally vital economic resource. Consequently, economically underdeveloped and weak timber interests failed to generate political support in other ministries to counteract the alternative epistemic community that is directing forest policy.[59]

By contrast, international factors seem to carry more weight in the policy outcomes of Mexico and Costa Rica. This is clearest in the comparison between Costa Rica and Chile. As previously mentioned, in both cases alternative epistemic communities dominated the state institutions directly charged with formulating forest policy. In both cases, initial policy formulations in the late 1980s and early 1990s conformed more to the alternative than to the market-friendly view, although this was more pronounced in Costa Rica than in Chile. However, in Costa Rica, a small Central American state, the U.S. government exerted a more direct influence than in Chile. Nevertheless, domestic opposition was also important.[60]

In Costa Rica, market-friendly social forces—agricultural and timber interests along with some ENGOs—were unhappy with the general, progressive, alternative cast of proposed environmental legislation, including forest policy.[61] Moreover, the latter was quite advanced in the Costa Rican Congress, which has significant powers. However, it appeared that the market-friendly forces alone could not stop the legislative bill. The USAID mission, aware of this circumstance, came to their rescue. It provided the funding for a study that would form the basis for a market-friendly bill to rival the one already in the Congress, and it contracted a market-friendly ENGO to carry out the project. Sympathetic representatives then introduced their competing bill in the legislature and managed to derail the original.[62] In short, this is an example of a complicated alliance of domestic and international market-friendly actors in a country where the external actors, the U.S. government in particular, traditionally exert significant direct power.

External actors also played a significant role in the environmental and forest policies of Mexico, although that influence was intimately tied to internal policy choices of the Mexican government. The Mexican government's decisions to engage in market-oriented economic restructuring and to open up to trade and investment with the United States heavily colors its forest policy. In this context, both the planning and the agriculture ministries began to devise market-oriented policy—including in the forestry sector.[63] In other words, the available evidence suggests that Mexico has a relatively cohesive market-oriented epistemic community in the environmental and natural resource management sectors.

Despite this trend, the case of Mexico and other examples throughout the hemisphere show that coalitions of actors interested in the alternative approach also manage to form and that they can be successful in translating their views into projects and policies. A number of studies have revealed that mixtures of international NGOs, European government development agencies, and the United Nations Environmental Programme together with local communities, unions, domestic NGOs, selected state actors, and progressive political parties can make a difference. This has been seen in the extractive reserves legislation in Brazil, the Nohbec community forestry project in the Mexican state of Quintana Roo, the biosphere reserve program in Venezuelan Amazonia, and many other examples.[64] In the final analysis, in most countries these forces will have to struggle constantly to open political space for their vision. It is unlikely that they will ever dominate the policy agenda, but they may find opportunities in discrete policy interstices. They will remain subordinate to other dominant trends, but this is nothing new in Latin American politics.

NOTES

1. For representative studies, see Dennis Mahar, *Government Policies and Deforestation in Latin America: The Politics of Sustainability* (Washington, DC: The World Bank, 1989); Robert Repetto, *The Forest for the Trees? Government Policies and the Misuse of Forest Resources* (Washington DC: World Resources Institute, 1988); Garrett Hardin, "The Tragedy of the Commons," *Science* 162 (December 13, 1968): 1234–1248; Judith Gradwohl and Russell Greenberg, *Saving the Tropical Forests* (London: Earthscan Publications, 1988); John Browder, *Fragile Lands of Latin America: Strategies for Sustainable Development* (Boulder: Westview Press, 1989); and Anthony Anderson, ed., *Alternative to Deforestation: Steps Toward Sustainable Use of the Amazon Rain Forest* (New York: Columbia University Press, 1990).

2. For this methodological approach in political economy, see Stephan Haggard and Robert Kaufman, *The Political Economy of Democratic Transitions* (Princeton: Princeton University Press, 1995); Peter H. Smith, "Crisis and Democracy in Latin America," *World Politics* 43, no. 4 (1991): 608–634; and Hector E. Schamis, "Reconsidering Latin American Authoritarianism in the 1970s: From Bureaucratic Authoritarianism to Neoconservatism," *Comparative Politics* 23, no. 2 (1991): 201–220.

3. Peter Haas, "Epistemic Communities and International Policy Coordination," *International Organization* 46, no. 1 (1991): 143.

4. Marianne Schmink and Charles Wood, eds., *Frontier Expansion in Amazonia* (Gainesville, FL: University of Florida Press, 1985); Alexander Cockburn and Susanna Hecht, *The Fate of the Forest: Developers, Destroyers, and Defenders of the Amazon* (London: Verso, 1988); and Stephan Schwartzman, "Deforestation and Popular Resistance in Acre: From Local Social Movement to Global Network," *The Centennial Review* 35, no. 2 (1991): 397–422.

5. Brundtland Commission, *Our Common Future* (New York: Oxford University Press, 1987).

6. Global Tomorrow Coalition, *Sustainable Development: A Guide to Our Common Future* (New York: Oxford University Press, 1989).

7. For this breakdown of the concept, see James Weaver and Kevin O'Keefe, "The Evolution of Development Economics," unpublished mimeo (Washington, DC: The American University, 1991). There is, of course, quite a debate over whether it is possible to have economic growth and be able to protect the environment. For this, see Herman Daly, "Environmental Carcinogenesis Reviews," Part C of *Journal of Environmental Science and Health* 8, no.2 (1991): 401–407. There are also a number of more eco-centered definitions focused on concepts such as through-puts, steady states, and carrying capacity.

8. For the dominant view, see World Bank, *World Development Report 1992: Development and the Environment* (New York: Oxford University Press, 1992).

9. For similar arguments, see Michael Redclift and David Goodman, eds., *Environment and Development in Latin America: The Politics of Sustainability* (Manchester: Manchester University Press, 1991); Jaime Hurtubia, "Seminario nacional sobre instrumentos y estrategias de financiamiento para la política ambiental chilena" (Santiago, Chile, 1991, mimeograph); and Barry Commoner, *Making Peace with the Planet* (New York: Pantheon, 1990).

10. For critical assessments of these projects and what they represent in the context of North-South relations, see Bruce Rich, "Multilateral Development Banks and Tropical Deforestation," in Suzanne Head and Robert Heinzman, eds., *Lessons of the Rainforest* (San

Francisco: Sierra Club Books, 1990); "Multilateral Development Banks: Their Role in Destroying the Global Environment," *The Ecologist* 15, nos. 1–2 (1985); and David Goodman and Anthony Hall, eds., *The Future of Amazonia: Destruction or Sustainable Development* (Basingstoke, England: Macmillan Press, 1990).

11. For these approaches, see Repetto, *The Forest for the Trees*; Mahar, *Government Policies and Deforestation in Brazil's Amazon Region*; and Hardin, "The Tragedy of the Commons."

12. For environmental cost accounting, see World Resources Institute, *Accounts Overdue: Natural Resource Depreciation in Costa Rica* (Washington, DC: World Resources Institute, 1991).

13. For similar views on the alternative approach, see Redclift and Goodman, *Environment and Development in Latin America*; Hurtubia, "Seminario nacional sobre instrumentos y estratégias para la política ambiental chilena"; Commoner, *Making Peace with the Planet*; Manfred Max-Neef, *A Human Scale of Development: Conception, Application, and Further Reflections* (New York: Apex Press, 1991); and Browder, *Fragile Lands of Latin America*.

14. For a clear articulation of this idea, see Michael Redclift, "Sustainability and the Market: Survival Strategies on the Bolivian Frontier," *Journal of Development Studies* 23, no. 1 (1986).

15. Hurtubia, "Seminario nacional sobre instrumentos y estratégias de financiamiento para la política ambiental chilena."

16. See Aarón Cavieres, "Conservación y utilización del bosque nativo chileno," *Síntesis Parlamentaria Partido por la Democracia/Partido Socialista* 2, 1991.

17. Harald Schmidt, "Disminución de la superficie, calidad y capacidad productiva de los bosques naturales" (paper prepared for the Comisión del Medio Ambiente PAF-Chile, 1992); and "La leña como herramienta en el manejo silvícola del bosque nativo" (paper prepared for the seminar on "La problemática de la dendroenergía en el desarrollo rural," Universidad de Chile, Santiago, 1991).

18. For the development of the forest industry, see Robert N. Gwynne, "Non-Traditional Export Growth and Economic Development: The Chilean Forestry Sector Since 1974," *Bulletin of Latin American Research* 12, no. 2 (1993); and Fernando Hartwig, *Chile, Desarrollo forestal sustentable* (Santiago, Chile: Editorial Andes, 1991).

19. Gwynne, "Non-Traditional Export Growth and Economic Development"; also see Patricio Rozas, "Concentración de mercados y grupos de control en la industria forestal," and Vicente Paeile, "La recomposición de los grupos económicos en el sector forestal," both in *Agricultura y Sociedad* 4 (1986).

20. Instituto Nacional Forestal (INFOR), *Boletín Estadístico*, 21 (August 1991); Corporación Nacional Forestal (CONAF), *Memoria Anual, 1992* (Santiago: República de Chile, 1993); and Corporación de la Madera (CORMA), *Chile, país forestal* (Santiago: Editorial Interamericana, 1991).

21. Comité Pro-Defensa de Fauna y la Flora (CODEFF), "El futuro del bosque nativo chileno: Un desafío de hoy," (CODEFF Working Paper, 1992).

22. CONAF, *Memoria Anual, 1992*.

23. Programa de Acción Forestal-Chile, "Análisis sectorial forestal" (working paper, March 1992); and *Informe final: Comisión de Medio Ambiente* (Santiago, Chile: n.p., 1992).

24. CORMA, *Chile, país forestal*, and CONAF, *Memoria Anual 1992*.

25. See "Ley de Bosques," Decreto Supremo no. 4,363 (June 30, 1931).

26. See Decreto Ley 701 de Fomento Forestal (1974); and Nuevo Decreto Ley 701 (1979).

27. Ministerio de Agricultura and Corporación Nacional Forestal (CONAF), "Proyecto de ley de recuperación del bosque nativo y fomento forestal" (May 1992).

28. Leonardo Araya, Director, Department of Forest Management, CONAF, interviewed by author, Santiago de Chile, August 1993.

29. For further details, see CONAF, "Elementos centrales para un proyecto de ley de fomento a la forestación y recuperación de suelos" (Santiago, July 28, 1993, mimeograph).

30. Jaime Hurtubia, interviewed by author, Santiago, July 1992.

31. For the articulation of the alternative conceptualization of sustainable development in the forest sector in Chile, see Aarón Cavieres et al., "Especialización productiva, medio ambiente y migraciones: El caso del sector forestal en Chile," *Agricultura y Sociedad* 4 (1986); Luis Otero, "La depredación forestal," *Agricultura y Sociedad* 2 (1985); Harald Schmidt and Antonio Lara, "Descripción y potencialidad de los bosques nativos de Chile, *Ambiente y Desarrollo* 1, no. 2 (1985); Antonio Lara, "Los ecosistemas forestales en el desarrollo de Chile," *Ambiente y Desarrollo* 1, no. 3 (1985); Antonio Lara, Aarón Cavieres, Marcos Cortés, and Pablo Donoso, "Consideraciones para una política forestal en el gobierno de transición, 1990–1994," *Documentos Serie Forestal* 89/11, (CODEFF, November 1989).

32. Aarón Cavieres and Leonardo Araya (both of CONAF), interviewed by author, June 1992.

33. Among others, the forestry subcommission included Aaron Cavieres, Jaime Tohá, Juan Moya, Luis Otero, Fernando Bascul, Jorge Catemillán, and Ignacio Leighton.

34. Aarón Cavieres and Leonardo Araya (both of CONAF), interviewed by author, June 1992.

35. The proponents of these views have written extensively in the press, especially Guillermo Guell and Hernán Cortés, both of CORMA, and Fernando Hartwig. Some representative studies include CORMA, *Chile, país forestal*; Paulina Infante, "Roberto de Andraca: Los empresarios podemos compatibilizar desarrollo y medio ambiente," *Revista Industria* 1051 (April/May 1991); SFF, "Carta Internacional: Empresas para un desarrollo sostenible," *Revista Industria* 1049 (January 1992); Jaime Undurraga, "La industria minera frente a la demanda ambiental del país," *Ambiente y Desarrollo* 7, no. 3 (1991) and "Comentario," *Ambiente y Desarrollo* 5, no. 3 (1989); Centro de Investigación y Planificación del Medio Ambiente, *Propuestas de acción ambiental en cinco sectores productivos* (Santiago: n.p., 1992); Guillermo Geisse, "El desafío ambiental y la coparticipación pública y privada," *Ambiente y Desarrollo* 3, nos. 1–2 (1987) and "Cooperación pública-privada para la gestión ambiental en Chile," *Ambiente y Desarrollo* 7, no. 3 (1991); Rafael Asenjo, "La legislación ambiental y honestidad política," *Ambiente y Desarrollo* 6, no. 1 (1990); and Eladio Susaeta and Susana Benadetti, "El sector forestal y la conservación ambiental," *Ambiente y Desarrollo* 6, nos. 1–2 (1990).

36. Andrés Asenjo, "El debate público en torno al bosque nativo," *Ambiente y Desarrollo* 8, no. 1 (1992).

37. See "Presidente de CORMA: Sólo un tercio de los bosques se aprovecha económicamente," *Estrategia*, January 11, 1991; "Ministro de Agricultura: El bosque nativo chileno debe ser preservado," *El Mercurio*, April 4, 1991; "DL 701 y Ley sobre bosque nativo analizó Comisión Nacional Forestal," *El Mercurio*, April 11, 1991.

38. CORMA complained regularly about this. See "Presidente de Corma."

39. Aarón Cavieres, CONAF, interviewed by author, Santiago, June 1992; and CODEFF, "Uso actual y alternativas de desarrollo de los recursos forestales de campesinos en Linares y Curacautín" (CODEFF Working Paper, 1991).

40. For more details, see Eduardo Silva, "Capitalist Coalitions, the State, and Neoliberal Economic Restructuring: Chile, 1973–1988," *World Politics* 45, no. 4 (1993): 526–559; and "Capitalist Regime Loyalties and Redemocratization in Chile," *Journal of Interamerican Studies and World Affairs* 34, no. 4 (1992): 77–117.

41. See Brian Loveman, "*¿Misión Cumplida?* Civil-Military Relations and the Chilean Political Transition," *Journal of Interamerican Studies and World Affairs* 33, no. 3 (1991): 35–74; also see Silva, "Capitalist Regime Loyalties."

42. See Silva, "Capitalist Regime Loyalties"; also see Pilar Vergara, "Market Economy, Social Welfare, and Democratic Consolidation in Chile," in William C. Smith, Carlos Acuña, and Eduardo Gamarra, eds., *Democracy, Markets, and Structural Reform in Latin America* (New Brunswick: Transaction Publishers/North-South Center, 1994).

43. Aarón Cavieres, CONAF, interviewed by author, Santiago, August 1993.

44. Leonardo Araya, Angel Cabezas, and Carlos Weber, all of CONAF, interviewed by author, August 1993.

45. For the Terranova case, see A. Asenjo, "El debate público"; "Industria japonesa reducirá a astillas bosques nativos de Valdivia y Corral," *La Epoca*, April 25, 1988; Comité Forestal PPD, "Antecedentes técnicos y políticos sobre el proyecto Corral," *La Epoca*, August 26, 1990; CODEFF, "Posición de CODEFF sobre el proyecto forestal Corral de la empresa Terranova," *Ecotribuna* 4, October 1990; "Ominami aseguró que IPC de enero no superará señal de 0.7 por ciento," *La Epoca*, February 2, 1991.

46. For a summary of their positions, see "Posición de CODEFF sobre el proyecto forestal Corral."

47. For the composition of the interministerial commission, see Andrés Asenjo, "El debate público."

48. Francisco Zúñiga, head of the legal office of the Ministry of Agriculture, Santiago, interviewed by author, August 1993; and Patricio Rodrigo, head of the department of budget and planning of the Ministerio de Bienes Nacionales, Santiago, interviewed by author, June 1992 and August 1993.

49. Hernán Verscheure, CODEFF, interviewed by author, July 1992.

50. Confidential interview with a leading alternative epistemic community member.

51. These data from Cavieres, "Conservación y utilización del bosque nativo chileno," p. 151.

52. For more details on the consensus document, see "Consideraciones en relación a una legislación destinada a la recuperación del bosque nativo" (August 1991, mimeograph); also see "Política especial para el bosque nativo," *El Mercurio*, August 31, 1991.

53. Juan Moya, "El proyecto de recuperación y fomento del bosque nativo" (paper presented at the Primer Seminario sobre Bosque Nativo, Universidad Austral de Chile, 1992).

54. A number of interviewees pointed this fact out to me during field trips in June-July 1992 and August 1993. According to an interview with Carlos Weber of CONAF (Santiago, August 1993), Aarón Cavieres of CONAF basically wrote the presidential speech.

55. Francisco Zúñiga, head of the legal department of the Ministry of Agriculture, interviewed by author, August 1993.

56. CONAF, "Proyecto de Ley de Recuperación del Bosque Nativo."

57. See Cámara de Diputados, "Informe de las Comisiones Unidas de Agricultura, Desarrollo Rural y Marítimo y de Recursos Naturales, Bienes Nacionales y Medio Ambiente, sobre el proyecto de ley de recuperación del bosque nativo," *Boletín*, no. 669–01 (1993).

58. Aarón Cavieres, CONAF, and Joaquín Vial, Coordinador de Políticas Económicas, Ministry of Economy, interviewed by author, Santiago de Chile, August 1993.

59. For more details on the comparison between Chile and Venezuela, see Eduardo Silva, "The Politics of Conservation and Sustainable Development: Native Forest Policy in Chile and Venezuela" (paper presented at the XVIII International Congress of the Latin American Studies Association, Atlanta, March 10–12, 1994).

60. For general background on Costa Rican forest policy, see Jean Carriere, "The Crisis in Costa Rica: An Ecological Perspective," in Redclift and Goodman, eds., *Environment and Development in Latin America*. Also see Peter Utting, "Social and Political Dimensions of Environmental Protection in Central America," *Development and Change* 25, no. 1 (1994): 231–259.

61. For a quick review of proposed policies that reflected the alternative approach to sustainable development in Costa Rica, see Dr. Carlos A. Quesada Mateo, *Estrategia de conservación para el desarrollo sostenible de Costa Rica* (San José, Costa Rica: Ministerio de Recursos Naturales, Energía y Minas, 1990).

62. Enrique Barrau, USAID; Raúl Solórzano, Executive Director, Centro Científico Tropical; and Alfredo Peralta, President, Ejecutora, Consultora y Administradora Forestal, S.A., interviewed by author, San José, Costa Rica, May 10-May 17, 1993.

63. Diego Pérez, formerly on the professional staff of the Secretaría de Desarrollo Social (SEDESOL), personal communication with author, St. Louis, Missouri, February 16, 1994; and Carlos Muñoz, professional staff, SEDESOL, personal communication with author, Mexico City, May 19, 1993. Also see Secretaría de Agricultura y Recursos Hidráulicos, *Ley Forestal de 1992* (Mexico: Editorial PAC, 1993).

64. For studies that examine the political economy of grassroots development and ecology, see John Friedmann and Haripriya Rangan, eds., *In Defense of Livelihood: Comparative Studies on Environmental Action* (West Hartford, CT: Kumarian Press, 1993); Marcus Colchester and Larry Lohmann, eds., *The Struggle for Land and the Fate of the Forests* (London: Zed Books, 1993); Dharam Ghai and Jessica M. Vivian, eds., *Grassroots Environmental Action: People's Participation in Sustainable Development* (London: Routledge, 1992); and Eduardo Silva, "Thinking Politically about Sustainable Development in the Tropical Forests of Latin America," *Development and Change* 25 no.4 (1994): 697–721.

CHAPTER FIVE

■

The Environmental Movement in Brazil: Institutionalization, Sustainable Development, and Crisis of Governance Since 1987

Eduardo J. Viola

In considering environmental issues in Latin America, it is very important to have a clear concept of the continent's importance in the world. According to the World Resources Institute, 8 percent of the world's population lives in Latin America; the population is growing at about the world average of 1.8 percent yearly. Twelve percent of Latin America's land is used for agriculture and 13 percent for cattle ranching. Latin America has 23 percent of the world's total forests, 46 percent of the tropical forests, around 50 percent of the biodiversity, 31 percent of the surface water, 4 percent of the world's GNP, 20 percent of the world's hydroelectric energy potential, and 3 percent of the fossil fuel reserves; the continent is also responsible for 12 percent of the world's carbon dioxide emissions and 1 percent of chlorofluorocarbon emissions.[1] These figures demonstrate that Latin America is a vital region in regard to global environmental change, particularly when the changes result in tropical deforestation, loss of biodiversity, and, to a lesser degree, climate change.

During the 1970s, an incipient environmental mobilization at the grassroots level existed in only three Latin American countries: Brazil, Mexico, and Venezuela. The situation improved significantly during the 1980s when grassroots environmental initiatives extended to most Latin American countries and environmental movements developed in Brazil, Costa Rica, Mexico, Venezuela, and Uruguay.[2]

Like other regions of the world, Latin American countries exhibit a correlation between the United Nations Human Development Index (HDI) and strength of the environmental movement. However, this correlation is incomplete, and there are important modifications and exceptions.

Since 1990, the United Nations Development Programme has produced the Human Development Index in order to provide a broad base of measures by which to compare countries. Its final goal is to integrate economic affluence with social welfare and environmental quality. In 1994, the index combined four dimensions: real gross domestic product (GDP) per capita, adult literacy, mean years of schooling, and life expectancy.[3] (Lower scores indicate a higher level of human development.) The status of environmentalism in Latin American countries can be classified by measuring the level of development of the environmental movement, the public's receptivity to issues of environmental protection, and the involvement of transnational actors in environmental politics. Using these criteria and the HDI, the region can be divided into four groups.

The first consists of three countries—Brazil, Mexico, and Costa Rica—in which the environmental movement is well established, with a network of activists and organizations. Public opinion is receptive to the issue of environmental protection, the movement influences public policy, and transnational actors play an important role in environmental politics.

Brazil has a medium HDI rating (63˚) and rates strong in environmental movements because the movement is particularly strong in the more developed southern and southeastern regions and because the transnational players in the Amazon (and to a lesser degree in other tropical ecosystems) have also had a positive impact. Brazil has the richest biodiversity in the world, with five vast tropical-subtropical ecosystems: the Amazonian forest, which covers half of the country and is the largest tropical forest in the world; the Atlantic forest, mostly transformed by human settlement but with very rich biodiversity remaining in spots; the Pantanal, the largest freshwater marsh in the world; the Cerrado Savanna, which has been the most important agricultural frontier in the world in the last decade; and the semi-arid Caatinga Savanna (the only area that is not rich in biodiversity). Brazil also has two temperate ecosystems in the extreme south (the Araucarian forest and the Pampa Savanna) that have been almost completely transformed by human activity. The transition to democracy, along with the influence of returning leftists who had been exiled to Northern countries, has been crucial in promoting the environmental movement in Brazil.

Mexico also has a medium HDI rating (52˚) and has strong environmental movements because of the influence of the process of economic integration with the United States. This influence has enlarged the domestic arena of environmental politics through direct participation of the North American environmental movement. In terms of biodiversity, Mexico is one of the seven richest countries in the world. This has attracted significant Northern support for domestic NGOs working on the protection of tropical forests. Mexico is the only case in Latin

America in which the environmental movement developed under authoritarian rule. In the twenty-four countries surveyed in the Gallup "Health of the Planet" survey, Brazil and Mexico rank first among developing countries in the percentage of people (71 percent) who chose protecting the environment over economic growth.[4]

Costa Rica ranks high (39˚) on the HDI, and the environmental movement has grown very fast since the mid-1980s, when the Northern environmental community decided to concentrate efforts on that country because of the low cost of building a movement (small country, highly educated population, and weak nationalism) and high benefit potential (extremely rich biodiversity). Costa Rica is the Latin American example of the extent to which a consolidated democracy favors the development of the environmental movement (this has been the dynamic in most developed countries).

The second group consists of countries with a profile similar to the first, except for the lack of internationalization of environmental politics: Venezuela, Chile, and Uruguay. Venezuela has a medium HDI ranking (46˚), and the environmental movement has stagnated recently, undermined by the economic and political crisis. Today's dynamic is opposite that of the 1970s and early 1980s when the strength of democratic institutions and economic prosperity stimulated environmental protection.

Chile ranks high (38˚) on the HDI, and the environmental movement has been developing rapidly under the democratic government since 1990, following the constraints experienced during the period of military dictatorship. In the 1993 presidential election, the Green Party candidate got 5.5 percent of the vote, in a performance without equivalent elsewhere in Latin America and comparable only to Western Europe. Uruguay has the highest HDI ranking (33˚) in Latin America, and concern about the environment has strongly penetrated its revitalized civil society since the late 1980s. Chile and Uruguay rank third in public awareness about the environment among developing countries in the "Health of the Planet" survey and are the clearest examples of how transition to democracy favors the development of an environmental movement.

The third group consists of countries whose public is basically indifferent to environmental degradation: Argentina, Colombia, Ecuador, and Nicaragua. In these countries, networks of environmental activists have a significant capacity to protest but have no impact on public policy. Argentina is an exception to the correlation between HDI and environmental movement: It is high on the HDI (37˚) and has a moderately strong environmental movement, but this can be accounted for by the national obsession with economic growth. Argentina is the only Latin American country in which public opinion is favorable to nuclear energy (in the other two countries with nuclear power, Brazil and Mexico, there is notable antinuclear public opinion). However, pride in nuclear energy technology is a poor substitute for the long-term decline of the country in world affairs. (Argentina had been among the world's ten richest and most powerful countries in the 1920s.) Although its ten large ecosystems—ranging from subtropical through temperate to cold—make it the biologically most diverse country in Latin America, it has not attracted significant attention from North America because the temperate and cold ecosystems are similar to those in the United States and Canada.

Colombia ranks mid-range (50°) on the HDI and has a widespread network of environmental activists. Because Colombia is among the seven countries in the world with the greatest biodiversity, there has been strong Northern support for government and NGO efforts to protect tropical forests. The Colombian environmental movement has not been successful in influencing public policy to protect the urban-rural environment, even though there recently has been considerable progress in environmental legislation. Ecuador is also in the mid-range on the HDI (74°) and has an environmental movement that concentrates on the protection of natural ecosystems because of the important support received from the North. Nicaragua is low (106°) on the HDI, but it has a network of environmental activists that has been supported by Northern (particularly Western European) organizations in protecting the urban-rural environment. Colombia and Ecuador are clear examples of the imbalance in domestic environmental protection produced by Northern intervention in Southern countries (favoring natural ecosystems over urban and rural areas). Nicaragua represents the opposite example because the Northern effort (developed by progressive governments or NGOs) concentrated on improving the quality of life of the population.

The fourth group is composed of countries with groups of environmentalists that are isolated and have low public visibility: Panama, Bolivia, Paraguay, Peru, Guyana, Surinam, Honduras, Guatemala, El Salvador, and Belize. These countries rank low on the HDI, with the exception of Panama (47°). Because Peru is very rich in biodiversity, the North has supported domestic NGOs working in the Amazon, but these efforts were undermined by the civil war and the collapse of political authority in 1989–1992.

BRAZILIAN ENVIRONMENTAL POLICY

Having compared the HDI and environmental movements in Latin American countries, I now will introduce the general dimensions of Brazilian environmental policy and politics. Brazilian environmentalism began in the 1970s as an innovative sociopolitical response to the increasingly destructive impact of Brazil's dramatic economic growth. In its formative period between 1971 and 1986, environmentalism was a loose juxtaposition of grassroots mobilization without effective popular support. The strategic goals were limited to sensitizing public opinion to the effects of pollution and natural ecosystem devastation. The relationship with environmental state agencies remained simultaneously cooperative and adversarial—cooperative as an alliance against the state-level departments that promoted conventional development; adversarial because they considered the state environmental agencies too moderate in the enforcement of the law, especially in their treatment of big polluters.[5]

North American and European ecological traditions had a partial and diffuse influence on Brazilian environmentalism. Organizational capability and agenda definition (particularly strong in North American environmentalism) did not get enough attention from Brazilian activists, who virtually ignored the encompassing statements of environmental issues that were clear around 1970: preservation of natural ecosystems, conservationist use of natural resources, and pollution control.[6] At this time, a narrowly defined perception of the environmental issue on the part of governmental agencies restricted mobilization to the point of bypassing the possibility of rational management of natural resources.

However, the movement did not succeed in providing an adequate solution to the problem of population growth until the late 1980s. As in the other Latin American countries (with the exception of those in the Southern Cone), most environmentalists were able to recognize the existence of high fertility rates among the population; but the prestige and dogma of the Catholic Church and the ideological appeal of socialist culture until recently made the topic of family planning a taboo. The neglect of demographic factors, in addition to the population growth issue, reveals itself in the hesitant way the movement addressed questions related to increasing rates of rural migration to urban areas. The significant improvement in women's status during the 1970s and 1980s produced a dramatic decline in fertility rates (from 5.9 in 1970 to 3.0 in 1992)[7] and consequently a more rational approach to family planning from all sides of the political spectrum. The society thus came to favor family planning without environmentalism playing a significant role.

In the mid-1980s, two interrelated questions of economic growth and social equity remained decisive for the growth of environmentalism in Brazil (as was the case generally in the Southern Hemisphere).[8] A significant change with regard to the social equity question occurred between 1971 and 1986. At the beginning of the 1970s, environmentalists remained isolated from the masses, failing to convey the connection between environmental and social crises. From the late 1970s on, the movement was strongly influenced by the dissemination of a radical democratic discourse about movements struggling against the authoritarian regime. This led to a greater sensitivity to human rights issues and social equity. Around 1986, an important array of activists realized that connection with popular sectors should be treated as an important task. In many industrial cities, environmental groups were beginning to establish a dialogue with union activists about common problems.[9] Grassroots movements for a clean water supply and the establishment of sewage disposal on the outskirts of the cities were receiving support from environmental groups.[10] On the other hand, in the Amazon basin, rubber tappers and other indigenous peoples were supported by environmental groups from southern Brazil. In spite of this advance, the movement's commitment to radical democratic rhetoric blocked serious consideration of problems concerning political and technical efficiency.

As in all Latin American countries, most environmentalists were ill informed and naive about making connections between economic development and environmental protection. They rejected any dialogue with economists and perceived a strong contradiction between ecology and economics. For instance, the program for producing ethanol based on sugarcane received limited support from environmentalists even though this program can be considered one of the most important technological achievements for limiting dependence on fossil fuels.

From 1987 on, organizations became more complex in the context of a distorted transition to democracy.[11] Certain key groups became professional organizations with national influence and international connections. At the level of ideological commitments, a shift took place in the perception of environmental issues. The initial focus, directed toward pollution control and environmental preservation, was replaced with an active search for alternative patterns of natural resource use. In this way, environmentalists began to associate their struggle more closely with the erosion of dominant concepts and indicators of socioeconomic development. A multisectoral networking process took place, expressing the interplay of complex systemic trends.[12] Because of this increasing complexity, eight sectors have constituted the Brazilian environmental movement since the beginning of the 1990s: (1) strict-sense environmentalism, the core, made up of three kinds of associations (amateurs, semiprofessionals, and professionals); (2) social environmentalism, composed of unions, social movements, and NGOs that have other main goals but incorporate environmental protection as one important dimension of their activities; (3) technicians in environmental state agencies; (4) scientists researching environmental issues; (5) communicators (teachers, journalists, artists), who create public awareness and stimulate value transformation in relation to environmental issues; (6) politicians who work within parties to encourage the incorporation of environmental protection in their proposals; (7) members of religions and spiritual traditions linking the protection of the Earth with awareness of the sacred; and (8) the reduced sector of managers and entrepreneurs who incorporate genuine consideration of environmental sustainability into their decision-making process. The preparation for and realization of the United Nations Conference on Environment and Development (UNCED) and the Global Forum hosted by Brazil (1990–1992) influenced Brazilian environmentalism more than it influenced movements in other Latin American countries.

The Special Secretariat of the Environment (SEMA) was created in 1974 as a peripheral sector in the Ministry of the Interior. During the processes of liberalization (1974–1981) and democratization (1982–1985) of the military regime which held power from 1964 to 1985, SEMA had a very low profile as an executive agency, though it successfully promoted the design and approval of the National Environmental Protection Act (NEPA) in 1981. This act, based on the 1969 U.S. NEPA, prompted the creation in 1985 of the Federal Council for Environmental Quality (CONAMA), which has normative powers with relation to environmental issues and is composed of representatives of federal agencies, state agencies, and the public (including representatives of environmental NGOs).

With the establishment of the new civilian government of José Sarney (1985–1990), SEMA changed its line of activity, recognizing the growing environmental concern in civil society. The most important achievement was the implementation of CONAMA. Once under way, CONAMA began producing crucial resolutions for Brazilian environmental protection, such as the requirement for environmental impact assessments on new projects (industries, roads, airports, dams, and so on). Such assessments would include public hearings as a mechanism for social participation in decision making.

SEMA's new roles included: (1) promoting the dissemination of environmental issues through the state apparatus despite considerable internal resistance; (2) encouraging debate on the relationship between development and the environment; (3) supporting efforts from the multisectoral environmental movement to incorporate environmental protection in the new constitution passed in 1988; (4) promoting interaction between state environmental agencies and the scientific community; and (5) supporting exchange among various state-level environmental agencies, including the founding of the Brazilian Association of Environmental State Agencies, a unique organization that strengthened the federal profile of environmental policy. In spite of Messias Franco's dynamic administration of SEMA between 1986 and 1988, the secretariat's archaic, rigid bureaucratic structure, its peripheral position in the state apparatus, and to a large extent the Sarney administration's lack of understanding and its "defensive" attitude toward environmental issues, led to low efficiency in dealing with the magnitude of environmental problems confronting the country.

Among the first group of state governors elected in free and competitive elections in late 1982, only those of São Paulo and Paraná tried to build institutions and decision-making apparatuses appropriate for enforcing environmental legislation (particularly pollution control). Consequently, from 1983 to 1986, environmental state agencies in São Paulo and Paraná fought for the first time against industries and other big polluters.[13] After an environment-related catastrophe in Cubatão in 1985 (the most polluted city in Brazil, with a concentration of heavy chemical, petrochemical, and oil-refining industries), the São Paulo state environmental agencies implemented a pollution control program in that city, which achieved good results by about 1988.

Because there was an active presence of environmentalists in the 1986 state gubernatorial campaigns, many candidates made rhetorical commitments to environmental protection. Progress at the federal level in the latter half of the 1980s was copied by several state-level agencies in the Brazilian South and Southeast. In those areas, environmental issues assumed increasing importance on state agendas (several state environmental secretariats were established), stricter control of industrial pollution was implemented, and plans were drawn up for integrated management of river microbasins. This was reflected in the passing of pro-environment state constitutions in 1989 and in the implementation of the environmental impact assessment requirement.

Deforestation (mostly by burning) in the Amazon and the border areas of Cerrado reached around 25,000 km^2 destroyed in 1987. (There is controversy over deforestation figures, although there is consensus about the magnitude.) Deforestation increased exponentially during the 1980s, pushed by the settlement of poor immigrants coming from the South and Northeast, investments in real estate as a protection against rampant inflation, cattle ranching by big landowners and corporations, and the growing domestic demand for timber.[14] U.S. environmental NGOs (particularly the Environmental Defense Fund and National Wildlife Federation) and Brazilian environmentalist and social-environmentalist NGOs (particularly the Rubber Tappers National Council, Union of Indian Nations, Institute of Amazonian Studies, and Brazilian Association of Anthropologists) joined together against two big construction projects: the Northwest Pole Settlement Project and the paving of Western Road 364. Both of these projects, funded by the World Bank, overlooked negative environmental and social impacts and produced further alarm about Amazon deforestation, especially in Northern public opinion. The dry, hot summer of 1988 dramatically increased sensitivity about global warming in North American public opinion. In this context, a highly concerned population linked the new peak of Amazonian burning in the second half of 1988 with global warming (a deduction that was at least partially correct). In the view of many North Americans, Brazil was rapidly becoming the primary culprit in global warming (even though most carbon dioxide emissions are produced by industries and vehicles in the Northern Hemisphere). Consequently, Brazil was also held accountable for the murder of rubber tapper and environmental leader Chico Mendes in December 1988. This resulted in a major reaction against the Brazilian government.

The Sarney administration's reaction to international criticism was slow and contradictory. In January 1989, the government set up the Institute for the Environment and Natural Resources (IBAMA) by merging SEMA and other governmental agencies dealing with forests, fishing, and rubber tapping. The creation of IBAMA implied conceptual and organizational reform in defining the environmental issue, since environmental protection and conservationist utilization of natural resources were for the first time associated under one governmental umbrella.

In February 1989, irritated by a high-visibility, international meeting of Indians in Altamira (the eastern Amazon), the Sarney administration tried to launch a mobilization against developed countries, inspired by a successful nationalistic campaign in the early 1950s that favored the nationalization of the oil industry. Government rhetoric emphasized the exclusive rights of Brazilians to develop the Amazon without any consideration of the global environment.[15] Simultaneously, the Brazilian government appropriately blamed Northern industrialized countries for centuries of forest degradation. In this way the Brazilian government introduced considerations of equity and contributed to the opening of the complex debate about who should pay for the protection of the biosphere. The Sarney administration's nationalistic rhetoric produced diffuse sympathy in some sectors of the population, but it fell considerably short of creating the active mobilization needed to isolate and defeat pro-environment public opinion in Brazil.

The Brazilian government was condemned nationally and internationally. In April 1989, it shifted its policy by launching the Our Nature program, designed primarily by the military. This was the first Brazilian geopolitical doctrine for the Amazon that incorporates the concept of environmental protection. From April 1989 until its conclusion in March 1990, the Sarney administration struggled to create an image of environmental responsibility. This attempt unfolded along five dimensions: (1) increasing rigor in the monitoring and control of burning in the Amazon (the deforested area was reduced from a peak of approximately 30,000 km² in 1988 to 15,000 km² in 1989); (2) temporary suspension of tax incentives and subsidies for cattle ranching and annual cropping in the Amazon; (3) support for IBAMA president Mesquita in struggles with other government departments; (4) a decision favorable to holding UNCED in Brazil (there was strong opposition to this inside the government, due to the perception that the conference would undermine national sovereignty in the Amazon); and (5) a decision favorable to the creation of extractive reserves claimed by the rubber tappers and environmentalists.

During the 1989 presidential election, environmental debates ranked far below the issues of inflation, employment, education, security, income distribution, and state reform. Because environmentalists have always been somewhat associated with the political left, most of the pro-environment public voted for the leftist candidate Lula da Silva. Consequently, national and international environmentalists were surprised when the rightist candidate, Collor, in a world tour before assuming the presidency, repeated several times that environmental protection would be a major goal of his administration. In reality, Collor was committed to a modernization program (new flow of foreign investments, lower trade barriers, and transfer of sensitive technology) dependent on strengthening links with the North, and he opportunistically perceived how important it would be to illustrate his commitment to a responsible policy on the Amazon. It is important to consider that in the first half of 1990, concern about the environment peaked in the North (according to polls, it was among the three most important issues in almost all Northern countries).

Collor created a Secretariat of the Environment and appointed as its head José Lutzenberger, who was a founder of Brazilian environmentalism in the 1970s. During the 1980s, Lutzenberger was a crucial player in creating a coalition among Northern environmentalists, Brazilian environmentalists, and "People from the Forests" (largely indigenous peoples and rubber tappers). In the first months of the new administration, Lutzenberger made important decisions about Amazonian policy that gave Collor international credibility among environmentalists: continuity in the suspension of tax incentives and subsidies for cattle ranching and annual cropping, a halt to the pig iron smelters program for the eastern Amazon (a program of twenty-two smelters that used charcoal from the forest), increased monitoring and control of deforestation, a program for ecological-economic zoning of the Amazon, and openness to international cooperation in dealing with Amazonian issues. The Collor administration also uncovered and halted, in October 1990, the military's plans for building nuclear weapons. The administration's subsequent strong commitment against nuclear proliferation constituted an important shift from previous policies.

However, on the domestic side, Lutzenberger undermined the environmental community because of his negligence in the everyday management of IBAMA, his long stays abroad, and the precarious state of environmental protection outside the Amazon. By the end of 1990, Lutzenberger embodied contradiction. Inside Brazil he was viewed as the personification of unfortunate public relations by an administration not seriously committed to environmental protection, while internationally he was seen as an effective defender of the Amazon.

The strong pro-environment rhetoric of the Collor administration was not translated into a budget reallocation in favor of environmental protection. The fiscal crisis in 1991 cut by half the budget of the Secretariat of the Environment. The governance of IBAMA, already complicated because of the conflict among the competing forces that had merged in 1989, worsened due to decreased motivation (prompted by drastic wage reductions) and the delays in Finance Ministry approval of international funding for developing specific projects at the institute. On the other hand, the Collor administration made several environmentally sound decisions in its second year. The government put in place debt-for-nature swaps of up to US$100 million a year, something that was forbidden before May 1991. The National Development Bank supported the huge river basin cleanup and basic sanitation projects proposed by state governors from São Paulo, Rio Grande do Sul, Santa Catarina, Paraná, Rio de Janeiro, and Ceará. In November 1991, despite strong opposition from the military and the Amazonian elites, the government also demarcated the large Yanomami Reservation (90,000 km^2) in accord with Indian claims supported by environmentalists. And in February 1992, Collor convened two presidential meetings (one of the Southern Cone Common Market [MERCOSUR] and the other of the Amazonian Pact) whose final statements emphasized sustainable development and reform in the world order.

In 1992, there was a serious crisis of continuity in environmental policy, illustrated by the rapid turnover of environmental ministers. In late March, Lutzenberger was fired after a serious open disagreement with the Ministry of Foreign Relations over the UNCED preparatory meeting in New York. At times, Lutzenberger held a radical, almost biocentric, position that produced much discomfort in the Ministry of Foreign Relations, which had already moved from a narrow developmental and nationalistic position to a moderate pro-environment one. The Collar administration's position during the UNCED preparations was based on four principles. First, global environmental problems are highly relevant and have to be treated as a priority by the international community. Second, there are different levels of responsibility in the realm of global environmental problems. Northern countries must assume the major financial responsibility for solving them, but Southern countries are also responsible and must give priority to the issue. Third, poverty and radically unequal income distribution are important causes of environmental degradation, and so reform of the world economic order is vital. And finally, as host country Brazil must assume an active facilitator role.

José Goldemberg, an internationally renowned energy expert and one of the most powerful members of the Collor cabinet, was appointed as the replacement for Lutzenberger, combining the new job with that of minister of education. Goldemberg successfully took care of the final political and operational arrangements for the realization of UNCED, but did not attempt the difficult task of improving IBAMA.

During the Rio Conference and before it, the media exposed Brazilians to a vast amount of information about environmental issues, generally in a pro-environment framework. It was one of the most pronounced instances ever of an entire country being flooded with a vast amount of environmental news. This exposure contributed to the dramatic increase in public awareness about environmental issues that occurred in Brazil in the early 1990s.[16]

During the Rio Conference, the Brazilian government successfully completed the shift, initiated in 1989, toward a responsible policy regarding global environmental affairs. Brazil was one of the leading countries in the elaboration of the Biodiversity Convention, which takes a balanced approach regarding the interests of populations in Northern and Southern countries (particularly those of people from the tropical rain forest). In addition, Brazil was committed to a strong climate-change convention, which failed because of the veto by the United States and other fossil-fuel-producing countries. Brazil was irresponsible only to the extent that it supported the Malaysian leadership against a convention on forests.

Immediately after the Rio Conference, Goldemberg was replaced, and the Collor administration entered into a period of generalized crisis because of a congressional investigation into corruption. The public focused on the political crisis, and the interest in environmental issues declined dramatically. In October 1992, the Chamber of Deputies removed Collor from the presidency, and the Senate initiated the political process that would end in his impeachment that December. Vice President Itamar Franco, a provincial politician with a reputation for honesty (a very important quality for credibility in Brazilian society of the 1990s), assumed the presidency and appointed an extremely heterogeneous cabinet. The new minister of the environment, Coutinho Jorge, a senator from the Amazon state of Pará, had no expertise in environmental affairs and, in fact, was linked to interest groups involved in deforestation.

By mid-1993, the Franco administration had squandered its initial credibility, and inflation was rising at a rate around 30 percent a month. On the other hand, the economy was growing at 5 percent a year after a severe recession that lasted from early 1990 to late 1992. For the most part, private enterprise in the South and Southeast had completed organizational reforms by cutting employees and introducing new technologies and management, and they were more competitive in the international market (Brazilian exports were growing at the fastest rate in the world in 1992 and 1993). However, as in other regions of the world, economic recovery did not result in more jobs. On the contrary, unemployment was increasing due to the great number of young people entering the labor market annually, a product of the very high fertility rate in the early 1970s.

The Ministry of the Environment was almost paralyzed due to a convergence of negative factors: (1) environmental issues lost their importance in public opinion after a peak during the Earth Summit; (2) Franco was less sensitive to environmental issues than Collor; (3) Coutinho Jorge was motivated solely by his career as a professional politician and not by a commitment to protect the environment, although he did not allow local vested-interest groups to take over the ministry; (4) the Ministry of Finance delayed approval of available foreign funding for programs of environmental protection that were conditioned on the existence of equivalent domestic funding; (5) the corporatist interest of the IBAMA civil service blocked the organizational reforms necessary to increase the efficiency of the ministry; and (6) the general crisis of governance undermined long-term decision making and focused public attention on emergency issues (superinflation, urban crime, and the political crisis).

In August 1993, two events again put the Amazon at the center of government concerns, particularly among the military. First, U.S. armed forces undertook military training operations in Surinam and Guyana, close to the Brazilian border. Second, a group of gold miners massacred approximately twenty Yanomami Indians on their reservation in Roraima (later it became known that the killing occurred a few kilometers inside Venezuelan territory). This prompted immediate international criticism, particularly from NGOs. The killing of the Indians in addition to the murders of children and slum inhabitants, mostly in the state of Rio de Janeiro, undermined the Brazilian government's credibility on human rights. After these events, the military increasingly feared that Brazilian sovereignty over the Amazon was under threat from Northern interests spearheaded by the U.S. government. Franco, under military pressure, approved the purchase of a radar system to monitor the airspace in the Amazon, which—independent of the intentions of the military—also could be very useful for monitoring drug trafficking and activities of gold miners. In addition, Franco created a ministry for coordinating government activity in the Amazon (which, only a few weeks later, was merged with the Ministry of the Environment).

The ambassador to the United States, Rubens Ricúpero, a career diplomat with experience in environmental affairs, was appointed as the new minister of the environment and the Amazon. After more than a year of dealing with Jorge, the environmental community was now optimistic because Ricúpero was someone knowledgeable about the issues.

Ricúpero's optimistic vision of the Amazon was based on the opportunity for long-term international cooperation that would allow Brazil simultaneously to preserve around one-half of the Amazon through the National Park/Ecological

Reserve systems and to promote the rational exploitation of the resources of the other half of the region (extraction of nuts and other forest products, sustainable forestry, biotech labs, "clean" mining, ecological tourism, research institutes, and so forth). In April 1994, Ricúpero was replaced by Brandão Cavalcanti, who continued with the same approach. But Cavalcanti suffered from the general constraints of crisis of governance, state inefficiency, and high uncertainty produced by the upcoming October general elections. Ricúpero and Cavalcanti, along with their successor, Gustavo Krause (who started on January 1, 1995), face a difficult mission. A major cleavage in Brazilian government and society now exists about policy for the Amazon and Brazil's integration into the post-Cold War order. Representatives of both sides of the cleavage are located in every state institution. On one hand, there is the nationalistic current, oriented toward a more protected and state-regulated economy and inclined to exercise classical military sovereignty over the Amazon, including human settlement and expedited exploitation of natural resources. On the other hand, there is the globalist current, oriented toward a more open economy and prepared for large-scale international cooperation in the Amazon, including high-tech exploitation of biodiversity and restrictions on conventional human settlement. Neoliberals and social democrats are mostly globalist. Conservatives and socialists are mostly nationalist. Since late 1993 globalists are prevailing over nationalists.

In spite of the contradictory character of the Collor (1990–1992) and Franco (1992–1994) administrations, there has been progress in environmental policy, especially in the states of Ceará, São Paulo, Minas Gerais, Paraná, Santa Catarina, and Rio Grande do Sul. This progress is related mostly to the importance that basic sanitation and river cleanup projects had on the agenda of governors elected in late 1990. Impressive achievements have also been reached in several cities— Curitiba, Santos, Vitória, Belo Horizonte, Natal—in terms of municipal environmental policy under these governments. Many experts consider Curitiba, the capital of the southern state of Paraná, to be an "ecological capital" of the world. Its mayor, Jaime Lerner, has attained an international reputation and is considered a potential leader for the creation of a socially and environmentally progressive political coalition.

The Institutionalization of the Environmental Movement, 1987–1994

The growing awareness of environmental problems, both domestically and internationally, has favored a process of institutionalization and, since 1987, the formation of a complex, multisectoral environmental movement. The number of activist groups operating for more than one year grew from around 400 in 1985 to nearly 1,300 in 1992. Hundreds of groups also acted on local environmental degradation issues and then disappeared after their first year of existence.

From 1987 to 1994, between 80 and 90 percent of environmental groups were located in southern and southeastern Brazil, which together comprise 15 percent of the country's territory, 65 percent of the population, and 85 percent of the GNP. The state of São Paulo replaced the state of Rio Grande do Sul as the core of Brazilian environmentalism in the mid-1980s, with almost one-quarter of the organizations located there. Five metropolitan areas—São Paulo, Rio de Janeiro, Belo Horizonte, Porto Alegre, and Curitiba—have the highest density of environmental groups, which often experience problems dealing with the conceptual framework (the specificity of the megalopolis) that guides their activities. Groups in mid-sized cities and towns are less numerous, but are generally more visible and sometimes more effective, since they are dealing with less complex environmental problems.

In spite of the concentration of environmentalism in the South and Southeast, there has been expansion into other parts of Brazil. International attention and the availability of funding and technical assistance have stimulated the development of the movement in the North (the Amazon), where environmentalism differs from the type present in southern Brazil. Organizations representing local nonurban people (rubber tappers, Indians, fishermen) are the core of Amazonian environmentalism. They receive strong support from international environmental NGOs and scientific groups. Urban environmental associations have a peripheral position in the Amazonian region. In the Center-Western region, environmental groups have formed in areas most exposed to international communications such as Brasília and around the Pantanal. In the very poor Northeast, environmental groups face a very difficult cultural context that posits that development comes before environmental protection. However, environmental groups have emerged in all state capitals and in some cities of the interior.

The emergence of a complex environmental movement cut through the partial isolationism that characterized the foundation phase of the movement. In 1987, demands from those with a more professional and dynamic approach to managing the movement increasingly leaned toward institutionalization. By the mid-1980s, this institutionalization partially shifted the center of gravity from volunteerism to professionalism and led to the emergence of new organizations with a professional profile, the partial professionalization of previously volunteer associations, and, among the volunteer-staffed organizations (the majority), a concern about effectiveness.

Professional organizations represent a dramatic innovation in Brazilian environmental culture. They no longer have only the limited goal of creating public awareness but instead have a broad aim of formulating an alternative for the restoration of the degraded environment. The period between 1986 and 1993 saw the creation of about forty new national or regional professional organizations. Their specific goals include preservation of ecosystems, improvement of water or air quality, and environmental education. Some of the organizations are Brazilian branches of international NGOs: Friends of the Earth, World Wide Fund for Nature, and Greenpeace. The organizations are staffed by between five and fifty people. Most of the organizations do not rely solely on staff but also utilize volunteers. Financial support comes from four sources: funds transferred by international environmental organizations (World Wide Fund for Nature, Conservation International, Environmental Defense Fund, and the International Union for the Conservation of Nature and Natural Resources); memberships; grants from companies; and service contracts with government agencies. Most professional organizations are pragmatically oriented and avoid a political definition within the left-right spectrum. The rhetorical identification with radical democracy that was initially very important to most of the associations has been abandoned in professional NGOs, being replaced with a flexible hierarchy committed to efficiency. In the context of complex environmentalism, the professional organizations have exerted influence on the state environmental agencies, the legislative branch, the scientific community, and business. In addition, they represent a collective social agent that could introduce Brazil to a new administrative style that combines long-term efficiency and social interests.

Approximately 100 environmental associations professionalized their operations to some degree between 1986 and 1994. As new "semiprofessionals," their leaders are going beyond the goal of raising public awareness to actively carry out fund-raising. In these semiprofessional groups, staffing varies from one to five people, and most work continues to be done by volunteers. Concern about democracy is still very important, and there are mixed reactions to the traditionally professional NGOs. Although the capacity for achieving goals is admired, there is regret over the loss of a more idealistic personal commitment, which had typified life for most staff members in these organizations. Pragmatism has also significantly penetrated professional and, to a lesser degree, semiprofessional organizations.

By 1992, there were around 1,150 strictly volunteer environmental groups that had survived for at least one year. These organizations continue to educate the public about environmental degradation, and they vigorously seek to deter irresponsible actions on the part of polluters. The importance of nonprofessional organizations has decreased in the last decade because their previous role of raising public awareness has been absorbed by the media. On the other hand, they continue to be crucial in empowering people (both individuals and small groups) and aiding collective and individual actions aimed at mitigating environmental degradation. In general, environmental groups are made up of a more active nucleus (between two and thirty people) and a passive contingent of supporters (from 10 to 200 people). Certain members stand out because of their energy and commitment, public prestige, authority in relation to decisions made by the group, access to the media and governmental departments, personal interest in ensuring their work has high visibility, and accumulation of political capital. Members of environmental groups have a significantly higher educational level and per capita income than country and regional averages. Typically there are more men than women in the groups. One or two specific aims generally constitute the hub of activity in each, although the organizations operate as receiving centers for the grievances and complaints of individual citizens, informal groups, or associations.

Since the mid-1980s, the movement has sought political involvement in concert with other social movements, labor unions, and NGOs that consider the theme of environmental protection an important aspect of their activity. From this mixing arises "socioenvironmentalism," a label that covers a wide spectrum of political actors:

1. the rubber tappers, whose interaction with environmentalist groups allowed them to draw up a program for extractive reserves that became internationally relevant after Chico Mendes's assassination;

2. the indigenous peoples, whose exchange with environmentalist groups, particularly international ones, led them to explain better the environmental protection component of their struggle for land and for demarcation of reservations;

3. the landless farmers, who in some regions have moved forward in their proposal for "ecological agrarian reform";

4. communities affected by hydroelectric dams, which emerged in the South in the 1980s with a nationwide campaign that has forced the state corporation Electrobras to rethink its planning of hydroelectric plants;

5. those neighborhoods that have incorporated environmental protection into political platforms (through such activities as confronting factories that pollute, demanding public sanitation projects, caring for parks and squares, and cleaning up streams and lakes);

6. occupational health practitioners, who have brought together union activists and public-health practitioners to reexamine environmental issues both inside and outside the factory;

7. students, who have attempted to improve the environmental situation both on campus (i.e., pollution caused by laboratories and hospitals, waste, care for green areas, energy conservation) and in surrounding neighborhoods;

8. consumer advocates, most of who have members who also belong to the environmentalist movement, that have played an outstanding role in gaining approval of a consumer code in 1991;

9. the peace movement, which is small in terms of the number of members but has a strong influence on environmentalism and has played an important role in raising public awareness about the military's nuclear program;

10. groups working for the development of human potential (homeopathy, acupuncture, yoga, tai chi chuan, alternative schools, and so forth), which have emphasized the relationship between the environment and "personal ecology";

11. limited sectors of the women's movement, which have shown their willingness to coordinate feminist issues with environmentalist ones;

12. urban workers and unions that have begun to associate their demands for
improvements in working conditions with demands for a change in the
prevailing development model and, at the same time, have pointed to sustainable models in an attempt to link explicitly environmental and social issues, criticizing the isolation experienced by both protectionist environmentalism and economist trade unionism; and

13. beginning in 1990, an increasingly significant sector of the NGOs devoted
to social development and support for social movements, with an enormous capability and responsibility for forming public opinion and inter-
vening in the public sphere.

During the deliberations of the Constituent Assembly in 1987 and 1988, the
environmentalists, for the first time, systematically lobbied the representatives.
On the initiative of Fábio Feldman (the only environmental representative), the
Green Parliament Front (uniting 15 percent of the representatives) was organized
in 1987 and served to articulate environmentalist interests during the Constitutional Congress. As a result, the Constitution of 1988, one of the most advanced
in the world in terms of environmental protection, significantly increased the regulatory capacity of the state for protecting natural resources and the environment, established the universal right to a healthy environment, and incorporated
the mechanism of environmental impact assessment. The Front's success occurred partially because anti-environmentalist forces were unaware of the meaning of the legislation promoting rational environmental management.

From 1987 to 1989, at the federal and regional levels (but not in all the states),
only two political parties became substantially involved in the environmental
issue: the Party of Brazilian Social Democracy (PSDB) and the Workers' Party
(PT). The former arose in opposition to the Brazilian Democratic Movement
Party that had led the democratization process. The PSDB at that time boasted
two outstanding congressmen as representatives of the environmental struggle.
Under their influence, the party's general strategy shifted to include environmentally sound development options. The PT, on the other hand, developed its connections with environmentalists under the influence of the ecosocialist culture,
and certain congressmen became very sensitive to the demands of ecology. Since
the constitutional revision, environmentalists have failed to expand their programmatic influence to other political parties, even though some politicians have
worked in that direction.

At the time of the Constituent Assembly, environmentalists created the Green
Party (GP), taking the opportunity created by the increased public attention to
environmental problems.[17] Debate began in 1985, and by 1986 environmentalists
had staked out three positions. A small number thought the GP was desirable and
viable in the short term; others emphasized that it was not desirable, since it
would create difficulties for those working in the environmental movement because of dispersion of limited forces. Most environmentalists, however, believed
that the GP was desirable but not viable, at least in the short or middle term.

The group committed to the creation of the party, concentrated in the state of Rio de Janeiro, decided to launch the effort, making use of the opportunity of an alliance with the PT in the 1986 state gubernatorial elections. Although the alliance did well in the elections (receiving 8 percent of votes), most environmentalists outside of the state of Rio remained reluctant. Consequently, the GP remained mostly a Rio party with modest representation in the states of São Paulo, Santa Catarina, and Bahia. In the municipal elections of 1988, the GP candidates in those states performed poorly, and in the 1989 presidential elections, the GP had an erratic trajectory, including a failed attempt to be the most important partner in a leftist alliance led by the PT. That candidate ended up with just 0.2 percent of the vote.

The GP survived these disasters and, in 1990, finally elected in the state of Rio its first representative to the national legislature. In the 1992 municipal elections, the GP elected representatives in some cities and successfully reelected its national president, Alfredo Sirkisi. He became the municipal secretary of the environment of Rio de Janeiro in early 1993, when the GP formed a coalition government with the center-right Brazilian Democratic Movement Party.

Throughout Brazil, the GP remains badly organized. Its leadership holds an exceedingly loose conception of party organization. The party also reflects an excessively utopian ideology and has yet to address appropriately the question of sustainable development. The GP also has no program for metropolitan areas, where most potential constituents are concentrated. Finally, there was not enough effort inside the party to adapt the European idea of a green party to the Brazilian reality. The viability of the party is also in doubt because of the restrictive electoral law and because of its very poor results in the general elections in October 1994 (electing only one representative, from the state of Rio de Janeiro, to the Federal Chamber of Deputies.)

SUSTAINABLE DEVELOPMENT, UNCED, AND THE CRISIS OF GOVERNANCE

Until the late 1980s, most environmentalists rejected the idea of economic development. This may have arisen in response to the Brazilian authoritarian regime (1964–1985), which achieved high economic growth through unequal income distribution and severe environmental devastation. Through regulation and promotion of development, the public sector has played a very important role in the system set in place by the authoritarian regime. The democratization process during the 1980s was partial and contradictory, mainly because there was no change in unequal income distribution.

Democratization has shown its perverse dynamics through the severe decline in public-sector rationality and efficiency, which was deeply permeated by local and sectoral interests. Many popular social movements assumed an ideology based on the principle of social equity without considering economic and ecological efficiency. By the end of the decade, however, there was a growing receptivity among environmental activists to the concept of sustainable development. Worsening economic and public financing problems forced environmentalist organizations to take economic issues into consideration or risk losing the influence they had acquired. The existence of socioenvironmentalist organizations provided positive responses to newly arisen concern with economic issues. With strong international connections, newly professionalized organizations have been influenced by the strategy of conservation with consideration for local populations' economic problems. The Brundtland Commission Report, *Our Common Future*, was widely publicized and read attentively by members of the Brazilian environmental movement, one sector of which has drawn its main inspiration from the report while another sector of the movement, with socialist ideas, has criticized it.

Parameters for the Brazilian environmental debate changed in 1990. One no longer speaks of environmental protection apart from economic development. The thrust of the debate is how to attain a new style of development that can incorporate environmental protection. Although the majority uses the expression "sustainable development" and the minority rejects it, all agree that economic development is very important for Brazil. Thus, a new debate is emerging regarding the kind of sustainable development society is seeking.

In June 1990, the Brazilian Forum of NGOs for UNCED was created by fifty groups. Eight national meetings took place before the Rio Conference, progressively increasing the number of associations to around 1,200 by the beginning of 1992. These organizations participated in a process that combines effective organizational networking with destructive internal power struggles. The Brazilian Forum has served as an effective tool for activating the multisectoral character of environmentalism, resulting in its further growth. This has been especially true for the meetings between environmentalist and socioenvironmentalist organizations. Preparations for UNCED also resulted in difficulties arising from ideological heterogeneity. In spite of the obstacles, organizations from both sectors recognized that the process had extraordinary merit. It forced the various actors to situate themselves within the multisectoral space and direct their planning toward sustainable development, which offered a point of convergence among different interest groups.

The realization of the Global Forum of NGOs at the Earth Summit dramatically contributed to the Brazilian environmental movement's ability to network internationally. It also promoted a debate about politico-ideological positions. In 1992, Brazilian environmentalism and socioenvironmentalism split into three ideological orientations: reformist-globalist, reformist-nationalist, and radical.

The reformist-globalists (green social democrats) are in favor of global governance and a strong redefinition of the Brazilian state in order to achieve a gradual transition toward a sustainable society based on the idea of environmental revolution (the convergence between economic development and environmental protection through environmentally sound technologies). The redefinition of the state would imply the reduction of its economic functions (state-owned corporations and protectionism) and the expansion of its environmental and social functions. Reformist-globalists think environmental quality is essentially a public good that can only be maintained efficiently through incisive normative and regulatory state intervention complemented by market incentives. According to this approach, environmentalists should build a broad sociopolitical coalition. Reformist-globalists prefer drastic reductions in fertility rates and moderate reductions in consumption patterns. They take into account that equity considerations must be balanced with economic-environmental efficiency considerations.

The reformist-nationalists (statist green social democrats) are reluctant to support global governance because they fear Northern interests will prevail. They favor strengthening the national state, including its economic regulatory capabilities, and maintaining a strong sector of state-owned corporations. They oppose the use of market incentives for environmental protection. Like the reformist-globalists, the reformist-nationalists prefer a broad political alliance in order to reach a sustainable society gradually based on the idea of environmental revolution. Although they support decentralization, both reformist-nationalists and reformist-globalists favor the strong presence of the federal state apparatus in the Amazon because they consider state and municipal governments too weak to enforce the rule of law. Reformist-nationalists favor moderate reductions in fertility rates and consumption patterns.

The radicals support a utopian, extremely decentralized world government and are reluctant to establish alliances beyond the radical Northern environmentalists and the poor people of the South. The radicals generally reject states and markets and have a strongly communitarian approach, according to which only civil organizations, through value transformation, can play a definitive role in creating a sustainable society. They oppose environmental revolution and favor drastic reduction in consumption. According to this approach, equity considerations must prevail over efficiency.

Reformist-globalists are numerous and active in professional and semiprofessional environmental NGOs. They are the minority among volunteer environmentalists and socioenvironmentalists. Reformist-nationalists are strong in both environmentalism and socioenvironmentalism. Radicals are a minority among volunteer environmentalism and socioenvironmentalism and are marginal among professional and semiprofessional environmental NGOs. The recent trend has been a movement from radicalism to reformism, and reformist-nationalists now constitute the majority of activists in Brazilian socioenvironmentalism.

During the mid-1990s, the most important reformist-globalist leaders have been Fábio Feldman (the new secretary of the environment of São Paulo State and former PSDB representative in the national legislature); Jaime Lerner (the new governor of Paraná and former mayor of Curitiba); Werner Zulauf (secretary of the environment, City of São Paulo); Alfredo Syrkis (secretary of the environment, City of Rio de Janeiro); Fernando Gabeira (Green Party representative in the

Chamber of Deputies); and João Capobianco, José Pádua, Mary Alegretti, Mario Mantovani, and Eduardo Martins (NGO leaders). The most important leaders of reformist-nationalists are Cristovão Buarque (the new governor of Brasília); Victor Buaiz (the new governor of the state of Espírito Santo); José Genoíno (leader of the PT in the national legislature); Carlos Minc (PT representative in the House of Rio de Janeiro); Azis Ab'saber (president of the Brazilian Society for the Advancement of Science); and Litz Vieira and Waldo França (NGO leaders).

By the end of 1992, Brazilian environmentalists felt disoriented. Their activities were strongly tied to UNCED and the Global Forum and, in both cases, the outcomes of these activities did not meet expectations. Additionally, public interest in environmental issues declined dramatically as concern increased over the political crisis that would lead to the impeachment of President Collor. Beginning in late July 1992 (particularly compared with the two previous years), most environmentalists withdrew to less visible local activities. The capacity for recruiting new activists stagnated, although most of the associations created earlier were still in existence at the end of 1994. National meetings of environmentalists declined dramatically after UNCED because of the lack of funding. In 1993 and 1994, social energy and financial resources were channeled to support the "campaign against hunger." Led by the Institute of Social and Economic Analysis (IBASE), the largest Brazilian NGO, this campaign addressed the immediate needs of the 20 percent of Brazilians whose daily caloric intake is insufficient to sustain health. The campaign has produced good results. One of its specific goals is to overcome the waste of food in all sectors (production, transportation, stockage, and home). Because approximately 25 percent of the food produced in Brazil is wasted, the campaign against hunger is directly connected with the goals of environmentalism. Many environmentalists have directly engaged in the campaign that progressive political forces perceive as an indicator of the potential for social change in Brazil.

At the end of 1993, many environmentalists thought it would be good to participate actively in the upcoming general elections by producing a specific agenda to be negotiated with the presidential and gubernatorial candidates. However, by mid-1994, cleavages inside the environmental community prevented the creation of a unified position. Most environmentalists supported two presidential candidates, Fernando Cardoso (PSDB) and Lula da Silva (PT). The social democrat Cardoso was elected in October 1994 with 53 percent of the vote. His coalition has at its core social democrats (PSDB), with neoliberals and conservatives serving as complementary forces. The socialist Lula da Silva won 23 percent of the vote, and the third candidate, Eneas Carneiro, a conservative radical nationalist, won 7 percent.

The Brazilian economy has gone through a modernization process and has been growing rapidly since late 1992. This economic recovery has been accompanied by a stabilization program launched by Cardoso in March 1994, when he was the minister of finance in the Franco cabinet. One of the Cardoso administration's most complex challenges is to continue improving that stabilization program while giving continuity to the modernization agenda.

Cardoso, who took office on January 1, 1995, will probably be more committed to environmental protection and more oriented toward sustainable development than his predecessors. The PSDB, along with the GP, deeply incorporated environmental concerns in its program; and Cardoso, as an academic-politician, is acutely aware of the importance of environmental sustainability in the contemporary world, even though in everyday politics he supports a mainstream approach to development. The Cardoso cabinet is made up mostly of people committed to promoting economic efficiency, reforming the government, rebuilding long-term planning, and defending the public interest against lobbies and corporative pressures. New governors in Paraná, São Paulo, Minas Gerais, Rio de Janeiro, Rio Grande do Sul, Santa Catarina, Espírito Santo, Brasília, Mato Grosso, Pará, and Ceará are also sensitive, to different degrees, to issues of environmental protection. Finally, basic education, public health, sanitation, and scientific-technological development are top priorities in the new national agenda—all fundamental dimensions for environmental sustainability. To avoid excessive optimism, however, it is fair to state that all these concerns are subordinated to economic stabilization. During his short tenure as minister of foreign affairs (October 1992 to May 1993), Cardoso proved his concern for global governance issues. He will undoubtedly continue the transformation—initiated by the Collor administration in 1990—of traditional, nationalist-oriented Brazilian foreign policy. Cardoso's remarkable capacity will also help to extend MERCOSUR beyond Brazil-Argentina-Paraguay-Uruguay toward the whole of South America. Along with that, we can expect the creation of regional institutions that incorporate sustainable development.

In conclusion, it is possible to affirm that the Brazilian environmental movement has been significantly strengthened as the result of the general elections of 1994, in spite of its low profile as a differentiated actor during the electoral campaign. However, the environmental movement's long-term capacity to frame public policies and influence individual or business behavior will depend on the effective capacity of the new federal and state governments to overcome the crisis of governance in Brazil. This would have, in my view, five major dimensions: (1) gradual but sustainable income redistribution through progressive taxation and social policies (education, health, housing, and transportation); (2) reform of the state in order to eliminate corruption and increase efficiency; (3) new, more decentralized and responsible federal agreements capable of simultaneously encompassing the new regional identities and avoiding the disintegration of the national state; (4) building a democratic political culture based on balance between equity and efficiency; and (5) implementating of an economic policy that stimulates foreign investment and more efficiently adapts Brazilian industry to the global economy of the 1990s.

NOTES

This article was written with the collaboration of Gisela de Alencar. The author thanks Hector Leis, Terry Karl, Margaret Keck, Gordon J. MacDonald, Daniel L. Nielson, and Marc A. Stern for their very useful comments.

1. World Resources Institute, *World Resources, 1994–1995* (New York: Oxford University Press, 1994).

2. Eduardo J. Viola, "A degradação socio-ambiental e a emergencia dos movimentos ecologicos na America Latina," in S. Larangeira, ed., *Classes e movimentos sociais na America Latina* (São Paulo: Hucitec, 1990).

3. United Nations Development Programme, *Human Development Report* (Oxford: Oxford University Press, 1994).

4. Riley E. Dunlap, George H. Gallup, and Alec M. Gallup, "Of Global Concern: Results of the Health of the Planet Survey," *Environment* 35, no. 9 (1993): 7ff.

5. Eduardo J. Viola, "The Ecologist Movement in Brazil, 1974–1986," *International Journal of Urban and Regional Research* 12, no. 2 (1988); and Eduardo J. Viola, "O movimento ambientalista no Brasil (1971–1991): Da denuncia e conscientização publica para a institucionalização e o desenvolvimento sustentavel," in M. Goldenberg, ed., *Ecologia, Ciencia e Politica* (Rio de Janeiro: Revan, 1992).

6. John McCormick, *Reclaiming Paradise: The Global Environmental Movement* (Bloomington, IN: Indiana University Press, 1989); and R. Paehlke, *Environmentalism and the Future of Progressive Politics* (New Haven, CT: Yale University Press, 1989).

7. The total fertility rate for a country is the average number of children that would be born per woman if all women lived to the end of their childbearing years and bore children according to a given fertility rate at each age.

8. Eduardo J. Viola and Hector Leis, "Desordem global da biosfera e nova ordem internacional: O papel organizador do ecologismo," in *Ciencias Sociais Hoje ANPOCS* (São Paulo: Vertice, 1990).

9. Leila Ferreira, "A politica ambiental no Estado de São Paulo" (Ph.D. dissertation, Campinas, UNICAMP, 1992).

10. Pedro Jacobi, *Movimentos sociais e políticas públicas* (São Paulo: Cortez, 1989).

11. Viola, "o Movimento ambientalista no Brazil."

12. Eduardo J. Viola and Hector Leis, "A evolution das politicas ambientais no Brasil, 1971–1991: Do bissetorialismo preservacionista para o multissetorialismo orientado para o desenvolvimento sustentavel," in D. Hogan and P. Vieira, eds., *Dilemas socioambientais e desenvolvimento sustentavel* (Campinas: Editorial UNICAMP, 1992).

13. Ferreira, "A politica ambiental no Estado de São Paulo."

14. Susanna B. Hecht and Alexander Cockburn, *The Fate of the Forest* (New York: Verso, 1989).

15. Hector Leis, "A desordem ecologica Amazonica e a desordem politica-economica da ordem internacional," in Luis Aragon, ed., *A desordem ecologica na Amazonia* (Belem, Brazil: Edit. UFPA, 1991).

16. S. Crespo and P. Leitao, *O que o Brasileiro pensa da ecologia* (Rio de Janeiro: CNPq, 1993).

17. José Augusto Padua, "O nascimento da política verde no Brasil: fatores exogenos e endogenos," *Ciencias Sociais Hoje* ANPOCS (São Paulo: Vertice, 1990).

PART TWO

International Aspects of Environmental Policy

CHAPTER SIX

———————— ■ ————————

Free Trade and Environmental Policies: Chile, Mexico, and Venezuela

Heraldo Muñoz

In recent years, the Western Hemisphere has moved vigorously toward free trade and economic integration, while economic globalization and interdependence have generally intensified worldwide. Examples of the trend toward the opening of trade in the Americas include implementation of the North American Free Trade Agreement (NAFTA) beginning in 1994; trade liberalization involving Mexico, Colombia, and Venezuela; the free trade accord signed in 1991 between Chile and Mexico; and the MERCOSUR scheme encompassing Argentina, Brazil, Uruguay, and Paraguay.

Simultaneously, the region from Canada to Chile has witnessed a heightened concern for the environment. Today, unlike the recent past, environmental issues are a public policy priority on the agenda of almost every country in the Americas. Nongovernmental groups have emerged to study and lobby for environmental conservation, and public opinion polls demonstrate that citizens throughout the region assign great importance to the creation and implementation of sustainable development policies.

Some analysts suggest that the effects of trade liberalization are mainly negative because the overexploitation of natural resources resulting from the international movement and exchange of goods can directly harm ecosystems or pose hazards to the people or natural endowments of a country. According to such a view, the style of development associated with free trade policies tends to fuel the overexploitation of resources in which countries have comparative advantages, it simultaneously underutilizes a series of environmental resources that, properly wielded, could improve national and regional well-being.

A different perspective stresses positive effects on the environment stemming from liberalization of international trade and free market policies. By producing an increase in revenue, free trade presents countries the possibility of dedicating more financial resources to environmental protection; this, in turn, contributes to the establishment of, and compliance with, progressively higher environmental standards. According to this thinking, explicit incorporation of environmental issues into free trade negotiations is yet another benefit of liberalizing trade. As yet there are no conclusive answers; the environmental effects of liberalization are still ambiguous.

A study using a formal model for measuring the relationship between economic growth and environment—including growth derived from trade liberalization—concludes that conventional growth rooted in the expansion of production factors tends to be associated with environmental deterioration.[1] In contrast, research on ninety-five developing countries classified according to their income levels, growth rates, and degree of opening to the international market concludes that economies that grew rapidly but were closed to the outside saw a rise in pollution rates during the 1970s and 1980s; in more open economies pollution rates fell.[2]

Work on Latin America by Nancy Birdsall and David Wheeler also suggests that free trade policies have positive effects on the environment. Based on the case of Chile, they argue that, by increasing competitive pressures, external liberalization accelerates investment in new technologies which tend to be nonpolluting because they are imported from countries with stricter environmental standards. The researchers illustrate their argument by describing the adoption of clean technologies in the pulp industry. An additional exploratory analysis of twenty-five Latin American countries between 1960 and 1988 led these same authors to conclude that more open economies achieved cleaner industries.[3]

Gene Grossman and Alan Krueger, who sampled urban areas in forty-two countries in different stages of development, argue that more serious pollution problems are closely linked to low per capita incomes. In the earliest stages of growth, concentration levels of sulphur dioxide (SO_2) tend to increase along with incomes. This is followed, however, by a rapid decline: SO_2 levels begin to drop when per capita gross domestic product exceeds US$5,000 (in 1985 dollars), while increases in income beyond that point generate additional improvements in the quality of air.[4]

A study on the environmental impact of adjustment programs in the Philippines reaches a more uncertain conclusion. That work—which defines trade liberalization as the cornerstone of structural adjustment—contends that if the economic reform program in the Philippines had been fully implemented and had met the original goals it would have entailed an expansion of primary- and productive-sector exports harmful to the environment. The study points out, however, that safeguards can be incorporated into adjustment programs in order to offset pressures on the environment. In short, the study stated that "trade liberalization can have harmful environmental effects that undermine its contribution to sustainable development, especially if environmental and natural resources control measures are not strengthened through institutional and public policy reforms."[5]

The contrast between these viewpoints shows that there are major conflicts over the premises, purposes, and effects of the relationship between economic liberalization processes and environmental policies. To clarify this linkage, this chapter examines the cases of Chile, Mexico, and Venezuela. Since the 1980s, these three important Latin American countries have promoted deep-seated economic reforms aimed at economic opening and characterized by cutbacks in fiscal spending, reduction of the size of the state, and privatization of public enterprises (that is, control of inflation; widespread use of market mechanisms; decrease in external tariffs; and promotion of external investment and exports, especially in the nontraditional sector). Therefore, these three countries are appropriate cases for examining how the application of free trade programs concretely affects the quality of the environment and the environmental policies in each.

Just as there is little literature on the broader subject of trade and environment, there are few empirical studies on this linkage in Chile, Mexico, and Venezuela. On the other hand, newspaper stories and comments by interest groups abound. These accounts, for example, conclude that trade liberalization in Chile led to overexploitation of natural resources and serious environmental damage and that given the supposed absence of effective environmental controls in Mexico, NAFTA will turn Mexico into an "ecological dumping ground" for U.S. businesses.[6] One purpose of this chapter is to determine how true these claims may be.

Regarding environmental protection policies and their connection with trade liberalization, it would be useful to consider a tripartite typology. The elaboration and execution of *strategic* environmental protection policies respond to a conceptual design that incorporates the environmental protection factor into long-term economic growth policies. *Anticipatory* or pragmatic environmental protection policies are intended either to facilitate the economic insertion of the country in question into more competitive markets that enforce ecologically sound standards or to facilitate the negotiation of eventual free trade agreements with countries with strict environmental standards, thus neutralizing foreign pressures regarding the level of environmental protection in the developing country. Finally, there are *reactive* environmental protection policies that result from responses to criticisms and pressures, both external and internal, generally made within the context of free trade negotiations with countries having high environmental standards. These criticisms come from interest groups through public declarations or legal suits.

The following section analyzes the cases of Chile, Mexico, and Venezuela using these three categories. The evidence resulting from the exploratory analysis of the three cases is not entirely clear, definitive, or uniform. It reveals positive and negative effects resulting from economic liberalization processes. Each country has a unique a priori reality in regard to environmental issues, and each experiences a nuanced version of the same impacts observed.

Overall, this chapter attempts to develop a more systematic and rigorous understanding of the link between trade liberalization and environment, using the methodology of comparative politics.

CHILE

Chile was the first Latin American country to develop a model of market liberalization and opening to the international economy. Following the 1973 military coup, the government authorities implemented a set of tough economic measures directed toward the privatization of public-sector production activities. These activities included partial abandonment of the state's regulatory functions; decrease of public expenditure; external trade opening; attraction of foreign capital; and the liberalization of domestic prices, the financial system, and the labor market.

After a strong initial setback, the Chilean economy began to show signs of recovery, attaining an annual growth rate of 8 percent between 1977 and 1981. This positive trend suffered a sharp break in 1982 with the eruption of the external debt crisis. The Chilean government reacted by applying an "automatic adjustment" followed by a strengthening of economic liberalization and export strategies. Chile also entered into agreements with the international banking community, and, at the beginning of 1982, with the support of the World Bank and the International Monetary Fund, the government drew up a structural adjustment program for the 1983–1988 period.

Following these measures, Chile's economy entered a new stage of recovery in its macroeconomic indicators: exports climbed from US$3.8 billion in 1983 to US$8.1 billion in 1989. The favorable performance of the Chilean economy was reinforced after Chile's return to democracy in 1990. Under the government of Patricio Aylwin, liberalizing policies were tempered by important counterweights in social policy.

In the case of Chile, development of environmental policies clearly had no link to the implementation of economic liberalization. Until 1989, state involvement in environmental matters was marginal. It could be argued that throughout the authoritarian regime (1973–1989), not only was there no environmental policy but also its absence was considered an advantage in attracting foreign capital to Chile. Systematic formulation of environmental policy began only in 1990, coinciding with the initiation of the democratic government of President Aylwin in 1990.

Before 1990, the concern over environmental issues received formal expression only in Article 19 of the Constitution of 1980, which guarantees to all Chileans "the right to live in an environment free of pollution." The article also states that "it is the duty of the state to ensure that this right is not affected and to see to the preservation of nature."[7] In 1984, the military government created the National Ecology Commission (CONADE), which elaborated and submitted to the legislative body of that time—composed of senior officers of the armed forces and *carabineros* (uniformed police)—a preliminary draft of a "General Law on the Environment and Renewable Natural Resources." However, the draft never went any further. Overall, CONADE's activity had no perceptible public impact.

During this period of consolidation of the liberal economic model, Chilean public awareness of environmental issues grew considerably thanks to the public criticisms made by some nongovernmental organizations and scientific groups about specific cases of environmental degradation. Courts of justice issued decisions in favor of environmental protection. For instance, in 1985, the Supreme Court of Justice admitted the claim of people who opposed the use of the waters of the *altiplano* Chungará Lake—a formal biosphere reserve—for irrigation purposes; in 1988, the Court rendered a verdict in favor of the inhabitants of the locality of Chañaral that ordered the state copper company, CODELCO, to stop dumping the waste of the El Salvador mine into Chañaral Bay.

These constitute exceptional examples. The inclusion of environmental issues into the Chilean political debate occurred clearly and definitively in the context of the return to democracy. Thus, in April 1990, less than a month after the inauguration of the Aylwin government, the new administration created the Special Decontamination Commission of the Metropolitan Region, and in June of the same year it established the National Commission on the Environment (CONAMA). The new formalization was completed with the creation of Regional and Provincial Commissions on the Environment and of Ministerial Environmental Units.

CONAMA's activities were directed toward improving ministerial coordination on environmental matters, evaluating environmental conditions nationally, analyzing all environmental legislation in force, and developing new legal and institutional frameworks for the promotion of environmental well-being in Chile. This last goal was reached in September 1992, when the executive branch remitted to Congress the bill on Bases for the Environment. In a parallel move, the government introduced other important legislative initiatives, outstanding among them the Fishing Law and the legislation on Native Forests and on Waters. It also introduced rules and regulations controlling pollution in Santiago, the capital of Chile.

The environmental policy of the Aylwin government was criticized, among other reasons, for focusing on specific isolated problems and for excluding from CONAMA's mandate the ability to ensure strict compliance with environmental regulations. Nevertheless, it is widely acknowledged that the advance in environmental matters in Chile has resulted largely from the action of the new democratic government.

On the other hand, the case of Chile does not support the thesis that economic liberalization transforms countries into havens for pollution and depredation of natural resources. As to the industrial sector, data on the Chilean situation instead support the proposition that trade opening tends to have a positive impact on the environment. According to a study by Andrés Gómez-Lobo, in the period subsequent to economic reform in Chile polluting industries expanded at slower rates than less-contaminating ones.[8] Incorporation of clean technologies used in developed countries seems to be an important explanation for the positive impact of trade liberalization, since it is more convenient and less expensive for multinational companies to use in developing countries the same technologies they use in developed countries. This is evidenced, inter alia, by the cases of Minera Escondida (a copper company of Australian-British origin located in the north of Chile) and Forestal e Industrial Santa Fe (a cellulose-producing company located in the south of Chile, whose major owner is the Royal-Dutch Shell group).

In this same vein, Birdsall and Wheeler's work on the Chilean experience suggests that opening to free trade has positive effects on the environment.[9] The researchers argue that external liberalization, by increasing competitive pressures, accelerates investment in new technologies that tend to be clean because they are imported from countries with higher environmental standards. The Chilean wood pulp industry's adoption of clean technologies provides a case in point.

Furthermore, evidence indicates that a growing number of Chilean companies, both private and public, are making investments to reduce the adverse environmental effects of their productive processes and are carrying out environmental impact studies before installing new investment projects. According to figures made public by the Manufacturing Development Association (SOFOFA), the private sector invested over US$225 million in similar projects between 1991 and 1992. It is notable in this regard that in May 1992, 105 companies affiliated with SOFOFA delivered a public commitment to the Ministry of Economy of Chile (titled "Charter of Enterprises for Sustainable Growth") that was a proposal for their contribution to the protection of the environment.[10] Beyond offering a global conception of economic development by private entrepreneurs, the report may be perceived in the private sector and in the Chilean state partly as an inclination toward environmental protection policies that *pragmatically anticipate* Chile's accession to NAFTA. This accession would require them to take into account environmental restrictions in the developed markets of Canada and the United States.

Nevertheless, as the result of economic liberalization, certain sectors in Chile experienced a negative environmental impact. First, the Chilean export model continues to be based on products derived from mining, agriculture, fishing, and forestry exploitation. For instance, an overexploitation of the *concholepas*—an abalone sea resource—led the government to declare a permanent prohibition on its exploitation. Additionally, there have been reports of negative environmental effects derived from cultivation of salmon, one of the main nontraditional Chilean export products, and reports on the illegal use of dolphins as bait for the capture of crab, another Chilean export product. Similarly, Gómez-Lobo has mentioned in a context of growing forestry exports, a possible negative impact of the logging of native forests and their replacement with exotic species (radiata pine and eucalyptus) that may provoke significant alterations in the forest ecosystem and a loss in the tourist and cultural value of the native forests.[11]

In short, a brief survey of the case of Chile suggests that free trade has had variable effects. Those effects have not always been negative, and in many cases they have been clearly positive. Moreover, the effects have varied depending on the products and sectors involved and the time period under analysis.

With respect to the last point, two stages with dissimilar environmental repercussions may be distinguished in economic liberalization. The first, between 1973 and 1988, could be called the period of "primitive liberalization" characterized by strong consumption-oriented patterns, like those existing in the advanced countries, and by the depredation of natural resources. The second was a period of "liberalization with sustainable growth," in which the harmful effects tend to be smaller than in the first stage due to the implementation of specific environmental policies and the adoption of a *strategic* vision of economic growth that incorporates the environmental variable, equivalent to what we have called a "strategic environmental protection policy." In this second period, the presence of *anticipatory* motives related to Chile's eventual entry into NAFTA reinforced the formulation of sustainable development polices based on strategic reasons.

The recognition of two distinct stages suggests that beyond the processes of economic liberalization and opening to free trade, what is really essential for the environment is the model or style of development that each country implements. The case of Chile also shows that these processes, although they may have "green" (or environmentally beneficial) effects, are not the automatic solution for the environmental problems of the developing countries. Only a combination of external opening and the execution of modern and efficient environmental policy can overcome environmental problems in countries such as Chile.

MEXICO

Toward the end of the 1970s, the stability and growth that had characterized Mexico in previous years—based on a strategy of import substitution, state subsidies, restrictions to foreign investment, and, in general, protection of domestic industry—gave way to internal and external economic imbalances. The collapse of oil prices and the increase in international interest rates, among other factors, resulted in the 1982 debt crisis. Mexico owed US$86 billion to foreign creditors when in July of that year, it declared the suspension of payments on its external debt. In response, the international banking system discontinued its loans to the country.

By 1993, President Miguel de la Madrid was forced to reevaluate Mexico's protectionist policies. The government redefined the role of the state in the economy and undertook dramatic structural adjustment. At the same time, de la Madrid also ordered a reevaluation of Mexico's environmental situation. The economic liberalization and trade opening thus began in 1983 and was strengthened during the second half of 1985 when Mexico announced its entry into the GATT starting in 1986. De la Madrid gave a more liberal interpretation to the rigid rules on foreign investment and foreign trade. By 1988, laws were enacted that conferred greater juridical security and opportunities to the private sector.

The consolidation of the Mexican economy's opening occurred when Carlos Salinas de Gortari assumed the presidency in December 1988. During its first forty months, Salinas's administration privatized more than one thousand state enterprises; considerably reduced inflation, the budgetary deficit, and the external debt; increased international reserves; and reinforced the liberalization of international trade. For example, in 1985 the average percentage of Mexican tariffs on imports was approximately 20 percent, but in 1992 it had decreased to nearly 8 percent. Foreign investment in Mexico, which in 1983 amounted to only US$461 million, soared to almost US$4.7 billion.

The economic liberalization and external opening process in Mexico reached its clearest and deepest expression in the negotiation on NAFTA among Mexico, the United States, and Canada, which became effective January 1, 1994. The enormous importance of NAFTA for Mexico may lead to the conclusion that Mexican environmental policy has been a by-product of the NAFTA negotiation process, which included "green" pressures coming from the United States. Although this hypothesis—which will be discussed in more detail—makes some sense, it is worth noting that the design of the Mexican environmental protection strategy began in the 1970s, long before the economic liberalization process.

In 1971, Mexico enacted the Federal Law to Prevent and Control Environmental Pollution, which represents the first law addressing this issue in Latin America. In 1973, just a year after the Stockholm Conference on the Human Environment, the Mexican Congress approved an amendment giving federal-level organizations the responsibility and duty to control environmental pollution. The amendment also granted the General Health Council—a constitutional organization—powers to take measures aiming at preventing, controlling, and reducing pollution.

The 1971 law failed to meet the new challenges of sustainable development, however, and in 1982 Mexico passed the Federal Law on Environmental Protection, which sought not only to prevent and control pollution but also to foster the improvement and restoration of the environment. The strengthening of legislation and of institutional instruments for environmental protection in Mexico coincided with the country's economic liberalization. In February 1986, President de la Madrid issued the so-called Twenty-one Points, a series of decrees on reforestation, regulation of air pollution, water purification, relocation of industries, and environmental awareness. The gravity of pollution problems in Mexico City led de la Madrid to enact the Program of 100 Necessary Ecological Actions, emergency provisions for the capital. In the following year, Mexico enacted the General Law on Ecological Balance and Environmental Protection—a law currently in force—that changed the prohibitionist and centralizing emphasis of past legislation to a more pragmatic, functional, and decentralized approach. By the end of 1991, twenty-three state environmental laws had been passed, giving force to the emphasis on decentralization of the 1988 law.

In 1992, in order to ensure the enforcement of national environmental standards and in the context of NAFTA negotiations, Mexico established the Attorney

General's Office for the Protection of the Environment, an organization under the Secretariat of Social Development (SEDESOL), itself a ministry, which includes sustainable development in its mandate.[12] Prior to this, Mexico was often criticized for having many environmental laws but failing both to enforce them and to invest sufficient budgetary funds to meet environmental objectives. Thus, in the view of one expert the Mexican government's record on environmental policy regulation had "sought to defer high costs by responding to demands primarily through symbolic reform and by opting for low-cost, future-oriented solutions in the planning and development realm."[13] This began to change with Salinas, and a well-financed National Program for Environmental Protection was adopted for the 1990–1994 period based to a certain extent on similar programs implemented by the U.S. Environmental Protection Agency and the Organisation for Economic Co-operation and Development.

The new environmental activism of the Mexican government could also be perceived in its signature in October 1991 of the Convention on International Trade in Endangered Species of Flora and Fauna (CITES). Similarly, Mexico was the first country to ratify the Vienna Convention and the Montreal Protocol on Protection of the Ozone Layer; it is an active party to an agreement that establishes sanctuaries for the gray whale and prohibits the trade in sea turtles. The dispute between Mexico and the United States regarding tuna-dolphin fishing may be interpreted as an attempt by Mexico to both promote environmental protection and foster compliance with GATT regulations and trade liberalization. In this famous dispute, Mexico considered it essential to safeguard free trade and the GATT regulations against the unilateral application of another country's internal environmental legislation.[14]

The increasing emphasis on environmental protection policies in Mexico can also be clearly perceived in its budget. In 1993, public investment intended for the implementation of the national environmental plan amounted to approximately US$2.5 billion, a sum that is 139 percent higher than the public investment for such purposes in 1991 and over 6,000 percent higher than the US$16 million invested per year in environmental protection projects between 1980 and 1985.

Another interesting demonstration of Mexico's new environmental commitment was the 1992 SEDESOL-Petróleos Mexicanos (PEMEX) agreement on an environmental auditing program for the oil company, which covered eighty PEMEX facilities.[15] This followed the March 1991 closure of the state-controlled refinery "18 de marzo," the largest in Mexico City, at a cost of nearly US$500 million, leading to a 15 percent reduction in the industrial pollution emissions in that capital.

Cooperation between the United States and Mexico on environmental matters—including hazardous wastes and air and water quality—dates back to an early framework agreement signed by Presidents de la Madrid and Ronald Reagan in 1983. With the cooperation of the United States, Mexico maintains a program in the *maquiladora* region that regulates the transportation of dangerous wastes across the border.[16] Given Mexico's highly developed sense of nationalism, it was interesting that the U.S. Environmental Protection Agency's collaboration in the training of Mexican inspectors employed by SEDESOL (mainly for the purpose of border environmental control) was accepted by the Mexican government.

Obviously, Mexico's actions were strongly conditioned by the NAFTA negotiations. Trade liberalization had a positive effect on the deepening and reinforcing of the country's environmental protection policies. NAFTA added important ingredients to the formulation of Mexican environmental policy, especially in the area of environmental standards. Nevertheless, given that the formulation and development of Mexican environmental policy started long before the NAFTA negotiations, it would be an exaggeration to claim that concern in Mexico for ecological welfare is the exclusive result of trade liberalization with its northern neighbors.

The text of the agreement includes explicit references to environmental and health standards and goals. The preamble contains a commitment to sustainable development and to the preservation and protection of the environment, and specific provisions appear in four chapters: sanitary and phytosanitary measures (Chapter 7b), measures related to standards (Chapter 9), investments (Chapter 11), and settlement of disputes (Chapter 20). In brief, the purpose of these provisions is to ensure (a) the integrity of the signatories' internal systems of environmental regulations, (b) the implementation of efforts tending to improve standards, (c) the ecologically sensitive settlement of disputes related to environmental measures, (d) the protection of the trade provisions of international agreements, and (e) the avoidance of external investments that could allow the creation of pollution havens.

The NAFTA side agreement on the environment, titled "North American Agreement on Environmental Cooperation," provides for the creation of the bilateral Commission for Environmental Cooperation. The Commission is designed to serve as a focal point for environmental cooperation among Canada, Mexico, and the United States, and it is intended to ensure the environmentally proper application of NAFTA. The side agreement also establishes that the commission shall perform its duties through three entities: a Council, which is the main body; a Joint Advisory Committee, where private actors and concerned individuals can participate in the decision-making process; and finally, a Secretariat. Even more important, the side agreement provides that the Council may appoint arbitration panels, if requested by one or more member states, to investigate complaints relative to persistent patterns of noncompliance with the environmental laws of a given country. Should the panel decide that there are grounds for the complaint, upon completion of a consultation process aimed at solving the dispute it may apply penalties and, eventually, authorize the claimant country to apply punitive measures in the form of tariff barriers.[17]

NAFTA thus may be the first international agreement seriously to address environmental problems or negative consequences that may result from free trade among nation-states. It is, at the very least, the "greenest" free trade agreement ever known.

To sum up, in the case of Mexico, a free trade agreement between two developed countries and a developing one has promoted the strengthening of environmental policies in the latter. It could be argued, therefore, that the environmental impact of free trade agreements tends to be positive for the developing country whenever such agreements are concluded with nations having significantly higher levels of social and environmental development. Such an assertion would be supported as well by the fact that the issue of environmental protection is not included in the free trade agreement signed between Mexico and Chile.

In the case of Mexico, the state rather than private entrepreneurs has been the driving force behind the change to stricter and more effective environmental protection policies. At the beginning of the economic liberalization process, the private sector concentrated on the possibilities for trade expansion and economic growth.[18] Nevertheless, the liberalization requirements led many Mexican entrepreneurs to confront external competition and introduce more advanced and environmentally sound technologies.

In short, economic liberalization and trade opening seems to have been largely positive for Mexico. An exploratory analysis of the new situation of free trade under the rule of strict NAFTA environmental side-agreement procedures and a review of the active role of the state in establishing the legal and institutional bases of environmental protection prior to economic opening support the idea that the liberalization process was beneficial to Mexico's environmental well-being. Of course, Mexico still faces serious environmental problems arising from actions taken prior to economic liberalization. Mexico long ago set out on a development path that accumulated a great environmental deficit that in recent years has begun to be remedied.[19] In this respect, World Bank figures suggest that the increase of the national product in Mexico in recent years may be interrelated with the decrease in contaminating emissions levels, which leads to the assumption that the reinforcement of trade liberalization would both stimulate growth and have a positive environmental impact.[20]

Mexico is, therefore, a complex case. The positive impact of free trade cannot be exclusively attributed to the direct and indirect consequences of the NAFTA negotiations. Mexico is not simply an example of reactive environmental protection; it displays the complex outcome of *reactive* measures, motivated by the international pressures of NAFTA; *anticipatory* or pragmatic measures to position Mexico appropriately in international economic competition and in the trade negotiations with the United States; and unilateral *strategic* measures derived from an incipient vision of sustainable development since the 1970s by the Mexican state, encouraged by multiple political, economic, and cultural reasons.

VENEZUELA

Venezuela began its economic liberalization and opening to trade relatively late compared to other Latin American countries. Only in 1989 did the second administration of President Carlos Andrés Pérez make the so-called great turn of economic policy—traditionally based on the exploitation of hydrocarbons and import substitution—toward adjustment and liberalization. An article in *The New York Times* in 1991 included Venezuela as one of the successful cases of economic opening in Latin America, stressing its reduction of external tariffs, privatization of Venezuelan state enterprises, attainment of high growth rates, and the reduction of inflation.[21]

The great turn focused on reducing state interventionism—in an economy traditionally characterized by a hypertrophic role of the state and dependence on oil proceeds—and on eliminating protectionism by exposing the economy to international competition. The reorientation of the Venezuelan economy meant a substantial change in the foreign trade strategy and in the policy toward foreign investment, even leading to the generation of a public discussion on the participation of foreign capital in basic enterprises such as the oil industry controlled by the state.

The new trade policy had three pillars: the gradual opening of the economy in order to promote greater efficiency and competitiveness; an active strategy to negotiate trade agreements aimed at widening export markets and furthering investment; and the promotion and diversification of exports with a special emphasis on nontraditional exports.

The first years of the Pérez government saw substantial progress on the first point. Although Venezuela in 1988 had tariffs as high as 135 percent, by 1992 these had been reduced to a maximum of 20 percent. Over the same period, Venezuela's average tariff dropped from 34 percent to 10 percent, and the government eliminated nontariff barriers.

Venezuela advanced fast in its trade agreement with Colombia that became the dynamic core of the integration process of the Andean Pact. It entered into an economic association agreement with Chile, and by the end of 1993 it concluded in the framework of the Group of Three, a free trade agreement with Colombia and Mexico. Furthermore, in August 1990 Venezuela joined GATT.

With regard to the promotion and diversification of exports, progress has not been as solid as in the other areas of the new Venezuelan commercial strategy, even though export bonuses were eliminated, requisites for exporting were simplified, ports were privatized, and a Foreign Trade Bank was created. In an effort to reduce the traditional dependence of the economy on the exploitation of hydrocarbons, the Venezuelan government fostered programs for the development of petrochemical products, gas, coal, hydroelectricity, aluminum, steel, and forestry resources. Nevertheless, despite these diversification efforts, by the end of 1993 oil continued to prevail over any other export, generating more than 75 percent of Venezuela's export revenues. According to one source, if aluminum, iron and steel, and petrochemical products are excluded, the remaining nontraditional exports amount to only 5 percent of total exports.[22]

The environmental impacts of Venezuela's great turn are neither clear nor final. The country's environmental protection policies were initiated and consolidated long before the implementation of the economic opening; therefore, there is no causal relationship between economic liberalization and environmental policy in the Venezuelan case.

At least in regard to the environmental legislation and the creation of related institutions, the protection of the environment in Venezuela corresponds to a *strategic* vision dating back to the 1970s.[23] The basic laws on environmental protection had been enacted by 1976, including the Organic Law on the Environment (which unified environmental legislation). In 1977, the Ministry of the Environment and Renewable Natural Resources was established as the governing entity for environmental policy matters.

In 1983, the Organic Law for Spatial Planning, also a basic law, provided that the occupation of land and exploitation of natural resources for economic development should be made in accordance with sustainable development criteria. The same law reinforced the role of the Ministry of the Environment in the physical planning and management of Venezuelan territory. The Criminal Law on the Environment, passed in 1992, was intended to classify as a crime "those acts that violate the provisions relative to the preservation, defense, and improvement of the environment and prescribes the corresponding criminal penalties." This instrument, backed by Venezuelan environmental groups and considered an efficient tool for environmental protection, has, however, been criticized for being ineffective and poorly implemented.[24]

Other criticisms have referred to the supposedly minimal coordination among the state agencies in charge of the environment, the discretionary power that these government entities have, the limited influence of nongovernmental organizations, and the alleged existence of gaps and contradictions in the legal and operative schemes for environmental regulation.[25]

It should also be noted that throughout the Venezuelan opening, environmental issues have been conspicuously present. The government resolutely supported the creation of a High-Level Group on the Environment in the context of the trade negotiations with the Group of Three; acceded in 1983 to Decision 182 of the Cartagena Agreement relative to the commitment to protect the environment and natural resources; and in the framework of the integration with Colombia, promoted the joint approval of codes related to renewable natural resources. The environmental theme has also been present in the commercial policy of Venezuela toward the Amazon countries and the members of the Caribbean Community and Common Market (CARICOM).

Unlike the case of Chile, the Venezuelan private sector has not been active on environmental matters. For example, private entrepreneurs did not participate in the preparations for Venezuela's participation in the 1992 United Nations Conference on Environment and Development, and they generally did not take part in international entrepreneurial organizations active in environmental matters.[26] Conversely, government agencies are more active and directly involved in environmental protection initiatives, both domestically and at the international level. The state-owned Petróleos de Venezuela, S.A., has made investments in environmental protection (particularly in oil refining) anticipating the demand for ecologically sound products by developed country markets that could affect the supply of hydrocarbons and byproducts in those markets.

The case of Venezuela reveals that economic liberalization and trade opening have not had a significant impact, positive or negative, on the environment. This is due at least in part to the preponderance of the oil sector's influence on the domestic economy. In other words, until 1994 trade liberalization had not substantially modified the traditional productive axis of the country's economy despite the increasing importance of some nontraditional sectors. In due course, it would be convenient with the advantage of a longer time horizon to evaluate the indirect effects on the environment that the liberalization process may have in Venezuela. Special attention should be paid to fiscal incentives provided by the Law on Partial Reform of the 1991 Internal Revenue Law that benefit new investments in primary activities by granting, for example, tax rebates of 10 percent on income derived from new investments in mining activities, the rational management of forests, and the planting of new forests.

The case of Venezuela also demonstrates that the establishment of policies and institutions for environmental protection preceded the great turn toward economic liberalization and trade opening and reflects a long-term vision of the interrelationship between economic development and environment; that is, it constitutes a *strategic* environmental protection policy. Despite the criticisms of the implementation and effectiveness of enforcement of environmental laws by the juridical and institutional system, the existence and consolidation of such laws since the 1970s lead to the presumption that Venezuela will have an important comparative advantage in regulating possible harmful effects of economic and trade liberalization.

FREE TRADE AND ENVIRONMENT: TOWARD THE FUTURE

This brief survey of the cases of Chile, Mexico, and Venezuela makes it possible to conclude that the environmental impact of economic liberalization is not uniform and that these processes by themselves are neither detrimental nor favorable to ecological well-being. In the three countries analyzed, generally positive effects on the environment can be perceived as the result of economic growth and trade opening. But the dichotomy between free trade and environmental protection is clearly false, because the very essence of sustainable development is that it is necessary and possible to harmonize and reconcile both purposes. In the last analysis, the impact of economic liberalization on the environment in any country will be closely linked to the appropriate valuation of natural resources and to the effective implementation of suitable environmental regulation policies by governments making special use of both proper economic instruments and of official rules and regulations.

A broad conclusion is that even though in the three countries the relationship between trade and environment has been more or less adversarial, governments and private actors can and should strive to make international trade and environmental policies mutually supportive to promote sustainable development. To this end, efforts will have to be made toward harmonizing environmental standards at the international level; clarifying the role of the different international organizations dealing with such issues; promoting transparency and consistency with international obligations if trade measures are taken to attain environmental goals; and combating the root causes of environmental problems rather than applying restrictions or distortions to trade as a way to protect the environment.

Economic growth and trade liberalization are compatible with improved protection of the environment. As one author has rightly stated, "policies that internalize pollution externalities may well raise costs and reduce output in certain activities, and this approach is obviously preferable to an uncritical pursuit of growth at any price. But this is a matter of adjusting relative prices to reflect the social costs and benefits, not of inveighing against increased economic activity because it carries environmental costs and consumes scarce resources."[27]

Technical cooperation policies and market-oriented measures that favor innovation and create incentives for environmental protection seem to constitute the ideal way to attain environmental goals. Good environmental practice is also sound business practice because it represents good advertising. Image is increasingly important in attracting the general public, and it therefore has become a competitive factor for firms. Thus, the future of many companies may very well depend upon their ability to anticipate and satisfy society's new requirements in relation to ecologically friendly products.

The cases of Chile, Mexico, and Venezuela illustrate the concepts of *strategic*, *anticipatory*, and *reactive* environmental protection policies as they relate to the processes of trade reform and liberalization. An essential recommendation can be drawn from this study: developing countries should consider environmental policy not as a source of difficulties but as a driving force for innovation that encourages sustained economic growth. As Konrad von Moltke stated, "failure to integrate the environmental imperative into development strategies will lead to economies which are not innovative and, thus, not internationally competitive, and that will continue to depend on the markets and priorities of more developed countries."[28]

In the future, governments, international organizations, and private actors will have to undertake further policy adjustments and changes in matters related to both trade and environment. Only then will trade liberalization and the application of environmental policies be sufficient to ensure the achievement of the now-universal objective of sustainable development.

NOTES

1. See Ramón López, "The Environment as a Factor of Production: The Economic Growth and Trade Policy Linkages," in Patrick Low, ed., *International Trade and the Environment* (Washington, DC: The World Bank, 1992), pp. 137–155.

2. Robert E.B. Lucas, David Wheeler, and Hemamala Hettige, "Economic Development, Environmental Regulation and the International Migration of Toxic Industrial Pollution: 1960–1988," in Low, ed., *International Trade and the Environment*, pp. 67–86.

3. Nancy Birdsall and David Wheeler, "Trade Policy and Industrial Pollution in Latin America: Where Are the Pollution Havens?" in Low, ed., *International Trade and the Environment*, pp. 159–167.

4. Gene Grossman and Alan Krueger, quoted in James Sheehan, "Free Trade's Natural Benefits," *The Washington Times*, October 6, 1992, F3.

5. Wilfrido Cruz and Robert Repetto, *The Environmental Effects of Stabilization and Structural Adjustment Programs: The Philippines Case* (Washington, DC: World Resources Institute, 1992), p. 61.

6. See "Chileans Pay Dearly for Economic Growth," *The New York Times*, November 10, 1991.

7. According to a source consulted in the research on the case of Chile, the inclusion of this article in the constitution was practically accidental because it was a personal initiative by a political appointee, an ambassador of the military government.

8. Andrés Gómez-Lobo, "Las consecuencias ambientales de la apertura comercial en Chile," *Colección Estudios CIEPLAN* 35 (September 1992): p. 107.

9. See Birdsall and Wheeler, "Trade Policy and Industrial Pollution in Latin America."

10. Because opening to foreign trade occurred sooner in Chile than in other countries, experts believe that Chilean entrepreneurs also recognized earlier that it would be necessary to implement clean productive processes and to invest in sustainable development in order to compete internationally.

11. Gómez-Lobo, "Las consecuencias ambientales de la apertura comercial en Chile," p. 103.

12. This new agency replaced the Ministry of Urban Development and Ecology (Secretaria de Desarrollo Urbano y Ecologia [SEDUE]). Autonomous agencies of SEDESOL include not only the Attorney General's Office for Protection of the Environment but also the National Institute of Ecology.

13. Stephen Mumme, cited in Richard A. Nuccio and Angelina M. Ornelas, "Mexico's Environment and the United States," in Janet Welsh Brown, ed., *In the U.S. Interest: Resources, Growth, and Security in the Developing World* (Boulder: Westview Press, 1990), p. 46.

14. In this dispute, referred by Mexico to the GATT and decided in Mexico's favor, the United States justified its prohibition against imports of Mexican tuna, stating that the tuna-fishing fleet of Mexico accidentally killed more dolphins than the amount permitted under the U.S. Marine Mammals Protection Act.

15. From this perspective, the number of environmental impact evaluations carried out in Mexico has grown considerably since 1988, amounting to over 3,000 in the 1988–1992 period.

16. Since 1991, Mexico has introduced various environmental regulations on the trade of chemicals in order to reduce negative impacts resulting from commercial transactions.

17. The penalties are imposed on governments and not against enterprises or individuals, but the punitive trade measures are applied against the industrial sector involved.

18. A significant part of the environmental degradation is imputed to the *maquiladora* industrial program, involving the U.S. private sector in the Mexican region bordering the United States.

19. See Nuccio and Ornelas, "Mexico's Environment and the United States," p. 19.

20. See World Bank, *World Development Report* (Washington, DC: IBRD, 1992).

21. See "A Breath of Fresh Economic Air Brings Change to Latin America," *The New York Times*, November 13, 1991, A1, D5.

22. See Luis Zambrano, "Perspectivas macroeconómicas de Venezuela 1992–1996" (draft document prepared for the Workshop on Free Trade and Environmental Impact in Caracas, Venezuela, [July 8–10, 1992]), p. 12.

23. Analysts suggest that Venezuela's relatively early environmental concern was due more to a desire for international political protagonism at a time when environmental issues were becoming increasingly relevant than to a strategic conception of development.

24. See *Economía Hoy*, Caracas, October 20, 1992, 14.

25. See, for instance, María Pilar García, ed., *Ambiente, Estado y Sociedad* (Caracas: Universidad Simón Bolívar, CENDES, 1991).

26. A gradual increase in private-sector interest in environmental issues may be observed in the initiatives of trade chambers, such as the Venezuelan-American Chamber, as well as those of individual enterprises.

27. Patrick Low, "International Trade and the Environment: An Overview," in Low, ed., *International Trade and the Environment*, pp. 7–8.

28. Konrad von Moltke, "Environmental Protection and Its Effects on Competitiveness," in Heraldo Muñoz and Robin Rosenberg, eds., *Difficult Liaison: Trade and the Environment in the Americas* (New Brunswick, NJ: Transaction Publishers, 1993), p. 10.

CHAPTER SEVEN

■

Endowing The Environment: Multilateral Development Banks And Environmental Lending In Latin America

Daniel L. Nielson and Marc A. Stern

In the past decade, a rancorous debate has centered on the environmental conse-quences of World Bank lending.[1] To address the concerns of their critics, the Bank and the other multilateral development banks (MDBs) have launched an array of important institutional and procedural reforms. Yet the banks remain the focus of a pointed campaign by environmentalists intent on improving the MDBs' envi-ronmental accountability. As the greatest beneficiaries among all regions of MDB lending, Latin America and the Caribbean have received nearly US$82 billion in loans from the World Bank since the institution's inception.[2] Meanwhile, the re-gion alone contains 370 endangered species of mammals and over 450 million hectares of existing rain forest cover, approximately 63 percent of the world's re-maining rain forest.[3] Moreover, extensive air and water pollution, particularly in the growing urban centers, spill over into the public health arena by causing wide-spread illness and disease that affect the quality of life as well as the productivity of the region's residents. As a result of these problems, environmental issues in Latin America merit the highest priority for the region's leaders and the interna-tional development community. The Bank's efforts to address the environmental concerns of its critics thus have significant practical implications for the hemi-sphere. As discussed later in this chapter, in many respects the regional develop-ment banks, particularly the Inter-American Development Bank (IDB), have fol-lowed the World Bank's lead on environmental reform.

Recent reforms in environmental lending at the Bank have had two major effects. First, the Bank has funneled more resources into its "environment portfolio," either through freestanding environmental loans or through environmental components of traditional projects in the energy, transportation, health, agriculture, and mining sectors. Second, the Bank has been prodded to improve its adherence to its own internal environmental and social policies and guidelines as it implements loan projects. Most studies of the Bank's recent performance on the environment have addressed almost exclusively on the second of these two issues and have raised pertinent questions about the consistency of the Bank's talk and actions. However, few studies have looked at the first issue: the banks' lending specifically for environmental projects. In this chapter, we seek to close that gap by examining the Bank's environment portfolio since 1980. We attempt to determine what impact, if any, efforts to influence the Bank's policies have had on lending dedicated to the environment.

Our findings reveal that the Bank is neither as insensitive to the concerns of its critics as some claim nor as responsive to them as the Bank's own literature argues. Instead, our analysis suggests that the Bank has increased its lending for legitimate environmental projects throughout the developing world. However, this spending heavily favors infrastructure and tightly focused antipollution projects—called "brown loans"—over projects that provide for diffuse benefits such as protecting rapidly disappearing natural resources or strengthening environmental agencies—called "green loans." The data indicate that this pattern extends throughout Latin America, applying to most World Bank and IDB lending in the region.

The banks came under tremendous pressure during the mid–1980s to reform their lending practices along environmental lines, especially after the occurrence of several well-publicized environmental disasters that had been funded in part by MDB loans. With few exceptions, these criticisms were leveled by groups and individuals concerned with issues of natural resource degradation, habitat loss, and rain forest destruction. Although there is a tremendous deficit in infrastructure throughout the Third World, we find it curious that the Bank supported so many more of these projects over resource preservation (by a margin of between 4:1 and 2:1, depending on the year).[4] This is particularly puzzling in light of the predominantly green motivations of most of the Bank's critics.[5]

Our analysis of the brown-over-green lending pattern suggests that it can be best understood as the outcome of a confluence of interests. Officials at the banks and leaders of developing countries face compelling incentives to promote and pursue urban environmental infrastructure projects at the expense of natural resource preservation. Much of this chapter focuses on revealing those incentives. Thus, we argue that both the lenders' and the borrowers' incentives produce the pattern of environmental lending that we observe. Until the incentives change substantially for both parties, we expect the pattern to continue: Lending on urban-targeted infrastructure projects will continue to outpace funds marked for protection of natural resources such as forest lands or regions of high biodiversity.

OVERVIEW OF THE ARGUMENT

Adopting the Bank's own typology of environmental loans, we separate environmental lending into the categories of brown and green.[6] The Bank's brown environmental agenda addresses problems facing cities: energy use and efficiency, urban industrial pollution control, urban environmental management and the provision of potable water.[7] The green environmental agenda promotes sustainable natural resource management and the reduction of resource degradation. For reasons discussed later, we also believe that strengthening national environmental agencies falls into the green category. Because controversy exists over whether the Bank's forestry lending is pro- or anti-environment, we have tried to sidestep the dispute by excluding forestry loans from our study.

Figures 7.1 and 7.2 display the patterns of environmental lending at the Bank and the patterns of borrowing in the major Latin American countries. The figures indicate the percentages of total lending and borrowing comprised by environmental loans. If we were to include the absolute dollar amounts of loans, the trends would be even more pronounced. Environmental lending has increased as a percentage of total World Bank lending over time, especially since 1986. In the 1980–1986 period, environmental loans totaled US$2.91 billion and averaged 3.1 percent of total lending per year. That compares to a total environmental portfolio of US$8.84 billion for the 1987–1994 period, where environmental lending averaged 5.2 percent of total Bank lending per year.

In terms of environmental categories, although green lending increased substantially, especially beginning in 1990, brown lending continued to dominate through 1994. Green lending increased from US$132.2 million during the period 1980–1986 to US$2.78 billion during the period 1987–1994, representing an increase in yearly percentage of total Bank lending from 0.13 percent to 1.3 percent. Brown lending increased from US$2.78 billion (2.9 percent yearly average of total loans) during 1980–1986 to US$6.6 billion since 1986 (4.3 percent yearly average). Even since 1989, when green lending was augmented substantially, brown lending continued to dominate green by an average ratio of two dollars to one.

In this chapter, we ask two basic questions: What explains the substantial increase in Bank lending for the environment? and What accounts for the imbalance between infrastructure and natural resource conservation projects in the Bank's environmental lending portfolio? We hypothesize that both supply- and demand-side variables contribute to this pattern. By supply-side variables we refer to incentives within the lending institution to finance one type of project over another. Borrower preferences for certain projects over others create demand-side pressures.

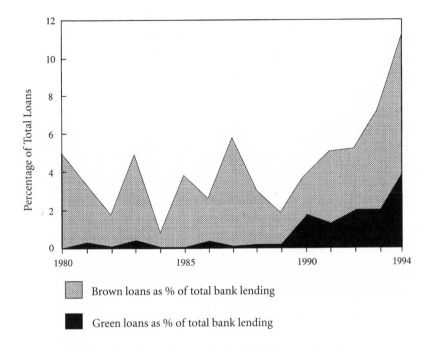

Brown loans as % of total bank lending

Green loans as % of total bank lending

FIGURE 7.1   Environmental Lending as a Percentage of Total World Bank Lending, 1980–1994.   SOURCE: *World Bank Annual Reports, 1980–1994* (Washington, DC: World Bank, 1980–1994).

Even though the Bank uses the brown-green typology for substantive reasons, we see an important analytic distinction between brown and green projects. Brown projects generally provide discrete benefits to a territorially limited and easily identifiable set of citizens. Green projects, by contrast, tend to provide diffuse benefits to society-at-large. This distinction is commonly described as private versus public goods, and it suggests a possible rationale for the imbalance in lending in these two categories.[8] We offer four propositions to explain the sharp increase in environmental lending at the Bank and the imbalance between brown and green projects within the environmental portfolio. The first and second propositions relate to the Bank, or the supply side of the lending relationship. The third and fourth propositions relate to the borrowers, or demand side.

First, pressure by the United States on the Bank led to increased lending for environmental projects. Concerns in the U. S. Congress about the environmental

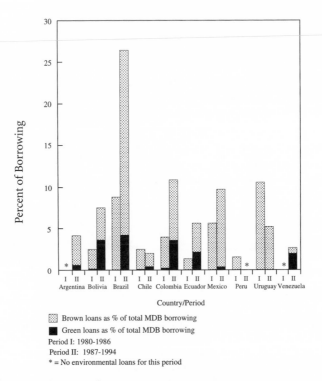

FIGURE 7.2   Environmental Borrowing as a Percentage of Total MDB Borrowing on Latin America.   SOURCE: World Bank Annual Reports, 1980–1994 (Washington, DC: World Bank, 1980–1994), and Inter-American Development Bank Annual Reports, 1980–1994 (Washington, DC: ICD, 1980–1994).

record of the Bank and the IDB threatened to cut off appropriations of funds for capital subscriptions and replenishments. Congress and Treasury officials began in the mid-1980s to press arduously for reforms, motivated by revelations that Bank projects had severely damaged natural resources such as the tropical rain forests of South Africa and Southeast Asia. We would expect to observe a corresponding change in Bank lending patterns beginning in 1985, when these pressures mounted.

Second, incentives for project managers at the development banks to move large amounts of capital as quickly as possible prejudice their lending preferences toward brown rather than green projects. Institutional incentives at the World Bank continue to reward staff for pushing big-ticket infrastructure projects rather than more complex resource-management or institution-building projects. Attempts by shareholders to impose their will on the Bank's management are hampered by the weak oversight mechanisms in place that could facilitate control over the Bank's actions. Unless and until these incentives change we expect brown lending to dominate green lending.

Third, in borrower countries where electoral rewards for pork-barrel spending are greatest the proportion of brown-to-green projects should be greater. Where political systems and electoral rules reward the construction of narrow rather than broad political coalitions, we expect politicians to prefer lending projects that permit them to funnel scarce resources to their political clients—that is, we expect brown projects to be favored in such systems. Conversely, where national parties are strong, client-focused pork-barrel spending is moderated by the parties' need to produce policies that reward broad political coalitions—that is, policies which provide public goods, such as green projects.

Fourth and finally, where environmental movements are strongest, lending for environmental projects in general should be higher. The larger and more institutionalized the environmental movement of a given country, the higher the probability that the country's policymakers will pursue environmental borrowing. Thus, we expect greater lending in both categories to countries where environmental movements are strong.

We explore these propositions in a discussion later in this chapter of the evolution of multilateral development practices and reforms and through brief discussions of several Latin American cases. This qualitative discussion is intended to lay the foundation for quantitative work in future iterations of this study. Our propositions, if correct, suggest that efforts to influence the environmental lending of multilateral development banks may need to be redirected toward reforming the oversight mechanisms available to Bank members as well as the incentive structure for Bank project managers. Furthermore, if lending patterns are strongly influenced by borrower preferences, then efforts to reform democratic institutions in the developing world and to help domestic environmental organizations thrive may be as important as lobbying to change bank policy directly. Regarding Latin America specifically, these propositions suggest that responsibility for the success or failure of MDB lending to address pressing environmental needs may rest as much with domestic political leaders as with the Bank's staff.

A NOTE ON PUBLIC GOODS AND
ENVIRONMENTAL LOANS

The distinctions we make between brown and green loans stem from concerns about the nature of specific public policies. Certain policies have a broader, more diffuse effect on constituents than others. This is typically understood as the problem of providing public goods. Pure public goods exhibit (1) nonrivalry in consumption (that is, consuming the good does not reduce another's ability to do so); and (2) nonexcludability (that is, it is impossible or very costly to prevent the consumption of the good).[9] Environmental protection policies are often considered archetypical public goods. Yet, it is clear that even environmental protection can display rivalry in consumption or can be excludable. The localized benefits of nature parks or preserves undermine the public nature of the good; clean air or clean water can be directed only to privileged districts or provinces. Some analysts have found it more useful to think of some environmental questions as common pool resources rather than as public goods.[10] Still, environmental protection policies exhibit less excludability and less rivalry than many other government policies. Complete populations of an entire area benefit from cleaner air, cleaner water, or nature preserves. This is much different than targeting specific tax loopholes, public works projects, or production subsidies among many other particularistic policies to privileged political allies and clients. Environmental measures are generally blunt policy tools, exhibiting a greater degree of "publicness" than many other areas of legislation.

Among environmental projects, however, some exhibit less excludability and rivalry than others. Brown projects are more easily divisible and excludable than green projects. Public works projects such as sewer construction can be used by politicians to benefit both those who are granted the contracts to build them and those communities that house the projects. This gives politicians tangible resources to distribute to political clients. Even cleaner air and water, depending on geographic conditions, can be targeted to catch basins or valleys, benefiting only those that live inside the domain of the pollution-abatement project. It is harder to exclude potential beneficiaries from the advantages of preservation projects, and enjoyment of biodiversity and protected lands by some does not normally limit the subsequent enjoyment by others.

ENVIRONMENTAL LENDING
AND THE WORLD BANK

To address our research questions, we first turn our attention to the accountability structures that motivate the Bank's management to satisfy the priorities of their shareholders. By casting the shareholder/management relationship as a classic case of delegation from principal to agent, we shed light on the oversight and accountability problems that underlie environmental policy reform at the Bank. Second, we review the incentives that motivate the Bank to "move money" at the expense of project performance despite shareholder preferences for projects that are smaller and demand additional staff attention to planning and design.

Throughout this section, we maintain a tight focus on the World Bank, although the NGO campaign had an impact on the regional development banks, too. Of the three regional banks, the IDB was the most affected by the activities of the U.S. Congress during this period. Indeed, the IDB undertook important environmental reforms because of these pressures.[11] For example, the number of full-time professionals dedicated to environmental issues at the IDB rose from eight in 1990 to thirty-two in 1993. Systematic review of project proposals has been instituted, and responsibilities have been decentralized to locate environmental expertise in regional operational departments. In another recent policy change, the Bank has adopted a new disclosure policy to ensure that most information on the Bank's operations is available to the public.

These reforms, of course, closely mirror the pathway of reform pioneered by the World Bank. Interestingly, the IDB has also mirrored the World Bank's pattern of environmental lending . By the IDB's own count, "loans for urban or 'brown' environment projects constituted some 65 percent of the Bank's environmental lending [for 1993] while 35 percent was directed to 'green' environment projects and environmental institution building."[12] The next year, 1994, saw little change in these priorities, with potable water and sewerage programs receiving the bulk of the IDB's environmental resources. This is not to disparage the IDB's new-found interest in incorporating environmental goals into its lending activities. Consultations with NGOs and local peoples have increased, and efforts to provide funding for small projects have born fruit. Nevertheless, this pattern of lending by the IDB offers additional reason to investigate our propositions to attempt to better understand the motives behind environmental lending by multilateral development banks in the hemisphere.

DELEGATION, AGENCY LOSS, AND THE BANK

Delegation of authority from principals to agents is a pervasive pattern in modern society: Voters delegate lawmaking to politicians and corporate shareholders delegate decision making to managers. Because delegation involves granting "authority to take action from the individual or individuals to whom it was originally endowed—the principal—to one or more agents," ensuring that agents serve their principals' interests, and not their own, is a central problem in social organizations of all sizes.[13] D. Roderick Kiewiet and Mathew D. McCubbins describe the natural tensions that arise between principals and agents and the tactics available to principals to mitigate the accountability problems (or "agency losses") that result.[14] Agency loss is compounded by the "congenial environmental for opportunism" present in the principal-agent relationship.[15] Agents typically possess information about their own performance or the results of their actions that is either difficult or impossible for a principal to obtain. Additionally, for delegation to work, resources and authority must be granted to the agent that could potentially be turned against the principal. In its early years, the Bank was largely an instrument used by the U.S. government to assist in the reconstruction of Europe following World War II.[16] Subsequently, the Bank's mission expanded to include channeling large quantities of development assistance to the Third World at interest rates only slightly above those available to the most creditworthy borrowers. In this undertaking, the Bank has essentially been delegated the authority both to borrow on international capital markets on behalf of the major industrialized countries and to implement a collaborative lending scheme among them towards the developing nations. Operational decisions regarding project identification, design, implementation, and oversight are essentially the responsibility of the Bank.

However, the institutional interests of the Bank diverge from those of its primary shareholders in several key areas. Where shareholders are concerned about project performance, lending objectives, and compliance with loan conditions, the Bank is motivated by loan repayment, lending targets, and remaining "part of the action." The Bank's motives stem from an overriding interest in maintaining its unblemished repayment record (in order to assure its AAA bond rating), expanding its overall lending totals, and preserving a working relationship with its best "customers." When tensions between the Bank and its shareholders emerge, the oversight mechanisms designed in 1944 at Bretton Woods strongly influence the resolution of conflicting priorities.

Oversight of the Bank is assigned to a Board of Governors, comprised of one representative from each member nation (usually the finance minister or central bank president). Because the governors meet only once a year their day-to-day responsibilities are delegated to a Board of Executive Directors. This board is composed of five appointed delegates from the Bank's largest shareholders as well as nineteen elected delegates who represent groups of smaller shareholders. The executive directors must approve all lending by the Bank and all major policy decisions. A director's voting share is based on the contributions to the Bank made by the represented country, with the United States possessing the largest share. The Bank's president, who also serves as the Chair of the Board of Executive Directors, formally serves under the direction of the Board of Governors. Historically, however, the U.S. government has named the successful candidate (in every case a U.S. citizen) to this office.

Despite these mechanisms for the shareholders to exercise control over the Bank, the Bank enjoys an advantage vis-à-vis its shareholders that is common to all delegation relationships—it possesses information about its performance that is either unavailable to the shareholders or very costly for them to attain. As a result, the Bank's staff can either use this information strategically or simply keep it hidden when it is politically expedient to do so. Examples of this behavior abound in the Bank's dealings with the Board of Executive Directors concerning its environmental performance.[17] The oversight problems of the executive directors are compounded by the demands that coordination and consensus building among donor countries place on the board. The collective action problems of the board have been mitigated by the effective delegation of leadership to the U.S. executive director for much of the Bank's history. As the U.S. voting share continues to drop, however, coordination among the executive directors is likely to prove more difficult, further complicating efforts to hold the Bank's management accountable to the board.

The weakness of the board vis-à-vis the Bank's management staff has attracted the attention of analysts for more a decade.[18] As the board becomes more restless with respect to the Bank's lending practices, what measures are available to it to compel greater accountability by management staff? Some control mechanisms are in place to minimize agency losses for the Bank's shareholders. The Bank faces incentive payments of a sort when it approaches its shareholders with new issues of capital subscriptions and when it negotiates replenishments of the International Development Association (IDA, which provides mostly interest-free loans to the poorest developing countries). Difficulties in negotiating either contributions or subscriptions, or in securing the appropriation of these resources, can undermine the confidence of financial markets where the Bank raises funds. Decisions on these appropriations are opportunities for major donor countries such as the United States to place demands on the Bank's management.

Difficulties in securing accurate information have recently captured the attention of the board. For example, an internal review of the Bank's lending practices completed in November 1992 (the now famous "Wappenhans Report") found that staff appraisal reports had become "marketing devices for securing loan approval" rather than "a disinterested, reliable, . . . professional assessment of a project or reform proposal."[19] In 1993, the board responded to this problem by establishing an independent inspection panel to provide affected third parties an avenue by which to challenge the Bank's noncompliance with its own policies and procedures.[20] If the panel operates as intended, it will alleviate the board's difficulties with monitoring the implementation of the Bank's internal policies in the field by harnessing the energies of affected third parties to assist them with oversight of the Bank's far-flung operations.

Moving Money and Internal Incentives at the Bank

Our second proposition turns on the internal incentives at the Bank and their consequences for lending priorities within the environmental portfolio. The institutional incentives that promote lending for large, infrastructure-intensive projects have been well documented.[21] The Wappenhans Report, for example, found a "pervasive preoccupation with new lending" within the Bank.[22] Outside analysts suggest that pressure on country directors to meet their lending targets stems from a pair of interrelated structural imperatives faced by Bank management: to assist developing countries to overcome pressing balance-of-payments crises and to avert a net negative transfer of resources from borrowers to the Bank.[23] Together these imperatives strongly motivate Bank management to emphasize moving money to borrowers. These pressures to maintain a continuous stream of large resource transfers to borrowers bias the loan appraisal process against smaller, more complex, resource conservation or institution strengthening projects. In fact, the Bank's own environmental report describes conservation projects as "inherently complex and requir[ing] major borrower and staff effort in design and implementation."[24] At the operational level, these pressures are translated into lending targets for country directors, and staff appraisal and promotion mechanisms that reward fulfillment of these targets. The Wappenhans Report, for example, documented "signals from senior management [that] are consistently seen by staff to focus on lending targets rather than results on the ground."[25] The Bank's culture, according to the same report, is attuned to loan approvals and disbursements "as the measure of success."[26] Our own recent interviews with Bank personnel indicate that these incentives favoring big-ticket items remain solidly in place within the Bank. Under these conditions, it should not come as a surprise that country directors and their staffs prefer to meet environmental directives through relatively simple and large-scale brown projects rather than through complex, smaller green ones.

Compounding the problem in Latin America is the region's particularly difficult net transfer position vis-à-vis the Bank. Table 7.1 demonstrates the magnitude of the problem in the region. According to the World Bank's own data, Latin American and Caribbean governments transferred nearly US$4.4 billion more to the Bank than they received in loans during 1994. Between 1990 and 1994, the total net transfer of resources to the Bank from the region totaled more than US$11.1 billion. Brazil and Mexico alone accounted for over US$2.3 billion in net transfers to the Bank in 1994.

Before proceeding, a note on the desirability of brown loans is in order. Clearly there is a need for urban environmental infrastructure projects in the developing world generally and in Latin America particularly, where urbanization has been so dramatic. Shortfalls in urban environmental protection directly affect public health, economic productivity, and quality of life. Projects focused on these issues can have tangible benefits, positively affecting growth rates and overall development. This is a serious consideration for MDB officials as they contemplate lending priorities. Brown lending is needed to overcome the glaring deficits of environmental protection in the cities.

TABLE 7.1   World Bank Net Transfers in Latin America and the Caribbean

	Millions of U.S. Dollars							
	Brazil		Mexico		Argentina		Latin America and the Caribbean	
	1994	1990–94	1994	1990–94	1994	1990–94	1994	1990–94
Gross disbursements	437	3,399	997	8,663	392	2,789	2,769	22,307
Repayments	1,292	6,139	1,007	4,588	441	1,691	4,489	19,714
Net disbursements	(855)	(2,740)	(10)	4,075	(49)	1,097	(1,720)	2,593
Interest and charges	544	3,177	907	4,157	276	1,090	2,658	13,711
Net Transfer	(1,399)	(5,917)	(917)	(82)	(325)	7	(4,377)	(11,118)

NOTE: IDA disbursements are included. Parentheses indicate negative values.

SOURCE: World Bank, *Annual Report*, 1994, Table 5–15 (Washington, DC: The World Bank, 1994).

However, it is curious that brown lending has outpaced green so predominantly. This might have occurred because brown projects are more expensive than green projects or because there is simply a greater need for such infrastructure development. We find little direct evidence that validates these explanations. Protecting forest lands and natural habitats—and even knowing what to protect—is a very expensive undertaking, as the hefty budgets for resource preservation in the developed world attest. The social and financial costs of species loss, destruction of forests, and increased global environmental problems would indicate that green issues are as important and pressing as brown concerns. The World Bank was receiving unmistakable signals from its principals that green projects merited much greater attention and a higher priority than they were receiving. The critics—core constituents of the Bank's principals—were motivated primarily by concern about the destruction of forests and habitats. They called for more green lending. The subsequent lending patterns do not appear to fully internalize these newly defined priorities.

To summarize, we offer two supply-side propositions. The first suggests that the Bank is best understood as an agent of its shareholders. Therefore, pressure for environmental lending from the most influential of these shareholders should motivate the Bank to respond in kind. Due to the difficulties that shareholders face in overseeing the Bank's behavior, the Bank has moved only reluctantly to satisfy the demands of its patrons. Our second claim is that internal incentives at the Bank motivate project managers to press for large, straightforward infrastructure projects rather than complex resource management or institution-strengthening projects. Overall, then, we expect the Bank's environmental portfolio to grow hesitantly in response to shareholder preferences and the composition of the portfolio to favor brown over green projects.

EXPLAINING THE BANK'S ENVIRONMENTAL PORTFOLIO SINCE 1980

Since the first articulation of an environmental policy at the World Bank in the early 1970s, the focus has been on mitigating the environmental impacts of its traditional project lending rather than providing support for freestanding environmental projects. The Bank's Office of Environmental and Scientific Affairs remained understaffed and marginal throughout the 1970s and well into the 1980s.[27] Limited environmental lending was targeted toward urban pollution issues through the Water Supply and Sewerage, Population Health and Nutrition, and Urban Development sectors. Other environmental lending during this period was focused on controversial forestry projects. By the 1980s, the Bank's environmental policy was under attack for its inability to halt ecologically destructive projects and for its lackluster performance in supporting new environmental lending. Largely as a result of pressures from U.S. ENGOs, the U.S. Congress held seventeen separate hearings in six different congressional subcommittees on the environmental performance of the multilateral development banks between 1983 and 1986. Because the United States holds the largest share of votes on the Executive board and has traditionally played a leadership role among the directors, the NGOs hope to gain influence over the U.S. director and thus the Bank's environmental policy by petitioning the U.S. Congress.

The NGOs approached Congress with a litany of complaints against the Bank. They maintained that environmental evaluations were insufficient and not taken seriously in the identification and preparation of projects; environmental conditions attached to project lending went unfulfilled and unenforced; funding for environmental conservation and rehabilitation projects was insufficient; and development strategies failed to incorporate ecological constraints.

Although congressional committees have no direct influence over the World Bank, they can impose restrictions on the activities of U.S. government officials and, more importantly, can withhold U.S. contributions to international organizations. As a result of NGO lobbying, formal recommendations were produced in December 1984 by the House Banking Subcommittee on International Development Institutions and Finance to improve the environmental efforts of the MDBs and strengthen the capacity of the Departments of State and Treasury to evaluate the environmental performance of the banks. Included also was guidance for the U.S. executive director to the Bank to consider environmental impact when voting on new project lending. As a result, the Treasury created a full-time position to oversee MDB environmental practices. To underline its seriousness, the subcommittee added that it would "frown on funding requests from institutions which did not seem to be trying to move forward in this area."[28] The large U.S. environmental organizations succeeded in gaining the support of the U.S. Congress by focusing their attention on the spectacular ecological and human costs of massive transmigration development schemes in Brazil and Indonesia. Enormous loss of tropical rain forest cover resulted from these projects. Meanwhile, natives of the affected regions were overrun by Bank-assisted settlers, raising additional criticism of the projects. Environmental and native reserves outlined in the loan agreements were largely ignored by the governments in question, a contractual breach that the Bank was unwilling to penalize until pressed to do so by public and congressional opinion.[29]

These and other environmental failures were attributed to the absurd understaffing of the Bank's internal environmental staff. Responsible for systematically reviewing the environmental impacts of proposed projects, the staff of the Office of Environmental and Scientific Affairs numbered only six individuals as late as 1985.[30] By early 1985, the strength of the NGO lobbying efforts had become clear to the Bank's management. With the subcommittee's recommendations written into law and the relevant House and Senate subcommittee chairmen outbidding one another to impose even stricter environmental conditions on the multilateral development banks, the Bank initiated new internal efforts to address its critics.[31]

As Figure 7.1 illustrates, by 1987 the Bank's lending portfolio reflected a new priority on exclusively environmental projects—two years following the first round of intense pressure on the Bank. (This lag of two years is consistent with the Bank's normal project identification and preparation process.)[32]

Not surprisingly, the new environmental lending was almost entirely composed of brown projects. From 1980 to 1987, green lending hardly grew. During 1986 and 1987, pressures on the Bank continued to escalate. By 1986, the seriousness of the U.S. position was underscored by the "no" vote on environmental grounds by the U.S. director on a US$500 million loan to Brazil. By 1987, additional legislation directed the U.S. representative to press the Bank to consult with NGOs in its lending activities and to promote greater public access to Bank documents. While committee hearings in the U.S. Congress on the Bank's environmental policies continued, Bank President Barber Conable announced a new set of reforms to address the environmentalists' concerns. He created a new top-level Environment Department to direct overall Bank policy, along with new environmental offices in each regional department at the Bank; he declared Bank support for national planning efforts in borrowing countries that incorporated environmental values; and he announced a major initiative to boost spending to combat tropical deforestation.[33]

This last initiative, the Tropical Forest Action Plan (TFAP) was intended to direct hundred of millions of dollars in new lending to "expanding priority work in forest management and reforestation."[34] NGOs quickly denounced the TFAP as a program designed to accelerate the harvesting of tropical forests rather than to protect them. By mid–1990, the executive directors, under pressure from an international mobilization against the plan, requested that all forestry lending by the Bank be halted until the policy could be redrafted, this time with input from NGOs. As Figure 7.1 illustrates, environmental lending sagged for three years following Conable's policy announcement. Not only did green lending remain moribund but also brown lending declined dramatically. It appears that the Bank was caught in a double-bind during this period. First, the reorganization initiated by Conable in 1987 disrupted project identification and preparation activities, thereby extending this process by a full year. Second, Conable had planned to offer green lending through the TFAP. When this effort collapsed, there were few other projects in the pipeline to present to the Board for approval.

During this period, NGO efforts continued to produce activity in the U.S. Congress. In September 1988, USAID was required to monitor MDB projects likely to have negative environmental impacts. More importantly, in December 1989, new legislation directed the U.S. representatives at the Bank and the IDB to vote against any proposed lending that would have a significant environmental impact unless the Bank provided a thorough environmental impact assessment at least 120 days prior to the vote, and this assessment was made available to affected groups and local NGOs. To ensure that officials at both institutions took these requirements seriously, they were included with the authorization of a contribution of US$82.3 million to the Bank's Fund for Special Operations and a US$9.2 billion increase in the U.S. subscription to the capital stock of the IDB. Furthermore, these authorizations were also conditioned on an expansion in both environmental staffing and freestanding environmental lending, as well as improved access to information for affected groups.

By 1990, the Bank finally responded to these demands with a substantial increase in funding for freestanding environmental projects and for green projects in particular. As Figure 7.1 demonstrates, the break with the practices of the 1980s is clear: three years following Conable's public statements, the Bank's environmental portfolio began a period of steady and deliberate growth. It is important to note in particular the expansion of green lending that occurred in 1990. Nevertheless, growth in brown lending was even more dramatic, particularly in 1991 and 1993.

International events contributed to the transformation of Bank priorities during this period as well. In November 1990, the Global Environmental Facility (GEF) was approved by the donor countries as a three-year, US$1.3 billion pilot program. In conjunction with the United Nations Development Programme and the United Nations Environment Programme, the Bank administers the GEF to address four global problems: climate change, biodiversity loss, international waters pollution, and ozone layer depletion. Indeed, the GEF is named as the implementing agency of both the Montreal Protocol and the Convention on Climate Change and is currently the main international organ designed specifically to provide financing for solutions to environmental problems of global consequence. Additionally, in the wake of the UNCED meeting in 1992, the Bank has frequently been called upon to assist in the implementation of sustainable development plans in its work throughout the developing world. This changing international context appears to have provided additional reinforcement to the direct pressures for environmental reform emanating from the United States during this period.

Our review of the Bank's environmental portfolio since 1980 appears to confirm both of the supply-side propositions that we offer. The Bank reluctantly moved to address the environmental issues being pressed by its primary shareholder, but only after extensive and sometimes dramatic efforts to hold the Bank accountable to its principals. Furthermore, the Bank responded to these concerns first by directing its attention primarily toward infrastructure projects that paid environmental dividends. When the Bank did attempt to address the green concerns of its critics with the TFAP, its efforts were criticized as little more than logging and development plans for the very forests the plan was intended to preserve. As the Bank moved to support green projects in response to pressures from the executive directors, brown projects grew even faster. In 1993, the gap between brown and green lending at the Bank reached 4:1. This apparent imbalance was reinforced by the demands of the banks' borrowers or clients.

DOMESTIC POLITICS AND
ENVIRONMENTAL BORROWING

As noted, this chapter generates arguments that attempt to account for the origins of the two patterns in multilateral lending. First, MDB financing of environmental projects has increased significantly since the mid–1980s. Second, brown loans to ameliorate urban environmental problems have outpaced green loans that go to preservation projects and national regulatory infrastructure. The previous section detailed our supply-side explanation for these trends. However, in a real sense these new patterns in MDB environmental lending are overdetermined. Changes in the demand side of the equation—at the level of domestic politics and policy making—have reinforced and amplified the supply-side impulse toward greater, but predominantly brown, environmental lending.

In focusing on the domestic politics and policies of borrower countries, we seek to redress a deficiency to date in the analysis of multilateral development financing. Many studies have noted the important role that motives, incentives, and expertise at the banks have played in determining lending patterns. We echo these concerns and have attempted to refine them. However, analyses of bank practices often occur at the expense of understanding the interests and demands of the borrowers themselves.

The announcement of a given loan is the culmination of a long and arduous process of proposing, rejecting, negotiating, and refining development project priorities. Developing country representatives generally propose projects to bank officials, who can offer counter proposals to promote projects of their own in the negotiations or modify proposed projects according to their interests. The country representatives can either accept, reject, or amend the counterproposals. For a given loan this process is complex, lengthy, and linked to other project loans. The loan as negotiated generally, therefore, represents an equilibrium outcome—an amalgam of bank and borrower interests. In multiple interviews with bank staffers, borrower representatives, and observers, there was a strong consensus that lending is a reflection of shared interests, the intersection of the diverse demands of bank and borrower officials. Loans are shaped by both borrowers and creditors, and although the leverage of either party can wax or wane for a given loan, the final outcome almost always represents a compromise of competing positions.

ENVIRONMENTAL MOVEMENTS

These compromises reflect a certain dynamism over time as both the banks' objectives and the borrowers' goals have evolved, particularly since 1985. In the developing world, environmental concerns matter now in a way that was inconceivable just a few years ago. The "third wave" of democracy has swept the developing world, and voices that were once muted or repressed completely are now broadcast widely and loudly.[35] Environmentalists often march at the vanguard of the new democratic social movements. The surge in Latin American environmentalism epitomizes this trend. As noted by Viola, Mumme and Korsetz, Torres, and Silva in this volume, environmental groups and movements have rapidly gained membership and have mobilized politically, but their access to decision-making circles varies from country to country.

Environmentalists have actively pursued their agenda by lobbying legislatures and bureaucracies; and they also have improved the information available to policymakers, demonstrated the political necessity of environmental reforms, and provided significant expertise and experience to decision makers seeking solutions to problems with electoral relevance. The organizing and information dissemination of environmental groups, who now act within a generally freer media environment, have sensitized citizens to environmental problems. To a greater degree than ever before, voters now expect politicians' policy agendas to include clean-up and preservation projects as priorities.

We suspect that this increased social strength and political leverage will translate directly into concrete environmental policy reforms. Of course, the ability of environmentalists to provoke political and policy action on the environmental agenda depends significantly on the size of their membership organizations, how well they are funded (and where that funding originates), and how professionalized their organization is. Where environmental groups are strongest (here we adopt Viola's categorization in Chapter 5 of the comparative strength of environmentalism in countries in the region), we expect that their influence will extend to greater borrowing from MDBs for environmental projects. We explore this proposition below.

POLITICAL INSTITUTIONS

Environmental groups do not act in a vacuum. We do not believe that policy directly reflects societal demands as if government were a vast cash register that totals up interest group pressure and then allocates and regulates accordingly. Instead, political institutions intervene in the actions of interest groups, setting entry barriers, privileging some interests over others, and shaping the incentives of politicians and bureaucrats who make decisions. By institutions we mean rules and decision-making procedures, the terrain that political actors must negotiate to reach desired policy goals. Although they vary from country to country, these rules set the bounds of public policy making.

Party-Centered Electoral Rules

Electoral rules shape the incentives of the politicians who make policy decisions. Certain types of electoral laws are more likely to motivate the provision of public goods, such as environmental protection. If electoral laws are structured in such a way as to privilege the interests of the party as a whole over the interests of individual rank-and-file members, then we expect policy in such systems to be more likely to favor public goods over particularistic policies, such as pork or patronage. If party leaders nominate candidates for election, set the order that candidates will be elected from the ballot, and exercise control over campaign finance, then we expect the incentives to provide public goods to be stronger than they are in systems where individual politicians control these aspects of elections.[36] Because party leaders are entrusted with caring for the party image, the collective reputation can rise or fall with voters' perceptions of the party's success or failure in providing public goods.[37] As noted, environmental protection is an archetypical public good. When party leaders have the ability to discipline the rank and file, as they do when they control nominations, ballots and campaign finance, then they are better able to enforce party discipline and keep individual politicians in line with the pursuit of collective goals. Examples in Latin America of party-centered electoral systems include Mexico, Venezuela, and Costa Rica. As it happens, all three countries also boast relatively strong environmental movements in Viola's categorization, and so we should expect relatively high ratios of environmental lending per capita in the countries.

Leaders of Mexico's governing PRI have broad sanctioning powers over rank-and-file members, including full authority over nominations for elected office, the order of the ballot, and campaign finance—and this is true down the municipal level of elections.[38] According to many accounts, Mexico has yet to reach the status of full-fledged democracy, although terms such as "semi-democratic" are often employed to describe the country's political system. Although significant inroads toward greater democracy were made during the 1994 presidential elections, the political system, particularly at the state and local level, must still undergo reforms before elections can be considered fully free and fair. Still, despite the semi-democratic nature of the system and the corruption that apparently pervades the political system in general (and the governing party in particular), there is still evidence to support our claim that the governing party is moving collectively, led by the president, to attract a general constituency. The president and other party leaders are attempting this partly through the provision of public goods, specifically environmental protection. It is likely that the current PRI leadership is using a public-goods campaign to build a popular base of support that is moving away from the party's traditional constituency.

Like Mexico, Venezuelan and Costa Rican political institutions are highly centralized. The party lists are closed, leaving nominations, campaign finance, and ballot control in the hands of the dominant parties. Votes are pooled within parties, and district magnitude (the number of legislative seats per electoral district) is high, which, coupled with closed lists, further centralizes the parties. In Venezuela, although voters could split tickets between president and legislative races, they could vote only at the level of the party, and their single-party vote counted simultaneously in the elections of three legislative bodies: the Senate, the Chamber of Deputies, and the state legislature. Voters often did not know which individual politicians were on each list, and party leadership determined almost entirely who got elected. Although this system has been changed along the lines of the German compensatory-member electoral districts, the electoral rules foster a "nearly ironclad party discipline" in which parties are so centralized that roll-call votes are rarely called in the legislative bodies.[39] Lacking Venezuela's state governments and federal structures, Costa Rica's politics are even more centralized, and authority is strongly concentrated in the hands of party leaders. Legislative elections in both countries almost entirely hinge on the collective reputation of the parties, which is often decisive not only for congressional elections but also for presidential elections.

Anecdotal evidence supports the initial proposition that party-centered electoral rules encourage greater attention both to the provision of public goods and to environmental protection in general. Venezuela and Costa Rica are known for their relative environmental responsibility in the region. Environmental concerns were raised as salient political issues in Venezuela long before environmental protection became politically relevant elsewhere in the region. The Venezuelan president even formed the region's first environmental ministry and endowed it with cabinet-level status. Costa Rica has often been at the vanguard of the developing world in pursuing sustainable development projects and in promoting its growing ecotourism industry. The two countries lead the developing world in percentage of territory dedicated to protection and preservation. In terms of environmental borrowing, neither country has received as many loans or loan dollars per capita as many other countries in the region. But a good portion of their environmental loans are focused on resource preservation issues. Two of Venezuela's three environmental loans since 1986 have been green.

Mexico, however, has received comparatively fewer green-loan dollars per capita than either Venezuela or Costa Rica, although we expect that pattern to change. However, a good deal of Mexican borrowing for green projects is often subsumed as a component of larger brown projects. The best example of this recent pattern is the massive Northern Border Environmental Project, which is aimed at tackling huge environmental problems along the U.S.-Mexican frontier. Just under 20 percent of the project's US$233 million in foreign lending and more than 25 percent of the US$528 million in local funds is dedicated to institutional strengthening (which we categorize as public-goods spending and hence green), including money set aside for the demarcation and administration of protected lands and nature preserves. Perhaps more importantly, the border project funds are administered centrally by the federal government. We believe that this feature provides fewer opportunities for distributing rents from the project to privileged political clienteles than would a more decentralized administrative mechanism. This is a problem that is faced more frequently in lending to countries with candidate-centered political institutions, to which we now turn.

Candidate-Centered Electoral Rules

Party leaders' prerogatives are greatly reduced and the importance of party reputation and nationally focused public goods underemphasized when individual politicians nominate themselves for election through petitions or by paying a filing fee, voters choose individual candidates from party lists, or individual candidates raise and control their own campaign funds. Under electoral systems that provide significant autonomy to the rank and file, policy choices are more likely to benefit narrowly defined groups of political clients rather than the general public. In such systems, individual candidates cultivate personal reputations in addition to the reputations of the parties. They do so because such systems require them to win office by expending individual effort rather than allowing them simply to ride on the good reputation of their parties.

Such politicians may supply targetable benefits to the localities that they represent or to some narrow interest group within their broader constituencies. That is, they develop a "personal vote" and engage in pork-barrel activities and other services for which they can claim personal credit.[40] These types of incentives mitigate strongly against the promotion of public goods. Even when public goods such as environmental protection become politically expedient, politicians in personal-vote systems will seek ways to divide the spoils of the public goods. For example, if the environmental measure in question is cleaner water, politicians in personal-vote systems may try to assert control over the provision of the sewer-grid contract and to direct the grid through neighborhoods or precincts where they have developed personal loyalties and clienteles. Thus, systems with strong party leaderships will be more likely to pursue public goods, and systems with autonomous politicians will be more likely to pursue particularistic policies. Examples in Latin America of such candidate-centered systems include Colombia and Brazil. According to Viola, Brazil's environmental movement is highly developed and professionalized, but Colombia's remains incipient. This difference in strength of environmental movements should be reflected in the amount of environmental lending going to each country. Figure 7.2 shows that Brazil vastly outpaces Colombia on this measure.

In Brazil, national party leaders do not control nominations, ballots or campaign finance. Extreme individualism characterizes the behavior of Brazilian politicians vis-à-vis their parties. An electoral-system feature called *candidato nato*, (or literally, "birthright candidate") means that elected politicians are guaranteed a spot on the party ticket in the next election, even if they switch parties—a feature that emasculates leaders when they try to impose party discipline and control nominations for office.[41] Moreover, the Brazilian open-list system of proportional representation means that a party's candidates are ordered not by party leaders but by the electorate. This system promotes heated intraparty rivalry, with candidates competing vigorously against fellow party members on the basis of promises for pork and patronage.

Brazilian politicians have been known to distribute actual material payoffs to households (for example, they may give a left shoe or the bottom half of a pressure cooker before the election, and they follow up with the right shoe or the lid after the election if they carry the precinct) that vote for them. On a larger scale, politicians cut deals with businesspeople and other interest groups for campaign funds, which they pay back with specially tailored legislation or contracts. Notorious among the campaign donors in Brazil are the *empreiteiras*, or large construction companies, which profit greatly from securing government contracts for public works projects.[42] Each politician uses these tactics to stake out his or her own electoral bailiwick or *reduto eletoral* (electoral readout or fortress) within their individual states, which serve as large electoral districts. These tactics create to extremely weak and decentralized parties and highly individualistic politicians in Brazil. The upshot is particularistic policy making.

Colombia shares many of the decentralized features of Brazilian politics. Like Brazil, Colombia has weak parties largely because of the broad fragmentation and internal competition of multiple party lists. This is because Colombia's proportional representation rule applies to factional lists and not to parties. Colombian party leaders do not control either nominations or the ranking of candidates. Internal party competition is widespread, and electoral institutions put up only moderate barriers to entry for new parties. For election, politicians cut particularistic, local-level deals with party bosses or *caciques* for blocs of votes.[43] The key difference between Brazil and Colombia is the institutionalized nature of the major parties in Colombia. The Liberal and Conservative parties in Colombia are so important to individual Colombians, and characterize so much of political life in the country, that they have been likened to an ethnicity of sorts, with the schism between the two parties becoming the major political issue cleavage in the country.[44] Because of the entrenched nature of the major parties in Colombia, the two parties there have marginally greater incentives to establish programmatic agendas than do the multiple, loose associations that characterize parties in Brazil. In all, these personalistic electoral features in Brazil and Colombia work powerfully against the sustaining of policy programs aimed at the provision of public goods.

This particularistic bias carries over into the realm of environmental policy. Colombia's environmental projects have been few; and often rents from the projects appear to be funneled directly to bosses' clienteles. In Brazil, this tendency has achieved notorious heights. Several large, internationally financed projects, including the efforts to clean up Guanabara Bay in Rio de Janeiro and the Tietê River in Sao Paulo, have been riddled with controversy and charges of corruption. Environmental groups have accused the *empreiteiras* that have won the contracts of "supervaluing" their bids, charging absurdly more for their labor and materials than it will cost them to actually complete the projects. Questions over the bidding procedures and administration of the projects have, at least in part, caused significant delays in the project cycle for both works.

Such problems have prompted the banks to tighten their contract requirements and to press the Brazilian federal government for more aggressive legislation to control corruption on public works projects. Perhaps the most famous instance of the twisting of the intent of a World Bank loan toward local, corrupt interests concerns the efforts of the Planaflora Project to ameliorate environmental damage in Rondônia, a state of the Amazon region. The Planaflora Project was intended in part to provide environmental protection and public health assistance to the region, where rapid deforestation and public health disasters had occurred in the wake of the failed transmigration project mentioned above (the project had been sponsored in part by Bank funding). Almost since the project's inception, environmental groups have leveled charges of fraud, corruption, and diversion of funds at local and national leaders and at Bank officials. Their efforts caused a temporary delay in dispersal of funds, and investigations have been performed and testimony heard by affected groups before the Bank's newly formed inspection panel. The experience with Planaflora in Brazil seems to indicate that, even where money is dedicated to green projects in the country, vast potential exists for using the funds for particularistic political purposes. This brief discussion of cases is suggestive and indicates that the propositions noted above are potentially fruitful. Our further studies in this on-going project will perform more rigorous empirical and quantitative analysis of multilateral bank lending patterns.

CONCLUSION

Our analysis suggests that efforts to influence the environmental lending of multilateral development banks (MDBs) may need to be redirected toward reforming the oversight mechanisms available to donor countries and refashioning the incentive structure for Bank project managers. The steps made toward the first goal so far have been significant, and the pressure on the Bank has appeared to have resulted in more dollars being dedicated to environmental projects. This in and of itself is significant. However, these findings do nothing to address the claims of several MDB critics about the content and implementation of specific loans and loan provisions. Our study was much broader than previous criticisms; it only says something about which direction the money is flowing and nothing about the environmental quality of the outcomes that the money produces. As such, this study complements, but does not supplant, previous critiques of MDB lending practices. Regarding the incentives of bank staff members, it appears likely that established patterns of environmental lending will continue unless efforts are made to reshape the reward system for project managers. As long as big-ticket infrastructure projects are rewarded at the expense of more complex and smaller projects, we believe that brown lending will continue to dominate green. Again, we believe that brown projects are worthy of funding and should continue to be strongly supported by international financing. However, this pattern of MDB lending may not, in fact, reflect preferences of the donor countries. Until internal incentive structures change, we doubt that bank practices can be fully aligned with the interests of the banks' shareholders.

Furthermore, if lending patterns, as our analysis suggests, are strongly influenced by borrower preferences, then efforts to reform democratic institutions in the developing world and help domestic environmental organizations thrive may be as important as lobbying the Bank directly. Regarding Latin America specifically, this analysis suggests that responsibility for the success or failure of MDB lending to address pressing environmental needs may rest as much with domestic political leaders as with the banks' staff. If incentives for politicians continue to benefit the interests of specific locales and clienteles over the interests of national constituencies, then we suspect that public goods, such as environmental protection in general and green projects in particular, will continue to be undersupplied.

Still, this study suggests that there is room for measured optimism. The amassed pressure on the MDBs apparently did have significant results, even if those results fall short of the expectations of the banks' critics. Environmental lending has increased dramatically since 1987. Green lending likewise increased substantially as a percentage of total environmental lending, even though brown lending continued to dominate green. In particular, the 1993 reforms at the World Bank can be expected to have an impact on the quality of the information that shareholders and observers can obtain from the Bank, and this should affect positively the overall implementation of the environmental provisions of Bank loans. The notion that the MDBs are organizational fortresses that cannot be penetrated is only partially correct. When pressure from environmental groups got the attention of the MDBs' shareholders, the changed priorities of those principals were incorporated, albeit partially, into MDB operations. There is reason to believe that this trend can persist as the priorities of donor and borrower countries continue to evolve.

For Latin America, the implications of our study extend to broader policy questions regarding natural resource management throughout the region. As Ascher and Silva document in this volume, domestic political and economic pressures can substantially undermine sound resource management practices. Under these circumstances, international assistance for conservation can bolster political, bureaucratic and public resolve to protect the region's rich ecological endowment. Even though the multilateral development banks are beginning to demonstrate a new commitment to fund environmental projects in their lending, they currently appear reluctant to tackle conservation issues with the same energy as they dedicate to urban pollution problems. Attention should be directed to the incentive structures that support such a bias, with an eye toward aligning funding priorities with the objective needs of the region. The banks have begun to underwrite critically needed baseline studies of the environmental problems that face their borrowers. Hopefully, these documents will provide the framework for future environmental lending in Latin America and elsewhere in the developing world. In the absence of structural reforms to address the perverse incentives discussed in this chapter, however, such studies are likely to be overlooked by political leaders and Bank staffers more concerned with their personal motives than the broader environmental needs of the region.

NOTES

1. See, for example, Bruce Rich, *Mortgaging the Earth: The World Bank, Environmental Impoverishment, and the Crisis of Development* (Boston: Beacon Press, 1994); Raymond F. Mikesell and Larry Williams, *International Banks and the Environment: From Growth to Sustainability* (San Francisco: Sierra Club Books, 1992); Robert J. A. Goodland, "Environmental Priorities for Financing Institutions," *Environmental Conservation*, 19, no. 1 (Spring 1992): 9–21; Philippe Le Prestre, *The World Bank and the Environmental Challenge* (Toronto: Associated University Press, 1989); Robert W. Kasten, Jr., "Development Banks: Subsidizing Third World Pollution," *The Washington Quarterly* 9, no. 3 (1986): 109–114; John Horberry, "The Accountability of Development Assistance Agencies: The Case of Environmental Policy," *Ecology Law Quarterly* 12 (1985): 817–869; Bharat Dogra, "World Bank vs. The People of — Reforestation or Deforestation?" *Ecologist* 15, no. 1/2 (1985).

2. *World Bank Annual Report*, 1994, p. 288.

3. World Resources Institute, *World Resources: 1994–95* (New York/Oxford: Oxford University Press, 1994).

4. This figure is calculated according to the Bank's own reporting in its Annual Reports. Grants from the Global Environment Facility (GEF) are included in these calculations.

5. For a summary of the congressional oversight hearings held between 1983 and 1987 that ultimately led to the 1987 reforms, see Rich, *Mortgaging the Earth*, ch. 5.

6. See, for example, *The World Bank Annual Report 1994*, p. 7.

7. Ibid.

8. See Mancur Olson, *The Logic of Collective Action* (Cambridge, MA: Harvard University Press, 1965).

9. Ibid.

10. See Elinor Ostrom, *Governing the Commons* (Princeton: Princeton University Press, 1990).

11. See, for example, Environmental Management Committee, "Conceptual Framework for the Bank's Environmental Protection and Improvement and Natural Resources Conservation Activities" (report approved by the Coordination Committee, Inter-American Development Bank, Washington, DC, September 13, 1988).

12. Inter-American Development Bank, *Annual Report 1993* (Washington, DC: Inter-American Developmental Bank, 1993).

13. D. Roderick Kiewiet and Mathew D. McCubbins, *The Logic of Delegation* (Chicago: The University of Chicago Press, 1991), p. 24. See also, Arman Alchian and Harold Demsetz, "Production, Information Costs and Economic Organization," *American Economic Review* 62 (1972): 777–795.

14. Ibid.

15. Ibid., p. 25.

16. Edward S. Mason and Robert E. Asher, *The World Bank Since Bretton Woods* (Washington, DC: The Brookings Institution, 1973).

17. See Rich, *Mortgaging the Earth*, pp. 165 and 178–80. For an alarming example of information manipulation by Bank staffers, see Bradford Morse, Chairman, *Sardar Sarovar: Report of the Independent Review* (Ottawa: Resource Futures International, Inc., 1992).

18. Robert L. Ayres, *Banking on the Poor* (Cambridge, MA: The MIT Press, 1983), pp. 66–67.

19. World Bank, *Effective Implementation: Key to Development Impact* (report of the Portfolio Management Task Force, Washington, DC, November 3, 1992), p. 14.

20. See The World Bank, "The Inspection Panel News Release No. 1," Washington, DC, September 7, 1994.

21. Horberry, "The Accountability of Development Assistance Agencies," p. 824; and Le Prestre, *The World Bank and the Environmental Challenge*, p. 66.

22. World Bank, *Effective Implementation*, p. iii.

23. See Rich, *Mortgaging the Earth*, chs. 6 & 7; Hilary F. French, "Rebuilding the World Bank," in Lester R. Brown, ed., *State of the World 1994* (Washington, DC: Worldwatch Institute, 1994), pp. 156-174; and Paul Mosley, Jane Harrigan, and John Toye, *Analysis and Policy Proposals*, vol. 1 of *Aid and Power: The World Bank and Policy-Based Lending* (London & New York: Routledge, 1991), pp. 45–51.

24. *The World Bank and the Environment, First Annual Report, Fiscal 1990* (Washington, DC: The World Bank, 1990), p. 5.

25. World Bank, *Effective Implementation*, p. 23.

26. Ibid, p. 30.

27. LePrestre, *The World Bank and Environmental Challenge*, ch. 2.

28. House Committee on Banking, Finance, and Urban Affairs, Subcommittee on International Development Institutions and Finance, *Draft Recommendations on the Multilateral Development Banks and the Environment*, 98th Cong., 2d sess., 1984, pp. 1–2.

29. Bruce Rich, "The Multilateral Development Banks, Environmental Policy, and the United States," *Ecology Law Quarterly* 12, no. 4 (1985): 681–745.

30. Rich, "The Multilateral Development Banks," p. 707.

31. Pat Aufderheide and Bruce Rich, "Environmental Reform and the Mulilateral Banks," *World Policy Journal* 5, no. 2 (Spring 1988): 310; Bruce Stokes, "Storming the Bank," *National Journal*, December 31, 1988, pp. 3250–3253; and Rich, *Mortgaging the Earth*, ch. 5; and LePrestre, *The World Bank and the Environmental Challenge*, ch. 5.

32. Warren C. Baum, *The Project Cycle* (Washington, DC: The World Bank, 1982).

33. Barber Conable, "Address to the World Resources Institute, Washington, DC, May 5, 1987," *The Conable Years at the World Bank* (Washington, DC: The World Bank, 1991).

34. Ibid., p. 27.

35. See Samuel Huntington, *The Third Wave* (Norman, OK: University of Oklahoma Press, 1992).

36. John M. Carey and Matthew S. Shugart, "A General Scoring System for Leadership Rank-and-File Relations in Competitive Political Parties" (paper prepared for the Annual Meeting of the American Political Science Association, September 1993); and Daniel Nielson and Matthew Shugart, "A Liberal Dose: Electoral Reform and Economic Adjustment in the Wake of the Debt Crisis" (paper prepared for the 1994 Annual Meeting of the American Political Science Association, New York, NY, September 1–4, 1994).

37. See Gary Cox and Matthew McCubbins, *Legislative Leviathan* (Berkeley, CA: University of California Press, 1994).

38. Ann L. Craig and Wayne A. Cornelius, "Houses Divided: Parties and Political Reform in Mexico," in Scott Mainwaring and Tim Scully, eds., *Building Democratic Institutions: Parties and Party Systems in Latin America* (Stanford: Stanford University Press, 1995).

39. Matthew S. Shugart, "Parties and Rank-and-File: Electoral Reform in Colombia and Venezuela," *Electoral Studies* 11, no. 1 (1992): 21–45.

40. See Bruce E. Cain, John Ferejohn, and Morris Fiorina, *The Personal Vote: Constituency Service and Electoral Independence* (Cambridge, MA: Harvard University Press, 1987); Barry Ames, *Political Survival: Politicians and Public Policy in Latin America* (Berkeley: University of California Press, 1987); Scott Mainwaring, "Politicians, Parties, and Electoral Systems: Brazil in Comparative Perspective," *Comparative Politics* 24, no. 1 (October, 1991): 21-43; Richard F. Fenno, *Home Style: House Members in Their Districts* (Boston: Little, Brown, 1978); Roger B. Meyerson, "Incentives to Cultivate Favored Minorities under Alternative Electoral Systems," *American Political Science Review* 87, no. 4 (December, 1993): 856–69; and Kenneth Shepsle and Barry Weingast, "Politicians' Preference for the Pork Barrel: A Generalization," *American Journal of Political Science* 25 (1981): 96–111.

41. Scott Mainwaring, "Politicians, Parties, and Electoral Systems: Brazil in Comparative Perspective," *Comparative Politics* 24, no. 1 (October, 1991): 21–43.

42. Barry Ames, "Electoral Rules, Constituency Pressures, and Pork Barrel: Bases of Voting in the Brazilian Congress," *Journal of Politics* 57, no. 2 (May 1995): 331.

43. Shugart, "Parties and Rank-and-File."

44. Jonathyn Hartlyn, *The Politics of Coalition Rule in Colombia* (New York: Cambridge University Press, 1988).

CHAPTER EIGHT

■

Transnational Environmental NGOs: Linkages and Impact on Policy

Blanca Torres

In the twenty years between the 1972 Stockholm and 1992 Rio de Janeiro environmental conferences, there were noteworthy changes in attitudes and political discourse in Latin America regarding environmental protection. Growing concerns in the industrialized nations over the future consequences of the environmental degradation that began in the early 1970s were shared only by very small groups in Latin America. Societies and governments responded slowly, concentrating on other problems that were considered overwhelming. This is not surprising in a region where developmentalist ideas have deep roots and where rapid economic growth, resembling Western industrialized patterns as much as possible, was considered not only the best but possibly the only way to raise standards of living and to control demographic explosion.[1] Latin American elites and supporters or promoters of that pattern of development—foreign governments, international organizations, multinational companies, and even many foreign nongovernmental organizations (NGOs)—shared this conviction.

Nevertheless, since the 1980s, the region has experienced an increased level of awareness about the negative long-term consequences of environmental degradation. Changes in attitude initially came slowly, but recently the pace has accelerated. In spite of suspicion and reluctance, governments gradually made modest policy shifts and took concrete action. However, unevenness in response and timing by different countries is noteworthy.

How can we explain this turnabout in attitudes and policies? Were changes produced purely by domestic pressure or did international factors play a decisive role? Initial studies suggest that both external and internal factors led Latin American governments to introduce changes. Initial government measures were often related to the effects of environmental degradation on health—mainly air and water pollution—which indicates that domestic demand may have been key in fostering new attitudes since external demands did not focus on these problems until recently. State institutions, state actors, social groups, and international factors—including the transnational flow of ideas—have been mentioned as influencing the actual shaping of new policies. Analysts have attributed different levels of importance to each factor depending on the country, specific issues, and timing.[2]

Among international factors commonly mentioned as having influenced environmental awareness and policy shifts in the region are joint activities by NGOs from the developed world and their counterparts in Latin America. However, these transnational ties and activities have not been studied in a comparative way. This chapter seeks to explore why these linkages have been established and how Northern NGOs (NNGOs), mostly from the United States and Europe, have interacted with their counterpart Latin American NGOs (LNGOs) in three Latin American countries. It is difficult to measure the relative weight of transnational actors and the linkages and joint activities of NGOs on policy changes. Lack of sufficient empirical data complicates the difficult methodological problems encountered when trying to focus on Latin American countries, partly because these countries have undergone deep political changes in the last ten or twelve years. Therefore, at this stage I am attempting only to establish the patterns of influence and the conditions under which NGOs were influential rather than trying to measure the impact on policy.

By using examples from Costa Rica, Brazil, and Mexico, this analysis hopes to shed more light on the relevance of transnational linkages to the expanding role that many have attributed to NGOs. It is widely claimed that NGOs have been crucial "in shifting public and political attitudes toward the environment; in pushing up environmental issues on the internal and external agendas of many states; in publicizing the nature and seriousness of environmental problems; in disseminating scientific research; in organizing and orchestrating pressures on states, companies, and international organizations; and in providing one of the most important mechanisms for helping to ensure effective implementation of environmental agreements."[3]

Most of these elements are incorporated in the political-opportunity approach, which focuses on social movements but could also be useful in the study of NGOs.[4] Unfortunately, it is a somewhat static approach. Therefore, this chapter will follow it loosely by considering only certain questions it raises in order to give a general overview of a process that is dynamic. A rigorous comparison using the political opportunity approach would require for a given country either a focus on a specific issue or a comparison over time.

A good way to approach the complex issue of transnational linkages and their impact on policy is to explore how those linkages modify the "elements of influence" mentioned by scholars who have analyzed NGO participation in policy making in their own countries.[5] Some of these elements are directly related to the resources available to NGOs to engage in lobbying work. Others are related to the context in which decisions are made and implemented.

This exploration may also help us explain the unevenness in scope and timing of the response of Latin American governments to pressure for better environmental protection. Such unevenness is not surprising because most of those scholars who emphasize the importance of external factors in internal decision making accept that those factors are rarely the only ones, however strong they may be.[6] Countries, even under the influence of a hegemon, have some degree of choice. It is usually considered necessary to focus on domestic policies and structure in order to explain that fact. I share the belief that a country's size and its perception of the role it should play in the international arena also need to be taken into account.[7]

Costa Rica, Brazil, and Mexico are widely recognized as world leaders in biological diversity—diversity that many NNGOs considered to be threatened. For years, NNGOs made Brazil their highest priority because of the perceived link between deforestation, climate change, and ozone depletion and because of the importance of the Amazon and the rapid destruction of the rain forest during the 1980s.[8] Costa Rica has also attracted deep and continuous attention from NNGOs. It is one of the world's largest centers of tropical research and receives high marks for its conservation of protected lands, which comprise almost a fourth of its territory. NNGOs consider it a model not only for Central America but also for countries of its size elsewhere in the world. Mexico's proximity to the United States and the transboundary environmental problems shared by both countries have increased U.S. NGO interest in Mexico. These concerns were added to the more traditional interests in endangered tropical forests, coastal lands, and habitats for migratory species. Mexico is also a good case to use in examining NGO interactions when the issue is the link between free trade and environment. The negotiations for NAFTA presented an excellent opportunity for NNGOs to increase their leverage by introducing the environmental issue in the trade agenda.

The first part of this chapter will try to answer the following questions: Why and how do NNGOs and LNGOs interact with each other? To what extent have NGOs mutually influenced each other's attitudes and behavior, including the search for alliances with other domestic and external groups and organizations? How have these interactions modified the resources available to LNGOs? The second part of this chapter will explore how transnational linkages have modified the context in which LNGOs work, the strategies they followed, and the conditions under which their counsel was recognized.[9]

THE EFFECT OF NGO LINKAGES
ON INTERNAL RESOURCES

Until the beginning of the 1980s, environmental NNGOs' concern and activity focused on their own countries. Few organizations showed interest in the developing nations of the world. Although NNGOs—mostly U.S. or European—gradually became concerned about Latin America, the number was still small at the beginning of the 1990s. Working in Latin America are among the best known and largest U.S. organizations involved in the promotion of conservation. They focus on the establishment of parks and protected areas or on supporting scientific research in the region (e.g., the Nature Conservancy and the National Wildlife Federation). A handful of policy think tanks that specialize in scientific-technical or legal advice also works actively in Latin America (e.g., the National Resources Defense Council, the Environmental Defense Fund, the World Resources Institute). International NGOs, including Friends of the Earth, the World Wildlife Fund, and Greenpeace International, fund some affiliates in the region as well.[10] Among the European organizations, we can mention Gaia (very active in Brazil) and CARE (mainly operating in Costa Rica). The activity of the International Union for the Conservation of Nature, which integrates both government and nongovernmental organizations, has been very influential (Costa Rica serves as one of its two regional offices in Latin America).

NNGO concerns about the Latin American environment have been varied. Conjunctural issues, such as the transit or disposal of specific toxic wastes or the defense of a threatened species, have emerged side-by-side with more encompassing ones, such as population growth. Protection of tropical forests and the biodiversity they represent are two issues attracting consistent NNGO attention. Linkages between NNGOs and LNGOs have frequently arisen around the protection of specific areas in Latin America. At the outset, NNGOs contacted governments to offer them help to protect those areas, but soon existing domestic NGOs joined the effort. Later, partly due to suboptimal experiences with governments and the advance of privatization, NNGOs encouraged the establishment of local organizations.

It is therefore useful to focus on the linkages between NGOs that share a specific interest in tropical forest protection. The protection of these resources acquired increased relevance because of the shift to conservation approaches that link environmental depredation and the patterns of economic development with the new conception of the management of protected lands. The need to involve the community living on or close to those lands is now widely recognized, as are the relationships between marginal indigenous populations, poverty, and environmental degradation.

It is also possible to explore NGO perceptions of the links between free trade and environment and the consequent actions of these organizations. Although the issue of trade has emerged from time to time regarding the protection of certain species such as dolphins or turtles, environmentalists attention to that link was particularly strong during NAFTA negotiations. If NAFTA is widened to include other Latin American countries, as was discussed at the Summit of the Americas in Miami in November 1994, trade could again become a high-priority issue. Trade also provides a window through which one could observe the limits to NGO transnational cooperation, since NNGOs and LNGOs do not necessarily share the same perceptions on the issues.

Evolution of NGO Linkages

Since at least the nineteenth century, the immensely rich flora and fauna of Latin America have caught the attention foreign scientists. External influences have deepened recently as a result of U.S. government cooperation in the establishment and protection of Latin American national parks. Since the 1960s, the Peace Corps has been involved and, since the 1970s, NNGOs have systematically studied Latin American biodiversity and have worked on behalf of the protection of the parks, usually in cooperation with Latin American governments or research centers.[11] These groups tried to establish contacts with the few existing LNGOs, which were mainly scientific societies.

Although environmentalists in Brazil, Mexico, and Costa Rica argue adamantly that the national government or domestic conservation groups led the early efforts at conservation, this does not diminish the importance of the ideas and experience received from organizations in developed countries, whose patterns were followed more or less closely by local groups in the three countries. Domestic organizations often comprised individuals who had been trained abroad and who benefited from exposure to researchers and NNGO personnel. Even in cases where the domestic effort was considerable, as in Costa Rica, institutions such as the Organization for Tropical Studies (OTS)—which includes both foreign and Costa Rican scientists—played an important role in the earliest conservation efforts.[12] The three countries established park systems patterned largely on the U.S. model, although over time Latin American systems of protected lands diversified in order to adjust to local conditions.

The earliest major change in the pattern of interaction occurred in Costa Rica, which was one of the first Latin American countries to experience the economic crisis of the 1980s. Funds available for protection plummeted, land purchases ended, and staff was reduced.[13] Government officials, fearing that forest conservation efforts would be halted, actively sought foreign support. To improve bargaining power, some, including the director of the Park Service, left office and established NGOs. They thus initiated a flow of information between the government and these organizations. Costa Rican officials also encouraged the establishment of the National Park Foundation (Fundación de Parques Nacionales), making it responsible for channeling foreign funds in order to avoid bureaucratic controls in both the donor and recipient countries.

The large U.S. NGOs already working in Costa Rica—the Nature Conservancy (NC) and World Wide Fund for Nature (WWFN) among others—were ready to offer direct financial support or training in fund-raising.[14] That country received a large percentage of NNGO funds spent in Latin America, and the governments of Sweden, the Netherlands, and the United States also provided major grants. This concentration of resources is explained by the ready acceptance of foreign participation on the part of the Costa Rican government and society, the prevalence of a democratic political system, geopolitical considerations, and the rapid growth of domestic environmental NGOs.

Costa Rica soon stationed itself in the forefront of environmental education, ecological tourism, and private reserves.[15] Foreign and national NGOs played a significant role in this process to a much greater degree than in other Latin American countries, where advances in environmental protection relied more on research centers.

Within a few years, the democratization of several Latin American countries encouraged NNGOs to expand to other areas of the region and to explore joining forces with domestic NGOs. Brazil was particularly attractive. Domestic environmental organizations flourished there, and conservationists joined middle-class groups increasingly concerned with urban pollution problems.[16] Many exiles who had lived in developed countries favored the process. Groups with wider interests—usually involving national development problems—united with the environmentalists, creating a form of "social environmentalism."[17] Although NGOs grew more rapidly in Brazil and Costa Rica than in Mexico, the number of Mexican ENGOs also increased, a large percentage having foreign contacts or financial support.[18] According to a survey carried out in the late 1980s, 29 of the 40 ENGOs interviewed had foreign contacts; 13 received counseling; 11, information; and 13, financial support.[19] These numbers are high considering the reluctance of Mexican NGOs to openly accept such linkages.

As organizations in the three countries became better organized and better able to press for spaces of action and access, NNGOs took advantage of the new political conditions to strengthen their links with them. LNGOs possessed more direct information, wider contacts, better communication with local communities, and greater capacity to effectively design projects. The involvement of these domestic organizations also helped prevent xenophobic responses and suspicion in local communities. Such responses sometimes arose in reaction to the presence of large numbers of foreign scientists, advisers, and activists involved in the study of tropical forests.[20]

As the 1980s advanced, NNGOs became convinced that they had to widen their scope and interests in order to save individual species and protected areas in developing countries. They targeted huge development projects and the MDBs that had strong leverage over setting development priorities and making decisions on natural resource exploitation. Given their influence on MDBs, U.S. and other developed-country governments became targets too.[21]

Accordingly, NNGOs changed strategies to include several lines of action, including shifting who they targeted and what tactics they used. New tactics now included lobbying Congress, the executive, and the representatives of other governments or multinational organizations. Pressure was also brought to bear through consumer boycotts against multinational corporations and public education about environmental issues.[22] Perhaps the most important and successful NNGO tactic involved winning mass media support to publicize accusations and demands. Media coverage was decisive in sensitizing public opinion. The utilization of dramatic cases to illustrate Amazon deforestation was particularly effective.[23] Campaigns against the capture of dolphins by the tuna industry or exposure of appalling environmental conditions on the U.S.-Mexican border were also effective—although within a smaller regional scope.

When NNGOs incorporated environmental protection into the development agenda by focusing on MDBs, they found it useful to strengthen contacts with LNGOs. Given that the Reagan administration was unresponsive to NGO demands, U.S. organizations sought to influence Congress. NNGOs recognized the strength of the argument that development projects ameliorate harsh living conditions in Third World countries, and they feared that members of Congress would choose to neglect environmental concerns in favor of those projects. They further recognized that NGOs from the countries in question could be the best possible witnesses that megaprojects worsen environmental conditions; using them could dilute the criticism that NNGOs intervene in the internal affairs of developing countries.[24] National Wildlife Federation (NWF) and Environmental Defense Fund (EDF) staffs, for example, began to collaborate with Brazilian NGOs to oppose MDB loans for Amazonian development. The Brazilian NGOs proposed the creation of extractive reserves as an alternative to those development projects that were seen as threatening tropical forests. Such reserves would leave forests in the hands of local people who could support themselves by extracting nontimber products.[25]

Members of LNGOs were among the first to testify before U.S. congressional committees, and a handful acquired international prestige. The participation of Brazilians and Central Americans in those hearings was usually arranged by U.S. environmental organizations (NWF and EDF in particular). LNGOs also lobbied MDBs' directors and staff on extractive reserves and other proposals. Response was positive because the concern in the developed world was at its peak due to the growing evidence about such things as the depletion of the ozone layer, reduction of worldwide biological diversity, and signs of threatening climate changes. In 1987, the World Bank and IDB formally endorsed the concept of extractive reserves, and one of the development megaprojects was suspended. The banks also pressured the Brazilian government to negotiate with local rubber tappers and Indians.[26]

Developed countries immediately endorsed multinational instruments designed to face the most urgent environmental problems. The majority of Latin American countries were willing to adhere to those instruments, and some introduced more comprehensive legislation on the matter. Such acquiescence was caused not only by pressure but also by advances in learning about the environment. The industrialized world, however, did not consider compliance with these agreements as guaranteed, and given their urgency, many considered the terms of implementation to be too long. Some observers even claimed that the response from Latin American countries was mere lip service to foreign demands. Consequently, environmental NGOs, especially in the United States, increased pressure on their governments, and by politicizing environmental issues, they were able to advance them on the bilateral agenda between industrial and Latin American countries. Calls for better protection of the environment increased, in particular of those resources claimed to be common goods. Concern in the developed world over Latin American environmental practices was focused primarily on Brazil. But pressure was also brought to bear on other countries with declining tropical forests, including Mexico, Costa Rica, and Guatemala.

Foreign leverage was higher than usual because of the unfavorable economic conditions prevailing in the majority of Latin American nations. However, strong domestic resistance still existed to the implementation of environmental laws. Opposition came not only from the private sector but also from professionals, academics, and other middle-class groups, which did not reject environmental protection but resented foreign involvement. Suspicion increased because environmental NNGOs had powerful economic allies, including strong protectionist interests at home. Although those tactical alliances proved useful to NNGOs, they also provoked strong nationalistic reactions in Latin America, with many groups viewing the issue of environmental protection in terms of a North-South division. As they had during the 1970s, Latin Americans argued that, under the pretense of environmental protection, industrialized countries were intending to "freeze the structure of world power" and prevent the most advanced of the developing countries from improving their position.[27] Brazilians were the most explicit in these accusations, but the view was shared widely (though expressed more discretely) elsewhere. The environmental behavior of more than one industrial nation at that time did not help to dispel doubts.

Once again, the strengthening of linkages with LNGOs seemed useful. Transnational activity favored the spreading of important scientific information, it reinforced the effect of cross-border links between scientists, and it pushed toward the advancement of value sharing if not of consensus building. Although LNGOs were not crucial actors, they contributed to a better understanding and acceptance of foreign demands. They served as transmitters of information and needs by making Latin American governments more sensitive to foreign demands. Although NNGOs made mistakes in their search for allies, as I will mention later, their links with domestic NGOs helped legitimize actions taken by Latin American governments in response to foreign pressure by allowing the governments to present those actions to the public as responses to their citizens' demands.

The advancement of privatization in Latin America during the 1980s also encouraged NNGOs to reinforce transnational links with LNGOs. NNGOs saw their counterparts as "the entrepreneurs for conservation" and began to push for the transference to LNGOs of government activities in this field.

At the same time, transnational relations among environmental NGOs, though not always easy, helped to strengthen the domestic leverage of the Latin American organizations. Financial support, information, and training from outside sources supplemented available domestic resources. It is almost impossible to ascertain the amount of funds channeled to each country. Interviews with NNGO officials suggest that Costa Rica received the greatest portion of funding. Officials of that country talk about receiving US$100 million for conservation, but this amount includes the debt-for-nature swaps in which governments were involved. Joint NGO action in Latin America also favored the widening of domestic access to LNGOs. When domestic access was blocked, foreign sites were seen as alternatives for lobbying. In this way, NGOs had an indirect effect on domestic policies and on the broadening of LNGO access to decision making.

Choosing Partners

If the previous discussion helps to explain why NGOs found transnational links convenient, the question that follows is: What criteria were used by NNGOs when choosing their southern partners? Here we also find different stages. Latin American traditional conservationists were usually the first partners of NNGOs. Later, NNGOs approached a wider variety of the existing LNGOs or encouraged their creation. Size or experience was not taken into account as long as the NGO in question had a legitimate base in the community. Personal contacts were and have remained important. Many NNGOs cooperated with LNGOs who did not share their ideological views as long as there was similarity in the diagnosis of a specific problem and the design of solutions to it. Barbara J. Bramble and Gareth Porter mention, as an example, the close cooperation between the International Division of the NWF and the National Council of Rubber Tappers. The NWF membership is well known for its conservative positions, while many members of the Brazilian NGOs stood far to the left.[28] However, because they recognized the need for dialogue with entrepreneurs, some NNGOs showed a clear preference for groups that did not resort to confrontational strategies.

NNGOs paid a high price for their initial lack of discrimination in choosing allies. Sometimes they entered into formal or informal coalitions with domestic interest groups whose environmentalist credentials were, to say the least, doubtful. This frequently undermined effectiveness and deepened the distrust of certain Latin American governments. Consequently, NNGOs now work with only a few groups that have a proven record of commitment and efficiency. The majority of these are large, professionalized organizations, but they also include some promising small LNGOs.

In the late 1980s, several NNGOs established offices in Latin America. They still rely on partners, however, and choose to maintain only limited staff in the region. It is not uncommon to find variations in staffing size in the branches of the same organization in different Latin American countries; and staff positions in the majority of NNGOs increasingly are manned by citizens of the host country. More recently, Latin Americans have also accepted positions in the U.S. headquarters of NNGOs; a handful hold directive posts. This incorporation of Latin Americans has led to the perception that these organizations are no longer just *Northern* nongovernmental organizations but are now truly transnational.

The main split among LNGOs is between those that refuse any foreign support and those that are willing to accept it. The majority of those accepting help have been ready to receive funds, training, and information. However, a small number prefer to limit cooperation to information exchange, which is less constraining than accepting financial support. In all cases, wider margins of autonomy and respect are usually sought, though these conditions are not commonly achieved.

The Nature of the Relationship

NNGO paternalism is the most common complaint of LNGOs. However, the dynamics of the linkages between NGOs have been more complex; they vary from country to country and among organizations. Although influence exerted by NNGOs over LNGOs has been considerable, on some issues the direction of influence reversed.

The most obvious mechanism used by NNGOs to influence their Latin American counterparts is financial, taking the form of either grants to specific projects or contracting for services. NNGOs sometimes use their own funds; more often they play the role of brokers, receiving money from governments or foundations and distributing it among local groups. The less interventionist organizations tend to give institutional support and to finance programs of activities rather than specific projects. But the influence begins with the selection of partners.

NNGOs typically push their own agenda, which largely responds to the commitments they have to their own sponsors. Their priorities and proposals for action frequently differ from those of the recipient country or even of LNGOs. This has become more evident over time. For several years, weak and ill-prepared LNGOs, lacking a clear idea of national priorities, were willing to participate without discussion in specific projects proposed by NNGOs. As the latter focused on forest conservation, crucial problems such as soil erosion and desertification were often overlooked. In addition, the choice of specific areas to be protected almost always remained in the hands of the NNGOs. This was particularly evident during the implementation of the debt-for-nature swap in Costa Rica. Top government officials and even some influential LNGOs wanted to distribute funds throughout the country, but donors, including governments and participating NNGOs, chose certain specific ecosystems and insisted on investing most of the monies there.

NNGOs have also pressed Costa Rica to extend its private protected lands, which led to the establishment of the National Institute for Biodiversity (INBIO). Although most environmentalists eventually accepted this institution, its creation was controversial, and suspicion toward it has not totally disappeared. Sometimes NNGOs try to monopolize activities. For example, according to one Costa Rican cabinet minister, Conservation International (CI) asked for exclusivity in the management of the debt-for-nature swap. In the face of Costa Rica's refusal, CI turned its attention to Bolivia. There are, however, differences among countries' bargaining powers vis-à-vis NNGOs; Costa Rica probably has the least leverage.

Transnational links have also influenced the strategies and tactics of LNGOs, although the opening of the political systems in Costa Rica, Brazil, and Mexico also has much to do with the new choices. Many LNGOs gradually moved from denunciation to education and information campaigns, policy and legal advice, and scrutiny of policy implementation. For example, Mexican NGOs frequently demand environmental impact assessments and audits. The best organized LNGOs have worked to strengthen access to media. Boycotts occur rarely, probably because domestic organizations target governments rather than enterprises. LNGOs increasingly resort to lobbying in the executive and the legislative branches; once in a while they even lobby in the courts. In other words, in Mexico, Costa Rica, and Brazil, many domestic NGOs that have relied primarily on confrontational strategies are now adopting assimilative tactics. They revert to confrontation only when they perceive an absolute lack of government responsiveness.

The nature of the relationships between NGOs varies widely, ranging from an asymmetry characterized by strong NNGO interventionism in the activities of the Latin American partner to situations in which better equilibrium is actively being sought. The most important effect on NNGOs, according to scholars and officials in Mexican organizations, has been to shift the focus of Northern groups from protection of endangered species to conservation of ecosystems involving the active incorporation of local communities in reserve management. However, a prominent Costa Rican environmentalist admits that NNGOs initially encouraged this shift in that country, and some Brazilians suggest this was also the case in their country. The fact that NNGOs have become increasingly receptive to ideas promoted by LNGOs is also attributed to experience working with them plus the presence of Latin Americans working as staff in offices of Northern organizations. However, as will be mentioned later, influence in agenda setting, including internal reorganization and alliance building, is still largely in the hands of the NNGOs that provide financing.

Experience and New Directions

The NNGOs I examine here have as their main goal forest and biodiversity conservation, but they give priority to specific tasks. For example, the Nature Conservancy focuses on conservation of parks, CI concentrates on community development in buffer zones, and the WWF works in both areas by financing projects on alternative exploitation of resources and on agricultural methods aimed at stopping biodiversity depletion. Others prefer to promote environmental education, management training, or basic research activities. Sometimes they mix different activities within each organization. Emphasis changes from country to country.

For example, CI in Costa Rica focuses on community work, but in Brazil that organization is helping to develop a nationwide biodiversity conservation strategy. Although NGOs report many successful and encouraging experiences, my analysis focuses on the problems they have encountered in order to explain recent developments.

A common NNGO complaint regarding many LNGO partners concerns their elitist or technocratic attitudes and their attempt to impose measures from the perspective of the capital of their countries. In other cases, NNGOs claim that local organizations overly emphasize scientific views or raise objectives of pure conservation that are not easily accepted by people who rely on natural resources for their survival. However, there is a mutual recrimination regarding this issue, and LNGOs accuse their Northern counterparts of the same behavior. Another frequent NNGO complaint is the lack of commitment by LNGOs and their abandonment of projects that have provoked or deepened lack of community confidence. LNGOs most commonly complain about the paternalism of their Northern counterparts as well as the NNGOs maintaining excessive control over funds. LNGOs are aware of donor conditionality and resent it, although they admit that some conditions are reasonable. Tensions also exist over a perceived lack of respect for national sovereignty, legal systems, and political practices. Disagreements also arise over the best manner of protecting a resource or a particular species.

Consequently, new paths and priorities have been established. Institutional strengthening of LNGOs is now a priority for NNGOs. They recognize that many Latin American organizations were too weak or unprepared to carry out fully the responsibilities delegated to them by their foreign colleagues, foreign governments, and international organizations. The better organized LNGOs are overburdened by offers of new projects, which reduces their efficiency and limits time for contributing to the setting of national priorities or for formulating possible solutions.

Latin American domestic groups are also under NNGO pressure to become more professional in order to increase their capacity to mobilize other social groups and to strengthen their leverage vis-à-vis their governments. Closer contacts with research institutions are also seen as a way to improve the scientific knowledge of many NGOs. Until recently, the scientific community's relationship with LNGOs was tenuous in all three countries, and scientists frequently viewed NGOs with contempt. Certainly some Latin American researchers became militant environmentalists, but institutional relations were rare. Improved scientific knowledge may give LNGOs tools for denouncing deleterious practices and proposing solutions. LNGOs are also being encouraged to adopt a legal status that will enable them to obtain tax exemptions.

NNGOs have also become interested in preparing local partners for the task of independent fund raising, both in the developed world and domestically. The interest in strengthening LNGO monitoring capacity is also a new goal, shared by international organizations that are constrained from carrying out this job for reasons of sovereignty in the host country.

Related to institutional strengthening is the NNGOs' new goal of influencing overall environmental policies rather than carrying out specific projects. Isolation and marginality from mainstream politics is a problem for the LNGOs because it reduces their ability to accomplish new objectives. Therefore, LNGOs are being encouraged to create networks and to look for broader alliances. Network creation, however, is not an easy task. In all three countries, there have been recurrent attempts at networking, including the creation of fronts and federations, but these were short-lived. The most successful attempts may be found in Brazil, including the Foro Brasileiro and the ecological assemblies established in large cities. In Costa Rica, the Federación Costarricense para la Conservación del Medio Ambiente (FECOM) was created years ago, but infighting weakened it. In Mexico, the Pact of Ecologist Groups (Pacto de Grupos Ecologistas) was formed in the 1980s, but it split for political reasons. More recently, there have been attempts at forming smaller networks and fronts: for example, the Union of Environmentalist Groups (Unión de Grupos Ambientalistas) and the transnational Border Network on Health and Environment (Red Fronteriza de Salud y Medio Ambiente).

Divisionism has pervaded the environmentalist ranks because of differences in ideology, partisanship, and personal considerations. Partisanship has been a major obstacle in the case of Mexico. Although most Mexican NGOs insist that they are apolitical, members' political affiliations affect an organization's access to the Mexican government, and this continues to be a divisive factor. Centrifugal tendencies are strengthened because government relies on co-opting leaders or organizations.[29] The "exaggerated horizontals" of the relations among the members and organizations, according to some die-hard environmentalists, also weakens networking efforts in Latin America. Fierce competition for funds has been one of the main obstacles to joint action, just as it has been in developed countries. Reduced flow of funds following the Rio Conference exacerbated this problem.

Developing the skill to build alliances—not necessarily with like-minded organizations—is another new goal. NNGOs are targeting Latin American entrepreneurs as a way of strengthening leverage and local fund-raising capacity. Although a handful of LNGOs or foundations relying on entrepreneurial support have existed for some time, we now find more willingness in the Latin American private sector to finance NGOs. Brazilian entrepreneurs were the pioneers, followed by a handful of Costa Ricans. For example, the Brazilian Society for Sustainable Development, a business-promoted NGO, was created in 1991. It was an encouraging event because it involved companies like Petrobras, Varig, and Shell, which seem ready to incorporate environmental considerations in their policies.[30] Since 1992, powerful Mexican businessmen also have joined the effort to finance conservation. It is interesting to note that some prefer to channel the funds through U.S. environmental organizations with offices in Mexico, such as CI.

The debt-for-nature swaps served as an opportunity to open or increase collaboration with governments, a practice that was common in Costa Rica but less frequent in Brazil. Government service contracts have delegated to NGOs the management of conservation efforts, sustainable development community projects, and environmental teaching programs. More so than in the other two cases, Mexican NGOs (encouraged by NNGOs) work jointly with research institutions, the government, and occasionally with international agencies such as the United Nations Development Program. Even more peculiar to Mexico is the priority given by NNGOs, and especially by foreign foundations, to Mexican NGO projects focusing on promotion of social organization and political participation rather than on environmental protection itself. The argument behind this policy is that strong NGOs and effective government institutions are necessary for successful work on the environment.

NGOS AND FREE TRADE: TAKING ADVANTAGE OF A NEW OPPORTUNITY

When the NAFTA negotiations were announced, Canadian NGOs immediately mobilized against the proposal, and soon U.S. NGOs got involved. However, Mexican NGO interest was initially limited except for a handful of NGOs in the border zone and one or two in Mexico City.[31] It is unclear whether U.S. NGOs failed to approach them and simply started an anti-NAFTA campaign on their own or Mexican NGOs feared that the NAFTA issue would prove to be internally divisive. Political rivalries had just put an end to the "golden years" of Mexican environmentalism, which during the second half of the 1980s reached its peak in terms of strength, unifying efforts, and capacity to mobilize large segments of the population. For some time Mexican NGOs concentrated their attention and efforts on the preparatory meetings for the Rio Conference.[32] This limited and delayed their involvement in the NAFTA negotiations and reduced Mexican NGO influence over the environmentalist agenda, which came mainly to reflect the concerns of U.S. NGOs.

Later there was contact and exchange of information, and a handful of Mexican NGO proposals were picked up by NNGOs. As in the United States, domestic NGOs eventually split between those willing to support a treaty incorporating environmental concerns and those who directly opposed it. This rift was related to the perception of the links between free trade and environmental protection. Those who strongly opposed NAFTA argued that free trade encouraged greater and more irrational exploitation of resources. Those who supported a conditioned treaty argued that free trade would favor more rational production choices and generate greater income, some of which could be directed to enhancing environmental protection. North American NGOs also emphasized that economic interactions—de facto integration—between the United States and Mexico were increasing anyway and that leverage by the United States over Mexico to demand improved environmental protection would grow with a formal agreement.

The Union of Environmentalist Groups (UGAM), which was convinced that the treaty could not be stopped, tried to make concrete recommendations. They had less success when making proposals directly, however, than did U.S. NGOs. The Mexican Network of Action against Free Trade, which included Mexican environmentalists who opposed the treaty, participated in and even hosted trilateral meetings in which environmental NGOs participated; but its proposals on labor issues tended to surpass in quality and number the environmental ones. However, the Network provided information and made some proposals to the U.S. anti-NAFTA coalition.

U.S. objectives including preventing "unfair competition" from products coming into the United States from a country with lax enforcement of environmental laws because NGOs feared such competition would lower U.S. environmental standards. U.S. NGOs also wanted to prevent the further environmental degradation of the border and to guarantee ample environmental investments in the zone. Better informed groups exhibited concern over potential overexploitation of Mexican natural resources, but it was not a widespread fear.[33] U.S. NGOs emphasized the negative impacts on that side of the border. The concern of Mexican NGOs for the traffic of U.S. toxic wastes into Mexico and U.S. export to Mexico of insecticides banned in the United States were scarcely raised; even less interest was paid to soil erosion or desertification.

The requirement for U.S. congressional approval of NAFTA increased the leverage of U.S. NGOs, even before the beginning of NAFTA negotiations. Lobbying directly at the executive level was not overlooked. NGO success in having the press raise the environmental issue and in using the courts increased the pressure on Washington. Although the impact of their activities on Mexican politics and policies will be described later, it should be noted here that the Mexican government tried to anticipate and respond as rapidly as possible to certain U.S. NGOs' demands. Instead of resorting to the positions of the underdeveloped South versus the North, the Mexican government underlined its environmental commitment and gave reassurances that it would not become the feared "pollution haven."[34] Mexican NGOs largely were left out of this "dialogue." Nevertheless, organizations strengthened their linkages during the discussions on the side agreements, and these may be reinforced now that NAFTA is in place.

The process also left feelings of mistrust on both sides. The asymmetry between the two countries and among NGOs stood out. Mexican environmental groups felt that their perception of the problems for Mexico's environment, as well as the strategies proposed to overcome those problems, were not always shared or even raised by their counterparts in the North. Priorities were also a problem. For example, the U.S. demand for large investments in environmental remediation and infrastructure in the border zone sounds reasonable. However, Mexican NGOs point out that it would be unfair to the rest of the country if too great a percentage of scarce Mexican funds were directed solely to that zone. Moreover, this strategy could cause the same vicious circle that now exists in Mexico City, where more public expenditure and better public services have attracted more people and enterprises, increasing requirements for even more public services that in turn cost more. Most Mexican NGOs also rejected the introduction of fines for lack of compliance with NAFTA or its environmental side agreement. Commitments such as strict enforcement of Mexican environmental laws could be difficult to meet in the short run. Mexican NGOs also perceived, as never before, that other interests could easily hide behind legitimate environmental concerns. Even the Mexican chapter of an organization as combative as Greenpeace publicly opposed U.S. sanctions applied to Mexico in relation to the dolphin-tuna dispute. The most sophisticated NGOs also recognize that the emphasis during the NAFTA negotiations on competitiveness—on "leveling the playing field" for producers—did reflect genuine NGO concern about potential pressure from the U.S. and Canadian business communities for lowering environmental protection standards. They also perceived that pro-environmental arguments could be used for protectionist purposes.

The view spread among the U.S. NGOs that their Mexican counterparts were too feeble and depended excessively on the government, a perception that was voiced by one of the U.S. NGOs talking about co-optation. Mexicans resented this criticism, especially because of the revolving-door tradition in Washington, where NGO representatives move from government to nonprofit groups and back again.[35] In short, environmental NGOs rarely formed loyalties that cut across borders. Instead, organizations from the two nations defended what each considered to be in the interest of its own country.

LINKAGES BETWEEN NGOS AND THEIR IMPACT ON LATIN AMERICAN ENVIRONMENTAL POLICIES

Many factors produced shifts in the environmental policies in Costa Rica, Brazil, and Mexico. There is evidence that NGO linkages significantly influenced many of them. Some changes are related to the internal political contexts in which environmental NGOs work; the others have a more substantive character—including legal modifications—or are related to stricter enforcement.

The level of foreign pressure, including that coming from NGO transnational activity, was also affected by many factors: (1) the size of the country in question; (2) its vulnerability to economic pressures, mainly exerted through the conditioning of external financing or access to a given community of nations; (3) government sensitivity to foreign criticism and interest in preserving an image of a "civilized" or "democratic" nation; (4) the site in which the pressure was exerted; (5) strength and access to the decision-making process of those opposing an environmental policy or policies; and (6) environmental learning. The combination of these variables largely explains differences in degree and timing of response in Latin American countries.

Although aware of the conditionality attached to aid, Costa Rica, the smallest, most economically vulnerable, and most open of the three countries, was willing to accept NGOs' demands in order to receive help to improve the country's system of protected lands. However, Costa Rica was less responsive to foreign complaints about depredation in areas outside that system, as cattle ranchers and banana planters, among others, strongly opposed changes in policy that would affect them. It other words, there is a dual Costa Rican response to external demands. The government has been willing to improve the conservation of protected lands, but it has been much less ready or able to prevent deforestation in the rest of the country, which has reached one of the highest rates in the world. Costa Rican NGOs involved in urban pollution problems and those working against specific tourist projects have also emphasized the lack of responsiveness on the part of Costa Rican authorities.

A larger and relatively stronger Mexico maintained a cautious stance. Its government never blatantly opposed the need for environmental protection, and it resorted to its traditional limited preemptive measures and "inclusive" practices to prevent both stronger domestic and foreign demands. This reliance on preemption and selective incorporation of new actors has been a key characteristic in this system's longevity. However, its responsiveness to foreign demands increased with its interest in signing a free trade agreement with Canada and the United States.

Brazil, the largest and economically strongest of the three countries, openly rejected foreign demands and resisted external pressures. Eventually, the economic and political costs became too high to be overlooked. As Andrew Hurrell has suggested, the rising costs came in the form of threatened withdrawal of foreign financial support for huge developmental projects and a very negative impact on Brazil's broader foreign policy objectives.[36] Although the Sarney government started to modify its environmental policies regarding the Amazon when external pressures were at a peak, it still prevailed regarding the Yanomani indigenous territory, which was menaced by encroaching miners. Disregarding both strong international condemnation and a decision from the Brazilian Federal Court, Sarney divided the Yanomani reservation in Roraima into nineteen areas and allowed the free entry of miners.

The strength of external pressure does not adequately explain subsequent deeper changes. Fernando de Collor, Sarney's successor, returned the territory to the Yanomani Indians at a time when interest in the issue had significantly diminished.[37] This change is partly explained by Collor's interest in improving Brazilian relations with Northern countries, especially the United States, in order to facilitate economic modernization through liberalization.[38] Another critical factor, however, was the diminished access to the decision-making process by forces opposing changes in environmental policy.[39]

The choice of NNGOs' sites of influence and the role of the domestic NGOs in presenting or channeling demands varied depending on country size, degree of openness, and political style. Sometimes it has depended on expediency. NNGOs frequently deal directly with the Costa Rican government, usually the executive branch in San José, although they have also presented their demands and proposals through local NGOs. However, when they found President Rafael Angel Calderón less responsive to their demands than his predecessor, Oscar Arias (a situation that arose due to strong internal opposition), NNGOs were motivated to exert pressure abroad. In the Mexican case, until the NAFTA negotiations, NNGOs rarely had direct formal contacts with Mexican government authorities, limiting themselves instead to interviews or informal gatherings of top and middle-level officials. The exception has been the border zone, where U.S. NGOs have more contact with local authorities. A favorite NNGO site of influence was Washington, and it continued to be after NAFTA negotiations started, although by that time NNGO contacts with middle-level Mexican officials in Washington had become frequent.

The NNGO approach to Brazil was similar to the one followed with Mexico before NAFTA. NNGO direct contact with government authorities has increased, however, largely because some representatives and staff members in the headquarters of Northern organizations are now Brazilians—including a handful of former high- or middle-level officials of Brazilian government agencies charged with environmental protection. Evidence suggests that pressure exerted abroad was the strongest and most successful element in influencing the Brazilian and the Mexican governments (and perhaps even that of Costa Rica).

Broadening Political Access of Nongovernmental Organizations

In Brazil, Costa Rica, and Mexico, greater opportunities are arising for domestic NGOs to articulate demands and to participate in the decision-making process. More opportunities exist for alliance building with other NGOs, groups within society, and government officials working in the agencies related to environmental protection. This is largely because of changes in the political regime in Brazil and Mexico. But even in the long-lived Costa Rican democracy, it is possible to talk about a widening of NGO access to the public sphere and political decision making.

It is clear that better funded, informed, and trained domestic environmental NGOs have benefited from the new political conditions. It is more difficult to assess the contribution of NGOs to those major political changes. Data support the assumption that, enjoying a more favorable overall context, domestic environmental NGOs—acting unilaterally or jointly with NNGOs—accelerated the modification of the specific arena in which they work. Initially, LNGOs found sympathy for their demands only in feeble undersecretariats for environmental affairs (which were usually located within a ministry charged with several other tasks). In the 1980s, these agencies evolved into full-fledged secretariats or ministries focusing exclusively on environmental matters. Although these secretariats do not belong to the first-tier cabinet level, they have more power than their predecessors. (The exception was the SEDESOL in Mexico, which had significant strength when it was headed by a politician who was seen as a probable PRI presidential candidate.[40]) Well-known environmentalists head these and other new environmental agencies. In addition, at national, state, and municipal levels, governments in Brazil, Costa Rica, and Mexico established councils, commissions, and working groups that provide for NGO participation. Decrees creating institutions such as Brazil's IBAMA and the Mexican National Institute of Ecology established in the 1980s also designate a role for NGOs. Some professional organizations have also been signing service contracts with governments agencies.

In the three countries, the legislative bodies also established ecological commissions, which sometimes collaborated closely with environmental NGOs. For example, a handful of NGOs worked systematically with Brazilian congressmen to provide technical information and proposals for policy changes, analyze drafts designed to defeat dangerous legislation, and monitor law enforcement. Given their direct and fluid contacts with grassroots groups, NGOs proved to be useful channels of information for legislators. The Brazilian "green congressional bloc" promoted the inclusion of several environmental provisions in the 1988 Constitution. But strong congresses do not necessarily mean better protection or deeper environmental concern. Brazilian deputies and senators, mainly from the Amazonian states, actively participated in the political counteroffensive against the Collor administration's environmental policies. President Arias's administration in Costa Rica faced congressional resistance that forced the newly created Ministerio de Recursos Naturales, Engergía y Minas (MIRINEM) to work without the formal approval of Congress. Congress also approved generous compensation for miners to discourage them from entering and threatening important parklands. But this expenditure in turn reduced the funds available for park management.[41]

In both Brazil and Costa Rica, NGO access to the judiciary has been widened. The 1988 Brazilian Constitution provides for broader access to the legal system because a provision was promoted mainly by NGOs. The Sala Cuarta of Costa Rica, which oversees the constitutionality of laws, is another new avenue of legal resort. Mexican NGOs have not been successful in promoting legal changes of similar scope. However, the judiciary is undergoing significant reform to guarantee it a greater degree of independence from the executive, including power to declare laws unconstitutional. This trend may mean wider access and leverage for domestic NGOs in the future.

Although the widening of NNGOs' access to government in Mexico has been more limited, NNGO contributions to the widening of access to domestic NGOs is clear in the last years. During the NAFTA negotiations, national and state-level governments both established environmental councils, including the National Institute of Ecology and the Office of the Environmental Federal Attorney (Procuraduría Federal del Medio Ambiente). Citizens and NGOs can now present complaints or denunciations to the authorities. The Mexican government retains a large degree of discretion in choosing the NGOs to which it grants access to some of these new organs, however. The NAFTA side agreements provide for NGO participation in the newly founded North American Commission for the Environment and the Mexican-U.S. Border Environmental Cooperation Commission.[42] Many of the side agreement's provisions are limited or vague, but there is a significant margin for NGOs action, beginning with a more comprehensive interpretation of those provisions.

Foreign pressure to increase NGO access provoked resentment and suspicion both in the governments and some sectors of society in Costa Rica, Brazil, and Mexico. A similar effect occurred when domestic NGOs adopted strategies patterned after successful foreign endeavors, especially when these were alien in style to the country in question. As change takes place in government discourse—as more and more leaders commit themselves to environmental protection—and in the level of environmental awareness generally, NGOs may find their demands and activities legitimized.

The NGO Impact on Policy Change

Regarding NGO impact on substantive changes in policy, the existence of more fully developed democracies, with more open institutions and policy-making procedures in Costa Rica and in the late 1980s in Brazil, would suggest very large differences in relation to Mexico. Elite-initiated reforms in this country, consistent with its political tradition, have until now reduced the gap in final outcomes.[43] Nielson and Stern, in this volume, also emphasize that the characteristics of the Mexican system allow for the provision of public-goods-focused policy that counters the existing patronage-based relationships (see chapter 7).

In the three countries, the strongest domestic NGOs may have contributed to the wording of new legislation, although the scientific community probably was more influential in Brazil and Mexico as comprehensive environmental laws were introduced during the 1980s. NGOs also influenced the development of national environmental programs, and governments tried to respond to their concerns by signing several multilateral agreements.[44]

Changes in the direction of Brazilian policy toward the Amazon reflect NNGOs concerns that were shared by domestic NGOs as well. Costa Rican groups had influence in the creation of the National System of Conservation Areas (SINAC), in which local conservation groups, community organizations, and international and domestic NGOs should be involved. NGO participation in the elaboration of national conservation strategies for sustainable development, already completed in Costa Rica and in process in the other two countries, has been significant. However, LNGOs have not participated in economic planning, and the incorporation of environmental concerns into overall economic projects is still limited.

Although the projects sometimes incorporated environmental rhetoric, they did not provide for mechanisms to enforce commitments.

The governments in Brazil, Costa Rica, and Mexico adopted a limited number of concrete measures and mechanisms recommended by NGOs, such as ecological zoning to establish priorities and special protection for the most fragile ecosystems. They also provided for environmental impact studies and audits and the transference of these activities to private hands, including to NGOs. There was a significant increase in Mexico's budget allocations, as a percentage of GNP, for environmental agencies, and the government has made commitments for increased public investment in environmental infrastructure, particularly at the U.S.-Mexican border. The government has also introduced new production norms and is studying better enforcement mechanisms. Brazilian budgetary allocations, however, were cut almost by half at the beginning of the 1990s due to the fiscal crisis. But there have been other kinds of advances. Operation Amazon launched in this decade includes measures to prevent illegal burning and to destroy illegal runways. Largely in response to NGO concerns and demands, new policies included the elimination of subsidies for cattle ranching and cash crops as well as other tax incentives that encouraged deforestation. In addition, some of the state governments have invested in basic sanitation and river cleanup projects. The Brazilian government also increased support for research, including that carried out by domestic NGOs.

NGOs proposed and had a central role in arranging the debt-for-nature swaps. There was open hostility in Brazil to this program at the outset, and Mexico also expressed suspicion because the Mexican government envisioned both negative monetary effects and a larger degree of involvement of NNGOs. The latters' demand to have the choice over the specific area to protect and their rejection of the Costa Rican proposal to establish a countrywide conservation fund with that money was not well received by the national government. However, all three countries eventually accepted the programs.

NGOs and Policy Implementation

Implementation of policies has varied from country to country and among policy areas, though broadly speaking, in Mexico, Costa Rica and Brazil environmental legislation lack adequate enforcement mechanisms. Although NGOs participated more fully in Costa Rica and Brazil, those governments were not necessarily more efficient in the implementation of policies. Costa Rica was better able to implement policies, but major gains were confined to the core of protected lands.

Although state control over the economy is still quite strong in Brazil, the federal government capacity to enforce laws has been progressively undermined. When the Mexican government decided to improve the enforcement of its laws, it was relatively more successful than Brazil.[45] The Mexican government showed expediency when responding to U.S. NGO demands during NAFTA negotiations.

However, some of the measures, including those related to species conservation—hurriedly taken in the face of external demands—did not always consider potential negative effects on people. The resulting damage was extensive. Mexico still has a long way to go to achieve an adequate degree of environmental protection.

By means of the new institutions, NGOs gained a few more points of access at this stage of the political process. The ability to monitor activities has allowed them to halt altogether—or at least press for the modification of—large, potentially damaging infrastructures and tourist development projects.

In Brazil, for example, in addition to the well-publicized megaprojects such as the POLONOROESTE migration project or the Carajás mining project, NGOs successfully opposed several projects, including the placement of the São Paulo International Airport, initially planned for Caucaia do Alto. Similar successes occurred with road projects in the Mexican Southeast and on large tourist projects on the Costa Rican and Mexican coasts. LNGOs are more systematically demanding environmental impact assessments for new activities and the enforcement of norms. However, some domestic NGOs complain that the NNGOs request that LNGOs professionalize and take charge of specific projects has reduced their capacity to work as effective watchdogs.

CONCLUSION

Transnational linkages have increased the leverage of NNGOs in their countries and strengthened LNGOs' internal resources, helping them to broaden their internal scope of action. Transnational NGO activity has influenced Latin American environmental policies. NNGOs' leverage increased when they were able to introduce the environmental issue into the development and trade agenda. Evidence also suggests that the broadening of NGOs access to the decision-making process in these countries was influenced by governments' interest in maintaining an image of civilized, democratic nations.

Transnational relations for NGOs have not been easy. NNGOs' paternalism was resented by LNGOs, and suspicion about the ultimate objectives occasionally emerged. NGOs share a general objective, and they support the idea of sustainable development. However, their vision on crucial issues, such as the relationship between environmental protection and development or trade, is not homogeneous. Although many NNGOs are changing their stance on social justice or equity, they are still more conservationist than most LNGOs, as it became evident during UNCED. This encouraged the search for South-South linkages and in the future could lead to deeper divergences in priorities. Trust building has advanced but cleavages are still there. It also appears that environmentalism has not strongly undermined loyalties to the state.

Linkages between NGOs helped to prevent or reduce nationalistic reactions and to legitimize Latin American government responses to foreign demands, contributing to a higher degree of political responsiveness. But they have also made the process of objective priority setting difficult. Some environmental problems have been put aside in order to face others that, although important, are not vital for sensible environmental protection or which may have unexpected negative impacts. For example, species conservation measures, hurriedly implemented in response to external pressure, have not always taken into account potential negative effects on people, and the damage caused has not been insignificant.

It is noteworthy that NNGOs' influence over policy in Latin America has not always been the product of joint action with domestic NGOs. In fact, many of the changes experienced since the early 1980s resulted from NNGOs pressure, especially on the U.S. government or on multilateral organizations. NNGOs sometimes acted independently and at other times with the support of their southern counterparts. In their first lobbying efforts, NNGOs tended to act independently; later they realized that their leverage in their own countries or in international organizations would increase by incorporating NGOs from Latin America, although they reverted to acting alone when they considered it to be in their interest to do so.

In summary, the unified action of LNGOs and NNGOs has had a limited impact on policy changes regarding tropical forest and biodiversity protection in Latin America and on environmental commitments in NAFTA. There have indeed been changes in policy, although more limited than NNGOs expected and their successful politicization of the issue would suggest. Latin American governments and societies have not completely abandoned developmentalist ideas, but there is an effort to incorporate the most urgent environmental concerns; the idea of sustainable development is now being debated in several sectors. Environmental awareness, improved research, and policy changes can have significant impacts in the long run. Broader access for NGOs could enable them to play a larger role in the future. But advancing toward adequate environmental protection requires careful priority setting to maximize limited internal resources—human, financial, and technical—and perseverance, rather than costly symbolic measures introduced to please foreign demands, however sensible they may sound.

NOTES

1. Steven E. Sanderson, "Policies without Politics: Environmental Affairs in OECD—Latin American Relations in the 1990s," in Jonathan Hartlyn et al., *The United States and Latin America in the 1990s: Beyond the Cold War* (Chapel Hill: University of North Carolina Press, 1992).

2. Approaches to the complex interaction between domestic and international forces, including "inner direct linkages," were highlighted in Peter Gourevitch, "The Second Image Reversed: The International Sources of Domestic Policies," *International Organization* 32, no. 4 (Fall 1978): 881–912.

3. Andrew Hurrell, "A Crisis of Ecological Viability? Global Environmental Change and the Nation State," *Political Studies* 42 (Special Issue, 1994): 146–165, esp. p. 151.

4. According to this approach, political opportunity structures can encourage or restrain the capacity of social movements to engage in protest activity in several ways. Herbert P. Kitschelt, "Political Opportunity Structures and Political Protest: Anti-Nuclear Movements in Four Democracies," *British Journal of Political Science* 16, no. 57 (1985): 59–60, 62.

5. Alison Van Rooy, "The Altruistic Lobbyists: The Influence of Non-Governmental Organisations on Development Policy in Canada and Britain" (D. Phil. diss., University of Oxford, 1994), p. 12.

6. The exception would be outright occupation by a foreign country. Gourevitch, "The Second Image Reversed," p. 911.

7. See Andrew Hurrell and Benedict Kingsbury, "The International Sources of Domestic Policy: Brazilian Policy Making in an Interdependent World" (unpublished paper); and Kathryn Sikkink, "Human Rights, Principled Issue-Networks, and Sovereignty in Latin America," *International Organization* 47, no. 3 (1993): 411–441.

8. Andrew Hurrell, "The Politics of Amazonian Deforestation," *Journal of Latin American Studies* 23, no. 1 (February 1991): 197–215.

9. Data came from a variety of sources, including personal interviews by the author with more than fifty people in all three countries, many of whom were well-known members of NGOs, government officials, members of the environmental commissions of congresses, and scholars. The author also interviewed a handful of officials of international organizations.

10. Barbara J. Bramble and Gareth Porter, "Non-Governmental Organizations and the Making of U.S. International Environmental Policy," in Andrew Hurrell and Benedict Kingsbury, eds., *The International Politics of the Environment* (Oxford: Clarendon Press, 1992), pp. 318, 323.

11. Alvaro Umaña and Katrina Brandon, "Inventing Institutions for Conservation: Lessons from Costa Rica, U.S.," Overseas Development Council, *Third World Policy Perspectives*, no. 17 (New Brunswick, NJ: Transaction Publishers, 1992), p. 87.

12. For example, Allston Jenkins, from the Philadelphia Conservation League, proposed the creation of a national park service to the Costa Rican government. Mario Boza, who had been trained in the United States, and Alvaro Ugalde agreed to head the project. Ibid., p. 10.

13. Ibid., p. 87.

14. Although NC typically involves itself only in the training of fund-raising techniques, the presidents of that U.S. NGO and others participated in the campaign by inviting large donors for dinners to introduce Costa Rican officials. For a detailed history, see David Rains Wallace, *The Quetzal and the Macaw: The Story of Costa Rica's National Parks* (San Francisco: Sierra Club Books, 1992).

15. Some considered Costa Rica to be a "laboratory for innovative scientific research." Anne Hambleton, "A Survey of United States Government Funded Activities Supporting Biodiversity Research and Conservation in Costa Rica" (unpublished document, San José, U.S. AID, January 1994).

16. Roberto P. Güimaraes, *The Ecopolitics of Development in the Third World: Politics and Environment in Brazil* (Boulder, CO: Lynne Rienner Publishers, 1992), p. 100.

17. Eduardo J. Viola's chapter in this volume mentions that Brazilian ENGOs grew from forty in 1980 to 900 in 1990. Also see Eduardo Gudynas, "Los múltiples verdes del ambientalismo latinoamericano," *Nueva Sociedad* 122 (November–December 1992), p. 110; and María Pilar García-Guadilla and Jutta Blauert, "Environmental Social Movements in Latin

America and Europe: Challenging Development and Democracy," *International Journal of Sociology and Social Policy* 12, nos. 4, 5, 6, and 7 (1992).

18. Recent data in Mexico mention 130 ENGOs in the Federal District and 330 in the remainder of the country. There are also, respectively, 75 and 156 legal advisory institutions (*consultorías*). See *Directorio Verde* (Mexico City: SEDESOL/INE, 1994); Enrique Leff and Juan Manuel Sandoval, eds., *Movimientos sociales y medio ambiente. Memoria de la primera reunión nacional sobre movimientos sociales y medio ambiente* (Mexico City: Justo Sierra Program, Universidad Nacional Autónma de México, 1985); and Enrique Leff, "El movimiento ecologista-ambientalista en México," in María Pilar García-Guadilla, ed., *Ambiente, estado y sociedad* (Caracas: Centro de Estudios del Desarrollo, Universidad Simón Bolívar, 1991), pp. 397–408.

19. See Edith Kurzinger Wiemman et al., *Política ambiental en México. El papel de las organizaciones no gubernamentales* (Mexico City: Fundación Friedrich Ebert, 1991), p. 139.

20. See, for example, Umaña and Brandon, "Inventing Institutions for Conservation," p. 9.

21. See Chapter 7 in this volume.

22. Bramble and Porter, "Non-Governmental Organizations and the Making of U.S. International Environmental Policy," p. 325.

23. Hurrell, "The Politics of Amazonian Deforestation."

24. Margaret Keck and Kathryn Sikkink, "International Issue Networks in the Environment and Human Rights" (paper prepared for the XVII International Congress of the Latin American Studies Association, Los Angeles, September 24–27, 1992), p. 25.

25. Bramble and Porter, "Non-Governmental Organizations and the Making of U.S. International Environmental Policy," pp. 332ff.

26. Keck and Sikkink, "International Issue Networks in the Environment and Human Rights," pp. 22ff.

27. Oxford Analytica, *Latin America in Perspective* (Boston: Houghton Mifflin Co., 1991), p. 274.

28. Bramble and Porter, "Non-Governmental Organizations and the Making of U.S. International Environmental Policy," p. 348.

29. Gabriel Quadri de la Torre, "Una breve crónica del ecologismo en México," *Ciencias* (journal published by the Ecology Center, Universidad Nacional Autónma de México, special number 4, July 1990): 56–64.

30. Sjur Kasa, "Environmental Reforms in Brazilian Amazonia Under Collor and Sarney: Explaining Some Contrasts" (working paper, Center for International Climate and Energy Research, Oslo, 1993): p. 6.

31. For a summary of border problems, see Roberto Sánchez Rodríguez, *El medio ambiente como fuente de conflicto en la relación binacional México-Estados Unidos* (Tijuana, Mexico: El Colegio de la Frontera Norte, 1990).

32. Debase, A.C./Grupo de Estudios Ambientales, A.C., *El Foro Mexicano de la Sociedad Civil para Rio 92. Sistematización de una experiencia organizativa. Síntesis Documental 1–3*, (Mexico: Debase, A.C./Grupo de Estudios Ambientales, A.C., 1992).

33. Mary R. Kelly, Dick Kamp, Michael Gregory, and Jan Rich, "U.S.-Mexico Free Trade Negotiations and the Environment: Exploring the Issues," *Columbia Journal of World Business* 26, no. 2 (Summer 1991): 42–58; and Roberto Sánchez, "El Tratado de Libre Comercio en América del Norte y el medio ambiente de la frontera," *Frontera Norte* 3, no. 6 (1991): 5–28.

34. Blanca Torres, "El medio ambiente en la relación bilateral México-Estados Unidos," in Gustavo Vega, ed., *Liberación económica y libre comercio en América del Norte* (Mexico City: El Colegio de México, 1993), pp. 335–346.

35. Bramble and Porter, "Non-Governmental Organizations and the Making of U.S. International Environmental Policy," p. 321.

36. Hurrell, *The International Sources of Domestic Policies.*

37. Kasa, "Environmental Reforms in Brazilian Amazonia Under Collor and Sarney."

38. Andrew Hurrell, "Brazil and the International Politics of Amazonian Deforestation," in Hurrell and Kingsbury, eds., *The International Politics of the Environment.*

39. Kasa, "Environmental Reforms in Brazilian Amazonia Under Collor and Sarney."

40. In January 1995, the SEDESOL mandate for environmental protection was transferred to a new secretariat, which is also in charge of fishing. Although large, it may not for some time attain the level of influence previously held by SEDESOL.

41. Umaña and Brandon, "Inventing Institutions for Conservation," p. 91.

42. The agreements are the North American Agreement on Environmental Cooperation between the Government of the United Mexican States, the Government of Canada, and the Government of the United States of America and the Agreement Between the Government of the United States of America and the Government of the United Mexican States Concerning the Establishment of a Border Environment Cooperation Commission and a North American Development Bank.

43. Enrique Leff, ed., *Medio ambiente y desarrollo en México* (Mexico City: Centro de Investigaciones Interdisciplinarias en Humanidades, Universidad Nacional Autónma de México, 1990); Stephen C. Mumme, Richard Bath, and Valerie J. Asseto, "Political Development and Environmental Policy in Mexico," *Latin American Research Review* 23, no. 1 (1988): 7–34; Stephen Mumme, "System Maintenance and Environmental Reform in Mexico: Salinas's Preemptive Strategy," *Latin American Perspectives* 19 (1992), pp. 123–143; and Antonio Azuela de la Cueva, "Políticas ambientales e instituciones territoriales en México," in Antonio Azuela de la Cueva, Julia Carabias, Enrique Provencio, and Gabriel Quadri, eds., *Desarrollo sustentable: Hacia una política ambiental* (Mexico City: Coordinación de Humanidades, Universidad Nacional Autónma de México, 1994), pp. 83–104.

44. Alberto Székely, "Establishing a Region for Ecological Cooperation in North America," *International Transboundary Resources Center* 32 (Summer 1992).

45. For example, during NAFTA negotiations, the government was able to improve law enforcement. Temporary or permanent plant closures increased, stricter measures were taken, and more funds were rapidly allocated to the protection of lands and species that were of the greatest concern to U.S. NGOs.

PART THREE

Comparative Cases From Other Regions

CHAPTER NINE

■

Environmental Policy Making in Southern Africa: Learning the Hard Way

Larry A. Swatuk

Cooperation is a highly prized commodity. It enables policy makers to avoid conflict over issues, and it often leads to effective public policy. Moreover, capability for cooperation can be acquired over time: in other words, international actors can learn to cooperate on the basis of experience. And as Ernest B. Haas tells us, "changing perceptions of values and interests among actors are associated with changed behavior, though not in obedience to any pattern of rationality imputed or imposed by the observer. There is no fixed 'national interest' and no 'optimal regime.'"[1] Similarly, I would argue, there are neither fixed interests nor optimal ways of organizing inter- and intra state behaviors on issues of the environment and development. Positions change as information changes.

In recognition of such relationships, this essay examines two cases of "learning" to cooperate on environmental policy making. The first presents an overview of environmental policy making in Zimbabwe. It is centrally concerned with understanding the dynamics behind decisions on water-resource use in this landlocked, drought-plagued, Southern African state. The evidence suggests that Zimbabweans are struggling to cooperate on water-resource issues, but the needs for industrial and large-scale agricultural development as defined by state-makers and business elites continue to determine the agenda and dominate decisions taken.

The second case explores policy making in apartheid and post-apartheid South Africa. It focuses on the continuing conflict between the need for jobs and industrial development and the desire for ecological conservation. The evidence here suggests that, as in Zimbabwe, there is an attempt to open up the decision-making process and to listen to all sides of the debate. Also like Zimbabwe, however, it remains painfully clear that those most seriously affected by decisions over resource allocation and use are the least able to articulate their needs and grievances.

This chapter seeks to go beyond description toward prescription. It suggests that in spite of the countless barriers, there is evidence that cooperation on environmental issues in Third World states can occur and is, in fact, occurring. Granted, these are very small steps. But Southern Africa, like most of the Third World, faces daunting challenges: How can it overcome its marginal place in the global economy? How can it overcome the legacy of uneven and race-based capitalist development? How can it learn to cooperate now on environmental issues before being overtaken by them later?

States in the region cannot go forward alone. Each requires assistance from the global community on issues such as debt forgiveness, increased access to markets in the North for exports, and technical assistance and technology transfer (so that accurate data can be gathered and better decisions be made). But Southern African states also need to learn to cooperate now so as to avoid conflict later. Disputes over resource allocation and usage are currently limited to intrastate levels; there is no guarantee of their containment in the future.

ENVIRONMENTAL POLICY MAKING IN
HISTORICAL AND GLOBAL CONTEXT

Environmental policy making in Southern Africa has evolved much as it has in most of the rest of the world: haphazardly, on a state-centric basis, in top-down fashion and usually only after past practices were identified as having created severe problems.[2] More often than not, the resulting policy has led to conflict. This is because when we speak of environmental policy, we are really talking of two things: the allocation and the usage of natural, often scarce, resources. Environmental policy making throughout the world is a highly politicized and problematic endeavor; it is especially so in the Third World. Environmental management—the operational outcome of policy formulation and implementation—historically has been the preserve of the colonial masters. To be sure, in the post-World War II period this management paraded behind the label of "development." But, given the legacy of colonial and settler societies dispossessing indigenous people of land and blocking access to natural resources, "environmental management" in all its forms—conservation and national-parks creation, industrial and agricultural development, land tenure and zoning policies—is a term that leaves a bitter taste in the mouths of most people living in the Third World. Southern Africa is no exception. Indeed, the history of environmental policy making and management in the region "is one of policing of natural resources and criminalizing their illegal harvesting."[3] According to Sam Moyo et al., "To this day, for many African farmers conservation has not shed unpopular associations with coercion and restriction."[4]

Environmental management must also be understood in the context of capitalist development. Like the rest of the Third World, Southern Africa was incorporated into the emerging global economy of the late nineteenth century as a provider of raw materials and precious metals for markets and industries in developed countries. South Africa, with its gold, diamonds, uranium, titanium, and countless other precious and strategic metals, has held a privileged place in the global economy among underdeveloped African states. Indeed, many white South Africans deny the fact that their country is part of the Third World.

Yet, as can be seen in Table 9.1, South Africa's economic and social indicators read very much like any other Third World state, with one exception: The misery of the majority has facilitated the emergence of a highly privileged, mostly white, elite. Zimbabwe resembles South Africa on a much smaller scale.

Like all emerging states, so-called infant industries in Zimbabwe and South Africa were protected by high tariff barriers and coddled by the state. In addition, the development of indigenous industry and agriculture in both countries was boosted by the imposition of international sanctions against what were once considered to be brutal, racist regimes.

Following the coming of majority rule in Zimbabwe in 1980 and in South Africa in 1994, each state enjoyed a "honeymoon" period with Western donors. It quickly became clear, however, that global economic norms and factors would de-

TABLE 9.1   South Africa and Zimbabwe: Social and Economic Indicators

Indicator	Zimbabwe	South Africa
Population (Millions)	10.7	39.7
Per Capita GNP (1993 US$)	520	2,980
Per Capita GNP Growth (% for 1980–1993)	−0.3	−0.2
Life Expectancy at Birth	53	63
Total Debt (1993 millions US$)	4,168	63,600
Debt/Export Ratio (1991)	164.9	78.3
Human Development Index	0.539	0.705

SOURCE: Africa Institute of South Africa, *South Africa in Sub-Equatorial Africa: Economic Interaction* (Pretoria: Africa Institute, 1994); World Bank, *World Development Report 1995* (Washington: World Bank, 1995); United Nations Development Programme (UNDP), *Africa 2000 Network Zimbabwe: Annual Report 1993* (Harare: UNDP AF2N, 1994); and SARDC (Southern African Research and Documentation Centre), *Southern African Environmental Issues No.7: Water*, CEP Factsheet, 1994.

termine the degree to which each state could remake itself. For example, Zimbabwe, under Robert Mugabe, tried for nine years to institute fundamental changes regarding land use and allocation. Little was achieved. The global financial community argued that radical changes, however fair, were luxuries unaffordable to a debt-distressed, primary-commodity producing country like Zimbabwe. In late 1989, suffering also from the century's worst drought, Zimbabwe was forced to sign onto a structural adjustment program with the World Bank and the International Monetary Fund (IMF).[5]

South Africa is currently facing similar constraints. In attempting to implement its Reconstruction and Development Program (RDP), the Government of National Unity (GNU) has rushed headlong into the logic of neoclassical economics. So, in spite of the need for housing, potable water, sanitation, education, primary health care, and a fairer distribution of land and resources (85 percent of the people still reside on 15 percent of the land), the international financial community continues to warn South Africa that it must balance its budget and maintain a tight monetary policy. Less than two years into office, the GNU has already been reduced to tinkering at the margins.[6]

BEARING A TRIPLE BURDEN

In such an unwelcoming and unforgiving context, reconstruction and development, let alone environmental policy making, is extremely difficult. South Africa and Zimbabwe, like their Southern African Development Community (SADC) partners, bear a triple burden: first, the legacy of race-based and highly uneven capitalist development; second, the contemporary context of a global economy obsessed with monetarism and marketization; third, the emerging and demanding global norms about sustainable development.[7]

Under race-based and uneven capitalist development, the vast majority of South Africans have been displaced from their traditional homelands, alienated from their families by becoming migrant laborers, impoverished, and dehumanized; in the meantime, a wealthy white elite has enjoyed unfettered access to the region's natural resources. This dichotomy results in extensive environmental and human degradation through the reassertion of diseases such as tuberculosis, cholera, and bilharzia; through desertification due to overgrazing, overstocking, and overuse of fuelwood; through siltation of dams and riverbeds due to soil runoff from unsustainable agricultural practices; and in water and air pollution through the use of pesticides, toxic waste dumping, and inadequate controls on industrial emissions (to name but a handful of the problems of underdevelopment in South and Southern Africa).[8]

The global economic context makes it virtually impossible to address seriously any of these problems. Radical change is needed to alleviate the human misery of township, homeland, and squatter camp. Radical change is needed to control the virtually free hand of white-owned industry and agriculture that causes the over-exploitation of human and natural resources.

To be sure, the governments of Zimbabwe and South Africa are well aware of the changes necessary. This awareness has been articulated at the national level, through a series of five-year development plans in Zimbabwe; through the 1994 publication of the Reconstruction and Development Program in South Africa; and through the establishment of National Environmental Councils or Commissions in both countries. At the regional level, these governments have maintained membership in the SADC, which is working, in part, toward the establishment of a common position on and approach to sustainable development.[9] Notably, this includes the August 1995 signing by SADC member states of the Protocol on Shared Watercourse Systems.[10] And, awareness is demonstrated at the continental level by support for the African Ministerial Conference on Environment, which presented an African common position at the United Nations Conference on Environment and Development in 1992. However, monetarism and marketization favor the "haves" over the "have-nots" and ensure that unsustainable industrial and agricultural practices will continue unabated as debt-distressed governments seek foreign exchange.[11]

Last, as the case studies will show, the need for jobs and for continued exploitation of the natural environment contends with an emerging global norm that seeks to limit the capacity of Third World governments and peoples to do as their First World counterparts have historically done.

THE ROLE OF THE INTERNATIONAL ENVIRONMENTAL COMMUNITY

The search for development, sustainable or otherwise, in the context of this triple burden is an elusive quest. Nevertheless, the search continues, and there exists a positive role to be played by international environmental and development-oriented inter-governmental organizations (IGOs) and nongovernmental organizations (NGOs). The global trend toward talking about, if not always practicing, sustainable development has forced racist, exploitative, and often unscrupulous corporate and political elites in Southern Africa toward some sort of environmental accountability.[12]

In South Africa, decades of struggle against apartheid have resulted in a vocal and well-organized civil society. In the discussion of St. Lucia and Saldanha Bay later in this chapter, it will be seen that domestic forces, periodically assisted by international NGOs like Greenpeace, can be very effective in getting government and industry to learn new and more sustainable behavior. In Zimbabwe, civil society is less well developed.[13] Relatively inarticulate, under-empowered, and only partially formed social organizations must align themselves with more powerful global organizations, such as the United Nations Development Programme

(UNDP), the World Wide Fund for Nature (WWFN), and the International Union for the Conservation of Nature (IUCN). Together they have persuaded government and business to address and respond to environmental concerns. As seen in the case of Zimbabwe, these alliances, however nascent, offer hope for the future.

Although Zimbabwe and South Africa provide fertile testing grounds for building broad-based coalitions around sustainable development, there is a continuing tendency toward top-down decision making, particularly on development issues. The unequal distribution of resources, continuing problems with debt and economic decline, and a historical preference for the *pater familias* state inhibits policy makers from learning new methods of governance. As the case studies show, however, "elite-pacting" decisions only raise the ire of local groups and ensure the long-term failure of "delivered-development"—as opposed to grassroots-developed—projects. In the absence of social cost calculations and considerations, environmental policy making will continue to be marred by conflict rather than cooperation.

EVOLVING NATIONAL INSTITUTIONAL FRAMEWORKS IN ZIMBABWE

Until 1980, Zimbabwe was known as Rhodesia and was ruled by white settlers who, like their South African counterparts, had stripped indigenous peoples of the best lands and crowded them on to reserves. As farmers, white Rhodesians were concerned with land and water resources. These farmers, or *voortrekkers*, were drawn by the seemingly endless fertility of the soil. By the early twentieth century, however, severe erosion set in. Thus, the first environmental policy came in response to a crisis on white-held lands. In 1929, a conservation unit was established within the Division of Agriculture and Lands to deal with the problem of erosion.[14] For the next fifty years environmentalism was tantamount to the conservation and preservation of land for nearly exclusive use of whites for agricultural and, later, industrial purposes.[15] Indeed, the 1951 Native Land Husbandry Act sought not to improve the quality of land on which indigenous people dwelled but to further restrict their access to lands beyond the increasingly degraded reserves.

Not until 1981 and the advent of black majority rule did the government create a national development plan to redress the severe imbalances in resource access, allocation, and use. Inequalities remain severe today; indeed, after nearly a decade of structural adjustment, the gap between the haves and have-nots has widened. More equitable and sustainable forms of economic development remain unrealized. In addition to the global and historical factors, the domestic policy-making environment in Zimbabwe contributes significantly toward maintenance of the status quo. The state machinery is highly complex, rife with contradiction, too often corrupt, and generally lacking in human and financial capacity.

For example, water-resource decisions involve more than a dozen federal government departments (Water Resources and Development, Natural Resources, Wildlife), ministries (Agriculture, Energy, Finance, Mining, Tourism, Trade and Industry), and parastatals (Zambezi River Authority, Zimbabwe Electricity Supply Authority). These compete with each other and with district and city councils, individual members of parliament, NGOs, various trusts, representatives of agribusiness (tea, tobacco, forestry) and industry (mining, manufacturing), and an interested and extensive donor community.

The lack of transparency in the quasi-authoritarian government of Robert Mugabe does not encourage understanding of how decisions emerge out of this morass. What is clear, however, is that historically well-served interests (business and industry) command the lion's share of resources and are best able to reach influential people in forceful and persuasive fashion. In addition, the government of Zimbabwe's standing policy on the pursuit of self-sufficiency in key sectors (for example, food and energy) continues to privilege those ministries centrally concerned with power generation and food supply. They, in turn, favor overly technocratic and capital-intensive solutions, thus facilitating something of a corporatist alliance. As will be seen below, negatively affected communities must fight hard just to be heard.

FROM LAKE KARIBA TO THE OSBORNE DAM: FAILING TO LEARN

In a land-locked country inhabiting a region that chronically suffers prolonged periods of drought, decisions regarding water resources are high politics. Zimbabwe has no indigenous lakes. There are, however, roughly 8000 impoundments, of which 150 (besides Kariba) are considered to be large, defined as over one hectare in area. Of the total water consumed in Zimbabwe, over 90 percent goes to agriculture. Ironically, "because the pumping costs to areas with good agricultural potential would be prohibitive, almost no agricultural use is made of [the Kariba Dam]."[16] However, Kariba, like other large dams, was constructed primarily for hydroelectric power generation. At the same time, Lake Kariba forms one of the major tourist attractions in Zimbabwe. It is therefore a highly valued foreign-exchange earner, and contributes significantly to Zimbabwe's gross national and domestic products (GNP and GDP).

Dam construction, however, is not always so successful or so sustainable. In almost all cases, the social costs of construction, particularly where indigenous peoples are to be uprooted and resettled, are very high. Many Third World countries, however, tend to gloss over the social costs of dam construction and to overvalue hydroelectric generation, tourism, and other water-related industries. In fact, the vast majority of dams constructed are unusable after fifteen to twenty years.[17] Therefore, in assessing whether or not dam construction is ecologically, socially, and economically viable, an open dialogue among all affected and interested parties should ensue. Historically, this has not been the case. The potential for conflict at and around proposed dam sites, due in large measure to top-down types of agreements, remains severe.

The case of the Tonga shows how important lessons have been ignored. The Tonga, who numbered about 86,000 people, farmed the Gwembe Valley, producing two rain-fed or floodwater-fed crops per year. Fishing for consumption and barter was conducted along the banks and floodplains of the Zambezi River.[18] As H. M. Masundire points out, "the socio-economic life of the Tonga was intimately linked to the Zambezi valley." Resettlement took place between 1956 and 1959. The Tonga were forcibly moved to higher ground "with poor soils and terrain which was unsuitable for agriculture."[19] In all, roughly 45,000 people were resettled. According to C. Machena: "There was no compensation from the government. Agricultural risk became very high and even today drought and malnutrition are a continuous situation that the Tonga must face. In addition to loss of agricultural land, their social pattern was disrupted and there was a permanent barrier from their Zambian relatives. It was hoped, however, that the development of a fishery would at least absorb some of the displaced populations."[20] What was once a sustainable society has since developed into an impoverished *bantustan* on the margins of a major tourist center.[21]

Yet, these kinds of decisions continue to be handed down. Hundreds of families were displaced without adequate compensation prior to the construction of the Manyuchi Dam in the Mwenezi District of Masvingo Province. And the recently completed Osborne Dam, situated on the Odzi River 30 km northwest of Mutare in Manicaland Province, has displaced 1600 families.[22]

The desire for hydroelectric power is compelling and ultimately overwhelming. The provision of power for industrial development, the prospect of a steady source of foreign exchange (deriving from, for example, the sale of hydroelectric power, fish exports, and tourism, among other things), and the creation of numerous jobs in seriously debt-distressed national economies, are clearly hard to resist. Large-scale dam construction, in spite of localized negative effects and controversy, is likely to continue into the foreseeable future. There is only one option for civil society—engagement, not disparagement.

FROM ZACPLAN TO BATOKA GORGE: FAILING TO LISTEN

Engaging the state, however, does not necessarily mean that its representatives will listen. This is particularly so with regard to international waterways, where "high politics" tends to preempt or upstage state-civil society relations. In Southern Africa, the development of the Zambezi River Action Plan (Zacplan) is one such case.

The Zambezi is the fourth largest river basin in Africa, flowing eastward 3,000 km from its source on the Central African Plateau. It is shared by eight countries, and for some of these countries, like Zambia and Zimbabwe, it is the principal water source. Surface water resources include river systems, swamps (e.g., the Okavango, which is 26,750 km²; Kafue, which is 7,000 km²; and the Lubanga, which is 2,600 km²), and lakes, both natural and manmade. Groundwater resources are also numerous and varied.[23]

Thirty percent of the total population of the eight basin countries, in other words, 20 million people, live within the river basin. In the four main basin countries—Malawi, Mozambique, Zambia, Zimbabwe—the total rises to 94 percent of their total populations living in 79 percent of the total basin area.[24] Major industrial sectors exist in these countries: metal manufacturing, machinery, textiles, clothing, footwear, fertilizers, pesticides, chemicals, pharmaceuticals, furniture, plastic and rubber goods, cement, and food processing. Among the main water consumers and polluters are the coal and aluminum industries. According to Lazlo, "the negative effects of mining and industrial development are many. Worth mentioning are overexploitation of natural resources and pollution."[25]

In 1985, the UN, through its Environmentally Sound Management of Inland Waters Programme, established a working group to explore interstate cooperation on the sustainable use of the Zambezi River Basin. Myriad problems were identified—for example, inadequate monitoring, soil erosion, deforestation, lack of potable water and sanitation, lack of community participation, inadequate protection of wetlands, inadequate dissemination of information to the public— and Zacplan was formulated as an action program of SADC. The Southern African Research and Development Center (SARDC) wrote: "[SADC] initiated discussions among its members to preempt possible conflicts over sharing of Zambezi river water, or any other shared water bodies in the region. Started in 1985 as the Zambezi River Action Plan . . . discussion on ways to share water equitably among the Zambezi river states has grown into a draft treaty among all SADC members governing any shared watercourse in the SADC region."[26]

There are four major components of Zacplan, each comprising numerous subcomponents: (1) environmental assessment; (2) environmental management; (3) environmental legislation; and (4) supporting measures.[27] According to SARDC, "the treaty will be an important step for SADC. With several countries eyeing the Zambezi waters thirstily and other water-rich countries considering international trade in water, the potential exists for mutually beneficial cooperation."[28] At the international level, then, it seems that there is indeed a concerted effort borne of necessity to address in a consensus-building fashion the needs of the region. However, according to Tabeth Matiza, Zacplan is a failure not only because it ignores extant social needs and problems of rural basin communities but also because it exacerbates them.[29]

In its formulation, Zacplan was a government-controlled project where NGOs had no voice and stakeholders were not consulted. Interstate cooperation on

River Basin management paves the way for more Kariba-type solutions, including the marginalization of indigenous voices from the negotiating process and, ultimately, of peoples from the land. To this day, thousands of marginalized peasants practice small-scale gold panning throughout the basin area, particularly in north and northeastern Zimbabwe. This causes serious problems not only of erosion but of violent conflict—as internal migration pits individuals from beyond the district against indigenous peoples—and of AIDS, alcoholism, and accidental deaths when river banks collapse and bury panners.[30]

At the same time, plans by Zimbabwe and Zambia to construct a new hydropower station at Batoka Gorge, which runs between Victoria Falls and Kariba along the Zambezi River, have raised the interest of state and non-state actors around the world. Many people are concerned about the impact of this project on the falls. In Zambia's case, however, the possibility of an additional source of foreign exchange seems overwhelming. Jowie Mwiinga writes: "The state-run Zambia Electricity Supply Corporation (Zesco) and the Zimbabwe Electricty Supply Authority (Zesa) are determined to see that the project is implemented. 'I believe this investment is justified and has as much significance as the copper mines,' Zesco managing director Robinson Mwansa said. Mwansa said the station would earn Zambia much needed convertible currencies through power exports to Zimbabwe and other neighboring countries."[31]

The importance of water for regional cooperation is manifold. Its use involves people and institutions that transcend state boundaries and narrow, often narrowly scientific, perspectives. No longer, then, can people be satisfied with leaving Zambezi River management to Zesco and Zesa. It is imperative that a broad-based dialogue be encouraged around water-resource use.

TOWARD A BROAD-BASED DIALOGUE

It would seem that where water resources are concerned, particularly in a part of the world that suffers both chronic water shortage and highly skewed capitalist development, the state-capital coalition (a coalition that many define as "corporatist") invariably wins the day. However, there is some evidence from Zimbabwe that this may not always be the case.[32]

Dialogue has become a key element in several instances of water-resource use. Most often discussion involves international, high-profile groups (like IUCN and UNDP), which support an array of unorganized and underfunded community-based organizations. They do so by pushing states toward inclusion and negotiation rather than exclusion and confrontation and by lobbying for direct participation of community-based organizations at all levels of the policy-making process (including, in many cases, a central position for rural women in that process).[33]

Recent experience concerning the rehabilitation of the Save River catchment provides some evidence for this. The catchment extends over 4.2 million hectares, covers roughly 10 percent of Zimbabwe's land surface, and contains the country's major interior river. The river itself runs nearly 400 km from the central watershed to southeastern Zimbabwe and into Mozambique. According to Bruce N. Campbell, the Save River "encompasses about 20 percent of all the cultivated land in commercial lands of Zimbabwe and has 40 percent of the communal land population. The Save River is of national importance in Zimbabwe's agricultural development as it forms the basis of several of the major irrigation schemes in the country, notably those at middle Save and Chisumbanje. The southeast lowveld of Zimbabwe has the best potential for extensive irrigation development in the country."[34] However, in recent years the river system has "suffered from excessive siltation caused by increasing population pressure and the associated problems of deforestation, overgrazing, stream bank cultivation and soil erosion induced by poor land management."[35]

In mid-1994, the IUCN convened a seminar on the Save River catchment that attempted to address popular grievances over the manner in which problems and issues were being handled by government. The seminar would mark, it was hoped, an initial step toward establishing a broad-based dialogue concerning resuscitation of the river. Up until then, action on the Save had been marred by an elitist approach. For example, the UNDP through its *Africa 2000* program compiled two studies focusing on the need to involve indigenous peoples in the decision-making process and to approach resuscitation of the catchment on a regional basis, including Mozambique. These were presented to the Zimbabwe government, but the government made no response.[36]

As with Zacplan, governments still perceive other parties, legitimate though their interests may be, as competitors, not partners. So for example, problems of erosion and siltation due to streambank cultivation were supposedly solved by forcibly removing small-scale farmers from the area. The Save River rehabilitation scheme has entirely failed to address loss of woodland cover due to overcrowding on communal lands.

The seminar, in contrast, saw eighty-six groups represented, including many representatives from Zimbabwean-based local communities, the international donor community, conservationists in Zimbabwe and elements of the corporate sector representing low-veld sugar estates.[37] Little progress has been made beyond establishing a "catchment coordinating body." According to the IUCN, local involvement in the catchment area remains limited. However, without intervention from international actors like the IUCN and the UNDP, draconian state measures would have remained the order of the day. Here, then, is an inkling of change.

The IUCN intends to organize more of these types of meetings, particularly at the regional level, with one of the main aims being to encourage interracial and intraregional dialogue. [38] With the movement of white South African farmers into parts of western Mozambique and recent discussions about transnational game-parks management, the Save River seminar seems an important first step toward finding solutions to water-resource problems amenable to all interested parties.

CONSERVATION AND POLICY
MAKING IN SOUTH AFRICA

The history of conservation in South Africa is similar to that of Zimbabwe. Since the mid-nineteenth century, conservation policy and practice served racially exclusive needs. According to Koch, during the colonial period:

> Conservationist legislation was diametrically opposed to the holistic relationship between people and their environment that had generally characterized the culture of most indigenous African societies. Crop and livestock farming by local peoples were seen as "unnatural" and ecologically unsound. . . . Subsistence hunters became defined as "poachers"—often by the very same settler population that had once relied on this form of economic activity for its survival. The emergence of paramilitary conservation authorities, funded by the state and devoted to the armed policing of protected areas under their control, was a logical outcome of this preservationist way of conceiving the relationship between man and nature.[39]

Beyond Conservation

In the late twentieth century, this approach is no longer feasible. Resource conservation today must recognize that (1) economic growth is a driving concern of business, labor, and government; (2) as populations grow and make more demands on government, scarce resources will be utilized; and (3) conservation in its "traditional" sense is outdated and unrealizable. Indeed, given the legacies of racial domination in Southern Africa, it is essential that historical approaches to conservation be rejected as viable forms of natural resource management.

Ecological conservation has too long been associated with the marginalization of local communities from their lands and resources:[40] "If conservation means losing water rights, losing grazing and arable land and being dumped in a resettlement area without even the most rudimentary infrastructure and services, as was the case when the Tembe elephant park [near Kosi Bay] was declared in 1983 . . . this can only promote a vigorous "anti-conservation" ideology amongst the rural community of South Africa."[41]

Increasingly, where governments take decisions without consulting local communities, conflicts ensue; and, in the cases of conservation-area or national-parks creation, adverse impacts materialize: relocation of indigenous peoples, restricted access by indigenous peoples to park resources, disruption of traditional life often including a decline in traditional patterns of authority and reciprocity, and widespread hostility leading to the setting of fires, vandalism, and resource poaching.[42] In South Africa, conservation policy has long been a nexus of violent conflict.

Exclusionary practices may be coming to an end. As suggested below, in an openly democratic era there seems to be increasing willingness on the part of government to enter into broad-based dialogue with individuals and groups affected by potential policy directions. Also, in the case of South Africa, although the central government sets the overall framework for environmental policy planning, nothing is fixed in stone. The capacity of government to oversee all decisions is limited by the legacy of apartheid's numerous overlapping institutions. State and society are in transition, their interrelations are robust, and, like Zimbabwe, the policy-making community is complex and heterogeneous. Unlike Robert Mugabe's well-entrenched, corrupt, and somewhat corporatist leadership, Nelson Mandela's government continues to feel its way and to profess allegiance to the have-nots of society. There is much scope for policy to be initiated from the bottom-up, or, as in the Saldanha Bay case, for a seemingly straight-forward provincial government decision on industrial site rezoning to be transformed into a national debate on the relationship between regional economic growth and the overarching national goal of sustainable development.

In the case of conservation policy, the central state, particularly through the Ministry for Environment and Tourism, the Council for the Environment, and the National Parks Board, is meant to deal efficiently and effectively with questions of policy formulation, implementation and regulation. Such clearly articulated and streamlined decision making does not, in fact, exist. Indeed, so destructive was the legacy of apartheid decision making—from lack of transparency to unabashed collusion with environmentally unfriendly business and industry—that the post-apartheid state finds itself overwhelmed by the policy-making context. In the past, the state dealt with confusion with a heavy hand. At present, it is trying to listen to the needs and demands of all sections of the population.

POPULAR PARTICIPATION AND COMMUNITY-BASED ORGANIZATIONS: THE CASE OF ST. LUCIA

Despite progress, debates over natural-resource use continue to be dominated by those with the time and capital to devote to these issues. The multiyear debate over proposed mining of the dunes north of St. Lucia along South Africa's east coast is one example. Involved in this dispute were, on the one hand, Richards Bay Minerals (RBM), which sought to mine titanium in an area considered by many to be worthy of World Heritage Site status, and on the other hand, a number of environmental and labor groups either permanently or temporarily opposed to the plan. The issue first arose in the latter part of 1989 and was temporarily resolved four years later when an independent tribunal headed by Justice R. N. Leon found in favor of the environmentalists and decided to ban mining from St. Lucia. According to an International Research and Development Council (IRDC) sponsored study: "The St. Lucia wetland area comprises an estuary, a string of lakes and wildlife reserves, and is the cutflow point of a number of Natal's rivers. For almost a century, its wildlife areas have been managed by the Natal Parks Board, the complex of terrestrial, estuarine and marine systems include rare mangrove forests, turtle breeding areas, tropical forest systems, and coral reefs."[43]

RBM was keen to strip-mine titanium over a 1400 km² section of St. Lucia's dunes. The site seemed ideal: RBM already had a large mine and processing plant 25 km south of the dunes at Richards Bay Harbour. Moreover, its supporters argued, location of the mine in South Africa would allow the Republic to monopolize world supply of titanium.[44] (Titanium is used in the construction of military aircraft and weaponry, more specifically in the production of durable and lightweight aircraft skins and war-head coatings, and as a substitute for lead in paint.) Reserves of the strategic mineral were said to be worth R5 billion and the government revenues to be derived worth R1 billion. The site had been chosen over similar sites in the United States and Madagascar, in part because anti-mining environmental lobby groups had pressured the company to look elsewhere.

To many observers the mine seemed a fait accompli. The prospect of large foreign currency earnings for the government coupled with the strategic content of the product seeming to overshadow more "mundane" considerations of environmental conservation. Nevertheless, once the issue became public, a formidable coalition of environmentalists emerged to argue against mining and in favor of eco-tourism.

This confrontation must be understood in its global context, given that notions of eco-tourism became fashionable in the late 1980s, particularly in response to the widespread deforestation of Amazonia in Brazil. Indeed, South African environmental groups adopted global tactics in the fight against RBM. First, they attempted to have St. Lucia's dunes declared a World Heritage Site along the lines of the Okavango Delta in Botswana. Second, they turned to the Ramsar Convention on Wetlands and its designation of St. Lucia as an area of extreme biological diversity worthy of preservation. And third, they argued not only for conservation of the dunes area but for the practice of "sustainable development," a concept that had gained international notoriety following the 1987 publication of the Brundtland Commission's Report, *Our Common Future*.[45]

These emerging global norms and ideals, particularly that of sustainable development, combined with white South Africa's abiding interest in conservation, worked to turn informed public opinion against RBM. At the same time, under South Africa's system of Integrated Environmental Management, an environmental impact assessment (EIA) was commissioned for St. Lucia and carried out by the parastatal Council for Scientific and Industrial Research.[46] The study that emerged is widely regarded as a landmark in the struggle for sustainable development and as a step away from a mineral-based mentality in South Africa. It considered two options: mining in combination with some eco-tourism (favored by RBM), and eco-tourism only (favored by the environmental lobby).

The conservationists fought RBM not only in terms of the mine's capacity to spoil the environment but also in terms of what kind of economic development would be most profitable in the long term for the St. Lucia area. Tourists come to South Africa, it was argued, first and foremost for the flora and fauna. Tourism is very big business, bringing in an average 1.7 million visitors per year (in the pre-1994 period), directly employing 300,000 people (in other words, 1 out of every 14 "actively employed" South Africans), and generating R2.5 billion in foreign exchange per year. With an end to violence in the post-apartheid era, tourism's contribution to GDP will be larger than the mining sector. Moreover, tourism, and in particular eco-tourism, is an industry with an unlimited shelf-life. In contrast, mining involves the stripping of assets that are eventually exhausted. At St. Lucia, operation of the mine and its eventual rehabilitation would commence after 2000 and last for only 20 years.

As the issue dragged on, each side became more sophisticated in its argumentation and approach. Business in general had been feeling the heat in the period just before the 1992 UNCED meeting in Rio de Janeiro, Brazil. In October 1991, business leaders from South Africa, Botswana, Lesotho, Swaziland, Namibia, Zambia, Zimbabwe, and Kenya gathered in Cape Town for the first Southern African International Conference on Environmental Management (SAICEM I). SAICEM is now a regular event. Within South Africa, the Industrial Environmental Forum was created to bring together representatives from the country's top businesses.

Among environmentalists, the Group for Environmental Monitoring (GEM) emerged as the premier think tank for progressives. Two of its members, Jacklyn Cock, a professor of sociology, and Eddie Koch, a well-known journalist, published an influential and award-winning book *Going Green: People, Politics and the Environment in South Africa*. Another important 1991 book, *Green at the Grassroots: Politics and the Environment in South Africa,* was written by two labor leaders, Rod Crompton of the Chemical Workers Industrial Union and Alex Erwin of the National Union of Metalworkers.

In January 1993, the National Union of Mineworkers (NUM) announced a compromise position. In the short term they stood opposed to mining of the dunes. In the longer term, however, they suggested that mining may have to go ahead. Their decision was based, in part, on the desire to see the issue put before a post-apartheid government and thereby be reexamined in a more equitable context.[47] However, since there remained substantial differences of opinion within both NUM and the ANC, neither actor could make a definitive intervention. Indeed, according to the IDRC, "whilst ANC economists favored the mining option, President Nelson Mandela was one of 40,000 signatories who favored protecting the dunes."[48]

In March 1993, RBM released information outlining the benefits of a mixed mining and eco-tourism approach. In their 1989 claims, RBM stated simply that 130 jobs would be created, R1 billion in government revenues would be generated, and the mining company would contribute R8 million per year to "social responsibility programmes." In the post-Rio era, they were more sophisticated in their calculations:

> Mining combined with eco-tourism will generate R460 million for RBM as well as R196 million for the Natal Parks Board from tourism activities. This option will create more than 900 temporary and permanent jobs, 613 in the mining operations as

well as up to 392 posts in the tourism industry. The new mine will indirectly generate between 1275 and 4675 jobs through the multiplier effect, pay R157.1 million to the government in tax and earn R606 million in forex. The company will also spend R8 million on social upliftment programs in a region where poverty ranks with "the lower levels of the lower-income countries of the world."[49]

Supporters of the eco-tourism-only option came to see the EIA process as biased in favor of the mining option. For example, how could it be that during the scoping process the U.S. Embassy and the Atomic Energy Corporation were identified as "interested and affected parties" while indigenous peoples were completely ignored?[50] In September 1993, John Ledger, director of the Endangered Wildlife Trust, suggested that the environmental coalition face facts: At some point RBM would get the go-ahead, so it was imperative to think of a win-win situation in which members of the St. Lucia community could be involved in some form of sustainable eco-tourism.[51]

A continuing criticism of the EIA, in particular, and of the entire dialogue between business and the environmental lobby was that the voices and concerns of indigenous people were often considered irrelevant. Webster and Cock stated, "A criticism made by a number of commentators was that the views of only a small proportion of the South African public were presented in the Environmental Impact Report; that the views of local people had not been adequately reflected; that the attitudes of local communities needed to be canvassed and submitted to a Review panel. To address these concerns the Rural Liaison Program was subsequently established."[52] Yet, for Webster and Cock, this process "failed to achieve any deep and extensive process of consultation," having gone no further than "employed workers, traditional tribal authority structures, and one Inkatha official."[53]

To the surprise of almost everyone, the decision handed down by Justice Leon's Review Panel in December 1993 went in favor of the eco-tourism-only option. Environmentalists were amazed and delighted, and in spite of a promise by the Minister for Mineral and Energy Affairs to uphold the decision of the Review Panel, no decision was taken prior to the April 1994 election.

Although this decision obviously pleased environmentalists and the Natal Parks Board, David Fig, director of GEM, lamented the absence of communal groups from the decision-making process. Fig stated, "Unless local communities are given a full say, right from the start, in decisions about the different ways in which their land can be used for economic development it will be impossible to promote popular support for these projects."[54] The local community had sought return of the land for their own designated purposes.[55] At the same time, many community members, Natal Parks Board workers, and trade unionists favored development of the proposed mine and the jobs it would create. In the absence of popular participation in the decision-making process, Fig warned, "There is no doubt [the tribunal's decision on St. Lucia]. . . will be seen by these people as yet another autocratic decision to protect the rights of animals and wealthy tourists before those of ordinary people. They will resist it—and there is a grave possibility of violence." Ironically, new land dispensations introduced under the GNU suggest that those communities forcibly removed from the area in the 1960s may possess title to the affected land. The GNU is being "asked to reopen the Environmental Impact Assessment process and to widen the scope of participation."[56]

POST-APARTHEID "CONSERVATION": THE CASE OF SALDANHA BAY

Numerous parallels with the proposed mine at St. Lucia exist in the Western Cape, where Iscor hopes to build a R4.7 billion steel mill. The proposed site for the mill is "barely a kilometre away from Saldanha harbour" and environmentalists are concerned about the project's impact on the region's sensitive "Langebaan lagoon, the delicate Wetlands ecology and the local tourist industry."[57] The proposed project pits politicians and industrialists against environmentalists and local property owners concerned about groundwater pollution, the establishment of a serious eyesore in the form of a steel mill, and other conservationist issues. Missing from the debate, once again, are the voices of poor and working-class residents of the area. Policy options have been articulated in an either/or fashion: that is, either the development of the steel mill and pollution of the environment or the preservation of the environment and loss of over 4,000 temporary and several hundred permanent, jobs.[58] The initial decision, shrouded in secrecy, was taken at the top levels of business and government. Broad-based discussion and transparency were not initially on the agenda. Finally, as in the St. Lucia case, a tardy public outcry followed by a court injunction postponed construction of the mill, providing an opportunity to discuss its merits in a more inclusive and systematic way.

Like St. Lucia, the Saldanha Bay issue seemed to emerge out of nowhere— which gives some indication of how business is still conducted in post-apartheid South Africa. It rose to prominence following a May 1995 information meeting. Present were Naas Steenkamp, Chair of the Natal Parks Board; Johan Neethling, Director of the Western Cape Nature Conservation group; the Regional Planning Minister Lampie Fick; the Council for Scientific and Industrial Research EIA independent consultant John Raimondo; and chair of the Saldanha Steel Project Bernard Smith. At issue was the proposed May 31 target date for a rezoning decision that would alter the status of the Langebaan Lagoon from a conservation to an industrial site.

Several concerns were raised: What is the likelihood that groundwater will be polluted? What will be the visual impact (that is, how siting of the mill might affect Saldanha's sense of place)? What kinds of and how much hazardous waste will be produced? How will this waste be disposed of? Have any other sites been considered for the mill (e.g., a few kilometers inland from the harbour)?

Iscor was clearly uncomfortable with these questions, particularly because it had already ordered hundreds of millions of Rands worth of equipment. Wittedrift Trust, which owns property in the area, succeeded in postponing a decision by having an interdict drawn up that sought to have the matter "properly investigated by an independent board in terms of Section 15 (1) of the Environmental Conservation Act." The interdict asked the Western Cape government to hold back on a decision until the Cape Supreme Court decided if a probe was needed and if so, only after the probe was completed.

Bernard Smith attempted to mollify those bringing the grievance by promising to "draft a deed to set up an environmental monitoring trust with Saldanha Steel and outside role-players as trustees. The trust would establish a contractual right to apply 'certain sanctions' to the plant . . . 'if reasonable but demanding pollution criteria are exceeded.'"[59] Saldanha Steel, however, relied primarily on threats to take their money elsewhere, with Port Elizabeth in the Eastern Cape being the prime candidate.

The issue became tinged with the new "politics of regions" in post-apartheid South Africa.[60] The ANC, desperate for votes in the Western Cape, was keen to see jobs brought to the National Party-controlled region. At the same time, the Eastern Cape remains one of the poorest parts of the country and would welcome any new industry.[61] And, in the Saldanha area itself, those like ANC Member of Parliament Jenny Schreiner and mayor Ismael Nagardien, argued that the entire south west coast desperately needs development. Traditional forms of subsistence fishing had long been usurped by the big factory ships, so fishers were forced to work on farms for terrible wages to supplement already meager incomes. The mill's construction and permanent jobs were desperately needed, and those desiring a better life tended to favor development over conservation. According to Schreiner, "There is no pristine beauty anywhere in South Africa. It's a misconception to believe that people have left any part of the country untouched. Apartheid certainly did not touch it in a way that left if protected."[62]

For Schreiner, criticism of the proposed mill based on sense of place was not sufficient reason to stop it, particularly in the absence of a viable alternative. Ecotourism, she felt, was not such an alternative, because it added up to "a big zero" for local people.[63] Some, like Peter Mokaba, addressing the National Assembly environmental committee, questioned what he considered to be the "limited terms of reference."[64] Why simply address the question of the mill? Why not examine the potential environmental and social impacts of a total overhaul of the area, from expansion of the harbor to secondary industrial development?

In June 1995, Minister of Tourism and the Environment Dawie de Villiers appointed a board of inquiry to conduct another EIA. Antoine Geldenhuys and Richard Fuggle of the University of Cape Town were to chair the board. Opposing the steel mill was an international coalition that included, in addition to the Wittedrift Trust, the Cape Nature Conservation, the National Parks Board, the Wildlife Society, Earthlife Africa, the National Union of Metalworkers of South

Africa, and the World Wide Fund for Nature. As with St. Lucia, Saldanha Bay became a cause celèbre and was featured, among other places, on the South African Broadcasting Company program *Agenda* (which is similar to CBS's *Sixty Minutes* in the United States or CBC's *Fifth Estate* in Canada). The issue thus reached the masses.

Ultimately, the Cape Supreme Court barred a zoning decision until the board of inquiry had completed its EIA. Not to be outdone, however, Iscor provided a helicopter to ferry Water Affairs and Forestry Minister Kadar Asmal, Deputy Minister of Environmental Affairs Bantu Holomisa, the Provincial Planning Minister Lampie Fick, and the Provincial Finance Minister Kobus Meiring to Saldanha to meet with the mayor, residents, and property owners. Said Asmal, "Experts must be on tap, not on top."[65] Yet, as with St. Lucia, the issue continues to pit environmentalists who support conservation against capitalists who support development. Though both sides claim to speak for and support the needs of common people—jobs via eco-tourism versus jobs via steel processing—they tend to exclude those likely to be most seriously affected by construction of the mill. According to University of Cape Town Environmentalist Fareida Khan, "How many people are talking about the Saldanha mill? All you have right now are experts and environmentalists slugging it out. You never hear the views of ordinary people."[66] The issue was resolved in favor of the mill, and unlike St. Lucia the will of the common people, in alliance with big business, won out: Guaranteed job creation, no matter how few the jobs or how limited the terms of employment, from their point of view, is preferable to hypothesized benefits from eco-tourism.

INSTITUTIONALIZING DIALOGUE: SOCIAL IMPACT ASSESSMENT

Each of these South Africa-specific cases suggests that there is both space and hope for civil society, including community-based organizations, to effectively participate in decision-making processes on issues vital to their survival.[67] By extension, such developments bode well for similar kinds of dialogue to emerge regarding other regional and transnational resource development.[68]

To be sure, conflict is unavoidable, for resource use is ultimately about power relations. Yet conflict is not necessarily to be avoided. Where community-based interests threaten the interests of capital and/or the state, it has historically been the community that loses out.[69] An emphasis on technocratic and scientific approaches to development helps depoliticize highly political issues. The perceived "successes" of Zacplan as a model in interstate cooperation juxtaposed with the dire conditions among thousands of rural dwellers and gold panners highlighted earlier is a case in point.

There is therefore a need not merely for scientifically sound environmental impact assessments but also for social impact assessments. According to Derman and Whiteford, "Efforts to develop appropriate methodologies without confronting the political issues can only legitimize the projects, and ultimately, the status quo."[70] In the current Southern African context, however, to maintain the status quo is to maintain the road to ecological collapse and sociopolitical confrontation.

Through institutionalization of dialogue, conflict can be a transformative and positive force in development. According to Webster and Cock, a Social Impact Assessment (SIA): "is something of a hybrid: a method of policy analysis, a planning tool; an investigation of 'the social and cultural impact of development plans, programmes and projects'. . . It involves different research methods and techniques to investigate at least 4 major categories of impacts: demographic . . . socioeconomic . . . institutional . . . and community. SIA can provide better information for decision making."[71] For these authors, SIA can "provide a voice for indigenous communities who are most likely to be affected by a planned development but lack power and resources."[72] SIA, it seems, has inherent consensus building potential.

One should not overstate the positive possibilities inherent in SIAs. Popular participation is sometimes tantamount to cooptation of local elites by more powerful political and economic forces in society. Similarly, emancipatory actions taken in the name of the "community" may entrench inherently unequal social relations within that community, for example, between men and women.[73] Nevertheless, if we take cognizance of these sorts of issues and recognize the need to unbundle seemingly unitary terms—community, civil society—SIAs can help in assessing the conflict potential of specific kinds of developments. To entrench SIAs, along with EIAs, in development planning therefore is to move toward sustainable sorts of social endeavors and away from unsustainable and conflict-ridden practices.

CONCLUSION

This essay has presented a relatively limited picture of factors affecting cooperation in environmental policy making in two Southern African states. Nevertheless, there are important general points to be made that speak to the analytical concerns of this volume, some of which were outlined at the beginning of this chapter. These will be summarized in terms of (1) the impact of globalization on environmental concerns; (2) the role played by international, particularly financial, institutions; (3) the increasing importance of international and local NGOs in pursuit of sustainable development; (4) the fundamental importance of democratization in decision-making processes; and (5) the continuing problem of state incapacity to effectively manage the development process, coupled with an increased willingness to delegate power to those who can.

First, globalization is a multifaceted process. It presents contradictory effects upon and opportunities to Southern Africans in general and the region's policy makers in particular. On the one hand, it has brought the environment to center stage. In the cases discussed earlier this includes, among other things, a global constituency concerned with preservation of Africa's natural—as opposed to built—environment. International NGOs were instrumental in helping delay or sidetrack government-planned industrial development in both St. Lucia and Saldanha. They were also key in opening up discussion around proposed developments in the Zambezi River and Save River catchment areas. On the other hand, pressures for economic liberalization generally undermine conservationist concerns and measures. As seen above, international pressure for liberalization and debt repayment usually combines with a national desire for job creation and enhanced foreign-exchange-earning capacity to drive industrial development (for example, hydroelectricity schemes, mining, and steel mill developments). This may or may not run against popular, particularly local, opinion.

Second, this highlights the equally contradictory role played by international institutions in the development process. For example, while the World Bank and the UNDP continue to stress capacity building, particularly the ability to collect, store, and exchange information on the environment, they also tend to ignore or overlook both the potential impacts upon and the role of local communities in top-down decision-making processes. This has been most evident in the various Zambezi Basin initiatives that continually overemphasize the potential macro-contributions to development of enhanced electricity generation capacity and underemphasize the negative local, social impacts of such endeavors.

Third, international and local NGOs are finding common cause in pushing government, business, and industry to open up the decision-making process before decisions are taken. These may be odd alliances, with international NGOs pressing for environmental concerns and local NGOs and community-based organizations pressing for developmental concerns. These alliances can give rise to new concepts and approaches to sustainable development, as seen in the growing preference for "sustainable utilization," a compromise position between conservation and resource exploitation. This has been the case with rehabilitation of the Save River, where local and international NGOs have formed united and coordinated fronts against central government and have gained the cooperation of local district councils and federal Members of Parliament in the process. However, as in the Saldanha and St. Lucia cases, these forces found themselves at odds with one another.

Fourth, both the Zimbabwe and South Africa cases seem to suggest that such dialogue would not have been possible in a Cold War and apartheid context. Democratization, however varied its definition and practice in the region, has opened a space for communities and individuals to confront government particularly on issues of local resource use. In the Save and Saldanha cases, local city and district councils were enlisted by community groups in the fight for an open policy debate. In the Save case, these forces worked in alliance with local and international environmental NGOs. In the Saldanha case, they worked in opposition to them.

To be sure, community groups do not always win out. Indeed, the Batoka Gorge project is slated to proceed in spite of international and local protests. Nevertheless, more listening and learning—however slow—is taking place. These are positive, post-Cold War and post-apartheid developments.

This brings the summary to its fifth and final point. In an era of increased democratic governance, central-state incapacity seems to be leading toward devolution of policy making to local and district levels, particularly in those cases where local and district councils have clearly articulated their needs. Limited state capacity and contradictory international and domestic pressures led in the past either toward the status quo or the line of least resistance. The cases described in this chapter suggest that the line of least resistance, when that means popular participation and community empowerment, is the proper path to take.

These issues in almost every case transcend class, race, and state. They will continue to constitute sites of both cooperation and conflict. Formal institutional structures, like SIAs and EIAs, can foster dialogue and cooperation. SIAs can assess the gender, and other social implications of proposed projects.[74] EIAs can address their ecological sustainability; SIAs, their social-sustainability. It is imperative that proposed solutions seek to avoid zero-sum scenarios and search for variable and relatively equitable pay-offs. Stakeholders have different preference curves, so consensus and enhanced cooperation, though not easily achieved, in fact may be possible.

NOTES

1. Ernst B. Haas, "Words Can Hurt You: Who Said What to Whom About Regimes," in Stephen Krasner, ed., *International Regimes* (Ithaca, NY: Cornell University Press, 1983), p. 57.

2. For an overview, see Sam Moyo, Phil O'Keefe, and Michael Sill, eds., *The Southern African Environment: Profiles of the SADC State* (London: Earthscan, 1993).

3. SADC (South African Development Community), "The State of Southern Africa's Environment" (pre-publication draft, 1994 [see Chap. 3; box 3.2]).

4. Moyo, O'Keefe, and Sill, eds., *The Southern African Environment*, p. 308.

5. See Rob Davies, Phil Sanders, and Timothy Shaw, "Liberalization for Development: Zimbabwe's Adjustment Without the Fund," in Giovanni Andrea Cornia, Rolph van der Hoeven, and Thandika Mkandawire, eds., *Africa's Recovery in the 1990s: From Stagnation and Adjustment to Human Development* (New York: St. Martin's Press, 1992), pp. 135–155; and Howard P. Lehman, *Indebted Development: Strategic Bargaining and Economic Adjustment in the Third World* (London: Macmillan, 1993).

6. For a trenchant example of how neoliberal economic principles have insinuated themselves into the RDP, compare the organization itself with the RDP White Paper that emerged less than six months later. See African National Congress, *The Reconstruction and Development Programme* (Johannesberg: Umanyano Publications, 1994), pp. 2–4; and Government of South Africa, *RDP White Paper: Discussion Document* (Cape Town, South Africa: CTP, 1994).

7. Formed in 1980, and until 1992 called the Southern African Development Coordination Conference (SADCC), SADC's member states are Angola, Botswana, Lesotho, Malawi, Mozambique, Namibia, South Africa, Swaziland, Tanzania, Zambia and Zimbabwe. Namibia joined in 1990, South Africa in 1994, and Mauritius in 1995.

8. See SADC, "The State of Southern Africa's Environment"; Moyo, O'Keefe, and Sill, eds., *The Southern African Environment*; Jacklyn Cock and Eddie Koch, *Going Green: People, Politics and the Environment in South Africa* (Cape Town, South Africa: Oxford University Press, 1991); Mamphela Ramphele with Chris McDowell, eds., *Restoring the Land: Environment and Change in Post-Apartheid South Africa* (London: Panos, 1991); SADCC, *Sustaining Our Common Future* (special report for the UNCED Secretariat [Maseru, Lesotho: SADCC ELMS, October, 1991]).

9. See SADCC, *Sustaining Our Common Future*; SADC, "The State of Southern Africa's Environment."

10. SADC/IUCN/IMERCSA, "Water in Southern Africa" (final draft manuscript, Harare, 1996, chap 8).

11. For an insightful discussion of the global economic factors in Africa's environmental crisis, see Jennifer Clapp, "Global Economic Factors in Africa's Environmental Crisis" (prepublication draft in Amadu Sesay and Sola Ankinrinade, eds., *No Place to Hide: Africa in the Post-Cold War World: Essays in Honour of James Mayall*, forthcoming, 1996).

12. In terms of unscrupulous activity, the case of Thor Chemicals, a British multinational in South Africa, is perhaps the most widely known. In September 1990, it came to public attention that Thor Chemicals had imported 40 tons of mercury-based waste, mostly from American Cyanamid, 30 to 40 percent of which was "organic waste mercury." In the United States, it is illegal to recycle industrial material that has an organic waste content of more than 3 percent. Thor intended to recover the mercury for reuse. However, it was not until July 1993, following the death from mercury poisoning of a Thor employee, that the government decided to investigate. More than a year later, the government "had not yet decided on what course of action to take regarding evidence of alleged malpractice" by the company (according to the *Cape Times*, June 5, 1994).

13. For an informed and useful comparative analysis of civil society in South Africa and Zimbabwe, see Andre Du Toit, *State-Building and Democracy in Southern Africa: A Comparative Study of Botswana, South Africa and Zimbabwe* (Pretoria, South Africa: HSRC Publishers, 1995).

14. Moyo, O'Keefe, and Sill, eds., *The Southern African Environment.*

15. In the mid-1940s, land came to be categorized under the Natural Resource Act (1941) on the following basis: commercial farms, national parks, demarcated forest, urban expansion, mining, dumping and mine wastes, and flooding of reservoirs.

16. Moyo, O'Keefe, and Sill, eds., *The Southern African Environment*, p. 326.

17. H. M. Masundire, "Effects of Dam Building on Riverine Wetlands," in Tabeth Matiza and S.A. Crafter, eds., *Wetlands Ecology and Priorities for Conservation in Zimbabwe* (Gland, Switzerland: IUCN, 1994), pp. 87–102.

18. C. Machena, "Dam Developments and Their Environmental Effect: The Kariba Experience," in Tabeth Matiza and H. N. Chabwela, eds., *Wetlands Conservation Conference for Southern Africa: Proceedings of the SADCC Wetlands Conference* (Gland, Switzerland: IUCN, 1992), p. 28.

19. Masundire, "Effects of Dam Building on Riverine Wetlands," p. 97.

20. Machena 1994, p. 30.

21. Bantustans, also called "homelands," are native reserves to which indigenous peoples were forcibly moved from the 1950s through the 1970s as part of South Africa's and Rhodesia's policies of separate development.

22. *Herald* (Harare), July 15, 1994. A similar phenomenon has marked developments around the construction of the Katse Dam in Lesotho (Khabela Matlosa, interviewed by author, University of the Western Cape, Cape Town, June 1994). For a general discussion of costs and benefits of dam construction see also A.V.R. Massinga, "Dam Developments and Their Environmental Effects," in Matiza and Chabwela, eds., *Wetlands Conservation*, pp. 43–57.

23. David J. Lazlo, "Environmentally Sound Management of the Zambezi River Basin," *International Journal of Water Resources Management* 4, no. 2 (June, 1988): 81.

24. Ibid., p. 85.

25. Ibid., p. 88

26. SARDC, *Southern African Environmental Issues No.7: Water* (CEP Factsheet, 1994).

27. Ibid., pp. 92–102.

28. Ibid.

29. Interview with Tabeth Matiza, Harare, Zimbabwe, July 1994.

30. Ruth Marsh, New Zealand VSA, and Moyo-Mhlanga, UNDP (interviewed by author, Harare, Zimbabwe, July 21, 1994).

31. Jowie Mwiinga, "Environmentalists Oppose Power Project," *IPS Africa Environmental Bulletin* (1993): 7; See also *The Sunday Mail*, July 17, 1994; and Environment 2000, *Zambezi River Environment Project* (mimeograph, Harare, Zimbabwe, 1994).

32. Timothy M. Shaw, "South Africa: The Corporatist/Regionalist Conjuncture," *Third World Quarterly* 15, no. 2 (June, 1995): 243–256.

33. Moyo-Mhlanga, UNDP (interviewed by author, Harare, Zimbabwe, 1994).

34. Bruce M. Campbell, "The Environmental Status of the Save Catchment," in Matiza and Crafter, eds., *Wetlands Ecology and Priorities for Conservation in Zimbabwe*, p. 21–23.

35. Matiza and Chabwela, eds., *Wetlands Conservation Conference for Southern Africa*, p. 6.

36. Moyo-Mhlanga, UNDP (interviewed by author, Harare, Zimbabwe, 1994).

37. There were no representatives from Mozambican groups or farms at the seminar, though the Save/Runde floodplain borders on and extends into Mozambique.

38. Francois Droz, IUCN (interviewed by author, Harare, Zimbabwe, 1994).

39. Eddie Koch, "War and Peace: Changing Conservation Patterns in Southern Africa" (GEM [Group for Environmental Monitoring] Discussion Document, March 1995), p. 5.

40. Eddie Webster and Jacklyn Cock, "Looking Before They Leap: Environmental Impact Assessments and Social Impact Assessments" (unpublished paper, Johannesburg, South Africa, 1994). Webster and Cock theorize ways around this fact. One proposed solution is to introduce "social impact assessments" alongside "environmental impact assessments" when considering resource use.

41. *Weekly Mail and Guardian*, October 6–12, 1989. Anticonservationism or antienvironmentalism goes beyond the individual or community level. According to Barney Desai, senior member of the PAC, "For the majority of black states whose lives and aspirations are dictated by the struggle for survival, environmental considerations are regarded with indifference or hostility" (David Fig, quoted in the *Weekly Mail and Guardian*, November 16–22, 1990).

42. Webster and Cock, "Looking Before They Leap." Also, see the sectional, country-based discussions on "Resource Use Conflicts" in Moyo, O'Keefe, and Sill, eds., *The Southern African Environment.*

43. International Research and Development Council (IRDC) et al., "Environment, Reconstruction and Development in the New South Africa" (draft for discussion, August 15, 1994), p. 40.

44. RBM, which is jointly owned by Rio Tinto Zinc and by the local mining conglomerate Genmin, "is aiming to corner 25 percent of world market share. In anticipation of this, it has constructed a titanium smelting plant at Richard's Bay." See IRDC et al., "Environment, Reconstruction and Development in the New South Africa," p. 41.

45. Indeed, in the Environmental Conservation Act 1989 (73), which came to replace the earlier 1982 (100) Act, South African policy makers have clearly adopted the Brundtland Commission's definition of "sustainable development."

46. In 1982, the South African Council for the Environment was established under the terms of the Environmental Conservation Act 1982 (100). Among the council's executive committees and commissions is one concerned with Integrated Environmental Management, whose mandate is conservation and development. Conservation is defined as "management of man's use of the environment so that it may yield the greatest sustainable benefit to present generation while maintaining its potential to meet the needs and aspirations of future generations." Development is defined as "utilization of natural resources and the consequent modification of the environment by man to satisfy human needs and improve the quality of human life." The council considers conservation and development to be part of an integrated system of environmental management. See Government of South Africa, *White Paper: National Environmental Policy and Strategy* (Cape Town, South Africa: Government of South Africa, 1989), p. 7.

The Integrated Environmental Management system was established in 1984. It identifies three categories of proposed actions: policies, programs and projects. All proposed actions pass through four stages of development: (1) proposal generation; (2) assessment; (3) decision; and (4) implementation. Given that some proposals have more serious environmental implications than others, the system identifies three classes of assessment: (1) high impact; (2) some impact; and (3) negligible impact. The RBM proposal was clearly a class 1 proposal.

47. *Weekly Mail and Guardian*, January 22–28, 1993.

48. IDRC et al., "Environment, Reconstruction and Development in the New South Africa," p. 44.

49. *Weekly Mail and Guardian*, March 19–25, 1993.

50. Ibid., p. 41.

51. *Weekly Mail and Guardian*, September 17–23, 1993.

52. Eddie Webster and Jacklyn Cock, "Looking Before They Leap" (unpublished paper, Johannesburg, South Africa, 1994), p. 8.

53. Ibid., pp. 8–13.

54. *Weekly Mail and Guardian*, December 17–22, 1993.

55. The land to be mined was part of the traditional lands of the community that had been forcibly removed in the 1970s when the park was established. Clearly, indigenous peoples did not trust RBM, the Natal Parks Board that had failed to defend them against their earlier removal, or the EIA process.

56. IDRC et al., "Environment, Reconstruction and Development in the New South Africa," p. 42.

57. *Cape Times,* June 30, 1995.

58. *Weekly Mail and Guardian,* June 2–8, 1995.

59. *Cape Times,* May 31, 1995.

60. Roger Southall, "Levels of Understanding: Towards a Differentiated Canadian Perception of South Africa" (paper prepared for the symposium on "The 'New' South Africa in Africa and Its Implications for Canadian Foreign Policy," Halifax, Nova Scotia, October, 1995).

61. Southall provides the following data taken from a Development Bank of South Africa study: Although the Western Cape has a Human Development Index (HDI) of 0.76 and a real GDP of R15,772, comparable figures for the Northern Cape are 0.73 HDI and R2,727 GDP, and for the Eastern Cape they are 0.48 HDI and R3,788 (Ibid.).

62. *Weekly Mail and Guardian,* June 2–8, 1995.

63. *Weekly Mail and Guardian,* June 28, 1995

64. *Cape Times,* June 29, 1995.

65. Interview with Kadar Asmal, January 1996, Johannesberg, South Africa.

66. *Weekly Mail and Guardian,* June 2–8, 1995.

67. See the extended and informed discussions of community-based struggles around ecological problems in, for example, Cock and Koch, *Going Green*; Ramphele with McDowell, eds., *Restoring the Land*; and the GEM 1994 National Conference Proceedings.

68. There is much concern regarding the viability of creating transborder national parks, however. For example, South Africa, Zimbabwe, and Botswana have agreed to establish a transfrontier reserve along the Limpopo Border. Similar discussions have taken place regarding extension of the Kruger National Park into Mozambique. On paper, these seem to be relatively simple ways to enhance regional cooperation. In reality, however, the creation of such "super parks" impinges on the living spaces of indigenous peoples, a problem also experienced at the national level.

69. See Moyo, O'Keefe, and Sill, eds., *The Southern African Environment,* particularly pp. 299–301.

70. Quoted in Webster and Cock, "Looking Before They Leap," pp. 8–13.

71. Ibid., p. 8.

72. Ibid.

73. Ibid.

74. Ibid.

CHAPTER TEN

■

Environmental Degradation and Environmental Politics in the Former Soviet Union

Barbara Jancar-Webster

Perhaps no country elicits more international concern for its environmental future than Russia. A new state formed from the wreckage of an empire, Russia has inherited the severe environmental problems of its predecessor, the USSR, together with the socioeconomic, political, and administrative structures that in large part generated and perpetuated the problems. Since 1991, the country has been trying to transform an inefficient state-owned and state-managed economy into a market economy at the same time that its people are sorting out their lives in a more liberal—but not quite democratic—regime. This chapter attempts to show how the problems engendered and solutions undertaken during Soviet rule continue to hamper the development of a more efficient and effective response to environmental issues. While inadequate financing is a major impediment to serious implementation of new environmental regulations, the struggle on the part of former Communists to remain in power in the regional governments and in the Moscow governmental bureaucracies, the failure to privatize the centrally managed industrial monopolies, and the continuing ambivalence of the government toward all things Western have also contributed to the current inadequacies of the Russian environmental management system. In this unstable political climate, international assistance plays a critical role in sustaining Russia's fight against tremendous environmental odds.

The chapter will first look at the physical and sociopolitical environmental legacy of the former Soviet Union (FSU) and then show how indecision over jettisoning Soviet practice, and inexperience with democratic options now largely define Russia's environmental difficulties. The chapter concludes with a discussion of the importance of international efforts to assist Russia in tackling its environmental problems. It is hoped that the Russian experience may provide insights for Latin American countries into the problems and prospects a people faces when economic progress, necessary for integration into the global economy depends in turn on progress toward sustainable development.

THE LEGACY OF THE SOVIET PERIOD

Geographic and Spatial Aspects

The FSU covered a huge area that spanned thirteen time zones. It included the whole topographical spectrum: arctic tundra, northern forests, temperate forests, deserts, mountains, the *chernozem* or black-earth zone, Mediterranean climate around the Black Sea, and steppeland. A photograph of environmental degradation in that vast area would reveal severe pollution in highly concentrated areas interspersed with extensive open areas relatively free from human activity.

The last Soviet report on the environment, prepared for the UNCED Conference in 1992, utilized a new method of hierarchical classification of environmental degradation by zones and identified 300 with "very severe environmental conditions."[1] These areas covered 3.7 million square kilometers or 16 percent of the territory of the former USSR. If one includes the degradation of pasture, the amount rises to 20 percent. Based on this system of classification, 20 percent of the entire population and 39 percent of the urban population were judged to live in "unfavorable environmental conditions." (Some former Soviet experts say that as much as 60 percent of the population experienced these conditions.) Of the 300 areas, the report singles out sixteen "zones of ecological calamity." This most severe category of ecological degradation is defined as having a complex set of environmental problems produced by pollution emanating from huge industrial centers and the intensive consumption of natural resources. Many of these areas are further characterized by the siting of the metallurgy and petrochemical plants in large cities with huge concentrations of people. Leading the list were the Aral Sea and Chernobyl, followed by the Donbass coal basin and the industrial region of Dneprovodsk-Krivoi Rog now in Ukraine. At the bottom of the list is the Ust-Kamenogorsk region in eastern Kazakhstan, including the nuclear test site at Semipalatinsk.

The new state of Russia inherited all of these problems. It can divest itself of none, including those of Chernobyl and the Aral Sea beyond its borders. One of the most intractable environmental problems inherited by Russia is spatial. Today, as in the former Soviet Union, most energy and virtually all natural resources are in Siberia. Most industrial production takes place in the western part of Russia, necessitating the transport of Siberian energy over long distances. The Soviets attempted to mitigate this problem by building large industrial complexes in the east, an attempt that proved costly, destructive of resources, and inefficient in terms of labor and production. The 1960s and 1970s in particular saw the construction of large dams in the east and the promotion of nuclear power stations in the west. Both solutions proved disastrous, the former causing the inundation of 28 million acres of land, and latter prompting a devastating nuclear catastrophe.[2]

During the transition to democracy, conditions have continued to deteriorate at possibly a still more rapid rate due to the breakdown of governmental authority. The 1992 White Paper on environmental conditions in Russia cites 84 cities with at least 3 pollutants that exceed the legal norms by tenfold or more. The paradox is that because of the drop in industrial production, pollution is not statistically on the increase. A table drawn up by Philip Pryde, comparing 1992 with 1987 pollution data for the 20 Russian cities with the highest ambient air pollution, indicates that pollution has decreased in all cities except Norilsk, where pollution has increased by a modest 3.5 percent.[3]

The Socioeconomic and Administrative Legacy

The record of environmental degradation should not negate the considerable effort put forth by the successive Soviet governments to protect the country's fragile ecosystems. Under Soviet rule, vast open spaces were preserved and some kind of environmental protection activity characterized the rule of every Soviet leader from Lenin to Gorbachev. The Soviet period saw progress in the areas of conservation, legislation, the development of a Union-wide centralized management system, and the education of a corps of competent environmental scientists. Russia inherited these programmatic and institutional successes, along with the gigantic failures in implementation.

The reasons for the emergence of environmental tragedy during Soviet rule may be found in two areas. The first is common to all industrializing states: the failure to consider the economic value of resource use and environment protection. "Pollute now, ameliorate later" seems to be the universal pattern of industrial development. The second category relates to the specifics of Soviet industrialization.

The Soviet model of development was based on state ownership of the means of production and centralized planning. The five-year and one-year plans were legal documents that set explicit targets and production goals for each Soviet enterprise. Depending on its strategic significance, each enterprise was subordinated to either a Union-republic or Union ministry. Energy, weapons production, and the chemical industry were Union ministries. Wood processing, textiles, pulp and paper were Union-republic ministries. Every branch of the economy had a lead ministry that oversaw the operations of that branch. The result was a total absence of competition and the concentration in large metropolises of huge industrial complexes managed by a Union or Union-republic ministry. The size of these industrial monopolies, coupled with the permanent demand for their products, made them all-powerful at the local level, insensitive to the local needs, responsible only to bosses at the republican or all-Union level, and ultimately made them environmental time bombs. The larger cities contained many such complexes. Today, the largest of them all, Moscow, is the most polluted of the 126 most severely polluted cities in Russia.[4] This industrialization strategy directly led to the extremely high concentration of pollution in specific urban areas, a legacy inherited by Russia and the other newly independent states (NIS).

The reasons for the relative weakness of the Soviet pattern of environmental management arose as the result of eight general factors:[5]

1. Economic plans set goals and targets that were legally enforceable for all branches of the economy. But since every enterprise was state owned, there was no clear separation of functions. Frequently, one found producer-polluters and environmental monitors and enforcers in the same ministry.

2. Fragmentation of environmental responsibilities weakened management. For example, the Ministry of the Fishing Industry was responsible for fish conservation, the Ministry of Water Amelioration (MinVod) for water conservation, the forest agencies for forest conservation, and the petrochemical ministries for monitoring pollution in the oil and gas industry. With no external controls or system of outside reporting on these agencies, it was virtually impossible to determine either the extent to which environmental regulations were implemented or which agency had final authority in which area of environmental protection. Moreover, many agencies frequently had authority over the same environmental object.

3. Key branches of the economy were under central control. There was little or no opportunity for environmental considerations to come in, except at the very top of the planning process, where the Soviet leadership always gave priority to production targets.

4. The practice of industrial fiefdoms encouraged the wasteful use of raw materials. Absence of competition and monopoly of production eliminated incentives for greater efficiency, while the five-year agreements between enterprises and ministries on the quantity and quality of products sold and purchased made enterprise initiative in product reform totally irrelevant.

5. Soviet law required local government to monitor compliance with environmental standards and to take action against local polluters. The responsibility to draw up comprehensive local land use plans also fell to local government. But it was powerless to take on the ministries, with their economic and political connections in Moscow or the Union-republic capital and their huge financial resources allocated by the central government.

6. Toward the end of the Soviet period, pollution fines and charges for natural resource use, including water consumption, were introduced. But a study by Moscow University of a representative sample of enterprises located in the city found that if an enterprise had to pay over 9 percent of its planned profit in environmental remediation, it would go out of business. The Moscow environmental committee thus structured fines and penalties not to exceed 9 percent so that the

enterprise operation was never threatened, even though the enterprise was forbidden to include the cost of the fine in the price of its product.

7. The USSR was the leader among the former communist countries in establishing an environmental fund both at the federal and the local levels, using the fines and charges taken from industry. Because the fund came into being on the eve of the collapse of the USSR, we have no consistent data on how well the fund worked.

8. The absence of independent, organized, and experienced environmental nongovernmental organizations (ENGOs) also impeded effective environmental management in the FSU. Although the Soviet press reported sporadic protests by citizens groups against a polluting local activity, mass indignation and concern over environmental conditions did not really begin until after Chernobyl and Gorbachev's subsequent institution of glasnost. After 1986, environmental groups literally exploded all over the Soviet Union, numbering in the hundreds in Leningrad alone. Estimates indicate that as of March 1, 1992, shortly after the collapse of the Soviet Union, there were ninety one ENGOs in the Russian northwest alone and over one thousand in the territory of the USSR.[6] Among the Soviet nationalities and particularly in the republics, glasnost was quickly transformed into a demand for national independence. In many cases, in the interests of survival national environmental groups quickly took on the colors of the independence movements in the Union-republics in which they were located, particularly in the Baltics and the Ukraine. Even though the newly formed ENGOs played an important role in bringing down the Soviet regime, their role must be understood more as a vocal mass opposition to the tyranny of the central government in Moscow than as organized citizen activism aimed at remediating environmental problems. Independence movements were considered anti-Soviet up to the end of the FSU. Particularly in the union-republics, the environmental organizations became the screen behind which those fighting for national independence could hide.

ENVIRONMENTAL POLITICS AND MANAGEMENT
IN RUSSIA AFTER 1991

Russia inherited all the features of the old regime, including the fragmented environmental management system, political infighting and patronage within the one-party system, and a command economy. It also inherited the rising tide of nationalist sentiment during the last years of Gorbachev's administration. The abortive military putsch of August 1991 tried to reverse the conditions to the status quo ante and instead brought the Soviet Union to an end. The Union-republics were quick to follow Russia's example and declare independence. In December, the three new states of Belorus, Ukraine, and Russia formed the Commonwealth of Independent States.

The West heralded the unexpected demise of the Soviet Union and forecast the transformation of Russia into a democratic country with a market economy. Thus began the experiment euphemistically known as the transition: The transformation from a centrally planned command economy, managed by a single party elite that extended over the entire territory formed by the new states, into separate independent market-oriented democracies with sufficiently strong public and private institutions to handle social, economic, and political welfare issues that formerly had been the monopoly and responsibility of the ruling Communist elite in Moscow.

Systemic Problems of the Transition

In the first phase of the transition, the Communist party collapsed, and with it, its monopoly of political, social, and economic institutions. Old institutions remained fully staffed with no program and no public mandate. New institutions had to be created very rapidly. The economic adventurism of the Russia's new elites, coupled with the increasingly negative public attitudes toward government in general, augur poorly for the immediate future of environmental protection in Russia. The state-owned polluting complexes are still in business. The new entrepreneurs profess attitudes toward environmental protection that differ little from their Communist predecessors, while the lack of experienced, organized, and well-financed NGOs leaves the environment defenseless against further predation.

Perhaps the most destabilizing post-Soviet development has been the replacement of the defunct ideology of Communism with nationalism or neo-nationalism. The Russian government has tried to subdue the independence movements by dividing and conquering the opposition, or when that policy fails as it did in the Caucasus, by the use of force. Of particular concern are the environmental consequences resulting from the substitution of military campaigns for political solutions. So far there has been no official tally of the environmental cost of the war in Chechnya, where Russian military tactics have turned a poor and underdeveloped region into an environmental and economic wasteland.

The growing role of the Russian military in the conduct of government and in the determination of public policy is another feature of the transition period that influences the course of environmental protection. The post-Soviet Russian military is an institution divided against itself. With one hand, it works with the United States for a new nuclear nonproliferation agreement; with the other, it sells nuclear material to the highest bidder, using any available channel of transportation. The sale of weapons and plutonium-producing nuclear reactors to Iran is particularly disturbing. the demoralization of the Russian military introduces a fearful and unknown factor into domestic and global environmental affairs.

A final phenomenon of the transition that is especially relevant to contemporary Russian environmental politics is the lack of clear definition of (and agreement on) the terms of the new Russian federal bargain. Since 1991, power has steadily devolved from Moscow to the regional governments, all of which have proclaimed their autonomy and sovereignty. Because the central government has been increasingly unable to provide the subsidies to which the regions had been accustomed during the Soviet period, the transition made the rich regions richer and the poor regions—in the Russian far north, southern Siberia, the North Caucasus, and Pskov—much poorer.[7] In the attempt to reassert the authority of the central administration, Yeltsin has adopted policies designed to undercut the power of regional government.[8] The federal constitution, approved by referendum in December 1993, is a case in point. The more liberal press already speaks of new totalitarianism in the making.[9]

Much of the new policy may be interpreted as Moscow's attempt to secure Russian federal control over vital natural resources. The center-federal conflict negatively affects Russia's environmental future. With the collapse of strong, central administrative oversight of the environment, a region may promote or discourage environmental remediation, depending largely upon the character and interests of the regional leadership. As in the past, regional administrators tend to see production as the bottom line. For many, natural resources are the most abundant source of moneymaking. The environmental consequences of extracting these resources are secondary concerns.

The transition period has brought the average Russian citizen personal stress, heightened crime, increased economic deprivation, and political instability. Three years into the transition, Russia has yet to produce stable political institutions, to subordinate the armed forces to civilian power, to create a stable federal contract, or to dismantle the system of state-owned gigantic enterprises. The transition thus shares many of the features of the transitions from military to democratic rule that have occurred in Latin America. Given the Latin American experience of frequent shifts between the two types of regimes and the record of Russian history, the outcome of the Russian transition is far from certain.

Environmental Politics During the Transition

The transition's attendant chaos and turmoil have precluded any thoughts of restructuring the system of environmental management or any coherent attempt to tackle Russia's serious environmental problems. There is ample evidence that the environment has been relegated to second place. With inflation and the growing national debt, the Russian environmental ministry finds itself with less support from the new government than it had from the old. What is more, the public that mobilized in the thousands for the environment and helped bring down the Communist regimes has fragmented and disappeared, with each individual now concerned for his own survival. The problems of Russian environmental management are inseparable from the problems of the transition as a whole.

As the public health system has come under increasing stress from drastically reduced budgets and high inflation, monitoring and control have decreased. The result has been a rise in pollution-related diseases: salmonellosis (typhoid, food poisoning), diptheria, cancer, and tuberculosis. Since 1992, cholera has been reported in southern Russia and the Caucasus.[10] Life expectancy at birth had declined from 69 years in 1990 to only 67 years by 1993. During the same period, mortality in males from 40 to 44 years old had increased from 7.6 to 10.9 deaths per thousand; maternal mortality per 100,000 births went from 47.4 to 52; and infant mortality per 1,000 births from 17.4 to 18.8.[11] In 1994, official statistics registered a decrease in the total population in the federation, excluding migration, of 0.2 percent over 1993. Population decline was observed in 49 of Russia's provinces, as compared to 41 in 1992 and 33 in 1991. The number of births declined 13 percent, while deaths increased 18 percent.[12] At a conference on "Women, Ecology, and Politics" held in Moscow in June 1994, Russian doctors stepped up to the podium with extensive documentation on the deterioration of the health of women and children attributable to pollution, claiming the evidence proved that Russians were practicing eco-genocide upon themselves. Of the 300,000 people who were involved in cleanup operations after the Chernobyl accident, 1 out of 10 is said to be disabled, and 10,000 reportedly have died in Ukraine alone, although the exact figures are unknown.[13] Western newspapers report illegal trafficking in plutonium by Russian nationals in Germany, gigantic oil spills in the Russian northwest, and continuing environmental deterioration in the once-closed cities of the Urals.

Russian environmentalists are divided about the effects of the transition on the environment. There has been on-going tension between Aleksei Yablokov, former chair of the committee on Ecological Security of the Russian Security Council, and Viktor Danilov-Danilyan, the Minister of the Environment. Yablokov takes every public opportunity to hammer home the message that there is a near-catastrophic situation in the Russian environment. Danilov-Danilyan counters these attacks with data showing that pollution has not gotten worse and by enumerating environmental accomplishments in legislation and institution building.

The views represent the two sides of the critical question facing all the former communist countries, namely, whether it is possible to formulate and implement an effective environmental policy during the period of economic hardship, transition, and reform. Although as yet there is too little data to give a definitive answer, the question as it pertains to the transition per se appears to require an answer in the negative. But the groundwork is being laid for the development of an effective environmental policy when the transition ends. Criteria for laying this groundwork may be divided into four areas:

1. the degree to which the new management system builds on past Russian and Soviet experience, yet accommodates the development of democracy and a market economy, in constructing accurate pollution and natural resource degradation inventories and developing adequate data collection, monitoring, and inventory systems;

2. the way the conflict over management of natural resources is resolved between the center and the regions and between Russia and other NIS;

3. the outcome of programs developed domestically and with international cooperation to resolve the worst environmental hot spots inherited from the Soviet period; and

4. the completion of the transformation of environmental organizations from dissident, pseudo-legitimate opposition organizations to recognized, legitimate representatives of public environmental interests.

Policy Construction and Implementation

A closer look at the Yablokov/Danilov-Danilyan controversy reveals the extent to which Russian environmental professionals are divided on which direction to take in the restructuring of the environmental management system. Perhaps the most significant aspect of the public and political discussion about pollution is the division between those who believe that Russia's problems can be solved by incremental improvements of the former Soviet environmental management system and those who believe the Russian environment is in such a serious state of ecological devastation that a more radical approach is necessary. Such an approach should be based on Western legislative and environmental management practices.

What seems to be in progress in Russia is an environmental variant of the clash that divides elites in virtually all modernizing non-Western societies: namely, the extent to which Western values and practice can be imported to meet economic goals before the identity of a given state—as exemplified in its national beliefs, policies, and institutions—is destroyed. In Russia, the direction of economic reform has been debated by Slavophiles and Westernizers ever since the early nineteenth century.

The Russian Ministry of Environmental Protection and Natural Resources (Minpriroda) represents the Slavophile side of the debate. In his 1994 New Year report on the environmental situation in Russia, Danilov-Danilyan, the minister, said that by comparison with 1992 there had been no "substantive change" during 1993, although in his view, the situation in the country remained very serious. "Over 15 percent of the territory of Russia belongs in the category of 'zones of ecological calamity and deficiency'. . . Of 222 million hectares of arable land, almost one-half is not suitable for cultivation. Only a fifth of all the industrial toxic waste has been decontaminated. About 100,000 people live in regions with harmful radiation." Danilov-Danilyan attributed the continuing seriousness of the situation to lack of money. Because of the Russian budget deficit, the ministry received only 66.8 percent of its initial appropriation. It was thus unable to carry out a whole series of environmental protection measures.[14] Nevertheless, the minister assured the public that the ecological situation in Russia had not worsened in the past three years and that today one could be more optimistic than earlier. In his words, "we have the most dangerous areas under strict control."[15]

Minister Danilov-Danilyan's sober but optimistic report is contested by Yablokov, his most severe critic among the "Westernizers". According to Yablokov, the environmental situation in Russia is "catastrophic." His main concerns are the continued high level of solid contamination, including poisoning by radioactive isotopes, especially in the Moscow area; the rise in lawlessness and poaching that threatens endangered species such as the Amur Tiger; the pools of pollution resulting from the unchecked rupture of oil pipelines and drilling equipment; the serious pollution of Lake Baikal; the annihilation of traditional habitat of the indigenous Siberian peoples; and the rising threat of flooding due to widespread soil erosion. According to Yablokov, Russia's negative environmental situation shortens life by 30 percent, so that for every three years lived, pollution will decrease one's life expectancy by one year. He also deplores the reckless and increased tempo of the exploitation of natural resources, and he demands that the ministry carry out its mandate of ecological expertise to perform the requisite environmental impact studies on proposed new nuclear power plants.[16] Yablokov's criticisms end with a request for the resignation of the minister of Minpriroda if the latter is unable to carry out his functions.

Danilov-Danilyan's response to this attack on his integrity was energetic. He went to considerable lengths to refute the accusation that environmental degradation shortens life by 30 percent and to put his agency in the best light.[17]

The ongoing polemic between the two fathers of the first Russian "White Book" (the first *Annual Report on the Environmental Conditions and the State of Health in the Russian Federation*) is indicative of the degree of polarization of opinion among experts; and it is suggestive of the absence of both a singleness of will and institutional capability on the part of Minpriroda to take the requisite measures to improve Russia's environment. While Yablokov advocates change and borrowing from Western experience, the minister defends his more conventional Soviet-type organization. At stake is whether the weakness of the ministry is more properly attributable to the minister's continued adherence to the old ways of Soviet environmental management, as Yablokov suggests, or to attempts to transform the ministry into a Russian EPA without adequate funding, as Danilov-Danilyan might argue.

There is no doubt that the environmental budget has been gutted during the transition. For 1993, the Russian federal government set aside 37,100 million rubles for measures dealing with the consequences of the accident at Chernobyl and nuclear contamination at the test site of Semipalatinsk and in the Urals, but it provided no separate line for an environmental budget. By way of contrast, military expenses in 1992 were 751,695 million rubles, and the social-cultural budget was 439,601.5 million rubles.[18]

Beset by interagency strife and reduced budgets, the federation's environmental administration has nevertheless continued functioning. In December 1991, the Russian parliament passed a comprehensive environmental law that established a legal basis for natural resource use and stipulated that environmental protection in the Russian Federation would be regulated by law (Article 2, Section 1).[19] Another landmark law, on the Regulation of Natural Resources, was approved in 1993. If the legislation on environmental protection is fully implemented, it would provide an excellent framework for the rule of law in environmental matters. However, enabling legislation has been slow in coming, and it is an open question whether the law will be fully implemented in its present form. A final version must await the outcome of the struggle between administrations in all levels of government over jurisdiction and ownership of natural resources.

The environmental protection law clearly builds on past Soviet experience. The hierarchical organization of environmental protection, the continued practice inherited from the Soviet period of fining enterprises for within- and above-norm limit pollution emissions, the concept of an extra-budgetary ecological fund to finance environmental cleanup, and the related ideas of environmental responsibility and compensation for environmental damage—all basic components of the new law—either existed under Soviet law or were being developed prior to legal enactment before 1991.[20] Indeed, one of the chief criticisms of the 1991 law and the enabling legislation and regulations that followed it is that they make virtually no accommodation for the realities of a market economy. Environmental expertise (*ekologicheskaya ekspertiza*) continues to be the monopoly of Minpriroda, limits are set on the amount of above-norm fines an industry may be charged to ensure it an adequate profit so it will not go out of business, and damage assessments are far too low to encourage a firm to take precautionary environmental measures.

A second critical transfer from the Communist period has been the environmental management structure, which has remained virtually unchanged. As before, regional and local environmental committees are subordinated to the federal ministry in Moscow, and the federal ministry is responsible for appointments throughout the environmental administrative structure. Ministerial appointments have been a source of criticism. Critics have complained that the ministerial staff is bloated, particularly if one compares its numbers to the number of employees in the U.S. EPA. They further argue that the EPA does a more competent job with fewer employees than the does Russian ministry. Contested overlapping jurisdictions continue to be another area of concern. For example, there is an environmental committee subordinated to Minpriroda for the city of St. Petersburg, and there is the Leningrad *oblast* (county) environmental committee. Because of its size, St. Petersburg has been given status equal to the Leningrad *oblast*. Today, there is contentious debate over the enlargement of the port of St. Petersburg through the construction of new facilities on the Gulf of Finland. The city committee questions and the *oblast* committee endorses the environmental feasibility of constructing this new port. Tension between the two bodies has become a bureaucratic no-win hassle in which the environment is the loser.

The retention of Soviet institutional practice goes hand-in-hand with the increasingly visible growth of a new body of environmental law, based on Western

environmental management experience. Greater accommodation to the requirements of a developing democracy and a market economy may be found in the
1993 law on natural resource management, with its decentralization of management authority and sharing of revenues between the regions and the central government. (The provisions of the law are discussed somewhat more fully in the
section on relations between the center and the regions.) Pursuant to the Law on
the Protection of the Environment, the government issued important regulations
on, among other things, the Status of the State Environmental Commission and
the Measures of Economic Stimulation of Environmental Protection. Arbitration
courts at the local and regional levels are becoming active in the enforcement of
environmental law. In 1992, these courts reviewed about 6,000 cases, and viola-
tors were charged 2.8 billion rubles. Significantly, the number of environmental
cases involving local and regional courts appears to be growing. These indicators
would be high for the United States, but Russia is just starting to use courts for
environmental purposes. The main monitoring agency for the ministry and related environmental institutions, the Commission on Environmental Expertise,
has strengthened its position. In 1992 alone, the commission reviewed over
55,000 projects, approving without changes only 40 percent of them.

A recent case involving the copper-sulfur plant at Mednogorsk in the Urals is
worth noting. When the plant refused to compensate the damage caused by the
dumping of its wastes into the Dzereka River, the arbitration court of Orenburg
sent the case materials to the State Institute of Applied Ecology. After reviewing
them, the expert group at the institute deemed the plant was at a fault, and it had
to pay 26.6 million rubles, four times more than the amount originally assessed
by the local environmental protection committee.

Despite these developments, the legal profession as a whole has been slow to
take environmental cases to court, believing that they are neither significant nor
lucrative. However, change is coming here as well. A pioneering group of women
lawyers, Ecojuris, is fighting an uphill battle to get the courts to deal seriously with
infringements of environmental regulations or the failure of ministry professionals to perform adequate environmental impact statements (*ecologicheskaya
ekspertiza*). But Ecojuris' eight attorneys have shown extraordinary determination
and courage in representing environmental issues before the courts.

In 1993, Ecojuris won a landmark decision halting construction of Severnaya
TETS, a huge thermoelectric power plant north of Moscow. Construction work
had begun some time before 1991 but had progressed very slowly. Angry citizens
and local environmental groups expressed concern about the plant's projected
emissions of above-norm amounts of sulfur dioxide and nitrogen oxides, the impact of the plant's operations on an adjacent protected forest, and almost certain
contamination of the surrounding groundwater, which provided some of
Moscow's drinking water. Ecojuris argued that construction should be halted because the plant's developers had failed to obtain a positive "ekspertiza" from the
Moscow environmental committee. The court ordered that construction be

stopped, pending a new environmental impact review. As is frequently the case in such decisions, the developers ignored the court order and continued building. A suit for damage to natural resources is currently under consideration.[21]

Ecojuris has also been active in providing legal education and training to ENGOs, both in the drafting and analysis of environmental legislation and in four nuclear tort cases seeking compensation for soldiers, workers, and residents suffering illness allegedly associated with radiation exposure.

Federal-Regional Struggle over Management of Natural Resources

Among the most serious problems for effective environmental management in Russia today are the confrontation between the legislative and executive branches of government and the jockeying between the federal, regional, and local governments over ownership and management of natural resources. The decision by many of Russia's federated regions to declare themselves to be autonomous or sovereign in large part reflects the desire for sole control over natural resources rather than an ability to assume the costs and responsibilities associated with independent statehood. Tatarstan and Yakutia, or Sakhma, are cases in point. Since 1991, other regions also have tried to establish autonomy over natural resources within their territory. The administration of Sakhalin Island, for example, has sought control over the continental shelf off its shores, the Primorski has asked to be a special free economic zone, whereas the Nenets Autonomous Region has asked for separation from Arkhangelsk Province and the right to export 10 percent of all oil extracted from its territory.[22]

The new Law on the Earth's Interior (*o nedrakh*) attempts to meet the centrifugal pull of the regions. It goes a considerable way toward transforming the previous regime of resource utilization based on central control and administration to a decentralized system oriented toward a market economy. Under the new system, the state still owns the land, and the user receives a license for a specific parcel. The license comes with a written set of obligations and requirements regarding conservation and preservation of the environment to which the licensee is obliged to adhere, including how much may be extracted, the level of payments for extraction, the duration of the license, and a section on rights to geological information. Indicative of the more autonomous status of the localities and regions, the law allocates the distribution of royalties among the three levels of government. The allocation for hydrocarbon extraction is 30 percent to local government, 30 percent to the regional government, and 40 percent to the federal government. The allocation for other minerals provides for 70 percent to go to local government and 15 percent each to the other two. By contrast, the allocation of royalties for mining of the continental shelf assigns 60 percent to the federal government. The ability of the federal government to implement the new legislation depends on the degree to which it can be adapted to the current trend toward regionalism. But it is important that a new regime is in force.[23] There is considerable evidence of a severe breakdown in government control over land use. Russian scientist Zhores Medvedev writes about the plowing of the most "sacred" pieces of land for gardening, including the Napoleonic battlefield of Borodino and watershed protection areas.[24] The high-quality forests of the Primorski have suffered tremendous damage in the past few years, partly because of a three year drought and beetle infestation, and partly because of clear-cutting by foreign lumber companies.[25]

Cases of misuse of natural resources, valuable raw materials, and environmentally protected objects and areas are too numerous to be recorded here. In many instances, local administrations are actively involved in squandering these natural resources. The leading environmental periodical, *Zelenyi mir,* carries articles citing the willingness of the local authorities to disregard environmental considerations in order to enhance their own power. This tendency will doubtless continue until property rights are clearly defined and reliable mechanisms for their enforcement are established. In the new political climate in Russia, the role of local communities and individuals in the protection of the environment may increase only if the habitual pattern of seeking justice at the top of the government hierarchy is changed and if local communities are willing and able to accept responsibility for enforcing environmental standards.

Russians involved in the development of their country's vast natural resources are themselves divided over whether to keep investment and development in Russian hands or give foreign investors some control.[26] Russian bankers and the Federal Committee for Mineral Resources of the Russian Federation argue the advantages of a "Russia-only" strategy. Central to their argument is the belief that foreign capital sees in a weak Russia a "pollution haven," where natural resources may be exploited with little or no environmental constraints. By contrast, regional governments, private entrepreneurs, and the indigenous ethnic groups—like the Volga Tartars, the Nenets, or the Chechens—assert that foreign investment is essential for financial and technological reasons and for protecting the environment from further abuse.[27]

At the regional level, the turnover of environmental professionals has been very small. Most have retained their old jobs and continued their work as before. Some municipal environmental protection committees, particularly those of Moscow and Novosibirsk, have made a relatively easy transition to a more open polity and are determined to continue pressing city representatives and developers to stop environmental deterioration. On the negative side, the jurisdictional conflicts between St. Petersburg and Leningrad province have placed obstacles in the way of environmental amelioration there.

Because of its distance from Moscow and its reputation as the "last frontier" on the Eurasian continent, Siberia has generally been characterized by a more self-reliant, less bureaucratically minded population. This independence has translated into a do-it-yourself attitude among Siberian environmental personnel. During

an exchange of forest management experts in 1992 and 1993, U.S. Forestry officials were surprised by Siberian forest-service workers' autonomy from the central agency, especially as compared to the closer supervision by the U.S. Forestry
Service over its field workers.

While self-reliance is to be welcomed in many instances, the implementation of
an effective federal environmental policy requires consensus among central and
regional institutions on the division of jurisdictions and powers. Such consensus
has yet to be reached. The political conflict between the center and its parts has
been exacerbated by the conflict within the central environmental bureaucracies,
as noted earlier. Only time will tell what the final disposition of competences will
be. Now that regional differences have ignited into outright war, the Russian federal government can no longer expect ready acquiescence to its authority in any
region. In the non-Russian areas, hostility to Moscow is growing. If Moscow
wishes to lower the costs of maintaining its leading role in natural resource management, sooner or later it will have to recognize the reality of regional power and
private capital and adjust its administrative organization accordingly.

Environmental Hot Spots

The third area of concern relates to progress in environmental remediation itself,
namely, programs to resolve the worse environmental hot spots inherited from
the Soviet period; the completion of pollution and natural resource degradation
inventories; and the development of adequate data collection, monitoring, and
inventory systems. This area is the main recipient of international assistance. Between 1991 and 1993, the international community (including international financial institutions, the European Union, the Baltic states, and other individual
countries excluding the United States) allocated some US$489 million to environ-
mental projects in the newly independent states. The Russian Federation received
the most monies (US$432 million), then Ukraine (US$32 million), Belarus, and
Kazakhstan in descending order. Of all 1991–1993 international donors, the
World Bank was by far the largest, contributing 85 percent of the overall environmental assistance for that period. In second place was the European Union in
conjunction with the European Bank for Reconstruction and Development
(EBRD). Of the individual European countries, Finland was the largest donor,
giving US$9 million, mainly for clean-up in the Baltic and the Kola Peninsula.
Germany gave US$7 million, and Denmark, Norway, and the Netherlands lesser
amounts. While the amount may be small in ecus (European Currency Units),
Denmark has given proportionately more of its GDP to environmental remediation in the Baltics than any of the other European countries. A new source of
donor funding has been the GEF authorized by UNCED. Under extensive prod-
ding from Turkey, the Black Sea states signed in 1992 a framework Convention on
the Protection of the Black Sea from Pollution. Money to fund the new institutions and training sessions will come from GEF.[28]

Cooperation through reciprocal action agreements on specific environmental programs funded through internal U.S. agencies was in large measure superseded in 1992 by a much larger general assistance program. In September 1992, Congress passed the Freedom Support Act, in which the United States promised some US$1.6 billion to the NIS. Of this, US$38 million was spent on energy and the environment, of which US$7 million was specifically targeted toward the latter. In the summer of 1993, an additional US$2.5 billion in aid was designated: US$125 million went to energy and the environment, and US$75 million was allocated for environmental projects in all the NIS. The largest share of the US$75 million was allocated to Russia.[29] However, the total U.S. allocation comes to only 2 percent of the total aid package of around US$4 billion.

Significantly, the Freedom Support Act does not permit the United States to be directly involved in environmental remediation. No U.S. monies will be spent directly on further clean-up of Chernobyl or clean-up of the nuclear waste in the Urals. The Act distinguishes four separate categories of assistance for environmental projects: policy building and institutional reform, hot spots, encouragement of private sector technological support, and building public awareness and environmental accountability. The United States will provide monies for pilot projects, research, or the introduction of new technology aimed at the hot spots. The Office of Coordinator in the U.S. State Department maintains communication with all the major international donors to integrate international assistance, set priorities, eliminate redundancy, and maximize effort. Formal integration is provided through a consultative group process involving the World Bank, the EBRD, and the European Community. While representatives from the various institutions are supposed to meet regularly, the meetings have yet to become routinized.

Slowly but surely the framework for international assistance to Russia and the NIS is being constructed. While no large-scale clean-up has taken place, Western environmental agencies have been actively assisting in the all-important processes of inventory taking, review of monitoring, and environmental planning. Exchanges of environmental professionals with their Western counterparts are now routine. By tacit agreement, the Western community has divided up the NIS assistance program by country or area: The Scandinavian countries are providing major assistance in the Baltic area and the Russian Northwest, the European Union is primarily responsible for assistance to central Europe and western Russia, and the United States and Canada are most concerned with projects in Siberia. In addition, multinationals, including Exxon, Amoco, and Weyerhaeuser, have also become involved in environmental issues in Siberia and the Russian Far West.[30]

One of the most important aspects of international assistance, in my opinion, evolved from UNCED in 1992. After the Rio de Janeiro conference, ministers from eighteen East and Central European countries met in Sofia, Bulgaria. A statement issued after that meeting urged harmonization of national environmental plans in six areas: early warning systems, including a "green telephone hot line"; national environmental legislation and regulatory activity to accommodate the best achievable standards; information gathering and sharing, particularly in the area of the transboundary movement of toxic and hazardous materials; the development of guidelines for the allocation of responsibility in transboundary environmental damage; support for the accelerated development of environmentally sound technologies and products, particularly those related to military-industrial conversion; and the establishment of a protocol of priority action on specific steps to address the most serious regional and transborder ecological problems and zones of ecological disaster.[31]

Workshops to develop strategy and tactics followed. The end product was the UN-sponsored report *Guidelines on Integrated Environmental Management in Countries in Transition*.[32] Equally important was the development of national environmental action plans (EAPs) for every country in Central Europe and the NIS, which described each country's main environmental problems and identified policies, institutional measures, and investments needed to address them, based on the guidelines.[33] The EAP process is a major step in coordinating national and international responses to the former Communist countries' environmental problems. Its chief drawback is the omission of any discussion of the vast sums needed to implement the projects.[34]

A final aspect of Western assistance that must not be overlooked is the unique criterion of conditionality attached to economic development loans to Russia, the NIS, and Central Europe. Every loan that is approved, from whatever source, comes with a set of mandated environmental stipulations. No other First World or Third World country must submit to such onerous conditions, only the so-called countries in transition. Conditionality means that regardless of domestic politics, Russia may not disregard the environment if it wants foreign loans.

While there are those in international finance who believe conditionality imposes overly harsh terms on countries struggling to reform their economies, complaints from the former Communist countries have so far been few. One reason may be that the up-front capital cost of pollution controls for a new enterprise averages between 2 and 3 percent and is thus not a major cost in locating a business.[35] Retrofitting, by contrast, is far more expensive. Another reason is that conditionality and harmonization of environmental standards and action plans are seen as the prerequisites for entrance into the European Union. In their function and objectives, they may be compared to environmental clauses in NAFTA (with their intent toward upward harmonization of standards) and more especially, to the side agreement setting up the North American Commission for Environmental Cooperation.

Significantly absent from the North American and the European environmental policy plans is a social contract to mitigate the effects of compliance upon the populations involved. The economic costs associated with cleaning up the environment are high. Because of the seriousness of the situation, Russia and the NIS must undertake environmental remediation at the same time as they are making the transition to a market economy and reforming economic structure. More destabilizing politically and socially are the unavoidable future plant closings or plant replacements in the smokestack industrial sector. In much of Russia and the NIS, environmentalism is being perceived as a threat to sovereignty, and at a more mundane the level, a threat to jobs. Social safety nets are in place in only a few countries, and those function minimally. Concern for a potential social time bomb encourages countries to move cautiously towards binding institutional development, and in Central and Eastern Europe and North America, international institution building for the environmental area is proceeding very slowly.

Russian critics say that although there is a great deal of talk about funding environmental projects in Russia, most international funding goes to Third World countries. Of the money allocated to Russia, most has found its way into the hands of Western environmental experts, paying for their time and frequent travel to and from Russia to provide advice on problem identification and options for managerial and technical solutions. Western observers argue that international donors are reluctant to get more involved because of widespread corruption in the NIS. However, NIS citizens say the West has no real concern for the fate of their environment and secretly wants to see the FSU collapse totally.

The international projects underway today are certainly small in comparison to Russia's environmental needs. In all likelihood, there is not enough money available on the international market to begin to rehabilitate the critical hot spots. The task is overwhelming. Russians may rightly be discouraged by the seemingly low level of Western interest in their environmental problems. For its part, the West deserves credit for setting in motion, during a very turbulent period of Eurasian history, a long-term program of environmental assistance to the FSU, built on solid foundations and well-defined criteria.

The Transformation of the Environmental NGOs

The fourth and last aspect of our question addresses the completion of the transformation of environmental organizations from dissident, pseudo-legitimate opposition organizations to recognized legitimate representatives of public environmental interests. As in the areas of institution-building and center-regional relations, the Danilov-Danilyan/Yablokov conflict lies at the heart of the disagreements that are rending the Russian environmental movement today.

Caught between the "pro-Western" and nationalist political factions, the Russian environmental movement finds itself at a critical juncture. The reality of transition in Russia is that environmental goals need to be constructive rather than destructive, regardless of who pursues them (the greens, the government, the legislature, the regions, or the municipalities). Environmental issues must cease to be instruments of political struggle and be assessed for what they are. The shift is not an easy one.

After years of opposition to the Communist government, environmental groups now must learn to design and promote specific practical policies. One advantage of their opposition to the totalitarian pattern of industrial development is that the majority of them generally back the achievement of a market economy and democracy in Russia. Yet even the Socio-Ecological Union, the umbrella environmental organization, is sharply divided in its attitude toward Yeltsin's plan for the privitization of all property, including state and cooperative farms but excluding natural resources, state nature reserves (*zapovedniki*), and other protected areas. While environmental activist Andrei Bondarenko calls on the green groups to unite in opposition to the plan, another active member of the Union, Sergei Zabelin, who is also a member of the president's team of environmental policy advisors, points to the advantages of private land ownership in maintaining and preserving environmental values. Zabelin encourages Russians to put their trust in the Russian people. The people, he argues, understand the value of land and will not sell out thoughtlessly to foreigners—the major concern of many Russian greens.[36]

An inherent danger in the movement is that as the Socio-Ecological Union has consolidated its organizational hold over the smaller, local environmental units, it has become increasingly bureaucratic, with all the attributes of a Soviet-style bureaucracy. If the local groups want help or funding from the Union, they must play the Union's politics. In the process, they risk losing their own uniqueness, spontaneity, and—what is characteristic of environmental groups—their lack of structure and hierarchy. This problem is not confined to Russian environmental groups alone but is symptomatic of local organizations everywhere in the world.[37] The Russian dilemma is rendered more acute because many Russians perceive the present system in Russia not as a dramatic change from the Soviet regime but as a continuation of the old. The only difference is that the current one is more corrupt, and it exhibits less law and order. The ultimate irony may be that the movement that organized against bureaucracy and central domination must perforce succumb to them in order to survive.

Here is where Western assistance may be vital. Under the Soviet regime, approved societies for the protection of nature were assured of funding from the central government. When the Soviet Union collapsed, these organizations continued to receive funding, but the amount was drastically reduced. In Smolensk, for example, the provincial Society for the Conservation of Nature experienced a rapidly diminishing membership until in 1993, the Smolensk chapter consisted of only one or two part-time functionaries. The number of chapter-sponsored activities dropped as the formerly numerous volunteers disappeared.

However, the "old-type" Soviet societies had the advantage over the spontaneous ENGOs that proliferated after Chernobyl. There were meetings and demonstrations involving thousands of people all over the Soviet Union against dam construction, against pollution of lakes and rivers, and against nuclear power. When the USSR fell apart, relations between the official societies and the upstart NGOs varied substantially. In St. Petersburg, relations have been generally cooperative, and the Green Party was allowed to use the offices of the regional Society for the Protection of Nature. Relations in Vologada, on the other hand, have frequently been adversarial.[38] Among the issues causing tension between environmental groups, the most common are organizational rivalry, envy of the other's perceived "higher" or more "accepted" status, and most frequently, lack of funds, critical materials, and services.

Today, support from abroad has tried to make up for losses in central funding. That support has its advantages and disadvantages. The advantages are that the money makes possible the revival of those pre-1991 organizations that exhibited the most energy in attracting Western interest, soliciting Western funds, and adopting Western methods of administration. As noted above, the lead environmental organization today in Russia is the Socio-Ecological Union, an indirect outgrowth of the former *druzhiny* of Soviet times. The Union unites under its fairly loose umbrella the majority of local environmental organizations in Russia. In addition, Greenpeace has local chapters in Russian cities, as have Earthwatch and Friends of the Earth. Russian environmental groups that merge with these international organizations are assured of continued operation, access to international communication (through the Internet), and funding for activities.

USAID also has a mandate to fund other environmental organizations through the nonprofit organization ISAR, the former Institute for Soviet-American Relations. ISAR's role is to identify appropriate organizations and dispense funds. One beneficiary of this assistance has been the environmental legal organization, Ecojuris. Members of Ecojuris have visited the United States to study firsthand the role of the courts in environmental management and receive training in legal procedure and the function of the rule of law in environmental problem solving. Donations by international foundations enable environmental activists and professionals to familiarize themselves with Western monitoring and inventory practices, environmental administration and responsibility, and modes of political activism to promote environmental goals.

The value of Western support of local NGOs and international NGO activity should not be underestimated. The experience of Latin America indicates that both are essential in helping transform weakly organized national activists into an organization capable of influencing both the input and output of public environmental policy. Nevertheless, it would be remiss not to mention some of the very real drawbacks to current Western assistance to the Russian ENGOs. In the first place, international environmental organizations, such as Greenpeace and Friends of the Earth, have themselves become huge bureaucracies, separated from local chapters and caught up in the current issues of global environmental politics. At UNCED, these NGOs were allowed to participate to a degree that would have been unimaginable previously, but the result, not surprisingly, was "the hard sell" of the NGOs' global environmental agenda. In the process, many environmentalists thought the needs and realities of Third World *sustainable* development got lost.[39]

A similar result may be occurring from international NGO and foundation activity in Russia. Greenpeace goes to great lengths to publicize nuclear contamination around the island of Novaya Zemlya or the horrors of the oil spill in the Nenets Autonomous Province. For Greenpeace, these are global problems that require the mobilization of global opinion for adequate resolution. For the local Russian ENGOs, they are irrelevant. The ENGOs' concerns relate to local water quality, local air pollution, and birth defects from toxic chemicals spewing from a local enterprise. The agenda of the international ENGOs includes such issues only to the degree that they are (or are likely to become) global problems. So the Russian local NGO associated with the Socio-Ecological Union or a local chapter of an international ENGO finds itself being called upon to mobilize public opinion for global problems, but it receives little or no help when it tries to address critical local problems. To put it another way, there is a tendency for the international donor, be it a state or an international ENGO, to command the agenda. Organizations funded through international assistance participate in international conferences and global environmental information networks, at the price of losing contact with the grassroots organizations that alone are able to mobilize public opinion for local environmental remediation.

A second disadvantage lies in donor or foreign agency ignorance of the intergroup politics of the Russian environmental organizations. A typical group is led by a person who may or may not be charismatic but who claims good scientific credentials and has developed contacts in the Russian government. Some of these individuals are serious environmentalists; some are in the movement for what they can get out of it. Donors cannot know the situation. They can only take suggestions from Russian environmentalists they have come to know and make their evaluations based on appearances and prior experience with U.S., European, or other environmental groups. When a mistake is made, Russian scientists and environmentalists resent what they call the high-handedness of the foreign agency, which in turn increases the skepticism about the ability of the international community to help significantly.

A third problem is that as the lead organizations distance themselves from the grassroots, they become increasingly bureaucratic, like their international peers. As a consequence, they have a greater stake in playing what might be termed "status quo environmental politics" than in pushing a radical or militant environmental agenda. Volunteers become disillusioned and stop coming to meetings. The organization falls apart. Andrei Baiduzhy, of *Nezavisimaya gazeta*, assessed the consequences of the decline of public interest in environmental issues in these gloomy terms: "The actions of the people who possess the greatest ecological power in Russia only seem to be pointed in opposite directions; in fact, those actions indicate a situation in which the small band of environmentalists, both professionals and amateurs, has lost public attention and support once and for all and is left to face numerous problems one-on-one."[40] Ecology is doomed in Russia, he argues. There is no public sentiment for it.

CONCLUSION

Russia is in midstream of its transition period. It is unclear what kind of political or economic system will emerge from the current situation. Developments in environmental policy send mixed signals. Although the environment has lost its position of priority in the public's opinion, it has not been forgotten by the Russian government. Legal frameworks dealing with environment and natural resources are in place, and they can accommodate both the center and the regions under an environmental rule of law. Steps are being taken to integrate Russian environmental planning with international programs and plans. Out of the current disagreements among various environmental groups and personalities, the regions, and the center, a vision of Russia's environmental future is, one hopes, being forged. A solution to the either-or dichotomy between the pro-Western and Russian nationalist environmental factions lies in the critical decisions ahead regarding the scope and content of privatization, the degree to which the old Soviet environmental management system is modified, and the extent to which Russia is able and willing to import Western environmental management practices and technology.

Historically, Russia's leaders have made intermittent attempts to turn a reluctant population toward the West. In the past, regional attempts at greater autonomy have resulted in the Russian assertion of authoritarian centralized control. The renaissance of an imperial Russia may restore strong government to the Russian federation, but history again suggests that it will do nothing to rehabilitate the Russian economy or avert the environmental catastrophe predicted by Yablokov. The bases of a federal or confederal solution are private property and entrepreneurship, a citizenry armed with civil rights that guarantee their freedom to vote their views on the relationship between the federal and regional governments, and federal and regional governmental institutions capable of carrying out the electorate's wishes. These essential components of federalism are a long way from being in place in Russia today. The environmental legislation and the new role of courts and citizen activism in environmental issues are important pieces of this process.

What lessons may be drawn for Latin America from this brief review of the efforts to maintain and change Russian environmental management during the transition? Perhaps the most important lesson is the vital need for continuing expression of international concern and assistance in the face of all obstacles. This assistance must be maintained on two fronts. The first front is what may be called the purely environmental. Russia, together with all the newly independent states, has inherited a legacy of severe environmental problems, many of them global in scale. Gorbachev made his overture to the West with the argument that environmental security transcended the class struggle. The ups and downs of the politics of East-West environmental assistance should not diminish the international community's concern for the environment of the former Soviet Union. The second front is continued assistance to Russia for economic and democratic reform. Russia continues to be a great power with a capacity for exerting extraordinary influence in the international arena. She stands at a new crossroads in her long history. One road descends into the chaos of national strife. The second ends in the revival of the authoritarian state. The third leads to economic, democratic, and environmental renewal through expanding cooperation with the international community. U.S. environmental relations with Russia exemplify twenty years of productive cooperation. Russian environmental relations with the West will remain constructive if they continue to be characterized by mutual cooperation, rather than a donor-recipient relationship. Russia will not accept remedial programs designed and made in the United States or the European Union. The best alternative to the UNCED scenario of a Russian environmental doomsday is strong Western support of environmental programs made in Russia to Russian specifications but linked and harmonized with evolving European and other environmental action plans.

A second lesson is the importance of environmental education and the evolution of permanent and active ENGOs in all parts of the country. The United States and Germany provide good examples of the role that mobilized environmental organizations can play in making environmental legislation and in ensuring its proper implementation. Russia has a tradition of environmental activism going back into the nineteenth century. In those parts of the country where it exists, this tradition needs to be revitalized; where it does not, it must be created.

A third lesson is one learned in over thirty years of global experience in environmentalism. Governments and their peoples tend to be environmentally proactive in times of environmental crisis. No government to date has integrated environmental considerations into its economic agenda. In times of economic turmoil, popular interest in the environment tends to fade. In the United States, according to *The New York Times,* poor economic performance over the preceding two years saw the fall off of 1994 contributions to the Sierra Club, requiring the club's headquarters to lay off essential personnel.[41] This type of response may be compared to an opinion survey taken in the Russian Northwest in 1992, in which over 85 percent of the respondents were pessimistic and did not think the environmental situation would improve. Twenty-five percent said that there were more immediate problems such as finding food and money to survive, while less than five percent listed the environment as the most important problem.[42] It is crucial that environmental organizations and agencies be able to continue their activities, no matter how diminished these may become.

A fourth lesson is the need for communication and transparency at all levels of international environmental cooperation. Environmental management strategies and remediation tactics may not be imposed upon a country. The huge size and historic xenophobia of Russia preclude any solutions dictated by the West. Latin America shares Russia's skepticism about the intentions of its northern "yanqui" neighbor. International environmental assistance and agreements must be built on the self-identified needs of the recipient country, not on the environmental or economic agenda of the donor state.

The final lesson from Russia that may be of special relevance to Latin America is that international support of environmental actions at all levels of government is critical to maintaining sustained political pressure on the decisionmakers so that when times do improve, their first priority will be the environment.

NOTES

1. Gosudarstvennyi komitet SSSR po okhrane prirody (State Committee for Environmental Protection), *Proiekt: Natsionalnyi doklad SSSR k konferentsii OON 1992 goda po okrushaiushchei srede i razvitiiu* (Draft of National Report of the USSR for UNCED 1992, mimeograph).

2. Boris Domarev, *The Destruction of Nature in the Soviet Union,* trans. Michel Vale and Joe Hollander, with a foreword by Marshall Goldman (White Plains: M. E. Sharpe, 1980), p. 57.

3. Philip R. Pryde, ed., *Environmental Resources and Constraints in the Former Soviet Republics* (Boulder: Westview Press, 1994), p. 32.

4. The criteria defining the categories of pollution are described in *Proiekt,* p. 224. The sixteen zones of ecological calamity are described in Pryde, ed., *Environmental Resources,* pp. 224–232. The Moscow region is listed as the most polluted region in the entire FSU.

5. Barbara Jancar, *Environmental Management in the Soviet Union and Yugoslavia, Regulation versus Structure in Communist Federal States* (Durham: Duke University Press, 1987).

6. Oleg A. Andreev and Mats-Olov Olsson, "The Ecological Situation and Environmental Organizations in the Russian Northwest," CERUM (Centre for Regional Studies), University of Umea, Sweden, CERUM Working Paper CWP–1991, no. 15, p. 15.

7. Ilya Shkabara and Andrei Skvortsov, "Russia's Strong Regions Will Receive Additional Money—the Weak Ones Can Hope to Become 'Off-Shore Zones,'" *Sevodya,* May 14, 1994, p. 3. See also Dmitry Balburov, "Does Russia Need the North?" *Moscow News,* no. 49 (December 9–15, 1994).

8. *Sevodnya,* April 20, 1994, p. 2.

9. Vis Leonid Smirnyagin, member of the Presidential Council, "The Separation of Powers No Longer Exists at the Local Level," *Sevodnya,* August 2, 1994, p. 2.

10. *Izvestia,* August 18, 1994, p. 1.

11. Figures from "Socioeconomic Situation and Development of Economic Reforms in the Russian Federation in the First Quarter of 1993," *Ekonomicheskaya gazeta,* no. 17 (1993); "Socioeconomic Situation and Development of Economic Reforms in the Russian Federation in the First Half of 1993," *Ekonomicheskaya gazeta,* no. 31 (1993); and Judith Shapiro, "Health," *Socioeconomic Survey* 3, no. 7 (Russian Federation, Ministry of Finance, Monetary and Finance Unit, August 1993) as cited in Christopher M. Davis, "Health Care Crisis: The Former Soviet Union," *RFE/RL* (Radio Free Europe/Radio Liberty) *Research Report,* 2, 40 (October 8, 1993): 38.

12. *Nezavisimaya gazeta,* May 5, 1994, p. 6.

13. Aleksandr Avdoshin, "Eight Years Later: The Chernobyl Case is Closed," *Novaya yezhednevnaya gazeta* (*New Daily Gazette*), April 26, 1994, p. 1; and Lida Poletz, "Ukraine Plays a Waiting Game with G–7 on Closing Chernobyl," *Christian Science Monitor,* April 26, 1995, p. 5.

14. *Zelenyi mir* (*Green World*), no. 4 (1994): 3.

15. *Zelenyi mir,* no 5 (1994): 4.

16. Ibid., 4.

17. Ibid.

18. Decree on the Russian Budget no. 1979, passed in 1993.

19. *Spaseniye (Salvation),* no. 7, February 23, 1992.

20. Vladimir V. Petrov, "Postateinyi kommentarii k zakony rocciiskoi federatsii 'Ob okhrane okrushaiushchei prirodnoi sredy'" (paragraph by paragraph commentary on the Environmental Protection Law of the Russian Federation), *Zakonodatel'stvo i Ekonomika (Law and Economics),* nos. 16 (38) and 17 (39) (1992).

21. Unpublished report from Erika Rozenthal on Ecojuris activities for 1993; and Sergei Vasiliev, Deputy Chairman and Main State Expert for the Moscow Committee on Environmental Protection (interviewed by author, Moscow, summer 1994).

22. Viktor Filippov, "Divorce Nenets-style," *Izvestia,* February 24, 1994, p. 2.

23. Yelena Nikitina, "New Challenges for Russia's Natural Resource Management," *CIS Environmental Watch,* no. 3 (Fall 1993): pp. 22–25.

24. *Zelenyi mir,* no. 17 (1993): p. 7.

25. *Zelenyi mir,* no. 31–32 (1993): pp. 6–7.

26. Peter F. Drucker, *Managing the Future: The 1990s and Beyond* (New York: Truman Tally Books, 1993), pp. 86–87.

27. Irina Demchenko, "Where to Find Investors for Mining Mineral Resources?" *Moscow News,* no. 25, June 24–30, 1994, p. 9.

28. Martin W. Sampson III, "Black Sea Environmental Cooperation" (unpublished paper prepared for the ISA Annual Convention, Chicago, IL, February 1995).

29. "Tokyo-Package—July 1993: US-NIS Expanded Cooperation," report by the U.S. Department of State, Office of the Assistant Secretary for Public Affairs, August 5, 1993.

30. For a brief description of the U.S. Forest Service exchanges, see USDA memo of October 25, 1993, "USDA FS FY 1993 Activities Summary," particularly the section entitled, "USDA Forest Service FY Programs in Russia." Information about multinational involvement came from many sources: (1) Bill Freeman, EPA (conv. with author, Washington, DC, November 21, 1993); (2) Robert F. Lowery, Project Manager, International Reforestation, Weyerhaeuser Forest Products Company, "Weyerhaeuser Reforestation Trials in the Russian Far East (unpublished report, 1993), and personal communication to the author; (3) Herton H. Bill, Weyerhaeuser Forest Products Company, Finance, Planning and Administration (conv. with author, January 26, 1994); and (4) Roger Witherspoon, "To Save the Siberian Tiger," *The Lamp,* 75, no. 1 (Spring 1993): 24–29; along with conv. with author, January 23, 1994. Exxon also contributed to a seven-nation study of the humpbacked whale.

31. Viktor Loksha, "The Former USSR, Asian Part, Transboundary Environmental Problems," report prepared for the World Bank (August 1994), p. 1.

32. United Nations Economic Commission for Europe and United Nations Environment Programme, *Guidelines on Integrated Environmental Management in Countries in Transition* (New York: United Nations, 1994).

33. Regional Environmental Center for Central and Eastern Europe (REC), *Strategic Environmental Issues in Central and Eastern Europe,* 2nd ed. (Budapest, Hungary: REC/AQUA, August 1994).

34. Reuters, North American Wire Service, February 22, 1993.

35. Heraldo Muñoz and Robin Rosenberg, *Difficult Liason: Trade and the Environment in the Americas* (Washington, DC: North-South Center, 1993), chaps. 1 and 2.

36. *Zelenyi mir,* no. 15 (1993): p. 10.

37. For a discussion of this problem, see Gustava Estevas and Madhu Suri Prakash, "Editorial: From Global to Local Thinking," *The Ecologist*, 24, no. 5 (September-October 1994): 162–163.

38. Andreev and Olsson, "The Ecological Situation," p. 1.

39. Participation in the Global Forum that ran parallel to the UNCED Conference proved to be quite a learning process, after which many developed-country NGO members said they would seek to expand their own future agendas to take closer account of the concerns of the developed country NGOs. (Reported in Peter M. Haas, Marc A. Levy, and Edward A. Parson, "Appraising the Earth Summit: How Should We Judge UNCED's Success?," *Environment* 34, no. 8 (October 1992): 26–31.

40. Andrei Baiduzhy, "Should We Forget about Ecology?—Clean Air is the Price of Economic Survival," *Nezavisimaya gazeta,* March 16, 1994, p. 2.

41. *The New York Times,* October 25, 1994.

42. Andreev and Olsson, p. 23.

CHAPTER ELEVEN

■

Environmental Challenges and Policy Responses in Indonesia

Carl H. Petrich and Shelby Smith-Sanclare

Indonesia stands as one of the development dynamos of the world. Two decades of steady economic growth have helped maintain political stability, but political problems are mounting amid the relative prosperity. Along with the economic blossoming has come an ambitious program for environmental protection, but one that lacks meaningful compliance measures. The success in implementation of the new program is checkered. Deforestation of the world's second largest expanse of tropical rain forests continues, and severe pollution problems accompany rapid urbanization and industrialization. Environmental policymaking is squeezed in among the disparate needs to support economic development. Because Indonesia is a global biological treasure house, it experiences the added pressure of careful scrutiny by the world community.

Indonesia, a country of more than 17,500 islands, resembles a loose collection of nations such as the European Community more than it does a single country. Unified by recent historical events, its diversity has been managed by the charismatic and strong leadership of only two presidents: Sukarno and Suharto, the present leader. To be taken seriously, the environmental policy proponents must be viewed as another power interest competing with the power and alliances formed by the president and his family; the military as a dominant player in government outside the civil service; the religious leadership, particularly the Muslim; and the ethnic Chinese business and economic contributors.

These interests are dynamic, jostling continuously for power; and the balance constantly shifts. Two cultural norms serve to mask the intensity of power conflicts: deference to hierarchy and authority figures and the practice of avoiding, deflecting, recasting, or denying "bad news." Identifying the intention and true meaning "behind the mask" is a cultural given for Indonesians.

Unlike most Latin American countries that suffered a "lost decade" during the 1980s when economic activity dramatically slowed, Indonesia experienced social and political upheavals earlier, during the mid- to late 1960s. By the mid–1980s, Indonesia had liberalized its investment and trade policies, thereby stimulating high levels of economic growth that lifted the country from the lowest ranks of the developing world.

In the environmental arena, the Indonesian citizenry has few strongholds in government institutions, a situation similar to most South American countries. What is more, the process of true democratization is moving more slowly in Indonesia. As in Venezuela, multinational oil and gas companies in part provide some leadership to local companies in acting responsibly on environmental issues. Their high profile and international visibility necessitates use of modern technologies to control effluents and emissions. As with Brazil, Indonesia's expansive tropical rain forests and remarkable biodiversity place it prominently on the radar screens of international environmental organizations that help to pressure the government for environmental reforms and commitments. Like Brazil, Indonesia has strong pockets of environmental awareness and activity scattered throughout government agencies. Some strict legislation exists but has little impact on public policy due to lax enforcement and general lack of political will. Balancing environmental with economic concerns remains difficult because the middle class is still small and therefore unable to push grassroots issues.

The extreme hierarchy of the government of Indonesia (GOI), deference to superior authority, and cultural avoidance of "bad news" lead to reports being cast in ways least likely to disappoint or offend superiors: hence, the problem with accountability in the GOI as well as in nongovernmental institutions. Those at the center and near the top have considerable difficulty finding out what is really going on; most do not make the extra effort. Horizontal information flow is minimal. Policies and decisions made with information that is incomplete and/or inaccurate result in misjudgments and poor solutions. Because the press is weak and restricted, alternative information flows are also faulty and deficient. Corruption and waste have, therefore, assumed major proportions, leading from inefficiency to cynicism, alienation, and indecisiveness or inconsistency toward conservation objectives.

Indonesia's economy follows the classic market orientation, seeking environmental amelioration only when it finds itself with few other options politically or when a highly visible environmental impact captures world attention, thereby presenting an opportunity for an infusion of international financial and technological assistance. Although the country seems reluctant to acknowledge and is often slow to respond to adverse environmental conditions, the GOI is building capacity in technological and environmental expertise. Canada and the Netherlands provide the most prominent assistance.

GEOGRAPHY
AND HISTORY

Indonesia is the world's largest archipelagic nation, stretching 5,120 km from the Indian to the Pacific Oceans—the distance from Dublin to Moscow or from Seattle to the Bahamas. This geographic breadth contributes to the diversity that is critical to understanding the country's environmental policy-making.

Indonesia is also the world's fourth-most-populous country (196.6 million in 1994),[1] and its chief demographic characteristic is the uneven geographic distribution of its population: 56 percent of the people live on 7 percent of the land, on the island of Java. Population redistribution is now occurring, a significant proportion through transmigration and secondary immigration of family members. The population on Java is growing at a rate of 1.6 percent per year, while the population of Kalimantan (the Indonesian portion of Borneo and the country's least densely populated island, with only 9.1 million people) is growing by 3.1 percent per year. This distribution reflects the large number of development projects that have attracted workers and other new residents to what are known as the Outer Islands—the peripheral islands geographically, culturally, politically, and economically.

The Republic of Indonesia represents over 100 distinct ethnic groups, each with its own cultural identity, who speak more than 300 mutually unintelligible languages. Only 20 percent of the population speaks Indonesian as its mother tongue. As Indonesian becomes the *lingua franca,* there is more possibility for social mobility and ethnic interactions, a primary goal of the Indonesian government.[2] Although there is no state religion, all Indonesians are required to state a religious preference. The Muslim faith is the most common, comprising 93 percent of the population. Rapid urban growth has led to the existence of culturally, religiously, and socially disparate groups of people living closely together, exacerbating tensions spawned by inequalities in income and opportunities among the country's multiracial societies.

The nation's founder, Sukarno, under intense economic and political pressure, handed the government over to current military president, Suharto, in 1968. Suharto engaged in numerous policy reforms, including a push toward exports and foreign investment aimed at promoting faster economic integration with the world economy.

As in most developing economies, the first wave of investors in the 1970s focused on exploiting the country's natural resources: copper, tin, timber, and oil. Oil, as in Venezuela, initially provided more than 60 percent of the state's total revenues. The second wave, starting in the mid–1980s, set up urban-based manufacturing industries, such as textiles, sports shoes, clothing, and furniture, which stabilized the economy as oil revenue began to decline.

POLITICAL AND BUREAUCRATIC CONTEXT
FOR ENVIRONMENTAL DECISION MAKING

The Indonesian government is extremely hierarchical, nearly to the point of paternalism. As a culture that seeks consensus, Indonesia prefers to avoid acting under conditions of uncertainty, and maintenance of the status quo is the rule. Creativity and new ideas find little fertile ground.

The Suharto government's successes in maintaining political stability and economic growth are the foundation of its legitimacy. The strong centralized power that served the country through the nation-building years has, however, extracted a severe cost in terms of the people's sense that their participation is ineffective in political parties or legislative institutions—particularly local ones—or that they can achieve justice through the court system.[3] The government agrees there is need for restructuring, but all arguments focus on interpretation as to the degree of scope, speed, and intensity of openness.[4] Criticism and dissent are seen as obstructing legitimate national goals or even as subversive.

Given the hierarchical nature of the Indonesian culture, it is no surprise that the country's strong central government has fostered a culture that can create a reality whether it is valid or not. Thus it has adopted sustainable development in its environmental policies and through its participation in international environmental forums. As Steve Rayner suggests, hierarchic bureaucracies are masters at "combining conflicting goals and interests without ever resolving their apparent incompatibilities."[5] The idea that the Indonesian government can embrace sustainable development as a viable course of action to be pursued in even the narrowest of areas flies in the face of existing experience.

The hierarchical character of the culture also explains why the head of the executive branch is endowed with such enormous powers of institutional sovereignty in decisionmaking.[6] Presidential decrees since independence outnumber laws by an order of magnitude.[7] This authoritarian culture also explains why the government bureaucracy has so little use for programs in energy conservation, renewable energy, and other areas. The government wants big projects that it can control centrally, especially if they involve arcane information that "only" the government can understand. This also suggests why nuclear power is so appealing to the Indonesian government, despite data showing that other energy sources would be better suited to Indonesia's needs and conditions.

Agencies within the Indonesian government that are responsible for environmental issues are hampered by a lack of support for their activities. Take, for example, the Ministry of Forestry's Directorate General of Forest Protection and Nature Conservation (PHPA). PHPA is handicapped by inadequate budgets, poor strategic planning, unsupervised and poorly trained field personnel, and low public and government support and appreciation—all potentially corrupting influences.[8] PHPA is said to need at least a sixfold increase in its annual budget to protect just the existing top-priority forest reserves, without considering protection of lesser reserves or the creation of new ones. A critical piece of legislation, proposed in 1980 to protect buffer zones around protected forests and reserves, took ten years to enact and came too late to save many forests. Improvement in Indonesia's protection of its natural areas, even with higher budgets and better management practices, is unlikely until the government puts its weight and authority behind PHPA activities, enforces the existing laws, and actively inculcates a stronger conservation ethic within all its relevant branches.[9] The point made by Mumme and Korzetz (in chapter 3) regarding de facto commons is apparent in the buffer areas surrounding the swamp development projects and forest reserves in South Sumatra as well development projects on the other islands.

Environmental agencies also suffer from a lack of coordination and layers of bureaucracy. For example, the administration of sea fisheries is under the jurisdiction of the Directorate General of Fishery in the Ministry of Agriculture. In 1989, the ministry issued a decree designed to ensure a sustained fishing yield in Indonesia's territorial waters. The Ministry of Transportation's Directorate General of Sea Transportation and the Ministry of Foreign Affairs, however, have issued their own directives to manage the marine-related aspects of the national interest under their jurisdiction; and marine research is managed by the Indonesian Institute of Sciences, a nonministerial government institution. There has been no formal proposal to establish an interministerial board for coordination, integration, and optimization of efforts both to protect and to use the country's enormous maritime resources. However, other countries with far fewer maritime resources have cabinet-level agencies to protect their territorial waters.[10]

In Indonesia's civil-military bureaucratic form of government, political parties and the public have little influence. The two groups that play major roles are the military and the civil service, followed increasingly closely by business interests.[11] The military, chiefly the army, is the dominant interest group in government and has powerful business interests as well.

To explore further the issue of civil-service power (and its manifestation in culture) in Indonesia's environmental affairs, consider the bureaucracy and the way it functions. Indonesian bureaucracy reflects important aspects of the country's culture in the deference shown to age and seniority, the belief in decision making by consensus, and avoidance of open opposition to policies. Civil servants are relatively isolated from the rest of society; they are, for example, rarely seconded to the burgeoning private sector or even to other ministries in order to gain broader experience. According to John Henry and B. I. Djajmadja, the grossly underpaid official bureaucracy:

> tends to be passive in nature, slow in its decision making and in formalizing decisions, giving little weight to individuality or to personal initiative. Another important influence on how government actually functions is the use of informal relationships and linkages that exist at all levels of Indonesian officials' life. Relationships can be based on background, family-connections and loyalties, ethnic loyalties, educational backgrounds, religion, etc. These loyalties and connections are accentuated by the system of monetary rewards and incentives.[12]

Frequently in the autumn severe air pollution from massive forest fires in Sumatra and Kalimantan plagues Kuala Lumpur and Singapore as well as much of the rest of Southeast Asia. In 1992 and again in 1994, these fires were particularly damaging, burning an estimated 567,000 hectares of tropical woodland. Airline schedules were disrupted, schools closed, and the elderly were warned not to go outside. The Indonesian government blames the traditional slash-and-burn farmers for the fires, while NGOs blame government-favored plantation and logging companies. They allege that the timber companies are trying to cover their tracks after illegal logging or that plantation companies are looking for inexpensive ways to clear tropical rain forests in order to make way for more lucrative monoculture oil palm operations.[13] In early October 1994, a new publication was banned after one issue because it discussed, among other things, the reasons for massive fires in Kalimantan.[14]

The business community has recently become a new voice to reckon with in Indonesian politics.[15] The New Order society has given over to one in which, in the words of Sjahrir, managing director of the private Institute for Economic and Financial Research, "the monopoly of power and the monopoly of the economy are married to each other."[16] One observer says the economy now looks very much like "a return to the bad old days, when Indonesian capitalism meant wrangling a monopoly, then exploiting it."[17] Economic activity is dominated by "a dense, intensely personal network of public monopolies, private cartels, and bureaucratic fiddles."[18] Not surprisingly, a majority of these businesses are natural-resource based: forestry and agriculture products.

Foremost among the protected industries is the forest-products area. Here, the president's closest friends and family have long ago secured—and continue to amass—incredible fortunes through what are, essentially, unregulated logging practices, protectionist policies, favoritism, nepotism, and corruption. The creation, implementation, and enforcement of Indonesian forestry policy always takes into consideration the wishes of a handful of selected businessmen in this industry. The main obstacle to reform in this area, therefore, is the lack of political will.[19]

At international conferences, on industrial association boards, and in international trade discussions, these businessmen—despite their dubious credibility—are becoming outspoken advocates for the environment. Leadership of the newly formed Indonesian Business Council on Sustainable Development is prominently exerted by corporate captains of the forest-products industry. Yet the reality of reforestation, of balanced species replanting, and other efforts still resides only in presidential decrees and in legislation, not in practice.

Economic Context

Since 1986 Indonesia has experienced rapid economic growth—nearly 7 percent in real terms. In 1994, per capita GDP was US$860,[20] up from only US$70 in 1976 when the New Order began,[21] and up 18 percent from 1993.[22] In 1994, inflation was a respectable 8.2 percent and GDP grew in real terms by 6.5 percent. This has given the country more financial resources to address environmental problems. Despite a climate of high-return, rapid turnaround investments (whose initiators want little to do with longer-term planning and perspectives), economic growth also has given Indonesia more international visibility, accelerating international concerns about environmental ills. The positive economic indicators have attracted multinational companies that are both able and compelled to invest for the long term. These companies also employ responsible environmental management practices.

The Javanese provinces—and to a lesser extent the south Sumatran ones—dominate the peripheral provinces, especially those in eastern Indonesia. Sixty percent of the country's wealth is concentrated in the nation's most developed area: West Java and Jakarta, the capital city. The relationship of the outer provinces to the core—Jakarta in particular and Java in general—is one of almost colonial subjugation and exploitation because the core depends on the peripheral provinces for its resources. This development disparity is a legacy of preindependence history coupled with inappropriate contemporary national, regional, industrial, investment, and other public policies unleashing powerful economic and noneconomic social forces. These in turn hinder a more equitable distribution of the development process and its benefits.

Demographic Context for Environmental Impacts

Indonesia has made remarkable progress in controlling population growth. Indonesia's annual population growth has fallen from an average of 2.1 percent in the 1960s and 2.3 percent in the 1970s to only 1.8 percent in 1994.[23] Family planning measures have reduced the country's total fertility rate from 5.6 children in the period 1967–1970 to 3.0 in the period 1985–1993.[24] Nevertheless, Indonesia's population will double by 2050.[25]

The country does face some obstacles to further slowing its population growth. Because of the ethnic, educational, and socioeconomic diversity of the Indonesian population, recruitment of women into family planning has to be custom designed for target population groups. Many Indonesians fear family planning because it has "become associated with subtle persuasion as well as explicit force in recruiting women to use contraceptives with no guarantee for their long-term state of health."[26] Yet another impediment to lowering population growth rates is the persistence of rural poverty, which results in early marriages for women. The government is tackling this by trying to sustain its general antipoverty efforts and at the same time focus on better education for women as a means of raising their economic and sociocultural horizons.[27]

Transmigration Program

Indonesia's population is also shaped by a formal program of transmigration that dates back to colonial times. The entire program has been the subject of much criticism not only because of the social impacts but also because of the concomitant environmental ones.[28]

Demographic pressures provide much of the motivation for the program. Java already has more than 830 people per square kilometer.[29] Aside from city-states like Hong Kong or Singapore, no country has ever managed the population densities that Java is likely to experience by the middle of the next century. Indonesia's Broad Outlines of State Policy (part of the formally adopted five-year plans) seek to improve the balance in each region between the resources available and the human activity dependent on those resources. The government has argued that, for socioeconomic equity alone, densities should be increased outside Java in low-population areas rich in timber, mineral, or petroleum resources. These notions now guide Indonesia's population program and are inextricably linked to the government's environmental policies and the positions it has taken at international environmental forums. Unfortunately, the transmigrants have been directed toward much of the unused or abandoned land that for environmental reasons is better left unexploited or used with much less intensity than projected by the master plans. The economic commitments to prepare and maintain the land in environmental harmony for long-term productivity are missing from the equations.

With the population of Java increasing by about two million people per year, however, it is futile to try to control overpopulation by moving people to the Outer Islands. Clearly, there are additional motivations driving the transmigration program. Today, reasons for maintaining a formal program have expanded to include economic, social, political, and national security considerations.

One clear rationale for the program is that it provides manpower to develop the natural resources of the Outer Islands and reduce Indonesia's economic disparities.[30] Another economic motivation for the transmigration program is provided by Indonesia's large irrigation and hydropower projects, which require the resettlement of tens of thousands of families. New arterial roads can also generate significant resettlement needs. A social goal of the transmigration program is to pull the country's diverse ethnic groups together by integrating the country's dominant culture, Javanese, into as many ethnic enclaves as possible, particularly those least enamored with Javanese control. The political benefits of extending Javanese culture and allegiances to the Outer Islands have obvious attractions to the central government, even though most of these attempts to put a Javanese stamp on national identity have met with bitter resistance or have failed altogether.

National security motivations for continuing the transmigration program have more recent origins, coming in the wake of threats of nationwide fragmentation along several of major ethnic fault lines. The idea of securing solid economic and patriotic bases in restless outer provinces through the introduction of Javanese citizens is a transparent policy. Indeed, the Bureau of Planning stated in 1987 that "the frontier regions of Kalimantan, Irian Jaya, and East Timor have the priority for migrating military people for the purpose of Defense and Security."[31] During 1994, one-thousand Indonesians from other islands migrated to East Timor each week, more than at any time in the past. The new residents reportedly take the best jobs, the best land, and even the small shops. Only 30 percent of public service jobs are filled by East Timorese.[32]

At the same time, political dissidents on Java may find themselves the unwilling recipients of free one-way transport to remote sections of Irian Jaya, where free plots of dubious-quality land await their exploitation. The government has also expressed some concern that relatively unpopulated islands may attract the interest of other countries with limited territory. Government policy, according to the minister of transmigration, is to "fill the empty islands."[33]

Urbanization

The U.N. Population Fund predicts that the population of Indonesia's urban areas is expected to grow by nearly 4.5 percent per year,[34] a rate second only to very agrarian Laos. Jakarta, a city of 8.2 million in 1990, is expected to have 12 million residents in the year 2000[35] and 15 million by 2005.[36] The trend toward urbanization is not confined to Jakarta: about 30 percent of Indonesians currently live in cities or towns, up from only 10 percent in 1960. Urbanization is expected to rise from a current level of about 36 percent to 40 percent by 2000 and to 50 percent by 2016.[37] Meanwhile, rural population growth will continue to shrink the size of individual agricultural holdings, prompting further migration of unskilled workers to the cities unless there is countervailing development of rural manufacturing, trade, and construction. However, such development is unlikely in the near future.

Increased migration to cities will further stress urban infrastructure and exacerbate environmental problems, the most critical being urban air quality, safe and adequate supplies of water, and domestic sanitary and solid wastes. Growing urbanization also means exceptionally high rates of growth in energy consumption. The large number of young people will trigger an explosion in the size of the labor force lasting well into the next century. Already, two million people leave school each year and enter the job market.[38] The GOI sees forest development as a large supplier of new jobs in the Outer Islands and outside of cities. It also sees the need to generate jobs as a higher priority than environmental protection. The government's message at the 1992 Earth Summit in Rio de Janeiro was clear: The government refuses to slow development in order to solve environmental problems that were largely precipitated by earlier development processes of Western and Northern countries. Indonesia believes it has a right to address the abject poverty at home first, a belief reflected in Agenda 21 (Principles 2, 3, and 5, among others) developed at the Rio meeting.

INDONESIAN ENVIRONMENTAL
PROFILE AND TRENDS

Indonesia is the fourth most populous country on earth, yet like Brazil it is incredibly rich in biological life. The country occupies only 1.3 percent of the

Earth's land surface; but it is home to 10 percent of the world's plant species, 12 percent of its mammal species, 16 percent of its reptile and amphibian species, and 17 percent of the bird species. More than 4,000 known tree species grow there. Of Indonesia's 1,500 bird species, 430 can be found nowhere else; the same is true of 200 of its 500 mammalian species. Indonesia has the world's longest list of species threatened with extinction: 126 birds, 63 mammals, and 21 reptiles compared with 121 birds, 38 mammals, and 12 reptiles for Brazil.[39] The primary threat to these species is loss of habitat, particularly through deforestation.

The country has seven major biogeographical zones, whose ecosystems range from permanent equatorial ice fields in Irian Jaya to a wide variety of humid lowland forests, coral reefs, mangrove forests, deep lakes, shallow swamps, and subzones differing from one another not only in species composition but also in climate, relative isolation, and geologic history.[40]

Indonesia's forests are its most valuable remaining natural resource asset, and they still cover nearly two-thirds of the country. These are the most extensive forest reserves in Asia and are exceeded only by those of Brazil. Indonesia has about 10 percent of the world's tropical forests, 60 percent of those in Asia, and perhaps 90 percent of the remaining virgin stands in Asia.[41] The vast lowland dipterocarp (Philippine mahogany) forests of Borneo and Sumatra have been termed the most valuable remaining tropical forest estate in the world.[42] Irian Jaya is about 84 percent forested, while Java's coverage is below 10 percent. Rapid deforestation is occurring on Sumatra, in Kalimantan, and on Maluku, Nusa Tenggara, and Sulawesi.

Environmental Law and Presidential Support
for the Environmental Ministry

The establishment by Presidential Decree No. 16 of the National Committee on Environment was a direct result of the conclusions of Indonesia's report for the U.N. Conference on the Human Environment, held in 1972 in Stockholm. The country's first comprehensive environmental legislation (enacted into law in 1982), was drafted in 1978, when the State Planning Agency asked a technical team within the newly created State Ministry for Development Supervision and Environment (the predecessor of Indonesia's the current environmental agency) to take on the mission. The state ministry established contacts with the United Nations Development Programme and held discussions with the Indonesian delegation that had attended the Stockholm Conference.

Indonesia's first minister for population and environmental issues repeatedly stated that he did not want to force companies to reduce negative environmental impacts arising from their operations because he believed such an approach ran counter to the government's commitment to deregulation.[43] The minister preferred that industries regulate themselves, institute their own research programs for assessing environmental impacts, and promote environmentally sound construction and operational practices "throughout the entire Indonesian business community."[44] In short, he advocated free-market incentives to promote the implementation of clean technologies.[45]

The 1982 antipollution legislation stipulates that all disputing sides settle their conflicts through negotiations or mediation before seeking a legal settlement in court. A significant obstacle to enforcement of the law is the high value that Indonesian culture places on avoiding confrontation if there is any chance of achieving the desired ends through cooperation. However, the government is reluctant to pursue court settlements more aggressively because it often lacks the political will to do so. One observer put it simply: "Is there any mechanism that forces people to live by the rules?"[46] The 1982 law states that the polluter must pay compensation for damage to property, health, or the environment; but no one has ever been taken to court for such violations.[47] Nor does the law fix the amount of compensation. If enforcement were strengthened and led to sanctions for environmental damage and pollution, this could involve the Ministry of Home Affairs, the Ministry of Justice, the State Ministry for the Environment, the Attorney General, and the Head of the Police. Therefore, potential for problems of overlapping jurisdictions and lack of coordination are substantial.[48]

Forestry Policy

From 1967 to at least 1983, Indonesian forest policy was geared to one goal: maximization of wood production from the tropical forest. The implementation of the various policies supporting this goal was highly successful: by 1980, Indonesia was exporting a greater volume of tropical hardwood than all of Africa and Latin America combined, claiming a dominant 41 percent global market share.[49] Forestry products industries have developed even more rapidly since the government banned the export of logs in 1985. Indonesia is now the world's leading exporter of hardwood plywood, pulp, paper, and furniture.[50]

Nevertheless, a lack of financial and personnel resources has forced the Ministry of Forestry to turn over the de facto management of forests to the concessionaires.[51] These 530 companies, public and private, conduct logging activities on 90 percent of the country's forested lands classified as production forests. There is little or no impartial, professional field checking of concessionaire performance.[52] In a government survey of 334 concessionaires, fewer than 30 percent were operating in accordance with the government's guidelines on sustainable utilization.[53] The Minister of Forestry has even acknowledged that only a fraction of the forest concessionaires abide by logging regulations.[54] The government has estimated that inefficient logging and wood processing operations waste around 47 percent of available board-feet of trees.[55]

Concessionaires operate with twenty-year leases on forests theoretically managed for a silviculturally optimal thirty-five-year rotation. However, if sustainability is desired, this custom will prove untenable, especially given the government's limited capability to regulate and enforce the practices of concessionaires. Short leases provide no financial incentives for concessionaires to manage forests for long-term productivity. They respond to this unambiguous government signal by reharvesting every five to ten years, a practice ruinous to forest vitality.[56] Forest development supplies many new jobs, and if the government requires concessionaires to develop their holdings for periods of more than thirty-five years, the number of available jobs, at least as loggers, may be reduced.

The maximum allowable annual cut to maintain a sustainable forest yield is of the order of 29 million cubic meters (to be decreased to 22.5 million cubic meters by the year 2000). However, the forest-products and lumber industries have set yield goals of around 37 million cubic meters, and the government has allowed sawmills to be built with a total capacity of 52 million cubic meters per year. Because Indonesia's profitable industries do not leave their capital investments idle, the result is an annual harvest much higher than legally permitted. These actions are particularly damaging because industry planning typically ignores government-set allowable yields. In 1993, the World Bank estimated that the harvest of tropical forests in Indonesia was exceeding sustainable rates by 50 percent.[57]

Many of the regulations that do exist largely go unheeded. In theory, all lands above 500 meters and on slopes greater than 25 percent are not to be logged. In practice, concessionaires ignore this rule almost completely.[58] Moreover, the ecological structure of forests tends to change because the concessionaires "cream off" the most lucrative tree species, thereby damaging 40 to 50 percent of the residual stand. Current regulations call for forest concessionaires to prevent human encroachment, encourage regeneration, and prevent fires on their leased lands, "but in the absence of strict supervision and incentives, these obligations are generally ignored."[59]

Concessionaires are also required by law to submit environmental impact assessments of their existing forest areas. However, only two of the 117 concession holders in Kalimantan have completed the required reports; the others are doing nothing.[60] The Kalimantan environmental officer explains that companies are reluctant to spend money on such studies. He added, "These studies are also quite new for them so that forest concessionaires, who are often ignorant of the essence of development under a sustainable system, do not know where to start."[61]

Indonesia's transmigration program also has a significant impact on deforestation. For each family formally moved by the government, an average of 2.5 other families use their own resources to migrate. These self-motivated migrants are more enterprising and self-reliant than those individuals moved by the government. As "the single largest agent of land-use change" in Indonesia, the voluntary transmigrants are explicitly encouraged but not managed by the Ministry of Transmigration. They tend to move to areas where settlements are already well established and where infrastructure and communications are developed.[62] According to one foreign advisor, transmigrants are "the single largest cause of environmental degradation in Indonesia and have created an especially critical situation in Sumatra." They most often come in behind poor logging, land clearing, or infrastructure development, and "lacking the cultural traditions of local farmers, farm the soils to exhaustion before moving on in search of new land."[63]

At the same time, the government sees the establishment of timber estates linked to the transmigration program as a way "to help speed up the reforestation program."[64] The president personally briefed about 100 selected forest concessionaires on the importance of the program and the government's support for it through equity capital and low-interest loans. Interestingly, the budget for this support is taken from the reforestation levies on the volume of cut logs.

A comprehensive analysis by Malcolm Gillis on the effects of Indonesian government policies—forest and nonforest—on the country's forest resources concluded that Indonesian deforestation "would have been less rapid had government policies had more neutral effects on tropical land-use decisions; government policies and institutions have, jointly and separately, discouraged resource conservation." Gillis cautions that endemic poverty, along with misguided and uncoordinated policies, are chief destroyers of the country's tropical forests. "If the Indonesian forest is to face an apocalypse, then public policy is but one horseman. Poverty, institutions, and ignorance round out the quartet, 'interacting' to produce unforeseen and largely unwanted results."[65]

In contrast to the destructive nature of a production/extraction emphasis, Gillis suggests that local ethnic groupings could—by local standards—make an excellent living tapping the "non-wood products of the forest." For example, because a company controlled by one of President Suharto's daughters is developing an oil palm plantation in the tropical rain forest of Siberut (an island of unique evolutionary history off the western coast of Sumatra), the World Wide Fund for Nature has recorded all data concerning the healing properties and cultural use of the island's medicinal plants in hopes of protecting a nascent herbal collection industry.[66]

The Indonesian forest products industries are, however, controlled by people with too much political and financial clout to permit large-scale efforts in these directions. In Sumatra, for example, most of the land is not legally titled, meaning that the people working the land do not have rights of ownership. Those with influential connections to the president frequently negotiate land-use permits from the GOI in Jakarta, effectively forcing farmers to sell to the only available buyer or go head-to-head against a major corporation in trying to stay on their land.[67]

Because the country has committed itself to sustainable forest cutting by the year 2000—but not before, as the logging associations frequently stress—one gets the impression that the concessionaires intend to make as much money as possible within the next few years. Perhaps in 2000 there will be the creation and enforcement of serious government-backed sustainable policies.

Indonesia's Role in International
Environmental Fora and Agreements

Indonesia has a mixed track record in complying with either the letter or the spirit of international agreements regarding environmental issues, despite the commitment and actions of many well-meaning individuals both within and out-side government. This affects both its credibility in negotiations on global climate accords and its ability to advance its sustainable development agenda. When macroeconomic policies are compromised or cherished industries are threatened, the GOI has failed to regulate its natural resources effectively.

One of Indonesia's leading NGO officials noted that since the Earth Summit in Rio de Janeiro in 1992, developing countries have been reluctant to take the ini-tiative in coordinating actions to fulfill political and economic implications of their Rio positions. Dependence on developed countries for financial assistance in ameliorating development problems may underlie this failure. Criticisms have also been leveled at Indonesia's international negotiation skills. The state minister for administrative reform has been quoted as saying, "There are only a handful of Indonesian government officials who can negotiate international agreements." He said that incompetence in making legislation had hampered government officials in negotiating with foreign parties.[68]

In 1979, Indonesia signed the Convention on International Trade in Endan-gered Species of Fauna and Flora of 1973 (CITES).[69] The country faces severe tests in protecting extremely rare species and is holding its own fairly well in some instances. For example, the 500 or so remaining Javanese rhinos, the rarest rhi-noceros species on earth, all live in or near one of Indonesia's best-run game re-serves, the Ujung Kulon National Park in West Java.

On the other hand, Indonesia's record is also not so clear on other endangered species. Although CITES includes a ban on killing all turtle species inhabiting In-donesian waters,[70] Greenpeace maintains that 50,000 green and hawksbill turtles are slaughtered each year in Indonesia—half in Bali—for their meat, shells, and eggs.[71] Because there are large numbers of these turtles in Balinese waters, In-donesian government authorities believe there is no need for special protection, and they further maintain that the two species in question are not included in the commercial ban.[72] Major department stores in Jakarta, including state-owned ones, sell the shells of giant clams, chambered nautiluses, Triton's trumpets, and horned helmets—all quite rare and theoretically protected within Indonesia.[73] A scene in a British Broadcasting Company film on the sale of protected species showed its crew in Jakarta's largest bird market purchasing a baby orangutan, a species protected internationally since 1931. A 1990 New Zealand television show features the poaching of baby orangutans from tropical forests in Kalimantan to be sold in Jakarta or smuggled into the international black market.

The Ministry of Forestry authorities charged with enforcing the endangered species laws say they are overworked and so understaffed that they can do little more than distribute leaflets that identify protected species and detail the laws and penalties, make spot inspections, and occasionally arrest those trading ille-gally.[74] With 81,000 kilometers of coastline in Indonesia, it is incredibly difficult and expensive to mobilize the scarce resources needed to mount patrols that might reduce smuggling of endangered species to black markets elsewhere in

Asia. What is harder to understand is the apparent inability to patrol effectively the illegal markets that operate openly in the nation's capital.

Although Indonesia sees itself as having an important stake in international agreements, political will alone has proven insufficient for assuring effective implementation. As the world's largest archipelagic country, Indonesia has a keen interest in protecting its national waters. In the 1960s, the government set up various committees in preparation for Indonesia's formal role in the U.N.-sponsored Conference on the Law of the Sea in 1973. The International Law of the Sea Convention was completed in 1982, and Indonesia signed it in 1985. The process was considered a progressive step because the Indonesian government's efforts to have the archipelago principle recognized by the international community had succeeded. However, lack of coordination among its own agencies and excessive bureaucracy have hindered efforts to implement the Law of the Sea Convention. Indonesia also signed the Basel Convention on Waste Disposal in 1989, but it has yet to ratify the agreement. The Basel Convention would provide the legal framework for protecting the country's lands and waters against transboundary movements of hazardous wastes. Meanwhile, hazardous wastes continue to be dumped on Indonesian islands, which are too numerous to patrol effectively.

As a developing country, Indonesia is only beginning to tackle many of the difficult decisions that inevitably confront nations undergoing economic and political transitions. Compared to more pressing development imperatives such as sustaining high economic growth rates, negotiations on global climate change per se are not likely to be high on the agenda. Unless there are strong signals that negative environmental practices are undermining the development process itself, one should not expect to see Indonesia giving the subject significant attention beyond undertaking "no regrets" activities consistent with its efforts to implement more definitive sustainable development policies.[75]

As a participant in global-climate-change negotiations, Indonesia has linked its continued cooperation to specific commitments for foreign financial and technological support, especially by the developed countries. Indonesia agreed to abide by the Montreal Protocol and to meet the advanced chlorofluorocarbon (CFC) phase-out date of January 1, 1996, which was established in Copenhagen in November 1992. Indonesia does not produce CFCs or halons. Although air conditioners and refrigerators are used extensively in offices and households in urban areas, a recent survey revealed that the consumption of CFCs in 1990 was only about 0.02 kg per capita, far below the maximum limit of 0.3 per kg originally set by the protocol.[76] The use of CFCs in aerosols has been banned by the Ministry of Health since 1990. Because CFC use in Indonesia is limited, the country is, in effect, benefiting as a recipient of international goodwill for banning their manufacture and use.[77]

With its extensive coastal areas, Indonesia is clearly vulnerable to any rise in the sea level that might result from global warming. A recent NGO study projected that:

inundation of seaports, beach resorts, and inland or coastal fisheries, intrusion of saltwater into coastal freshwater aquifers and shallow groundwater, and changed tidal ranges would severely affect millions of Indonesians, if not by directly displacing them, by eliminating the industrial or agricultural zones or fisheries upon which their livelihoods and welfare depend, salinating their drinking water, overwhelming flood control and sewer systems, or disrupting marketing and transportation networks and their access to goods.[78]

Indonesia's vulnerability to projected global climate changes raises questions as to whether the country could cope with the impact of such damage. The country's resilience in the face of major climatic and meteorological deviations remains largely untested. Historically, it has escaped the Indian Ocean region's typhoons; however, the handling of the huge Kalimantan forest fires of 1983, 1992, and 1994 suggests the country is ill prepared to cope with environmental crises.

NGOS AND ENVIRONMENTAL POLICY

The military, the government, and big business exert the greatest influence on environmental policy formulation, implementation, and compliance. Indonesian NGOs also play a role, if only as a constant thorn in the government's side. Business, the bureaucracy, and the government-led political organization are very sensitive to world opinion regarding environmental matters and are keen to embrace what are often only cosmetic changes. To their credit, they are usually quite candid about their motivations.

AMDAL: Indonesia's Environmental Management Policy

Article 16 of the 1982 environmental law created the basis for Indonesia's environmental impact legislation, the environmental impact assessment (AMDAL) procedures. Although heavily influenced by the Canadian environmental protection processes, the social and cultural aspects of AMDAL were tailored to Indonesian conditions.[79] Indonesia's environmental legislation is acknowledged worldwide for its lofty statutory goals, including requirements to retroactively address environmental problems. Its implementation, however, is characterized by many missteps and false starts; this might be expected, however, anywhere that such comprehensive legislation is being applied for the first time, particularly in the context of an economy growing explosively. In 1993, Indonesia found it impossible to implement its retroactive edicts, and they were simply declared to be complete.

The State Ministry for Environment (the 1993 incarnation of the country's first environmental ministry) is charged with drafting policy on environmental issues but not with carrying out operational activities. These are largely handled through regional administrations and universities. BAPEDAL, the Environmental Impact Management Agency, under the ministry organizationally, is still preparing itself for full operational duties.

AMDAL has a strong legal foundation, but since it was established as law, it is difficult to amend in a timely way. The process has been "forced to function without either the guidance of more detailed policies and programs or the operational underpinnings, such as environmental information systems and regulatory permits, that would allow it to function most effectively."[80]

The State Ministry for Environment also has no authority to intervene in conflicts. Its role is merely to develop environmental policy and attempt to persuade sectoral ministries to participate in the process of achieving integrated environmental management in both the policy and implementation arenas. There is no government regulation giving a particular government organization clear responsibility for overseeing environmental management.[81] As one critic asserts, "Failure to address these problems will call into doubt Indonesia's publicized commitment to sustainable development."[82]

The State Ministry for the Environment coordinated environmental policies horizontally across sectoral ministries, but the individual ministers have the true power to influence environmental policy. Interdepartmental collaboration is difficult to achieve because responsibilities are unclear and there is usually competition between environmental and nonenvironmental interests. The intent of the 1982 legislation is to coordinate the various ministries' policy making. The penetration of AMDAL principles into each ministry's behavior is also impeded by the failure at the highest levels to engender the commitment of ministerial-level officials to the AMDAL process.[83]

The ministries that wield the most power in areas relevant to environmental issues are Mines and Energy, Transmigration, Agriculture, Public Works, Forestry, and Industry. Although the military's influence remains strong in most governmental operations, it generally keeps a low profile in the environmental area. Many military-supported projects, frequently infrastructure-related (such as dam building and transmigration settlement areas), have substantial environmental effects, both positive and negative. Provincial and local governments have some power over environmental policy initiatives, but they do so mostly under the guidance of the central ministries.

The Indonesian legal system is moribund, so one cannot rely on it to uphold environmental laws and provide leverage for NGOs seeking rigorous implementation of environmental policy. It has not succeeded in transforming Dutch legal traditions of colonial commerce into practices capable of regulating a modernizing, bureaucratic state. Given its pluralistic and heterogeneous composition, Indonesia is in desperate need of a flexible, accessible legal system. Other obstacles within the judicial system that impede its ability to support environmental activities include the following:

- Indonesia is virtually a "lawyer-free zone," with only 1200 lawyers for its entire population.[84]
- The legal system is greatly overburdened. The Supreme Court, comprising of forty-seven judges, one-third of whom are military officers, had a backlog of over 13,000 cases in 1993 and was falling more behind daily.
- Judges are underpaid, a situation that, "has not helped them to be honest and professional;"[85] they speed up and slow down cases, even alter verdicts.
- The system favors the executive branch despite a significant 1970 constitutional amendment that should have ended executive branch interference.[86]
- Culturally, overt confrontation is to be avoided, and the adversarial aspect of law sidestepped.

High-level officials see the need to perform at least some enforcement activities in order to get some teeth behind the environmental law, but commitment to action remains uncertain. Many Indonesian industries have little respect for the country's environmental law, regarding anything related to the environment as a cost-increasing item that should be avoided whenever possible.

The 1982 law on the environment allows the government to take action against polluters only after environmental damage is done. Even then, taking action requires the services of qualified environmental experts who can prove in a legal, evidentiary way that the environment has been polluted. Unfortunately, they are few and far between. Additionally, Indonesia needs legal sanctions for ignoring government warnings, violating environmental controls stipulated in business licenses, giving false or incorrect information to the government, and obstructing officials trying to carry out audits of waste-treatment facilities.[87]

The average individual has a hard time being heard in Indonesia. The mechanisms for public input are basically nonexistent. This creates tensions when international funding agencies require that potentially affected citizens help in the preparation of environmental assessments for projects. NGOs can be invited to participate actively in AMDAL review sessions at the ministerial level, but the government is very reluctant to invite them. However, NGOs work closely with citizens and communities, with scientists (especially graduate students), with legal experts, and with the business communities. This evidence of cooperation is encouraging and seems to have some momentum and dynamism of its own.

Still, the bureaucracies dealing with environmental policies are suspicious of NGOs and do not know which individuals (volunteers, paid staff, consulting scientists, lay members) to work with or how to work with them. They are always afraid that the NGOs will not be valid representatives of the people. When NGOs have to be involved in some meetings (for example, because of a funding agency requirement), the bureaucrats often do not know whom to invite (that is, who is "safe").

WALHI: THE INDONESIAN
ENVIRONMENTAL FORUM

NGOs do push the government to take a stand on certain environmental policies. WALHI, the Indonesian Environmental Forum, established in 1980, is a respected, environmentally committed association of professional organizations, amateur environmentalist groups, and public-interest groups with environmental agendas. It acts as a resource center, develops educational programs, and pursues environment-oriented community projects.[88] WALHI's climate-change study described earlier illustrates its ability to work with the public, private, and international NGO sectors. WALHI successfully pressured the government to agree to the 1982 antipollution law. At the Earth Summit, WALHI representatives also called on Indonesia to lead developing countries in urging industrialized countries, particularly the United States, to commit to reducing or stabilizing greenhouse gas emissions.[89] NGOs are very active in lobbying the government on its oversight of forest management practices, often using professional economic and technical analytical research techniques.

WALHI achieved an NGO "first" when it filed a suit in 1989 on behalf of alleged victims of severe environmental damage occurring as a result of practices by a pulp and rayon manufacturer. The suit was filed against both the government and the private company after they had failed to mitigate the damages. Although both the government and the company were exonerated, the NGO believes it achieved a milestone: The court acknowledged WALHI's right, as a community organization, to represent the public—to have standing, in the legal sense of filing suit on environmental issues.[90]

WALHI achieved another first in August 1994 when it attempted to bring suit against President Suharto. No other entity had ever challenged the president's authority in Indonesian courts. The lawsuit, filed on behalf of seven environmental and public interest groups, charged that Suharto abused his authority when he issued Decree No. 42 in June 1994 directing that US$190 million collected to replant Indonesian forests and plantations be lent interest-free to an aircraft company. The lawsuit was dismissed in December 1994 on the grounds that no court has the authority to try the chief executive.

DML: FRIENDS OF THE ENVIRONMENT FUND

A much lower profile is being taken by a group of business leaders from major Indonesian companies who, at the invitation of the minister for the environment, formed Dana Mitra Lingkungan (DML, or Friends of the Environment Fund) in 1983. DML has a fundamental goal of supporting environmental projects undertaken by the country's NGOs. For example, DML provides 60 percent of the annual operating budget for WALHI. In few other places in the world does the business elite raise funds for groups that may eventually attack their own companies, as has happened on several occasions in Indonesia.[91]

The DML has just undertaken sponsorship of a five-year program to evaluate the relationship between traditional cultures and the rain forest. In a collaboration with the Smithsonian Institution, the new study will bring together Indonesian and foreign biologists, anthropologists, and other experts to carry out academic research and to produce books and films for educational institutions and the general public.

ROLE OF NONGOVERNMENTAL ORGANIZATIONS

Neither the words nor the concept of "nongovernmental organization" translate directly into either the language or the culture of Indonesia. The term is understood in governmental circles as meaning "against the government."[92] For example, the Minister of Home Affairs recently urged NGOs to write a code of ethics for their operations so that the government's exercise of supervisory tasks "would prevent NGOs from betraying the country."[93] In fact, it is impossible for a given NGO to be "against the government" and still be functional because, according to the Law on Social Organization No. 8 of 1985, the GOI has the authority to suspend or dissolve NGOs that stray from strict guidelines, such as receiving aid from foreign parties without government permission.[94]

One of the country's first NGOs was the Indonesian Planned Parenthood Association, formed in 1953. It performed valuable ground-breaking work for what later became the highly touted government family-planning program.[95] Despite some positive contributions made by NGOs in Indonesia, the concept of NGO per se still is tenuous, and those active in community institutions walk a fine line of tolerance. Frequently, international multilateral and bilateral funding agencies exert leverage on the GOI's environmental policies and their implementation by writing NGO assistance and participation requirements into their projects' designs, assessments, and evaluations. This irks the Indonesian government and is one reason the government would like to end its dependence on foreign development assistance.

NGOs in Indonesia are, therefore, less activist and lower profile than their counterparts in the West. The GOI screens NGOs that receive foreign aid to "ensure the assistance goes to the right groups."[96] The GOI says that it fears the participation of Indonesian NGOs in international forums because "[they] will be dominated or even misused by NGOs from other countries to support a critical message which might be alien to Indonesian values."[97]

Before the Asian Pacific Economic Cooperation (APEC) summit meeting in November 1994, the GOI began to tighten control on the country's NGOs, allegedly to prevent them from expressing dissent or opposition to government policies.[98] A draft decree developed by the Directorate General of Social and Political Affairs of the Ministry of the Interior gave broad powers to the government to shut down any NGO deemed to be engaging in political activity or threatening the national interest.

FUTURE PROSPECTS FOR INDONESIAN NGO INFLUENCE

Indonesian NGOs have just begun to take up the responsibilities that the 1982 law and 1986 regulations conferred on them with respect to AMDAL. WALHI has initiated what it terms "barefoot AMDAL," a grassroots mechanism for encouraging the affected citizens to make themselves heard in official AMDAL procedures. Where international funds are involved in development projects, such tactics will inevitably have visibility and effectiveness as decentralization progresses, no matter how slowly.

The paucity of reliable, quality information coming from the Indonesian government provides strong opportunities for the NGO and local and international research communities to share what information they have that they generally believe is credible. There is a hunger for reliable, candid assessments of the country's environmental status, a first step in reaching consensus among domestic environmental groups on key issues. For example, there is a long-standing argument among environmental groups and development agencies about the rate of deforestation in Indonesia. Estimates vary by a factor of two. This has caused problems in communicating with the outside world about the capability of the country as a carbon sink and about the extent of the biodiversity problem in Indonesia. The situation is ripe for consensus building, a natural objective of the Indonesian culture. From there, perhaps a greater international constituency can be built as an initial step toward action in the areas of reforestation and energy conservation and in the demands for enforcement of logging regulations.

Indonesian NGOs must confront a country dominated foremost by the military and an entrenched bureaucracy, and increasingly monopolized by big business. They also must function within a multiracial, multiethnic, multireligious, highly fractionalized society that lacks a free press to provide visibility and convey strength in numbers. Furthermore, the culture rejects confrontation and legal maneuvering. Indonesian NGOs are inventing a unique path; they must walk the fine line between pushing for the environment and for citizens' right to be heard and at the same time not coming across so stridently as to be perceived to be challenging the existing order. Despite some occasional jailings and some coercion into silence, their progress continues. That an organization such as DML should be the primary source of funds for the country's largest NGO is a signal to the rest of the developing world about the potential for cooperation and trust among major domestic interest groups.

CONCLUSION

Indonesia typifies the problems with distribution of natural resource rents (particularly those from oil, gas, mineral, and forest products) that William Ascher describes in broad outline form in chapter 2. Conflicts among the military, bureaucracy, and favored private-sector interests over the allocation of surpluses from resource extraction skew the optimal allocation of economic resources, result in overly rapid exploitation of such resources, cause royalty rates to be valued below resource rents, undermine attempts to achieve sustainability, cause excessive environmental damage, create inadequate transfer payments to other favored downstream resource purchasers and consumers, and rarely result in the highest societal values being derived from publicly owned resources.

While the GOI participates to varying degrees in global discussions of sustainable development and protection of tropical forests, highest on the GOI agenda is economic development. Its environmental policymaking takes a backseat to development goals, and it will for considerable time into the future. With the elimination of severe poverty and establishment of a larger and more prosperous middle class will likely come the major opportunity to achieve realistic environmental goals. Progress toward becoming a more developed nation will, however, be hampered by two major challenges not faced as much by other Southeast Asian or Latin American nations. The first set of challenges encompasses the resource allocation and equity issues listed above. The second is related: political stability through the transition to a less Balkanized society and to more democratic structures and processes. In addition to the political instability caused by widespread income disparities, ethnic diversity, and religious clashes, the GOI faces severe threats to its future stability as it makes the democratic transition. It will likely have to face these pressures from the populace at the same time it makes a change from the thirty-plus years of Suharto's authoritarian rule to a successor government. So, to the four horsemen of the tropical-forest apocalypse that Malcolm Gillis identifies as working to undermine Indonesia's environmental policy making mentioned earlier one must add (1) the tensions and vagaries of a democratic transition within a context of a highly charged regime change likely to be characterized by power struggles among the military, (2) economic interest favored during the Suharto years, (3) the Suharto family's economic interest, (4) a civil service losing its public stature, and (5) Muslim interests.

NOTES

1. The Economist, "The World in Figures: Countries," *The World in 1995* (London: The Economist Publications, Ltd., 1994), pp. 83–90.

2. Ian Chalmers, "Introduction to This Issue," *Prisma: The Indonesian Indicator* 50 (September 1990): 3–6.

3. "Guests From Rural Poor," *Jakarta Post*, July 10, 1991; and "Sign of Growth," *Jakarta Post*, August 8, 1991.

4. "Pressure Rising for Political Reform: Juwono," *Jakarta Post*, June 20, 1991

5. Steve Rayner, "A Cultural Perspective on the Structure and Implementation of Global Environmental Agreements," *Evaluation Review* 15, no. 1 (1991): 75–102.

6. Ibid.

7. Marcus W. Brauchli, "Asian Paradox: Indonesia is Striving to Prosper in Freedom but Is Still Repressive," *Wall Street Journal*, October 11, 1994.

8. Regional Planning Program for Transmigration, "The Land Resources of Indonesia: A National Overview," report of the Land Resources Department, Natural Resources Institute, Overseas Development Administration, Foreign and Commonwealth Office (London) and Direktorat Bina Program, Direktorat Jendral Penyiapan Pemukiman, Departemen Transmigrasi (Jakarta), 1992.

9. Ibid.

10. John Henry and B. I. Djajamadja, "RI Needs System to Fully Explore Sea Resources," *Jakarta Post*, August 5, 1991.

11. Ibid.

12. Ibid.

13. Philip Shenon, "Indonesian Forest Fires Blanket Southeastern Asia with Smoke," *New York Times*, October 9, 1994.

14. Human Rights Watch/Asia, "Tightening Up in Indonesia Before the APEC Summit," Human Rights Watch/Asia 6, no. 12 (October 1994); available from apakabar@clark.net INTERNET.

15. Harry Bhaskara, "Asian Investors in Indonesia More Successful than Westerners," *Jakarta Post*, August 13, 1992.

16. Cait Murphy, "Indonesia's Long and Winding Road to Deregulation," *Asian Wall Street Journal*, November 14, 1991.

17. Ibid.

18. Ibid.

19. Bhaskara, "Asian Investors in Indonesia More Successful than Westerners."

20. The Economist, "The World in Figures: Countries," pp. 83–90.

21. "Indonesia: The Long March," *The Economist*, April 17, 1993, Survey 3–18.

22. "Indonesia's Personal Income," *Wall Street Journal*, September 13, 1994.

23. The Economist, "The World in Figures: Countries," pp. 83–90.

24. "Islam and the West," *The Economist*, August 6, 1994, Survey 3–18; and "Youths Need More Help in Dealing with Sexual Problems," *Jakarta Post*, June 18, 1991.

25. Linda Starke, "Fertility Rate Decline Stalls," in Lester R. Brown, Hal Kane, and Ed Ayres, eds., *Vital Signs: The Trends That Are Shaping Our Future* (New York: Worldwatch Institute and W.W. Norton & Co., 1994), pp. 124–125.

26. Ati Nurbaiti, "Family Planning Objective: Choice or Target?" *Jakarta Post*, July 8, 1992.

27. "Asia-Pacific Women Need Better Education, Says Emil," *Jakarta Post*, August 20, 1992.

28. See Bruce Rich, *Mortgaging the Earth: The World Bank, Environmental Impoverishment, and the Crisis of Development* (Boston: Beacon Press, 1994).

29. "The Question Rio Forgets," *The Economist*, May 30, 1992, pp. 11–12.

30. Sandra Burton, "Centrifugal Force," *Time*, November 11, 1992, 23–24.

31. Regional Physical Planning Program for Transmigration, "The Land Resources of Indonesia."

32. Barbara Crossette, "New Migrants Altering Face of East Timor: Indonesians Flock to Contested Area," *New York Times*, October 30, 1994.

33. Regional Physical Planning Program for Transmigration, "The Land Resources of Indonesia."

34. "Social Indicators," *Far Eastern Economic Review*, April 23, 1992, p. 14.

35. "Regreening Programs for Jakarta," *Jakarta Post*, May 7, 1991.

36. "Longest Lasting Headache," *Jakarta Post*, June 1, 1991.

37. Kartome Wirosuhardjo, "Population and Environment: The Intersection" (paper prepared for the Population-Environment Dynamics Symposium, The University of Michigan, October 1–3, 1990).

38. Tulus Tambunan, "High Population Growth Big Challenge to RI," *Jakarta Post*, July 11, 1991.

39. Regional Planning Programme for Transmigration, "The Land Resources of Indonesia."

40. Ibid.

41. The World Bank, *Indonesia: Sustainable Development of Forests, Land, and Water* (New York: Oxford University Press, 1990).

42. Malcolm Gillis, "Indonesia: Public Policies, Resource Management, and the Tropical Forest," in Robert Repetto and Malcolm Gillis, eds., *Public Policies and the Misuse of Forest Resources* (Cambridge: Cambridge University Press, 1988), pp. 43–113; and Stan Sesser, "Logging the Rain Forest," *The New Yorker*, May 27, 1991, pp. 42–67.

43. "Business Leaders Support NGOs," *Jakarta Post*, November 26, 1991.

44. Ibid.

45. "Good Ecology Is Good Economics," *Jakarta Post*, November 26, 1991.

46. Koen W. Toonen, *The Implementation of Environmental Impact Assessment in Indonesia* (Toronto: University Consortium on the Environment, Faculty of Environmental Studies, York University, 1990).

47. "Government Urged To Take Strong Action On Polluting Industries," *Jakarta Post*, July 4, 1992.

48. Toonen, *The Implementation of Environmental Impact Assessment in Indonesia.*

49. Gillis, "Indonesia: Public Policies, Resource Management, and the Tropical Forest," pp. 43–113.

50. Pandaya, "Indonesia Set to Sign Montreal Protocol on Environment," *Jakarta Post*, July 10, 1992; and "Indonesia: The Challenge of Growth," *The International Herald Tribune*, August 17–18, 1991.

51. Bhaskara, "Asian Investors in Indonesia More Successful than Westerners."

52. Ibid.

53. "Government Sets New Requirement for Inexperienced Forestry Concessionaires," *Jakarta Post*, May 17, 1991.

54. "Government Prepares Pilot Project for Forest Control," *Jakarta Post*, May 14, 1991.

55. "High Level of Waste Wood Industry Inefficient," *Jakarta Post*, June 12, 1991.

56. Gillis, "Indonesia: Public Policies, Resource Management, and the Tropical Forest," pp. 43–113.

57. "Sumptuous Sumatra," *The Economist*, September 24, 1994, pp. 33–34.

58. Bhaskara, "Asian Investors in Indonesia More Successful than Westerners."

59. Ibid.

60. "HPH Holders Unwilling to Make Environmental Study," *Jakarta Post*, May 21, 1991.

61. Ibid.

62. "Living Space," *The Economist*, June 27, 1992.

63. John Dick, *Forest Land Use, Forest Use Zonation, and Deforestation in Indonesia: Summary and Interpretation of Existing Information,* (background paper to the United Nations Conference on Environment and Development prepared for the State Ministry for Population and Environment [KLH] and the Environment Impact Management Agency [BAPEDAL], Prooyek EMDI, June 1992.

64. Hyginus Hrdoyo, "RI Starts Timber Estates Related to Transmigration," *Jakarta Post,* February 28, 1992.

65. Gillis, "Indonesia: Public Policies, Resource Management, and the Tropical Forest," pp. 43–113.

66. Claire Ellis, "Drug Firms Rush to Indonesia to Find Medicinal Plants," *Jakarta Post,* July 28, 1992.

67. "Sumptuous Sumatra," *The Economist.*

68. "Indonesian Officials Not Apt In Negotiations: Sarwono," *Jakarta Post,* September 28, 1991.

69. "Western Tourists Urged to Curb Turtle Slaughter," *Jakarta Post,* July 10, 1991.

70. "Korean Businessman Held for Smuggling Dried Turtles," *Jakarta Post,* May 11, 1991.

71. "Western Tourists Urged to Curb Turtle Slaughter," *Jakarta Post.*

72. "Turtles Not Endangered Species in Bali: Official," *Jakarta Post,* July 22, 1991.

73. Claire Ellis, "Shells: The Forgotten Endangered Species," *The Voice of Nature* 96 (August 1991): 36–41.

74. David L. Feldman, *Managing Global Climate Change Through International Cooperation: Lessons From Prior Resource Management Efforts,* Technical Memorandum ORNL/TM–010914 (Oak Ridge National Laboratory, Oak Ridge, TN, 1988).

75. Saswinadi Sasmojo and Dody Nawangsidi, "Policy Reorientation for Effective Energy-environment Integration in Asian Pacific Countries" (unpublished paper, Center for Research on Energy, Bandung Institute of Technology, Bandung, 1991).

76. Pandaya, "Indonesia Set to Sign Montreal Protocol on Environment."

77. Ibid.

78. Agus P. Sari, "Indonesia Country Report," *Climate Change in Asia* (Asian Development Bank, Manila), as reported in *Climate Alert* 7, no. 4 (July-August, 1994).

79. Toonen, *The Implementation of Environmental Impact Assessment in Indonesia*

80. John Dick and Lynn Bailey, "*Indonesia's Environmental Assessment Process (AMDAL): Progress, Problems and a Suggested Blueprint for Improvement* (report of the Environmental Management Development in Indonesia Project, Jakarta and Halifax, Canada, June, 1992.)

81. Toonen, *The Implementation of Environmental Impact Assessment in Indonesia.*

82. "The Question Rio Forgets," *The Economist*, May 30, 1992, pp. 11–12.

83. See Toonen, *The Implementation of Environmental Impact Assessment in Indonesia.*

84. Ty Ahmad-Taylor, "Looking for a Lawyer? Dial Reykjavik (and Forget Jakarta)," *The New York Times,* October 21, 1994.

85. "Industrialization, ABRI's Presence Hinders Democracy," *Jakarta Post,* August 28, 1992.

86. Deborah A. Gordon, "YLBHI Focuses on Public Interest Cases," *Jakarta Post,* August 1, 1992.

87. Tabita Sima Gunawan, "1991 Nightmare Year for Polluters," *Jakarta Post*, December 28, 1991.

88. "DML Funds Wide Range of Projects," *Jakarta Post*, November 26, 1991.

89. "Government Urged to Lobby Developed Nations on Gas Emission Reduction," *Jakarta Post*, May 21, 1992.

90. Gordon, "YLBHI Focuses on Public Interest Cases."

91. "Business Leaders Support NGOs," *Jakarta Post*, November 26, 1991

92. Toonen, *The Implementation of Environmental Impact Assessment in Indonesia*

93. "Non-Governmenal Groups Agree to Write Code of Ethics," *Jakarta Post*, January 20, 1992.

94. Toonen, *The Implementation of Environmental Impact Assessment in Indonesia.*

95. "NGO Ethics," *The Jacarta Post*, January 20, 1992.

96. "Minister Tells NGOs to Stay Out of Politics, *Jacarta Post*, November 6, 1991.

97. August Rumansara and Peter van Tuijl, "*RI Needs to Match Progress with Stability*," *Jakarta Post*, August 7, 1992.

98. Human Rights Watch/Asia, "Tightening Up in Indonesia Before the APEC Summit."

CHAPTER TWELVE

— ■ —

Conclusion: Latin American Foreign Policy and International Environmental Regimes

Gordon J. MacDonald and Daniel L. Nielson

Chapters in parts one and two of this volume have identified some of the complex elements that affect environmental policy in the Latin American region. The chapters in part three presented the cases of Indonesia, China, and Russia as points of comparison. Through this discussion, a picture has come into focus of the important roles that foreign pressure and global market forces play in shaping domestic environmental policy. Likewise, environmental policy reflects a complex mix of internal domestic political, economic, and social dynamics.

This chapter attempts to close the circle. That is, now that we better understand what shapes environmental policy domestically, we feel it a worthwhile exercise to turn our attention to the roles that Latin American countries play in forming the global environmental agenda. Our discussion centers on the actions of Latin American governments in international environmental forums, focusing on Latin American interests and strategies in building multilateral environmental regimes. This chapter does not represent a comprehensive study of Latin American foreign environmental policy; rather, it is intended to serve as a broad survey, drawn from our vantage point as participants in and observers of international environmental negotiations. Our collective impressions should contribute to the understanding of Latin American involvement in global environmental issues.

Especially beginning in the mid–1980s, Latin American countries have become some of the key players in the formation and modification of major global environmental agreements and institutions, such as those dealing with ozone depletion, hazardous waste, climate change, and biodiversity. In all of the major environmental agreements and amendments negotiated between 1985 and 1995,

Latin American nations played important—sometimes even vital—roles in shaping the ultimate outcomes. They have taken lead roles in many of the negotiations and have served as organizers of negotiating blocs and developing-country positions, as well as being hosts and facilitators of the international events themselves.

Although the increased importance of the environment to Latin American foreign-policy making may reflect growing global environmental activity, in other ways it demonstrates radically changed domestic priorities. The increased importance of environmental questions in Latin America is well documented by Mumme and Korsetz, Silva, Torres, and Viola in this volume. Moreover, the changing domestic priorities toward environmental concerns have been heightened by international pressure and evolving global market conditions, as noted in this volume by Muñoz, Nielson and Stern, and Torres. It is only natural that these changed priorities would manifest themselves in more assertive positions in international environmental negotiations. What is perhaps less predictable is the extent to which these changed priorities have actually come to influence deeply the course of international environmental diplomacy.

The next section summarizes the importance of the changed domestic and international priorities in shaping multilateral environmental agreements and discusses the general importance of Latin America as a region in global environmental issues. The third section provides examples of the important involvement of countries from the region in the major environmental negotiations of the past ten years. The conclusion looks forward to potential sources of conflict and cooperation in international environmental questions to be settled in the future.

SHIFTING PRIORITIES AND
LATIN AMERICA'S IMPORTANCE

The conclusion of the Cold War has elevated numerous items on the list of global priorities, including human rights, democratic governance, education, and health. However, few issues have benefited more from the increased attention of the global community than the environment. Some analysts have gone so far as to dub the environment "the third major issue area in world politics, along with international security and the global economy."[1] Although it would be overstating the matter to insist that the environment is on equal footing with those other issues in international negotiators' minds, it certainly has gained international respect as a vital issue area in its own right. Moreover, it has become clear that the environment is strongly linked to security and economics. Environmental problems have spilled into the security domain, at least partially provoking, for example, the civil war in Somalia and political instability in Haiti. Moreover, the costs of environmental degradation are increasingly manifest on economic ledgers. As noted in the introduction, air pollution, water pollution, and natural resource degradation are clearly associated with severe losses in productivity and efficiency.

However, power in the international environmental arena is perhaps more difficult to determine than in security and economics, and it stems from very different sources. It is not a matter of counting armaments or calculating gross national product. In the environmental issue area, natural resource stores and current and potential pollution matter greatly when determining which nations will influence international policy. When the question on the negotiating agenda addresses preserving global biodiversity, for example, then the interests of the nations whose territories encompass the greatest stocks of biological riches must be acknowledged and dealt with explicitly in negotiations. Furthermore, when international efforts are directed toward reducing atmospheric emissions of carbon dioxide or chlorofluorocarbons, the negotiations must deal not only with current producers of the gases but also with future and potential producers. In these regards, the balance of environmental power is definitely shifting toward developing countries, whose influence has traditionally been muted in international security and economic negotiations. The Third World's vast resource stores and enormous development potential make developing countries crucial players in setting priorities for alleviating global environmental problems.

Latin American nations have become core actors in negotiations over new international environmental regimes. As noted elsewhere in this volume by Viola and Nielson and Stern, Latin American nations encompass areas of vital concern to the international environment. Latin America holds more than 63 percent of the world's remaining tropical rain forest. Deforestation in the region has devastated vast swaths of virgin rain forest, with an average of more than 7.2 million hectares disappearing annually between 1981 and 1990. That deforestation appears to have peaked in 1987, when more than 9 million hectares of rain forest were cleared in Brazil alone. The disappearing forests threaten the globe's biological diversity. Latin America is host to 370 endangered species of mammals alone, most of which are threatened because their habitats are being destroyed. Major portions of the world's stocks of biological diversity are contained in the rain forests of Latin America. As deforestation continues, these stocks are diminishing at an alarming rate.[2]

Moreover, deforestation clearly contributes to world carbon dioxide emissions and is now seen as a major contributor to projected global climate change. In addition, energy consumption in Latin America is escalating significantly and can be expected to contribute substantially to global carbon dioxide emissions. Mexico's energy use added 74 million tons of carbon dioxide to the atmosphere in 1986, but that total is expected to climb to between 157 and 233 million by the year 2025, which will place the country among the top emitters of carbon dioxide on the planet. Similarly, Brazil's emissions, 52 million tons of carbon dioxide in 1986, are expected to increase to between 71 and 142 million by 2025; Venezuela's emissions are projected to increase from 26 million tons to between 86 and 112 million tons; and Argentina's from 26 million to between 30 and 41 million.[3] Compared to developing countries, the region's carbon dioxide emissions are relatively small; but Latin American countries' potential emissions remain large, posing grave concern to those advocating reducing emissions in order to stave off the potentially destructive effects of global climate change.

In addition to the concern over Latin America's climate change and shrinking biodiversity, more than one-fourth (26.4 percent) of the entire planet's renewable freshwater resources exist in the region. Although this water is largely located in the Amazon basin and remains generally unaffected by human disruption—aside from massive hydroelectric dam projects, of course—urban pollution is threatening the region's remaining water resources. The population growth rate in the region is 2.1 percent, well below Africa's rate of 3.0 percent; but the rate of urban population growth from 1960 to 1990 was a staggering 3.8 percent. In Brazil alone, during that period as many as one million people per year flooded urban centers such as São Paulo, Rio de Janeiro, and Belo Horizonte. This rate of urbanization places immense pressures on urban infrastructure, particularly sewer systems. As rural migrants crowd squalid shantytowns throughout the region's population centers, their wastes are discharged almost completely untreated into urban waterways and catchbasins. The result has been massive pollution of rivers and bays, severely threatening public health in Latin America.[4]

Water, forests, and carbon emissions are only three of the environmental issues affected by Latin American countries that have gained importance to domestic policy makers and international negotiators. As noted throughout this volume, Latin American decision makers have dealt with the problems domestically with a wide variety of policies and with varying degrees of success. Their efforts in international forums have also been extensive. A professionalization of environmental diplomacy has taken place throughout the region. The Mexican Foreign Ministry has gained great expertise and interest in the issue and often leads discussions in international negotiations. Perhaps to a lesser degree, a similar point can be made of the international efforts of Argentina, Chile, Colombia, and Venezuela—each of which has taken active diplomatic roles in different international environmental questions.

Brazil's experience with environmental diplomacy is more difficult to categorize. In the years leading up to the Earth Summit, the interest of Brazilian bureaucrats in global environmental issues heightened substantially, as noted by Viola in this volume. In the early part of the Collor administration, environmentalism—or at least the environmental image projected to the international community—was seen as a key virtue. José Lutzenberger, Collor's first environment secretary, was an environmentalist of international renown who energized pre-Earth Summit meetings with his fiery environmental advocacy. His fervor eventually created a fissure in the Collor administration between him and the Foreign Ministry, leading to his ouster on the eve of the Earth Summit. He was replaced by José Goldemberg, a much more moderate environmentalist, but one who also had a substantial international reputation. Goldemberg and experienced scholar-diplomat Celso Lafer, Brazil's foreign minister, directed the events and diplomacy of the Rio Conference with considerable aplomb. The Brazilian team received high marks from the diplomatic community for its skill in bringing off the meeting with relative success.

However, after the Earth Summit the Brazilian commitment to progressive environmental diplomacy seems to have waned substantially. With the exception of Rubens Ricúpero, who held posts as environment minister and finance minister in 1993 and 1994, most of the bureaucrats who have held high-profile jobs in the Brazilian executive branch have seemed relatively uninterested in pursuing a strong environmental agenda in the international arena. Although Brazil still remains an active voice for tempering environmental concerns with development objectives, the bulk of the government's attention in recent years has focused internally on the pressing concerns of macroeconomic stability and the crisis of governance.

Latin American countries' interests in the environment appear to have been heightened by the linkage of environmental questions to trade issues. The experience of NAFTA, with its accompanying environmental side agreement, has sensitized the region's governments to the importance of the environment not only to the interaction of environment and trade concerns but also to the relevance of environmental questions when the U.S. Congress votes on trade agreements. The NAFTA experience signals that future members of the Western Hemisphere trade regime are most likely to be admitted only after passing environmental muster. Thus, as Muñoz discusses in chapter 6, international pressure and opportunities have significantly raised Latin American attention to environmental issues. All of these trends and experiences demonstrate that Latin American government representatives have gained interest and expertise in environmental issues and leverage over the international environmental agenda. We address several examples of Latin American involvement in international environmental forums in the next section.

LATIN AMERICA'S ACTIONS IN THE GLOBAL ARENA

Ozone Depletion

In 1974, two researchers at the University of California, Irvine, published a study claiming that the chlorine in CFCs could be depleting the thin layer of stratospheric ozone that shields the earth from excessive levels of ultraviolet radiation. Since the chemicals are used commonly in aerosol spray cans, refrigeration, fire extinguishers, foam insulation, and computer chips (among other applications) the news was cause for grave concern. It took several years for a corpus of research to build and a scientific consensus to form around the findings. It took even longer for the international community to take action. In 1981, the governing council of the United Nations Environment Programme (UNEP) began working toward a global convention on the protection of the ozone layer. The negotiations took several more years, and in 1985 the Vienna Convention for the Protection of the Ozone Layer was agreed upon.

In what would become a model for subsequent environmental negotiations, the framework convention was intended to foster scientific and technical exchange and information gathering, and it allowed mechanisms for updating and strengthening the agreement. However, it set no firm targets or reduction schedules. In 1985, the "ozone hole" over the Antarctic received international media exposure, and the increases in the use of CFCs during previous years meant that prior atmospheric models had to be revised. The upshot was a much greater sense of urgency concerning the creation of an international agreement to halt ozone destruction. In 1987, the international community completed negotiations over the Montreal Protocol. The protocol was significant because it established substantive schedules for reducing the production of CFCs over a multiyear period.

Despite the apparent urgency, several developing countries remained highly dissatisfied over the structure of the agreement. In particular, Brazil, China, and India argued that the arrangement penalized Third World countries for their late development, forcing them to pay the high costs of switching to other technologies to solve problems they did not create. It also made no provisions for the transfer of all-important substitute technologies. Argentina, Mexico, and Venezuela strongly supported this position. Brazil and Mexico pressed even harder for technology transfer assistance because they had already begun to explore CFC alternatives. Mexican firms had begun adopting alternative aerosol propellants, and Brazilian researchers were working on a better heat-exchange fluid for refrigerators. Although developing countries shared common interests in a revised protocol, of the Latin American countries just mentioned, only Brazil failed to sign the protocol after negotiations. Mexico was the first country to sign. China and India joined Brazil in its recalcitrance.[5]

The obstacles to the Montreal Protocol were compounded when, shortly after it was approved, new scientific evidence surfaced that showed the problem to be much greater than previously envisioned. At the subsequent meetings in London during 1990, it became clear to industrialized-country representatives that pushing the agreement further would require concessions to the developing-country position. The London talks ended in an agreement to facilitate technology transfer and to establish a cooperative fund to assist developing countries in their adjustments to CFC substitutes. The talks also produced a much stronger agreement that called for a total ban on CFC production. At Copenhagen two years later, the phaseout schedule was accelerated, and a total ban was projected for January 1996.[6]

Hazardous Waste Trade

With the rise of environmental regulations in the developed world came an obvious temptation: If toxic garbage can't be dumped at home, then what about dumping it in somebody else's backyard? During the 1980s, the extent of foreign dumping became manifest, and several examples surfaced of the problems caused by global trade in hazardous waste. In Koko, Nigeria, the "backyard" dumping was literal: An Italian businessman rented the yard of a local citizen for roughly US$100 per month and used it to dump more than 8,000 drums of hazardous waste, which, of course, leaked. The waste created significant health and environmental dangers for surrounding residents and cleanup workers. The waste issue also was highlighted by the more-than-two-year voyage of the famous garbage barge, the *Khian Sea,* which circled the globe—visiting five continents—searching in vain for a place to dump its 14,000 tons of incinerator ash.[7]

By the end of the 1980s, it became clear that global efforts would be required to resolve the hazardous waste trade. Many developing countries, particularly a cluster of nations in Africa, wanted to enact a total ban on North-South movement of hazardous wastes. Their position grew to encompass many nations of the developing world, including leaders of the G–77 such as Brazil, India, and China. Developed countries tried to press negotiations into mere regulation of waste trading. This sentiment was strongly opposed by many representatives of the developing world, as well as by Mostafa Tolba, the executive director of UNEP. The developing-country group felt that regulating the waste trade would be tantamount to legitimizing it.

Under Tolba's leadership, in 1985 a working group of UNEP issued the Cairo Guidelines and Principles for Environmentally Sound Management of Hazardous Wastes, which were adopted by the UNEP governing council in 1987. The UNEP document represented the first effort to control the transboundary movement of hazardous wastes and became the baseline for subsequent negotiations. These negotiations culminated in a conference in Basel, Switzerland, where the Basel Convention on the Control of Transboundary Movements of Hazardous Waste and Their Disposal was issued.[8] Although the Basel Convention put strict limits on waste trading, it left open several loopholes, including the potential for trading for recycling purposes.

In the initial negotiating period, Mexican representatives first sided with the position of developed-country representatives. The Mexicans favored management of waste trading, not a complete ban. This position probably reflected Mexican interests centered on the *maquiladora*—or in-bond assembly plant—industry in the Mexican-U.S. border zone. This industry proved to be a source of hazardous waste. Moreover, Mexico, along with Bolivia, did not accept hazardous waste for disposal but did accept it for recycling and recovery, a fact which also may have influenced Mexico's representatives.[9]

Still, Mexico's position was not entirely set, and the nation's negotiators later joined the developing-country bloc in opposing North-South trade altogether. In 1994, the Basel Convention was strengthened to include the complete ban of trade in hazardous wastes from countries belonging to the Organisation for Economic Co-operation and Development (OECD) to non-OECD countries. Interestingly, this ban says nothing about waste trading within the OECD or among developing countries. This loophole works to the advantage of countries such as Brazil, Mexico, and Uruguay that are listed as sources of hazardous waste.

Climate Change

In the 1960s and 1970s, a series of scientific studies, largely undertaken by researchers at Scripps Institution of Oceanography at the University of California, San Diego, revealed a disturbing set of patterns. The amount of carbon dioxide in the atmosphere was increasing, and the mean global temperature was rising as well. Since established scientific understanding holds that atmospheric carbon levels are directly linked to global warming and cooling, the new findings raised alarm in the scientific community. Climbing temperatures could spur a rise in the sea-level, and the increased global temperatures could effect cataclysmic changes in the planet's climate and storm patterns. As the scientific findings mounted, they gradually caught the attention of government decision makers. By the late 1980s, political momentum had gathered for a serious effort to mediate the atmospheric trends. Negotiations began on a framework convention for the control of climate change.

Industrialized countries faced a formidable challenge: preserving lifestyles for their populations that are largely supported by vast energy consumption while mitigating the potential effects of global warming. A likely solution would have been to squeeze the developing nations by limiting their future emissions to offset energy consumption in the developed world. Developing countries were very sensitive to the probability of this manipulation and thus were highly resistant to emissions targets that they perceived would limit their development. Led by representatives of China, India, and Brazil, among others, developing countries called attention to the fact that it was consumption patterns in the industrialized world that had largely caused the dilemma that the globe was facing. They refused to accept emissions reductions that were not accompanied by financial and technical assistance from the developed countries.

For example, representatives of Brazil, which had already been chosen to host the Earth Summit, sought a "pragmatic middle ground" in the negotiations.[10] They called attention to developed nations' contributions to the problem while avoiding the heavy rhetoric that characterized the actions of some of the other members of the G–77. Brazilian negotiators wrote off the U.S. concerns regarding deforestation as "a direct threat to national sovereignty" and sought to direct attention to "binding limits on emissions of greenhouse gases from industrialized countries."[11] Brazil made it clear that reaching agreement would require significant concessions and transfer payments by industrialized countries to the developing world.

By the time the negotiation process neared its conclusion a few weeks before the Earth Summit, developing countries had obtained a portion of their objectives. A proposal by Norway for "joint implementation" of the climate change agreement allowed developed countries to offset some portion of their commitment by facilitating the reduction of emissions in other countries (presumably those in the developing world) through technology transfer and codevelopment of advanced technologies. Furthermore, developed countries agreed to provide "new and additional financial resources" to developing countries to help them fulfill their commitments under the agreement.[12] This transfer of funds and technology can only be seen as a diplomatic victory on the part of developing countries, which reflected their leverage over issues of global environmental concern.

Biodiversity

In the mid-to-late 1980s, populations throughout the developed and developing world were bombarded with media accounts of burning rain forests, endangered species, and diminishing natural habitats. Moreover, it became increasingly clear that the world's stock of biodiversity was not only something that should be preserved for its own sake but also could be the very key to the survival of human beings. Pharmaceutical and biotechnology companies depend on the world's genetic and biological diversity for inputs to and models for their products. However, developing countries believed that if their resources were being tapped for profits, they ought to have some say in how the products were extracted and should participate in some way in the gains from product sales. Some developing countries and multinational industries cut mutually profitable deals, such as that between the National Biodiversity Institute, (a research institution sponsored by the Costa Rican state) and pharmaceutical giant Merck & Co. Merck agreed to pay US$1.1 million up front to the institute for the rights to its research on native biology and promised future royalties on products stemming from Costa Rican biodiversity.[13]

Unfortunately, such private industry-government agreements were few, and concern mounted over the proper balance between foreign and domestic interests and over the rapidly disappearing stocks of genetic diversity. As the issue gained notoriety, the date of the 1992 Earth Summit grew nearer. Interest in a convention on biological diversity intensified. Developing countries, including biological treasure troves such as Brazil, Colombia, Costa Rica, Mexico, Peru, and Venezuela, demonstrated interest in negotiating the convention only if mechanisms existed for financing conservation efforts and for sharing the patents and profits of products resulting from biodiversity exploration. Some of the larger developing countries had an increased incentive to support the treaty. Brazil and Mexico, for example, had already been investing significant resources in developing their own biotechnology industries. Mexico's research community had made significant inroads in developing genetic engineering techniques and in researching nitrogen fixation. Brazil's firms had begun developing joint ventures with firms in other Latin American countries, including Argentina and Cuba. Venezuela had also launched a significant biotech effort.[14]

After some significant wrangling (and with the conspicuous resistance on the part of the United States), the Biodiversity Convention was issued. Articles 20 and 21 provide for financing of developing-country conservation efforts through the Global Environmental Facility (GEF). The convention also notes that profits, research, and technology should be shared with developing countries, but the language is soft—the technology transfer and profit-sharing provisions are not mandatory. More significantly, the treaty deals directly with the question of sovereignty, making it explicit that developing countries have broad rights to control research within their boundaries and can restrict access to foreign biodiversity prospectors.[15]

INTERNATIONAL INSTITUTIONS AND CONSPICUOUS OVERSIGHTS

The influence of developing countries—Latin American nations in particular—over the course of international environmental diplomacy has likewise been manifest in the decisions regarding international institutions, particularly the GEF and the Commission on Sustainable Development. During the UNCED negotiations over Agenda 21, which is the overarching agreement governing many aspects of multilateral environmental policy coordination, a definite fissure opened up between the developed and developing nations over the question of financing environmental amelioration. The industrialized countries proposed that financing for UNCED agreements be carried out under the umbrella of the GEF, which is a grant-making organization of UNEP and the World Bank. The GEF was governed at the time by weighted voting of donors to the fund, much like the World Bank and the International Monetary Fund. Developing countries' ability to influence granting decisions within the GEF was therefore constrained.

The developing countries favored a new "Green Fund" that would focus specifically on the stated needs of the Third World, including technology transfer, capacity building, and sustainable development issues not already covered by international agreements. Perhaps most importantly, grant-making decisions in the green fund would be governed by equal voting of donor and recipient nations. Argentina, Brazil, and China were the most ardent advocates of the green fund.

In addition to the green fund, developing countries pressed hard for a commitment on the part of the industrialized world to allocate 0.7 percent of GNP to go to overseas development assistance. The financing issues at UNCED proved to be among the most contentious of the entire conference. Negotiating sessions dragged well into the night, and for several days no apparent resolution was evident.

In the end, developing countries achieved only a portion of their objectives regarding financing, but even those victories can be viewed as significant. The GEF was retained as the funding mechanism for the UNCED agreements, but its role was to be heightened and refurbished. Importantly, voting rights on the GEF were restructured a little more than a year after UNCED, with decisions requiring a "double majority" of weighted votes according to donor share and majority votes according to membership. Although membership in the GEF is somewhat re-stricted, developing nations have more control over its decisions than they do in other multilateral lending institutions such as the World Bank, the IMF, and the regional development banks. Although Agenda 21 did not include a firm commit-ment of 0.7 percent of GNP to development aid on the part of industrialized countries, this appeared to be mostly due to the obstruction of the United States. Several major donor nations, including Japan and France, announced unilateral commitments of 0.7 percent of their GNP at the Earth Summit after the isolation of the United States was made plain.[16]

Developing-country influence over international financing was paralleled by Third World control over the establishment of an international body to oversee global sustainable development efforts. In the meetings prior to UNCED, called PrepComs, Bangladesh proposed the establishment of an intergovernmental co-ordinating body to oversee the implementation of Agenda 21 and propose subse-quent environmental agreements. This motion initially was scuttled by the United States, which argued against the creation of new international institutions. How-ever, at the final PrepCom, Venezuela again proposed the establishment of the or-ganization, to be called the Commission on Sustainable Development. It was to be a high-level commission charged with reviewing national environmental reports, monitoring progress on Agenda 21, reviewing progress on technology transfer and financial commitments, and, perhaps most importantly, receiving the input and information of nongovernmental organizations. Despite some developed-world opposition to the creation of the new body, the commission was established at UNCED to carry out these relatively high-level functions.[17]

Possibly as important as what developing countries have been able to accom-plish in international agreements is what they have successfully blocked. The most notable example of Latin American veto power is the forestry treaty, which was initially projected as a framework convention on a par with the biodiversity and climate change treaties; the forestry treaty was scheduled for passage at UNCED. Two overlapping blocs of developing nations mobilized against such a far-reaching convention. In Latin America, the representatives of the group of Amazon nations met in the years and months running up to the Earth Summit and issued strong statements opposing the encroachment on national sovereignty that they perceived stemming from foreign concern over Amazon deforestation. Members of this group, particularly Brazil, joined forces with Southeast Asian na-tions such as the Kuala Lumpur group that similarly opposed attempts to dictate forest conservation at the expense of needed development. Significantly, although the United States repeatedly tried to raise the forestry issue before and during the Earth Summit, Brazil and the other tropical-forested nations reversed the charge, claiming that the United States had previously deforested almost an entire conti-nent during its own development and now was trying to block developing nations from doing the same thing. Brazil and its associated bloc strengthened their case when they criticized clear-cutting logging practices in the U.S. Pacific Northwest as being close analogues to tropical deforestation practices. The joint action on the part of forest nations and the charges of hypocrisy leveled at the United States proved successful. The only action on forests at UNCED was the meager issuing of the soft and nonbinding Statement on Forest Principles.

CONCLUSION

Clearly, Latin American nations have been very active and relatively successful in promoting their agenda on international environmental negotiations. From this brief survey of environmental diplomacy beginning in the early 1980s, it appears that Brazil and Mexico were not only core players in the developing-country bloc but also keys to the G–77 position in many instances. Argentina, Colombia, Costa Rica, Venezuela, and Uruguay have similarly been active on the issues, though perhaps with somewhat less influence over other nations.

In the near future, Latin American nations will again have opportunities to flex their environmental muscle, and there exists serious potential for conflict with developed countries on core international issues. The last word has yet to be said on a forest agreement. Given the importance of logging, development, and settlement to the governments with territory in the Amazon region, we can expect them to resist strongly any future international attempts to dictate conservation efforts. The situation of Brazil is even more complicated by the national congress in the country, where fully one-third of the federal senate comes from Amazon states. Those politicians have tended to oppose vehemently what they perceive as foreign encroachment on their nation's sovereignty. Some Amazon governors and senators actually have been elected on virtually single-issue platforms of antienvironmentalism. In addition, attempts to strengthen the provisions of the biodiversity and climate change conventions can be expected to continue to provoke conflict over financing and responsibility for fixing related environmental problems.

Still, despite the inevitable conflict, Latin American countries also have great potential for leadership on international environmental issues. The brief survey of Latin America's involvement in international agreements discussed earlier in this chapter makes one point quite clear: There has been an enormous change in global perceptions and attitudes toward developing-country interests in environmental issues. Although international agreements previously had little in the way of provisions for financing or acknowledgment of development concerns, the current paradigm reflects far more closely the tight linkage between environment and development. Sustainable development, rather than environmental preservation at all costs, is the current dominant concept. Latin American representatives to international forums were crucial players in shifting that paradigm. We expect this trend toward the tight integration of concerns for both development and the environment to continue and accelerate.

In addition to shifting attitudes and negotiating positions, Latin American nations have been important sources of institutional innovation. The proposed green fund, the restructuring of the GEF, and the organization of the CSD were largely the initiatives of Latin American countries. The region's representatives can be expected to propose further creative methods of financing environmental improvements and adapting existing organizations and technologies to developing-country needs and interests. Moreover, Latin American countries remain vast, largely untapped sources of citizen participation in international and domestic environmental initiatives. As political liberalization and economic growth continue, public interest in the environment—already high in many Latin American countries—will increase. Latin America's constructive engagement in international environmental forums can only be expected to grow as well.

NOTES

1. Gareth Porter and Janet Welsh Brown, *Global Environmental Politics* (Boulder: Westview Press, 1991).

2. World Resources Institute, *World Resources* (New York: Oxford University Press, 1990–91 and 1994–95).

3. J. Sathaye and A. Ketoff, "Emissions from Major Developing Countries: Better Understanding of the Role of Energy in the Long Term," Interim Report, LBL–29507, Lawrence Livermore Laboratory, Berkeley, CA, August 1990.

4. World Resources Institute, *World Resources*.

5. Marian A. Miller, *The Third World in Global Environmental Politics* (Boulder: Lynne Rienner Publishers, 1995), pp. 73, 81.

6. Ibid., pp. 68–81.

7. Ibid., pp. 88–89.

8. Ibid., pp. 88–95.

9. Ibid., p. 95.

10. José Goldemberg, "The Road to Rio," in Irving M. Mintzer and J. Amber Leonard, eds., *Negotiating Climate Change: The Inside Story of the Rio Convention* (New York: Cambridge University Press, 1994), pp. 175–185.

11. Ibid., p. 178.

12. Irving M. Mintzer and J. Amber Leonard, "Visions of a Changing World," in Mintzer and Leonard, eds., *Negotiating Climate Change*, pp. 3–44.

13. Miller, *The Third World in Global Environmental Politics*, pp. 111–118.

14. Ibid., p. 120.

15. Ibid., p. 119–123.

16. Betram I. Spector, "The Search for Flexibility on Financial Issues at UNCED: An Analysis of Preference Adjustment," in Bertram I. Spector, Gunnar Sjöstedt, and I. William Zartman, eds., *Negotiating International Regimes: Lessons Learned from the United Nations*

Conference on Environment and Development (UNCED) (London: Graham & Trotman/Martinus Nijhoff, 1994).

17. Lawrence E. Susskind, "What Will It Take to Ensure Effective Global Environmental Management? A Reassessment of Regime-Building Accomplishments," in Spector et al., eds., *Negotiating International Regimes*, pp. 221–232.

—————————— ■ ——————————

About the Book

Across Latin America in recent years, environmental policy has progressed from rhetoric to substance. In a fundamental shift away from the perception of environmental concerns as a luxury only affluent nations could indulge, leaders throughout the hemisphere now recognize that ignoring the need for environmental protection carries steep and often compounding costs. Although the pace of reform varies from country to country, progress in addressing both the enormous environmental deficits created by past development and the need for controls on present and future growth is evident in virtually every nation in the region.

In this volume, scholars and policymakers from throughout the hemisphere consider the domestic and international factors that shape the process of environmental policymaking in Latin America. Particular attention is given to domestic political institutions, growing domestic and transnational environmental activism, the role of the international development community, and the effects of sweeping neoliberal economic reforms on environmental policy. The volume also offers a set of comparative essays on environmental policy and politics in other regions of the world that demonstrates the common challenges confronting policymakers in many rapidly industrializing nations.

■

About the Editors and Contributors

William Ascher is professor of public policy studies and political science at Duke University. He is also director of Duke's Center for International Development Research and the Duke-UNC Latin American Studies Program. From 1986 to 1990, he was the editor-in-chief of the journal *Policy Sciences*. His research covers policy making, Latin American political economy, and forecasting methodologies. His books on developing countries include *Scheming for the Poor: The Politics of Redistribution in Latin America* (1984) and, coauthored with Robert Healy, *Natural Resource Policymaking in Developing Countries* (1990). As project director of the International Commission for Central American Recovery and Development, he edited *Central American Recovery and Development: The Task Force Studies* (1989). Ascher is currently directing research projects on the political economy of natural resources, including both the role of the state in oil and mining sectors and the potential for community management in forestry.

Barbara Jancar-Webster, professor of political science at the State University of New York at Brockport, is a specialist in the environmental policy and political-economic systems of East Central Europe and the former Soviet Union. She has conducted field research on these issues and is the author of numerous articles, chapters in books, and papers. Her recent publications include *Environmental Management in the Soviet Union and Yugoslavia: Structure and Regulation in Federal Communist States* (1987), for which she won the International Studies Association Sprout Award in 1990 for the best book in the area of international environmental policy. Jancar-Webster has traveled widely in Eastern Europe and the former Soviet Union and was in 1992 exchange professor in the Department of National Resource Use, Faculty of Economics, Moscow University.

Edward Korzetz is a doctoral candidate in the Environmental Studies program of the Political Science Department, Colorado State University. He is currently engaged in dissertation research on indigenous peoples and protected reserves in Latin America, with special emphasis on Ecuador and Guatemala.

Gordon J. MacDonald is Director of the International Institute for Applied Systems Analysis in Laxenburg, Austria. He is on leave from the Graduate School of International

Relations and Pacific Studies, University of California, San Diego (UCSD). His principal professional interests have been in scientific and technical research, education, environment, and national security issues that affect East Asia. MacDonald's current research focuses on such topics as international environmental policy and conflict resolution, as well as the physics of climate change. Immediately before joining UCSD, MacDonald was vice president and chief scientist of the MITRE Corporation. Previously, he held tenured professorships and had various administrative responsibilities at the Massachusetts Institute of Technology; the University of California, Los Angeles; the University of California, Santa Barbara; and Dartmouth College; and he has served in government at the federal and state levels, including service on the Council on Environmental Quality from 1970 to 1972.

Stephen P. Mumme is professor of political science at Colorado State University, where he teaches in the graduate-level Environmental Studies program. His research focuses on Mexico-United States environmental relations and Mexican environmental policy. His works include: *The United States-Mexico Boundary* (1981); *Statecraft, Domestic Politics, and Foreign Policy Making: The El Chamizal Dispute,* coauthored with Alan C. Lamborn (1988); *Apportioning Groundwater Beneath the U.S.-Mexican Border* (1988); and *Innovation and Reform in Transboundary Resource Management: a Critical Look at the International Boundary and Water Commission* (1993).

Heraldo Muñoz has been a distinguished visiting professor and a visiting scholar, The University of North Carolina (Chapel Hill); the Latin American program of the Wilson Center; the Friedrich Ebert Foundation in Bonn; the School of International Studies of UCSD; and other universities and academic institutions in the United States, Europe, and Latin America. Muñoz is founder and director of the Programa de Seguimiento de las Políticas Exteriores Latinoamericanas, Santiago, Chile, and professor of the Instituto de Estudios Internacionales, Universidad de Chile. He is author, coauthor, or editor of several books and numerous articles published in academic journals of various countries. Among his books are: *From Dependency to Development* (1981), *Amistad Esquiva: Las Relaciones de Estados Unidos y Chile* (1987) coauthored with C. Portales; and *Latin American Nations in World Politics,* 2d. ed. (1996), coedited with Joseph S. Tulchin.

Daniel L. Nielson is assistant professor of political science at Brigham Young University, Provo, Utah. His current book project examines the links between international shocks, domestic politics, and developing-country policies regarding economic adjustment and public-goods provision. His other projects focus on political institutions and public policy in Latin America and on environmental lending by multilateral development banks in the developing world. Nielson was cofounder and editor-in-chief of the *Journal of Environment and Development.* He received his Ph.D. from the Graduate School of International Relations and Pacific Studies at UCSD.

Carl H. Petrich is head of Technologies for Strategic Development in the Energy and Global Change Analysis Section at Oak Ridge National Laboratory in Oak Ridge, Tennessee. ORNL is the U.S. Department of Energy's largest multi-program laboratory. Mr.

Petrich has consulted in energy and environmental planning in developing countries since 1985 through both the Oak Ridge National Laboratory and Lahmeyer International (Frankfurt, Germany). He served in residence as head of a nearly two-year environmental training project in Jakarta in the early 1990s. Mr. Petrich has been with Oak Ridge since 1976 after receiving a master's degree in landscape architecture from the University of Michigan. Prior to that he earned a B.S. in botany from Duke University. In June 1995, he received an MBA from the University of Chicago.

Eduardo Silva is assistant professor of political science and a fellow of the Center for International Studies at the University of Missouri-St. Louis. His works include *The State and Capital in Chile* (1996). He is coeditor of *Elections and Democratization in Latin America, 1980–85,* and his articles on Chilean political economy have appeared in *World Politics* and the *Journal of Interamerican Studies and World Affairs.* Silva's recent research has concentrated on the politics of conservation and sustainable development in Chile, Costa Rica, Mexico, and Venezuela.

Marc A. Stern is a doctoral candidate at the Graduate School of International Relations and Pacific Studies at UCSD. His research interests include the role of international economic integration in promoting environmental protection in developing countries and the effects of environmental lending by multilateral lending banks in the developing world. Stern was cofounder and editor-in-chief of the *Journal of Environment & Development.*

Shelby Smith-Sanclare is owner of Sanclare Associates and ReVisioning(s) in Oak Ridge, Tennessee. Smith-Sanclare has consulted in environmental and regional planning and in personal and corporate strategic development since 1984. She served in residence as head of a two-year project in Jakarta to develop environmental design guidelines for swamp and irrigation projects for the Government of Indonesia. Smith-Sanclare received her Ph.D. in Environmental and Regional Planning from the University of New Mexico in 1976. She has taught at the University of New Mexico, University of Georgia, and the Master Extension Program for Systems Management at the University of Southern California.

Larry A. Swatuk is senior fellow and research team leader at ACDESS, the African Centre for Development and Strategic Studies, Ijebu-Ode, Nigeria. Dr. Swatuk received his doctorate from Dalhousie University in Halifax, Canada, and has been an SSHRCC Post-Doctoral Fellow at the Centre for International and Strategic Studies, York University, Toronto, Canada. He has published numerous articles, monographs, and book chapters on aspects of Southern African political economy and foreign policy. Most recently, he coauthored *Reordering the Periphery: An Essay on North-South Relations* (with Amitav Acharya, forthcoming), and he coedited *Beyond the Rift: the "New" South Africa in Africa* (1996) with David R. Black.

Blanca Torres is senior fellow and former director of the Center for International Studies at El Colegio de México. She has published books, articles, and book chapters on post-World War II U.S.-Mexican relations. More recently, she has focused her research on the management of transboundary problems. She has been Visiting Fellow at St. Anthony's College (Oxford University), Duke University, and the Center for U.S.-Mexican Studies at UCSD.

Eduardo J. Viola is a political scientist working on Brazilian and international environmental politics. He was Tinker Visiting Professor at Stanford University from January to July 1994. His permanent position is professor in the Department of Political Science and International Relations, University of Brasília, Brazil. He has been visiting professor at many universities, including the University of Amsterdam, the University of Colorado at Boulder, the University of Notre Dame, the University of Campinas (Brazil), and the University of Buenos Aires. He has published more than 20 articles on issues of social movements, democratization and the environmental movement in Brazil and the international politics of the environment.

Index

Activism. *See* Environmental organizations
African Ministerial Conference on Environment, 189
Agenda 21, 245, 272–274
Agriculture, 34, 66, 190–192, 224
  See also Forestry
Amazon forest, 32–33, 35, 89, 274
  burning of, 95, 96
  environmental organizations, 9, 96, 101, 162, 175–176
  parks and reserves, 82, 99–100, 162
  rational exploitation of, 100
  sovereignty over, 163, 270, 273, 274
  See also Forestry
AMDAL policy, 252–254, 257
Amoco, 226
Aral Sea, 212
Argentina, 90, 265, 268
Arias, Oscar, 173, 174
Ascher, William, 2, 8, 152, 258, 277
Aylwin, Patricio, 61, 65–80, 116–117

Baiduzhy, Andrei, 231
Banks. *see* Multilateral development banks
Basel Convention on Waste Disposal, 251, 268
Batoka Gorge, 194
Belize, 42(table), 91
Biodiversity, 9, 271–272
  in Brazil, 89
  in Chile, 72, 79
  Convention on Biodiversity, 2, 98, 272
  in Indonesia, 245–246
  in Latin America, 88, 265
  in Mexico, 89
Biotechnology, 271
Birdsall, Nancy, 114, 118
Black markets, 250–251
  See also Law enforcement
Bolivia, 4, 17, 42(table), 91, 269
Bondarenko, Andrei, 229

Brazil, 44, 90, 92, 103
  biodiversity, 89
  biotechnology, 271
  budget, 176
  bureaucracy, 53–54, 94
  democratization, 43–44, 89, 105–106
  economic crisis, 98–100
  economic recovery, 108–109
  electoral system, 149–150
  environmental organizations, 43–44, 89, 95, 100–104, 158, 160–163, 166–167, 172–177
  environmental policy, 91–105
  forestry, 32–33, 35, 82, 95–96, 175–176
  globalist vs. nationalist interests, 100, 106–107
  government agencies, 42(table), 93–97, 99
  greenhouse gases, 265, 268
  Human Development Index, 89
  impediments to environmentalism, 48, 51–54, 94, 108, 163, 270, 273–275
  indigenous peoples, 92, 95, 97, 99, 101, 103, 162, 172
  judicial system, 174
  mass media, 8, 38, 98, 102
  oil industry, 95
  park system, 99–100
  policy recommendations, 109
  political parties, 44, 48, 104–105, 108–109
  pollution, 8, 93
  population control, 92
  resource rent, 32–33, 35
  socioenvironmentalism, 105–108
  sovereignty of, 163, 270, 273, 274
  sustainable development, 105–109, 168
  and UNCED, 2–3, 8, 93, 96–98, 106–108, 266–267
Browder, John, 32
Brundtland Commission, 4, 63, 106
Bureaucracy
  in Brazil, 53–54, 94

283